Buddhism and Islam
on the Silk Road

ENCOUNTERS WITH ASIA

Victor H. Mair, Series Editor

Encounters with Asia is an interdisciplinary series dedicated to the exploration of all the major regions and cultures of this vast continent. Its timeframe extends from the prehistoric to the contemporary; its geographic scope ranges from the Urals and the Caucasus to the Pacific. A particular focus of the series is the Silk Road in all of its ramifications: religion, art, music, medicine, science, trade, and so forth. Among the disciplines represented in this series are history, archaeology, anthropology, ethnography, and linguistics. The series aims particularly to clarify the complex interrelationships among various peoples within Asia, and also with societies beyond Asia.

A complete list of books in the series is available from the publisher.

Buddhism and Islam on the Silk Road

Johan Elverskog

PENN

UNIVERSITY OF PENNSYLVANIA PRESS

PHILADELPHIA · OXFORD

Published by
University of Pennsylvania Press
Philadelphia, Pennsylvania 19104-4112

Printed in the United States of America on acid-free paper
10 9 8 7 6 5 4 3 2 1

Library of Congress Cataloging-in-Publication Data
Elverskog, Johan.
Buddhism and Islam on the Silk Road / Johan Elverskog.
        p.   cm.—Encounters with Asia
Includes bibliographical references and index.
ISBN 978-0-8122-4237-9 (hardcover : alk. paper)
1. Islam—Relations—Buddhism.   2. Buddhism—Relations—Islam.
3. Islam—Silk Road—History.   4. Buddhism—Silk
Road—History.
BP173.B9 E48   2010
294.3′35095 22
2009044830

For my mother

A man came to the Prophet and said, "O Messenger of God! Who among the people is the most worthy of my good companionship?" The Prophet said, "Your mother." The man said, "Then who?" The Prophet said, "Then your mother." The man further asked, "Then who?" The Prophet said, "Then your mother." The man asked again, "Then who?" The Prophet said, "Then your father."

—*Hadīth of al-Bukhārī*, No. 5586

Even if one should carry about one's mother on one shoulder and one's father on the other, and while doing so should live a hundred years, reach the age of a hundred years; and if one should attend to them by anointing them with salves, by massaging, bathing and rubbing their limbs, and they should even void their excrement there—even by that would one not do enough for one's parents, one would not repay them. Even if one were to establish one's parents as the supreme lords and rulers over this earth so rich in the seven treasures, one would not do enough for them, one would not repay them. What is the reason for this? Parents do much for their children: they bring them up, feed them and guide them through this world.

—*Aṅguttara Nikāya*, II, iv, 2

CONTENTS

I was ordered to fight all men until they say "There is no god but Allah."
—Prophet Muhammad's farewell address

The ascetic Gotama roars his lion's roar, in company and confidently,
they question him and he answers, he wins them over with his answers,
they find it pleasing and are satisfied.
—*Mahāsihanada Sutta, Dīgha Nikāya*

THE BUDDHIST MONASTERY of Nalanda was founded in northeast India in the early fifth century. Over time it became the premier institution of higher learning in Asia and, much like leading universities today, Nalanda had a world-renowned faculty working on the cutting edge of the theoretical sciences and a student body drawn from across the Buddhist world.[1] This prestige also brought with it ample gifts from the rich and powerful. Not only had local rulers in northeast India bequeathed entire villages to help finance the running of Nalanda, but the king of Sumatra had also offered villages for the monastery's endowment,[2] and a special fund had been created to support students specifically from China. At its peak Nalanda had an extensive faculty teaching a diverse student body of about three thousand on a beautiful campus composed of numerous cloisters with lofty spires that "resembled the snowy peaks of Mount Sumeru."[3] Then suddenly the serenity of this Buddhist institution was shattered. In the fall of 1202, Muslim soldiers on horses rode in and hacked down teachers and students where they stood. The once majestic buildings were left in ruins.[4] The savagery was so great it signaled the end of the Dharma in India.

This powerful story has been told countless times. Today it is ubiquitous, being found in everything from scholarly monographs to travel brochures. Indeed, by its sheer pervasiveness, this one episode has in many ways come to encapsulate and symbolize the entire thirteen-hundred-year history of Buddhist-Muslim interaction. And on account of this, whenever the topic of Buddhism and Islam is ever mentioned it almost invariably revolves around the Muslim destruction of the Dharma.[5]

This is problematic for many reasons, not the least being that the story of Nalanda is not true. For example, not only did local Buddhist rulers make deals with the new Muslim overlords and thus stay in power,[6] but Nalanda also continued as a functioning institution of Buddhist education well into the thirteenth century.[7] One Indian master, for example, was trained and ordained at Nalanda before he traveled to the court of Khubilai Khan.[8] We also know that Chinese monks continued to travel to India and obtain Buddhist texts in the late fourteenth century.[9] Indeed, contrary to the standard idea promoted by the above story that Nalanda's destruction signaled the death of Buddhism, the fact is that the Dharma survived in India at least until the seventeenth century.[10] Or, in other words, Buddhists and Muslims lived together on the Asian subcontinent for almost a thousand years.

Why is this not better known? There are numerous possible explanations for this and they range from Buddhist prophecies of decline to the problems of contemporary scholarship.[11] However, rather than addressing such concerns, one can begin simply with the power of story. As noted above, the destruction of Nalanda offers us a clear-cut narrative with good guys and bad. It avoids entirely the complex shades of gray that most often color the messy fabric of history. And this is certainly what the Buddhist historians who cobbled together this story wanted to do as they tried to make sense of the Dharma's demise in India.[12] Indeed, rather than exploring the complex economic, environmental, political, and religious history of India, or simply the Buddhist tradition's own failings, it was clearly much easier to simply blame the Muslims.

In this regard the Buddhists established a precedent that was to subsequently drive South Asian history.[13] The British, for example, used the same claims of Muslim barbarity and misrule in order to justify the introduction of their supposedly more humane and rational form of colonial rule.[14] In turn, while Indian nationalists questioned the moral righteousness and glory of the British Raj, they nevertheless continued with the historical model of blaming the Muslims. The humiliating imposition of colonial rule was thus not the result of Indian weakness per se, but rather the fault of the effeminate and voluptuous Mughals.[15] And this view is readily perpetuated in the rhetoric of today's Hindu nationalists who want to re-create some imagined Hindu utopia by eradicating all traces of Islam in India, by violence if necessary.[16]

This pervasive anti-Muslim view is, of course, not unique to medieval Buddhist and contemporary Hindu historiography. It has also been a part of the Jewish and Christian tradition ever since Muhammad received God's final revelation through the angel Gabriel in the early seventh century. Many have also argued that the modern western construction of itself as the paragon of righteousness was often done at the expense of Islam. Yet even though such "orientalism" has been roundly critiqued by decades of scholarship, these earlier views persist.[17] Indeed, the valiant attempt of contemporary scholars and museum curators to overturn these stereotypes by means of books and lavish museum exhibits highlighting Muslim tolerance and periods of Islamic exchange with Christian Europe has not really been able to diminish our "orientalist fear."[18] Of course, today's contemporary geopolitical environment may not be conducive to such a reevaluation no matter how necessary it may actually be. Thus if we take into consideration all of these disparate strands it is perhaps not at all surprising that the story of Nalanda and the attendant one of Islam destroying Buddhism are so readily accepted. To many they just make sense. Moreover, they fit our preconceptions about these two religious traditions. While Buddhism is a good, rational, post-Enlightenment philosophy, Islam is an inherently violent and irrational religion.[19]

Indeed, in the popular imagination there are probably no two traditions more different than Buddhism and Islam. One is synonymous with peace, tranquility, and introspection, the other with violence, chaos, and blind faith. One conjures up images of Himalayan hermitages and Japanese rock gardens, the other primitive and dirty villages with burqa-clad women. And while Buddhism is seen as modern, its teachings even in tune with the most cutting-edge science,[20] Islam is backward, its teachings and punishments redolent of the Middle Ages.[21] Yet as with the whole enterprise of orientalism and the construction of Islam as innately evil, this image of Buddhism as the perfect spirituality for the modern age is also a Western fantasy, or construction, of the nineteenth century. In fact, it was during those heady days of empire and modernity that Buddhism came to be conceived as the philosophy that could solve all the world's problems.[22]

This modern Buddhism had many authors, from British colonial offi-

cials to Asian nationalists and German philosophers to Russian Theoso-
phists.[23] All, however, agreed that this tradition shorn of rituals, doctrines,
and communal structures was clearly the spiritual philosophy for the age
of secular humanism. Of course, such a philosophy was not what Buddhists
in Asia actually practiced. They had apparently lost touch with the true
teachings of the Buddha and instead descended into a nightmarish morass
of ritualism and superstition. That this story coincided neatly with Protestant apologetics[24]—namely, the teachings of Jesus being deformed by
pagano-papism and then redeemed by Martin Luther—as well as nineteenth-century debates about Aryans and Semites was not coincidental, and
certainly provided a powerful narrative arc.[25] It also made Buddhism, the
meditative path for individual liberation, the very antithesis of Islam.

With this in mind it makes sense why so few question the story of
Nalanda's destruction. It is a perfect story with the requisite and well-
known actors playing their appropriate roles. Moreover, in recent years this
story has not simply been some event long lost in the fog of history, or an
abstract frame with which to map and order the chaotic progression of
history, but rather a concrete reality. During the month of March in 2001,
it played out on television screens around the world when the Taliban used
tanks and anti-aircraft weapons to demolish the colossal Buddha statues of
Bamiyan (figures 1 and 2).

This wanton act of destruction not only reenacted the story of Nalanda,
but also reaffirmed all of our stereotypes. What better image could one have
to encapsulate Buddhist-Muslim history than a group of fanatical Muslim
militants senselessly mauling the peaceful and passive representations of the
Buddha in the name of Islam? That is invariably how it was presented in
the international media. Little thought, however, was given to the possible
historical contingencies shaping this event; much less the fact that the statues had until then somehow survived thirteen-hundred years of Muslim
rule.[26] This was another of those inconvenient facts that somehow muddied
the story. It was perhaps better not to think about it since, if one did, it
opened the door for the whole messy reality of history to come rushing in,
and this could very well challenge, possibly even shatter, the conventional
narrative that has been told these last one thousand years.

Shining a light on the history of Buddhist-Muslim interaction is precisely the aim of this book. To this end the following history moves beyond
the spatial and temporal boundaries shaping the conventional history of
Buddhist-Muslim interaction. Its focus is thus not on India but the so-

Figure 1. Large Buddha, fifth–seventh century, in 1970. Photo: Volker Thewalt.

Figure 2. Large Buddha, after its destruction in 2001. Photo © Corbis.

called Silk Road, or more precisely Inner Asia, the wide swath of territory stretching from Afghanistan to Mongolia. And instead of dwelling on the early period and the imagined demise of Buddhism it covers the interaction of these two traditions up through the nineteenth century. Moreover, to provide the story a structure the chapters are arranged chronologically and to create a narrative drive each chapter is focused on a thematic issue. These separate issues provide not only a framework through which to organize the material, but also opens up the meeting of the Buddhist and Muslim worlds to larger theoretical concerns.

The first chapter explores the earliest contact between Buddhists and Muslims (ca. 700–1000 c.e.) through the lens of trade and the linkage between religious thought and economic regimes. The second chapter takes the same time period as its focus but moves beyond the economy of salvation in order to explore how these two traditions tried to understand each other. Chapter 3 moves beyond this early period to the time of the Mongol empire (ca. 1100–1400 c.e.) and investigates Buddhist-Muslim interaction in relation to cross-cultural artistic production. Chapter 4, on the other hand, moves away from the realm of art and the Mongol empire and investigates instead the political and economic background of the post-Mongol period (ca. 1400–1650 c.e.) and the conflicts it engendered between the Buddhist and Muslim worlds. Finally, Chapter 5 explores Buddhist-Muslim interaction during the Qing dynasty (1644–1911) as seen through the issue of religious foodways.

By presenting Buddhist-Muslim history in this way the hope is not to simply reveal an overlooked chapter of human history. The aim in what follows is to use the meeting of these two traditions in order to explore three interlocking themes. The first of these, and indeed the essential thread that runs throughout what follows, is the question of what happened when Buddhists and Muslims actually came into contact with one another. In particular, how were both of these traditions transformed as a result of this encounter? Moreover, by exploring the meeting of two traditions that are not often paired together in this way it is also the aim of this work to challenge some of the conventional divisions that shape our understanding of the world—such as the notion of East–West, and Middle East–East Asia, as well as the modern phenomenon of the nation-state—all with the aim of exploring how these conceptualizations potentially distort historical realities. And finally, by situating the history of Buddhist-Muslim interaction in terms of everyday activities, such as making money and cooking, I hope to generate new insights about not only the fraught intersection between religious thought and human life, but also the actual possibilities of cross-cultural understanding within such a meeting. Whether these goals are achieved in what follows I will leave to the reader. Though I do hope what follows is not only a good story, but also reveals how rather than being diametrically opposite Buddhism and Islam are actually very much the same.

CHAPTER ONE

Contact

O ye who believe! Eat not up your property among yourselves in vanities:
but let there be amongst you traffic and trade by mutual good-will.

—Qur'an 4:29

The wise man trained and disciplined
Shines out like a beacon-fire.
He gathers wealth just as a bee
Gathers honey, and it grows.

Like an ant-hill higher yet.
With wealth so gained the layman can
Devote it to his people's good.
He should divide his wealth in four.

One part he may enjoy at will,
Two parts he should put to work,
The fourth he should set aside,
A reserve in times of need.

—*Sigālaka Sutta, Dīgha Nikāya*

A BUDDHIST STUDIES JOKE has it that the Dharma in the West
should not be called the Middle Way, but the Upper Middle Way.[1]
Indeed, the seeming preponderance of wealthy Euro-American
Buddhists, who are able to escape the daily grind by jetting off for a meditation retreat on Maui, has become a stock figure of ridicule in American

popular culture.[2] The joke, of course, lies in the contradiction between the image of a Buddhist monk who has renounced all worldly possessions and the pampered, jet-set Buddhist. Yet is there really such a contradiction between being both Buddhist and wealthy?

If one looks at the question historically the answer is no. From the very beginning and throughout the millennia it has always been the rich and powerful who have kept the Dharma in business. For some this may seem incongruous. Wealth, power, and violence are the very things Buddhism supposedly rejects. Indeed, it is this absence that most often sets the Dharma apart in the contemporary religious marketplace. Buddhism is namely the one tradition that seemingly transcends all the things that generally give religion a bad name. Yet, as noted in the introduction, this view of Buddhism is a selective reading of Buddhist doctrine and history.

Thus if one were so inclined it would be very easy to dredge up the seamier underbelly of the Dharma. For example, one can readily point out Buddhism's misogyny.[3] Or in contradistinction to the standard claims of Buddhist peacefulness one can look at its history of violence as evidenced in the following command given by the Fifth Dalai Lama to his Buddhist death squads:[4]

[Of those in] the band of enemies who have despoiled the duties
    entrusted to them:
Make the male lines like trees that have had their roots cut;
Make the female lines like brooks that have dried up in winter;
Make the children and grandchildren like eggs smashed against
    rocks;
Make the servants and followers like heaps of grass consumed by
    fire;
Make their dominion like a lamp whose oil has been exhausted;
In short, annihilate any traces of them, even their names.[5]

To find such Kurtzean images connected with the Dalai Lama may be jarring to some; however, the fact of the matter is that Tibetan history accords less with the popular Western image of Shangri-La and more with the religious chaos and violence of Reformation and post-Reformation Europe.[6] Yet in looking for such examples of Buddhist violence one need not venture into the past, as is clear from the ongoing civil war in Sri Lanka.[7]

Thus contrary to the popular understanding Buddhism is not innately above and beyond the horrors found in the other "world religions." In fact precisely for this reason scholars have in recent years reveled in exposing some of these less-than-savory aspects of the Dharma. But this scholarship has not had much of a trickle-down effect on popular perceptions. Buddhism still retains its aura of being as pure as the driven snow. Whether this is true or not, however, is not the point to be argued here. Rather, the point is simply to reveal how the popular vision of the Dharma potentially shapes or distorts the story of what happened when Buddhism came into contact with Islam.

Such misconceptions are not the only thing to bear in mind as we begin unraveling this history. It is important to note two other points as well. The first is that Buddhism is not one teaching, school, or tradition. Rather, as with any religion it developed over time into an array of widely divergent and competing schools of thought. By the time of Islam's appearance in South Asia the Dharma had in fact broken off into three radically different traditions: the Nikaya schools, the Mahayana, and Tantric Buddhism. Muslims thus did not come into contact with a monolithic "Buddhism," but with a wide array of Buddhists with diverse beliefs and practices.

Similarly, no one unified group comprised "Muslims." What it meant to be a Muslim was very much under debate at the time Islam came into contact with the Dharma. Indeed it is vital to recognize that most of the ideas and practices that we today identify as "Islam" were articulated only in the ninth and tenth century. Thus Islam as it was understood and practiced before then was something different, and in approaching the history of Buddhist-Muslim interaction it is important to keep such realities in mind. In particular, we need to recognize that Buddhism and Islam were not two monolithic and static entities crashing into one another. Rather, both religions were diverse and ever-developing traditions that were not only grappling with their own internal theological developments, but also trying to understand the world outside their own particular communities.

In addition to keeping these larger realities in mind we also need to take into consideration the issue of economics. Whether religious traditions want to recognize it or not, the fact is that as with any social institution, a community of faith cannot survive without financial support. Indeed, as history has repeatedly shown, only those traditions that successfully raise capital survive. Those that do not receive money inevitably disappear. For example, of the sixteen Nikaya schools of early Buddhism only one survives, the Theravada, which is now practiced largely in Sri Lanka and Southeast

Asia. In approaching the issue of Buddhism and Islam we therefore cannot overlook the interrelationship between religions and the economic systems that support them. And this is especially important in regard to the Dharma. Although the linkage between Islam and the world of trade is rather well known, it is less so with Buddhism.[8] Namely, with its ultimate quest being the overcoming of desire, the Dharma is often seen as being antithetical to, or at least unconcerned with, the everyday realities of making money. This is a mistake.

The Buddha, or perhaps more aptly his disciples who codified his teachings, were astute theoreticians of economic realities. The Dharma is thus intimately tied into the changing socioeconomic world of early India and it is precisely on this account that Buddhism resonated most with the new, urban trading class. They were the ones who supported the Dharma and fostered its spread on the trade routes across Asia. Buddhism thus came to be—much as it is today—the religion of choice for the urban, cosmopolitan elite. It would in many ways hold this position for nearly a millennium. Only then would it be challenged by Islam, a new religion also supported by an urban cosmopolitan elite operating within the expansive economic regime of the Caliphate.

The Economy of Salvation

Having been told in various media—from texts to statues, paintings to film—the life story of the Buddha is well known. He was born Siddhartha Gautama, the son of a king who ruled a territory that is now in southern Nepal. His birth involved several miracles and so his father summoned his priests in order to interpret these portentous omens. They in turn declared the child would either be a renouncer and great religious teacher, or else a powerful king and world conqueror. Fearful that his son would not continue in the family business of politics, and instead follow some half-naked and dreadlocked guru, the king ordered Siddhartha to never leave the palace. His father also spoiled him rotten. Siddhartha had everything a boy and young man could ever want: toys, food, chariots, and women. But Siddhartha was curious, and one night with the help of his manservant he snuck out of the palace. What he saw shocked him, especially the sight of a sick man, an old man, and a corpse. Only then did he realize that this was his and everyone else's fate. He wondered what could be done about it.

At that point he saw a renouncer, someone who was trying to answer this question, and he decided to follow the religious path. Abandoning his father's palace he studied with various teachers over the next several years but none of their ideas or practices really answered the big question: the meaning of life. He therefore decided to go it alone. While sitting in meditation under a large banyan tree he had three visions. The first was about the nature of time as evidenced in all his previous births; the second revealed the nature of space as witnessed in his visit to the six realms of existence (gods, demi-gods, humans, animals, hungry ghosts, hell). Then finally he had the ultimate realization of enlightenment: no-self. The Buddha encapsulated this new wisdom in the Four Noble Truths:

1. There is suffering
2. Suffering comes from desire
3. Nirvana is the solution
4. Nirvana can be achieved by means of the Eight-fold Buddhist Path.

Siddhartha preached this Dharma for the next forty years.

The biography of the Buddha is a wonderful story. It is another issue entirely, however, whether it has any historical validity. The truth of the matter is that we know virtually nothing about the historical Buddha, not even when he lived.[9] This fact, however, does not mean that the biography is meaningless. Quite the opposite. By means of parables and metaphors it encapsulates the entirety of the Buddha's teaching, its cosmology, doctrines, and communal structures. For example, the initial prophecy of the two paths the Buddha could take in life explains the two interdependent components of the Buddhist community: the religious specialists who renounce the world, and those who live in the world and support them. The Buddha's imprisonment and debauched early life is, of course, a parable of desire, the material world, and the cycle of samsara that enlightenment enables one to transcend.

The biography of the Buddha is therefore not history, but myth. These two different realities may or may not intersect, but nevertheless each still creates meaning. In this regard one can also note that as the Dharma changed over time so too did the Buddha's biography. The Buddha's crass abandonment of his pregnant wife when he set out on his religious quest, for example, did not sit well with later family-values-type Buddhists and this episode was thus re-envisioned. The Buddha still left his wife, a central component of the story that could not be changed, but he did so in a loving and compassionate way. Moreover, the child she carried in her womb remained there until the moment of the Buddha's enlightenment, thereby linking forever the birth of his son with the Dharma.[10] Whether his wife or any woman would want to be pregnant for six years was of not much concern since as with most religions Buddhism was very much a man's world and such women's issues were beside the point.

Yet what were the concerns of the Buddha? What was the environment or historical context that not only shaped him, but also that he was engaging or challenging with his teachings? What was he responding to? What was he reinterpreting? The fact that we do not know precisely when the Buddha lived certainly hinders our attempt at answering these questions. In fact one scholar has recently lamented, "an adequately detailed and historically sensitive account of just what the critique enunciated by early Buddhism meant within the larger intellectual and cultural history of the subcontinent remains an important desideratum for Indological scholarship."[11] And although this may indeed be the case, we are not wholly ignorant of the historical context in which the Dharma was formed.

Most notably we know that during this period of time (600–300 B.C.E.), the so-called "axial age," India was undergoing enormous changes politically, economically, culturally, and technologically.[12] All of these intertwined developments had a profound impact on not only the structure and nature of Indian society, but also on how people understood the very nature of human experience. It was within this changing milieu that the Buddha and others like him, such as the Hindu Upanisadic thinkers and the Jains, were trying to answer the big questions about the meaning of life. And in this regard the Buddha's fundamental idea that everything changes well captured the tenor of the times.

One such change involved the nature of political structures. As reflected in the Buddha's biography and the nature of his father's kingdom, India at the time was supposedly divided into small lineage-based republics (map 1).[13] These small republics, however, were gradually being challenged, and ultimately they were defeated and absorbed into more complex kingdoms. While these kingdoms were still ruled by families, these larger entities were also inevitably becoming more genealogically diffuse. As a result these new states needed more abstract ideologies of legitimacy than the earlier clan-based political structures.[14] Moreover, in order to maintain these new states the ruling elite needed not only ideological innovations, but also a greater

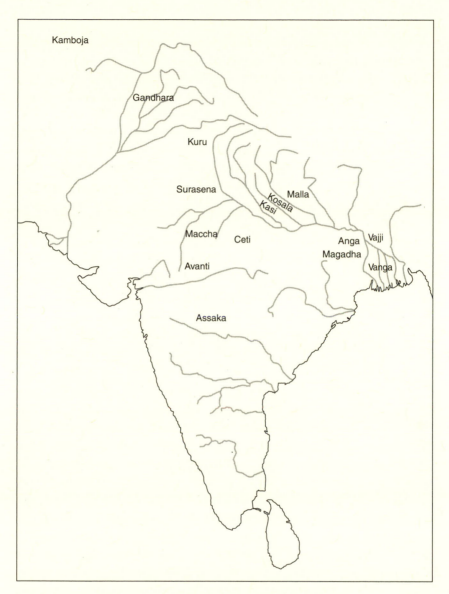

Map 1. Sixteen "great countries" of India at time of Buddha.

resource base with which to finance the structures that sustained this new entity. In particular, the court needed to pay their burgeoning bureaucracies, and also their armies.

Coincidentally these demands arose at the same time that iron was introduced into India. The ability to forge iron led to two major innovations. The first was the development of the iron plow that enabled the widespread cultivation of rice, which in turn led to a shift from nomadic pastoralism to farming, which in turn fostered the rise of cities. Urbanization itself invariably brought with it enormous changes as well, including the rise of trade and a merchant class. Moreover, the development of cities and a complex economy also demanded the need for protection. To safeguard these new enterprises of business and state-formation armies were necessary and of course iron made far better weapons.[15]

In short, all of these innovations were developing in tandem and they fostered the development of centralizing states. And these states were developing in relation to these changes. Namely, on account of agricultural surplus and increasing financial transactions these states could establish a regular system of taxation that could in turn pay for both an educated bureaucracy and a standing army. And all of these intertwined technological, social, economic, and political developments came together during the formation of the Mauryan Empire (322–185 B.C.E.), which was to control the largest territorial expanse of India until the coming of the British (map 2).

Forging such an empire certainly depended upon many factors; however, one of the most important was the creation and circulation of financial capital. Thus in tandem with the innovations noted above one of the key developments that transformed India during this period was the introduction of money. Monetization has always had a profound impact on all facets of a society, and not only in regard to the economy. Indeed, it is not a coincidence that the intellectual reevaluations of the Greek philosophers occurred shortly after the minting of coins in the Mediterranean.[16] Nor is it "coincidental that two of the more memorable episodes from the accounts of Jesus' life—his encounter with the moneychangers in the Jerusalem temple, and his remark about rendering unto Caesar that which was Caesar's—involved coins."[17] The reason for this is that money allows for a leveling of reality that puts everything, even things categorically different—an avocado, a day's labor, a temple—on the same plane and thus makes them comparable. At the same time the introduction of money introduces a new level of abstraction, especially through usury, that funda-

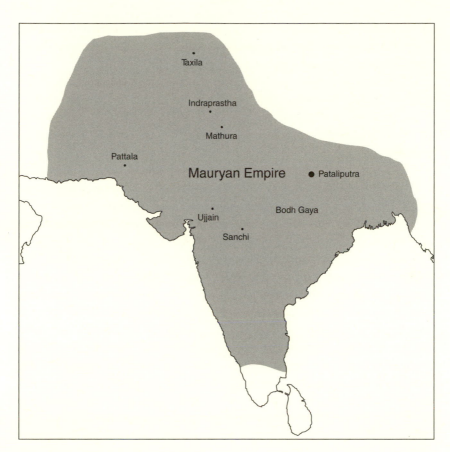

Map 2. Mauryan Empire.

mentally changes the nature of the world; and therefore this new reality and its intellectual implications needed to be explained.

The leveling of reality and abstraction that the introduction of money generates, however, are not only an intellectual problem. As evidenced in today's world and the spread of neoliberal capitalism, such changes in economic regimes bring enormous challenges to the standing order. In particular, the introduction of money and a market economy engenders massive social transformations by reformulating not only preexisting social orders, but also their underpinning conceptualizations and moral values. The acquisition of wealth, for example, promotes individualism and mobility

and thereby challenges traditional family structures. In short, the introduction of money is enormously disruptive, and it was precisely within this
changing world that the Dharma was formulated.

The Dharma is therefore not only a reflection of these transformations,
but also an interpretation. And within this conceptualization the Buddha
came to be presented as a radical progressive. But not necessarily in the
way he is often imagined: as a social critic of the caste system, or as an early
exponent of some kind of premodern Marxist utopia. Rather, the Buddha
was a thinker who fully supported the new market economy and all it
entailed: urbanization, trade, familial reordering, and new political structures. Thus instead of clinging to an idealized or romantic notion of the
past he urged his followers to move forward and embrace these new economic and social transformations. For example, if this meant giving up
nomadic pastoralism and thereby changing completely one's social and
economic world, then do it.[18] However, in the Buddha's estimation the best
plan of action was to leave the farm, the family, and all the old traditions
behind entirely and instead move into the city and create a new religious
identity within the world of business.

It was within this urban world of trade that the Dharma thrived. It is
therefore no surprise that the Buddha's teachings are filled with references
to this world. Early Buddhist scriptures even contain rates of currency conversion.[19] Moreover, debt and trade are used as similes and parables of
one's spiritual hindrances. Wealth is a sign of goodness, while if one is bad
then one will go bankrupt.[20] Indeed, the accumulation of wealth and its
display through material possessions is well captured in the Buddha's
description of an ostentatious mansion of the day: "A wealthy businessman
or his son has a house with a gabled roof, plastered inside and outside with
well-fitting doors and casements. Therein a couch is spread with a costly
skin of antelope, having a canopy overhead and a scarlet cushion at each
end. Here is a lamp burning and four wives wait upon him with all their
charms."[21]

Making money and being rich was therefore not a problem for the
Buddha. Quite the opposite, in fact, because the production of wealth came
to fundamentally shape Buddhist doctrine and practice.

Buddhist literature and art are therefore filled with elements related to
the new world of trade that flourished in the monetized Mauryan Empire.
Indeed, the linkage between the Dharma and this economic realm is well
captured in a special stipulation of the monastic code: namely, the Buddha

had initially decreed that all monks must stay in one place during the rainy season, and it is from this practice that the monastic institution itself actually evolved. However, in recognition of the link between the demands of business and the Dharma, the Buddha allowed monks to violate this regulation if they were traveling with a merchant caravan or trading vessel.[22] In fact, over time the Buddha himself came to be portrayed in Buddhist art and literature as a merchant caravaneer.[23] And stories abounded of how he saved merchants lost at sea or in the desert.[24] From these stories it is clear that the Buddha, or his later disciples who codified his teachings, were acutely aware of the socioeconomic changes unfolding at the time. Yet the Dharma did not only mirror these developments. It also tried to analyze them by looking at "the processes that underlie need and desire, production and work, giving and taking, hierarchy and equality, coming into being and dissolution."[25] Thus while the Buddha's teaching came to ultimately critique the material world, it also recognized that the world of trade and money could not be entirely rejected.

In this regard he differed importantly from other thinkers of the time. Hindu philosophers in India and the Confucians in China, for example, were both profoundly wary of a monetized economy and its social implications. In particular, they wanted to prevent the massive social transformations that a market economy invariably brought with it. Both of these traditions therefore clung conservatively to the past and bemoaned how these new developments threatened society's very moral order. As a result, both of these traditions argued that the market economy should be resisted. Confucian thinkers, for example, created an idealized four-fold hierarchy of society with merchants at the bottom.[26] Hindu law codes did the same. The Brahmans condemned activities essential for business, such as international travel, and also strictly regulated the new merchant class. For good measure these law codes also placed businessmen among the people who needed to be avoided, like drunkards, sadists, and lepers.[27]

The Dharma, however, took the opposing view. The Buddha and his disciples realized that a monetized economy and the new business elite were the future, as is clear from the story of Trapussa and Bhallika, the Buddha's first lay disciples. These two businessmen were not like the Buddha's former mendicant colleagues, who upon hearing the Dharma in the Deer Park wanted to become monks. Trapussa and Bhallika did not want to give up the comforts of everyday life. In return for a donation the Buddha therefore offered them a list of deities who, if prayed to, would protect them while traveling on business. This exchange established the social and ritual dynamic between the monastics and the laity that still defines the Buddhist community today.

Yet the Buddha went even beyond this mapping out of the social order. He even incorporated the very act of wealth-creation into Buddhist doctrine and practice since in his view the best way to generate positive karma is through the production of wealth, which can then be used to support the Dharma. Making money is thus a fundamental part of being Buddhist. It is nothing to be ashamed of. In fact it is essential to create merit, and wealth itself is a sign of good karma.[28] Indeed, this dynamic and the new realities of social mobility in the market economy of early India are well captured in a remarkable story from the *Milindapañhā*. In this story a prostitute has acquired so much merit, and thus power, that she can make the Ganges River flow backwards. The famous Buddhist king Asoka is so astounded at this display of power that he wants to know how it was done, and the answer he receives is the transmutation of financial capital into merit. However, the most remarkable aspect of the story involves why this particular prostitute was so successful: she treated all her customers the same regardless of caste or class. As she explains to Asoka, "Whoever, sire, gives me wealth, whether he be a noble or a Brahman or a merchant or a worker or anyone else, I minister to each in the same manner not thinking there is any special elegance in a noble or anything contemptible in a worker. I serve each lord of wealth without approval or repugnance."[29] Thus as one scholar has astutely observed, the Buddha did not really challenge the caste system as is often claimed, but rather he critiqued it economically since in a market system "receiving services is not conditioned by one's position in the status hierarchy, but on one's ability to pay for services."[30]

Money and its acquisition therefore mattered to the Buddha and his followers. But the Dharma was not simply an early form of prosperity theology. It also recognized the harsh realities unleashed by a market economy. Early Buddhist texts thus reveal not only the realities of economic specialization, but also the inevitable disparities in wealth they generate.[31] The early Buddhist canon, for example, recognizes six classes of financial being: very wealthy, wealthy, faring well, faring poorly, poor, and destitute.[32] In turn it was these distinctions and the sufferings created by the system itself that the Dharma was ultimately critiquing. But at the same time the Buddha also recognized that the material world of wealth was a necessary evil until the final utopia of universal Nirvana had ultimately been achieved. The

Dharma thus skillfully both legitimated and undermined the creation of wealth. As a result, the teaching of the Buddha not only came to resonate with the merchant classes of early India, but also continues to do so with today's urban, wealthy elite in both the West and East.

At one time this was also the case with Islam. For centuries Islam was the cosmopolitan religion par excellence. Moreover, much as Buddhism had done in its time, Islam came to both represent and resolve the concerns of a new urban elite that was created in tandem with the enormous economic and social transformations unleashed by the Arab conquests. As a result, if one is to understand the early history of Buddhist-Muslim interaction, it is important to recognize that Islam arose in the same context of social, political, and economic upheaval as did the Dharma.

Unfortunately, just as in the case of Buddhism, the origin and early history of Islam is obscure since we do not have any contemporary sources. The earliest extant biography of Muhammad, for example, was written over a century after the Prophet's death.[33] As one scholar has recently noted, it is difficult to know much of anything about Islamic history before the end of the eighth century since "none of the Islamic texts available to us yet existed."[34] This, however, is not to say that traditional Muslim scholars as well as contemporary scholars have not tried. And thus as with the biography of the Buddha there is now an established narrative of the Prophet Muhammad.

He was born around 570 C.E. into the Banu Hashim, a once prominent family of Mecca that had fallen on hard times. After both his mother and father passed away Muhammad was raised by his beloved uncle, Abu Talib, with whom he also learned the family business of trading as they followed the caravans up and down the Arabian peninsula. In his mid-twenties, however, Muhammad settled down in Mecca and married the forty-year-old widow Khadija. Then, after fathering six children, Muhammad began to retreat to Mount Hira in order to meditate. It was in a cave during one such retreat during the month of Ramadan that Muhammad first received God's revelation through the angel Gabriel. At first he was afraid he was going crazy; however, after confiding in his wife Muhammad realized that these were true revelations.

After receiving more of them over the course of several years Muhammad then began to preach. At first the people of Mecca did not mind; however, over time they became openly hostile toward Muhammad. It was at this time, around 620 C.E., that Muhammad made his miraculous journey to Jerusalem in one night. On the back of the magical steed Buraq he also toured heaven and hell with the angel Gabriel. He also spoke with the earlier prophets Abraham, Moses, and Jesus. The Meccans, however, were unswayed and the situation grew tense. Fortunately, two years later the twelve clans of Yathrib invited Muhammad to come to their city as a neutral mediator to resolve their long running feuds. Muhammad accepted the offer and with his followers he set about establishing the first Muslim community. Yet as this group expanded, relations between the recently established Muslim community in Medina, the "City of the Prophet" (*madīnat al-nabbī*), and Mecca deteriorated. Fighting broke out and only in 630 did Muhammad and his Muslim army emerge victorious and seize Mecca. Two years later Muhammad passed away after having made his final pilgrimage to the Ka'ba.

As with the biography of the Buddha it is unclear how much of this is historically accurate, or how much of it is a mythic formulation in relation to later Islamic doctrine. Indeed, since most of it was codified only when Muslims were much later required to explain to others who Muhammad actually was, it is an open question whether this story reflects historical realities or else the concerns of later Muslims who projected their ideas back into the past.[35] Moreover, as Muhammad came to be conceived as the paragon of human action in later Islamic thought there was also an explosion of stories about what he said and did since such episodes were seen as establishing guidelines for what it meant to be a Muslim. Thus, for example, if Muhammad had a beard, a Muslim should have a beard. Of course, as can well be imagined in the context of conflicting views about what it meant to be Muslim, differing stories about the Prophet also arose. As a result, when the Sunna, or traditions of the Prophet, were collected during the eighth and ninth centuries a central preoccupation of the compilers was whether a particular story, or Hadith, was legitimate or not. And this concern still continues today since it is precisely these stories that in addition to the Qur'an are the fundamental textual materials that define Islamic practice and exegesis.

Approaching this material from a historical perspective can therefore be quite problematic. Numerous scholars have in fact shown that the traditional story of Muhammad and early Islam is not only rife with oversights and simplifications, but also largely shaped by the concerns of later historians, scholars, and jurists each promoting their own, often competing interpretations. Much recent scholarship has therefore been aimed at challenging the Islamic tradition's own narrative and problematizing the formulaic idea that Islam was fully articulated during the lifetime of Muhammad. Scholars have therefore pointed out that fundamental components of Islam, such as the theoretical basis of Islamic law in which scholars have the authority to interpret the Sunna and Qur'an, was fully developed only in the ninth century. Moreover, many "aspects of Islam—its theological positions, the adoption of Islam as a religion by individuals and communities, the development of Shi'i Islam in its various forms—confirm that many of the important features we regard as typical, and by which we identify Islam as a distinct tradition of monotheism, only became established in the third/ninth or even the fourth/tenth century."[36]

Some scholars have even tackled the thorny issue of the Qur'an's creation, which strikes at the heart of the central Muslim belief that it is the eternal and unadulterated word of God as revealed to Muhammad and codified under Caliph Uthman (644–56 C.E.). Undaunted by such claims some intrepid scholars have used philology and the higher criticism of Biblical scholarship to show that the Qur'an, just like the Bible or the Buddhist canon, not only drew upon earlier sources, but was also compiled over time.[37] The most famous piece of evidence in this regard is the Qur'anic inscription on the Dome of the Rock. The passage is the earliest extant verse from the Qur'an yet it does not accord with the parallel passage found in the standard received version of the Qur'an itself. Numerous explanations have been offered to explain this discrepancy;[38] however, the central point to be drawn from all this material is that Islam, just like any religion, is a work in progress.

And in this regard it is important to note that many of the factors that played a role in forging the Buddhist tradition were similar in the case of Islam. These include not only the social and political dislocations inherent in the shift from the tribal society of the Arabian peninsula to that of an urban imperial milieu, but also all of the new ideas and technologies that the Arabs had to grapple with and make sense of as their empire expanded. Indeed, what is remarkable in this regard is how successful the Arabs were in accommodating themselves to these new realities. While the open and malleable nature of Islam certainly contributed to this success, another was the unprecedented economic boom facilitated by the unification and pacification of an enormous territory under Muslim power.

Arabs, of course, had always been involved with trade. For those in Mecca and Medina it may not have been as much, or of the kind maintained in traditional accounts,[39] but in the wake of the Arab conquests international trade exploded. The Caliphate was in fact the first empire in history to successfully link and integrate the trading networks of the Mediterranean and Indian Ocean. Moreover, the Arabs took all the gold and silver hoarded over the centuries by the Byzantine and Sassanid Empires and put this money into circulation. The fact that all this newly created money was standardized in the gold dinar and silver dirham also meant that the Muslims created a unified economic zone in which one could easily travel and trade across three continents.[40]

While this was clearly an enormous achievement it also brought with it enormous changes. Much as had been the case in India a thousand years earlier, these developments brought with them massive social upheavals. For example, the development of international trade ushered in urbanization and all the consequences that Hindus and Confucians were afraid of, such as social mobility and the rise of individualism. As a result early Muslim thinkers had to face the same issues that early Buddhists had to deal with, and in time the Islamic tradition in fact came to confront these issues head-on with a powerful message of moral order, universal equality, and social justice.

Yet, much as Buddhism, so too did Islam both skillfully reinforce and condemn the social and economic transformations of its time. Thus as Islam moved further and further away from its tribal origins, it developed into an urban religion grounded in the world of trade.[41] As Emperor Jahangir of the Mughal dynasty summarized it: "Of all the professions, only trade is respectable in the eyes of Islam."[42] Thus much like Buddhism, the Islamic tradition came to be both shaped and articulated within this framework, especially during the early Abbasid period (752–1258 C.E.) when most Muslim scholars and jurists were drawn from the families of the cosmopolitan elite.[43] It is therefore perhaps not surprising that Islamic law and theology came to be defined by the concerns of this merchant class.

Islamic law, or *shari'a*, therefore came to value things that would make one successful in the world of trade. These included practices that are today more commonly identified with the "Protestant work ethic," such as individual property, responsibility, and thrift. In fact, the value of trade and the commercial spirit was so important in early Islam that much of the *shari'a* is devoted to supporting it. "One of the more colorful examples is found in a treatise, *Kitāb al-Kasb* (roughly, "on earning"), attributed to the Hanafi jurist al-Shaybani (d. 804), which reports a story about 'Umar ibn al-Khattab. The caliph saw a group of pious and penitent (and inactive) men and, told that they were *mutawakkilūn*, 'those who patiently rely upon God,' responded: No, they are the *muta'akillūn*, 'those who eat up [other people's money].'"[44]

Of course, the tension between creating wealth and sincere "non-productive" piety is not unique to Islam. It was precisely this issue that the Dharma resolved by creating the two interdependent wings of the Buddhist community, the monastics and the laity. Islam, on the other hand, never developed a monastic tradition. Nevertheless, even though it differed greatly from Buddhism in this regard Islam was also clearly grappling theologically with the social transformations ushered in by radical economic and political developments brought on by the Arab conquests.

Even though the solutions ultimately offered by the Buddha and Muhammad were not the same, both traditions were remarkably adept at not only recognizing the contemporary social transformations and accepting them, but also weaving these new realities into the very doctrinal and social fabric of their respective traditions. In this way both religions spoke to a new, urban, merchant class, which was unsurprisingly often despised by the earlier society that was itself being undermined by the very forces Buddhism and Islam supported. As a result, both traditions offered this new class of people a means of validating itself in this new socioeconomic world by means of religion; and thus it is not surprising that it was precisely in this context where Buddhism and Islam first came into contact.[45]

Shifting Trade Networks

With its intimate connection to the world of business it is no surprise that the spread of Buddhism coincided neatly with the expansion of trade routes, cities, and ultimately imperial domains.[46] Of course, this linkage also meant that as trade networks shifted and empires crumbled so too did the Dharma. In order to begin the project of unraveling the impact that the new globalized economic religious imperium of Islam was to have on the Buddhist world, it is therefore necessary to recall that more than a thousand years had passed between the Buddha and Muhammad. This is an enormous span of time and during it, just as the Buddha had preached, everything changed. Not only did the Dharma itself fracture into distinct and often antagonistic traditions, but the trading networks enabled by the unifying laissez-faire states of early India, which had sustained the Buddhist tradition, had also passed away. Thus rather than coming into contact with a monolithic and triumphant Buddhism, the first Arab Muslims appeared in South Asia at a time of economic reorganization and Dharmic theological diffusion.

It had not always been so. As noted above, the Dharma was both a creation of and reaction to the developments of monetization, urbanization, and political consolidation during the several centuries before the Common Era, all of which were captured within the Dharma, and as we have seen, the Buddha's message was most appealing to the landed gentry and the urban merchant elite. These were the people who could generate and reinvest financial capital, which generated not only religious merit, but also in turn helped institutionalize the Dharma since monasteries functioned as banks in this early period.[47] And it was these same financial resources that also underwrote both the Mauryan Empire and its successor state of the Central Asian Kushans (first to third centuries c.e.). And even though neither one of these empires was specifically Buddhist—preferring instead to support all the religions within their domains—the ruling elite of both the Mauryan and Kushan empires were clearly aware of the importance the Dharma and its trading networks had in generating tax revenues for the state. Traveling Buddhist merchants could also bring back valuable goods, ideas, and technologies from abroad. The Mauryas, for example, adopted numerous practices from the Achaemenid Empire of Persia. It was thus on account of these interconnections that a powerful symbiotic relationship developed among these states, the merchant elite, and the Dharma, all of which resulted in the rapid spread of Buddhism within what one scholar has called the "Buddhist international,"[48] namely, a Buddhist world system that functioned as a communication network within "which ideas, commodities, and peoples circulated throughout Eurasia."[49]

Within the Buddhist international's nexus of trade, empire, and religion there was one region that was to play a pivotal role: northwest India up to the Hindu Kush (which now includes much of Afghanistan and Pakistan) and Central Asia (the area north of the Hindu Kush stretching to the Kazakh steppe and flanked in the west by the Caspian Sea and the Tianshan mountains in the east, which is now largely comprised of the five post-soviet states of Turkmenistan, Kazakhstan, Kyrgyzstan, Uzbekistan, and Tajikistan). These two areas were perfectly situated to function as the hub of the global economy since they linked not only the overland trade between Rome and China, but also connected this east-west trade with the maritime trade of the Indian Ocean through the port of Bharuch/Barygaza, now in Gujarat. Thus as the economy expanded under the Mauryas and Kushans there was an attendant expansion of the Dharma in these areas. In particular, the resident elites used their new wealth to support the building of monasteries, the production of Buddhist literature, and most famously the creation of Buddhist sculpture. Indeed, the sculptures of Gandhara, with their blending of east and west, are a world-famous monument to the cosmopolitan core of the Buddhist international (figure 3).[50]

Above and beyond this artistic florescence, however, what was remarkable about the economic expansion in the area of northwest India was that it went on for centuries. The economy and the Dharma even continued to flourish as the Indian dynasty of the Mauryas gave way to the Central Asian Kushan dynasty. In fact it was under the Kushans that economic activity and the support of Buddhism in northwest India reached its apex (map 3).

Moreover, it was during this time that Buddhist traders and missionaries actually ventured forth all the way to China and established what was to become a most fruitful mission both economically and spiritually.

But the situation in northwest India and Central Asia started to slowly unravel in the third century c.e.[51] There were several interlocking reasons for this downturn, but it was most likely set in motion by a series of military conquests. In 232 c.e. the Kushans lost parts of northwest India and Central Asia to the new Persian dynasty of the Sassanids (240–651 c.e.). Yet their hold on power was short-lived on account of the Hepthalites, or White Huns, another Central Asian dynasty that conquered the area north of the Hindu Kush and ruled it for more than two centuries (350–550 c.e.). Regardless of the differences between the Sassanid and Hepthalite regimes both had clearly invaded this predominantly Buddhist area in order to take control of the lucrative trade routes and the revenue they generated. And to a certain extent they succeeded. Even the White Huns, who are often portrayed as being purely destructive, tried valiantly to keep the economy going.[52] In the early sixth century they even secured a huge amount of silver from the Sassanids in order to monetize the economy.[53] Of course, this cash infusion and its economic impact may have been what drew the Turks to invade and conquer the region fifty years later.[54] Shortly thereafter came the Chinese and Tibetans and finally the Arabs, all culminating in the famous Battle of Talas in 751.

While this historical sketch is brief it nevertheless brings to the fore the central consequence of the Kushan's loss of the northwest and their retreat

Figure 3. Gandharan Buddha, Pakistan, ca. third century (1982.33). Reproduced courtesy of The Trammell and Margaret Crow Collection of Asian Art.

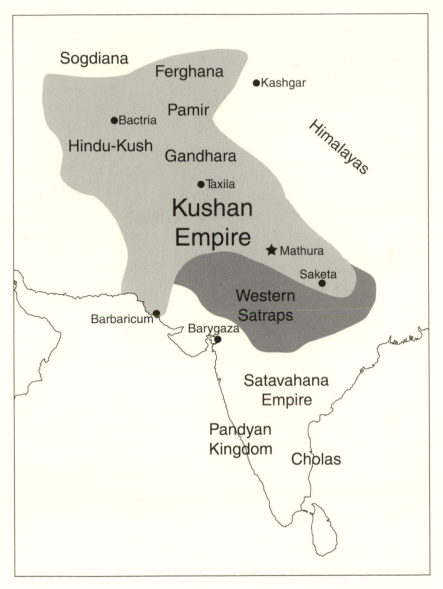

Map 3. Kushan Empire.

to the south: the removal of northwest India and Central Asia from the Indic orbit. This was a radical development because this area had been the center of gravity for Indian civilization for centuries. By moving south the Kushan dynasty therefore not only left an economic and social vacuum in their wake, but upon their arrival in north India they also had to come to terms with the new realities of an overwhelmingly Hindu world. It was therefore in this context that a new civilizational model arose that moved away from the Dharma and was instead grounded on the use of Sanskrit and drew political inspiration from the Hindu epics of the *Mahābhārata* and the *Rāmāyaṇa*.[55] Yet while this so-called "Sanskrit cosmopolis" was to have an enormous impact from India to Vietnam over the coming centuries, it had little impact on northwest India. And one of the key consequences of being left out of the new Sanskrit cosmopolis was that the old Buddhist economy of northwest India collapsed.

The Chinese pilgrim Faxian (ca. 337–422 C.E.), for example, recorded the shift of trade routes toward Kashmir in the early fifth century.[56] Two centuries later the famous Tang-dynasty pilgrim Xuanzang (602–64 C.E.) simply noted that the earlier trading cities of northwest India, such as Taxila, were in ruins.[57] In fact it was in this dilapidated state that Muslims found the area when they invaded shortly after Xuanzang had passed through, which is a reality the ninth century Muslim historian Baladhuri captures well. Rather than describing Buddhist riches he writes that "there was a scarcity of water in India, dates were bad and bandits daring. A small contingent of army would be liquidated, and a large army would die of starvation and hunger."[58] Yet the Arabs persisted with their incursions into this area. A valid question is why? The fact of the matter is that Baladhuri's description has more to do with military logistics than any real cultural or economic analysis. Other sources, for example, note that Muhammad al-Qasim, the conqueror of northwest India, actually brought back to Iraq a war booty of 120 million dirhams.[59] Money was thus certainly there, but not necessarily Buddhists'. Indeed, as Xuanzang lamented, many of the old trade routes in the valleys south of the Hindu Kush where Buddhism originally flourished had gone bust.

One reason Buddhism failed in this region was, as noted above, the move of the Kushans to the south and the creation of a specifically Hindu cultural and political sphere that was to dominate South Asia for a millennium. Yet another important factor driving this change was the environment. In particular, when the cities of Loulan and Niya in the southern Tarim Basin succumbed to environmental degradation, the main artery linking northwest India and China disappeared (map 4).

As a result, northwest India lost its relevance as a key hub of international trade. Of course, the trade did not end; it simply relocated. In particular, when the southern route dried up the trading networks moved to the northern side of the Taklamakan Desert along the southern edge of the Tianshan mountains. In tandem with this shift the economic center of gravity also shifted away from northwest India to Central Asia, whereupon the local Sogdians, an Iranian people living in the area around Samarkand, came to dominate international trade.[60] These developments, however, did not signal the end of the Dharma entirely. Rather, as one would expect, enterprising Buddhist merchants followed these economic shifts. Thus as Buddhist institutions waned in northwest India there was a simultaneous building boom in Central Asia at places like Adjina Tepe (Tajikistan), Kuva in Ferghana (Uzbekistan), and Ak-Beshim near Bishkek (Kyrgyzstan).[61] Yet it was not only Buddhist merchants who were involved in this shift. The

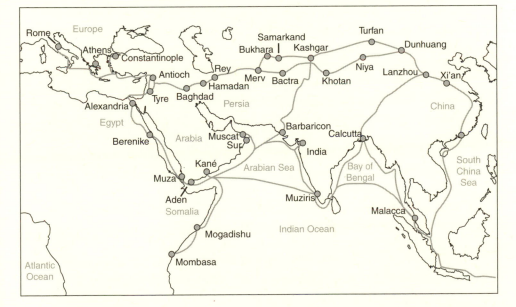

Map 4. Silk Road.

Chinese state recognized the linkage between Buddhism and trade and therefore supported the building of Buddhist monasteries in Central Asia in order to advance their foreign policy.[62]

Yet at the same time that both trade and Buddhism were moving north, new trading networks were also developing in the south. During the third and fourth centuries C.E., in tandem with the rise of the powerful Gupta dynasty in India (320–550 C.E.) and the consolidation of Sassanid power in Iran, there was an expansion of maritime trade across the Indian Ocean. Trading networks thus not only moved down the Konkan coast to Sri Lanka,[63] but also flourished between India and Iran with the Aksumite Empire of Ethiopia, whose control of this east-west maritime trade was to be challenged only with the subsequent rise of Islam. But before the Muslim conquests Buddhist merchants had handled much of this trade—so much so that objects from Africa, such as ostrich eggs, came to be housed in Buddhist monasteries.[64] It is thus clear that the rise of maritime trade resulted in Buddhist migrations toward these new trading networks in both the north and south along the rim of the Indian Ocean. The Chinese pilgrim Xuanzang, for example, came upon more Buddhists in his travels along the Persian Gulf in what is now eastern Iran and Pakistan than in the former Buddhist heartland of northwest India.[65] Moreover, it is also known from Muslim sources that Buddhists were not the only ones interested in this trade, because Arabs from Oman settled in this area as well. They were in fact to become an important beachhead for the subsequent development of Muslim maritime trade.

Nevertheless, this shift toward maritime trade did not entail the end of either east-west or north-south trade; however, both were rerouted toward the west as much of this trade came under the control of the Sassanids in Iran. And in tandem with this shift Buddhist merchants and their institutions also began to move westward.[66] It was in fact at this time that Buddhist centers expanded greatly in what is now Afghanistan, most notably Bamiyan.[67]

Buddhist merchants made an intrepid lot. They moved themselves and their financial capital in order to maximize their profit. And at this time probably the greatest arena in which to do so was the broader Sanskrit cosmopolis of the Gupta Empire that had conquered the Kushan dynasty. This newly unified cultural and economic zone of north India was a bonanza not only because of the enormous wealth that circulated within it, but also because it was predominantly Hindu and thus in various ways antibusiness. Buddhists could thus once again monopolize the expanding market economy.[68] Indeed, such a cycle of events played itself out numerous times in Indian history, as evidenced in eighth-to-twelfth-century Malabar, where Hinduization coincided with growth in trade with the Islamic world. Yet because Hinduism imposed restrictions on maritime travel and social interaction, Hindu involvement in the new economy was actually minimal. The burgeoning market therefore came to be controlled by Buddhists, Jains, Muslims, and Jews whose status and social ranks derived not from the caste system but from "the tradition of physical mobility and participation in trade."[69] And the situation was the same during the Gupta period because, in addition to the growth of temple Hinduism based on the new *Purāṇa* scriptures, this period also witnessed an expanding economy and the growth of a new urban cosmopolitan culture.

Indeed, this development is perhaps best captured in the most famous text from the Gupta period, the third-century manual for the man-about-town, the *Kāmasūtra.*[70] Of course, if one was to follow the advice of this lifestyle manual and while away the day drinking tea and reading poetry, and then at night engaging in wildly imaginative sexual gymnastics, it would certainly be helpful if one had a well-endowed trust fund, and apparently many did. Moreover, the one group that was very successful in this new gilded age were the Buddhists, and as a result the Dharma expanded at this time not only within the economic networks of India, but also across the broader Sanskrit cosmopolis into Southeast Asia.

New Times, New Ideas

Before looking further at these shifting trade networks and the concomitant territorial contraction and expansion of the Dharma in the centuries before Islam's arrival in South Asia, we need to recall that Buddhism itself was also transforming. In many ways this may not have been anything new, since apparently from the beginning there had been disputes about what the Buddha had actually taught. In fact to settle these disputes Four Councils had purportedly been held, but disagreements persisted and what is known as the sixteen schools arose.[71] Each school presented their own interpretation of the thorniest issues of Buddhist doctrine—such as if there is no soul, or no-self, who or what is actually reincarnated?—and invariably, as with any religious dispute, certain factions were successful and received institutional support, while others simply faded away.

In spite of these disputes, however, certain key principles were never challenged within the early Buddhist schools. But this was to change with the appearance of what came to be known as the Mahayana, the "Great Vehicle." Unfortunately, the origins of the Mahayana are now lost in the proverbial fog of history.[72] The date of its origin is placed anywhere from the first century B.C.E. to the fifth century C.E. Some claim it arose in India's northwest and others the southeast. Moreover, the old theory that the Mahayana developed among the laity has recently been challenged by evidence that it was not only a sort of puritanical monastic movement,[73] but also one supported by the wealthy women of the Gupta age.[74] Even so, what is known is that Mahayana thinkers turned the teachings of the Nikaya schools on their head. They did this by taking the Buddha's central idea of no-self and extrapolating it to the point where everything was taken to lack a permanent, inherent reality. Everything is instead empty (śūnyatā).[75]

Nevertheless, the central problem remained the same: we do not recognize this reality; and as the Buddha claimed, it is this mistake that is the fundamental problem, because when one makes the assumption that one exists then one will invariably want to have one's desires satisfied, which will lead one to act, thereby producing karma, which is the engine that drives the perpetual cycle of birth and death. In turn, the only way to break the cycle is to experience enlightenment, which enables one to overcome desire and thus end the production of karma. For only when no karma is produced will no future being be reborn, and only then will there be no suffering in the world.

This is the standard Nikaya interpretation that the Mahayana challenged with the new theory of emptiness, though it did not challenge the fundamental Buddhist claim of human misperception. In both the Nikaya and the Mahayana traditions the central problem is the same: people desire things and thereby act in the world and thus produce karma. But the idea of emptiness could also be taken in numerous directions, and in the larger Hindu context of Gupta India it is perhaps not surprising that it went toward a monist conceptualization. Thus the nihilistic emptiness of the early Madhyamika philosophers, who largely used it as a tool of logical argumentation, was transformed into a divine reality. Emptiness was thus not "empty," but rather the underlying nature of reality; it was the ultimate reality, which was none other than the Buddha, or Buddhanature.

This was a profound development since it enabled the Buddha in the Mahayana tradition to become an eternal and powerful entity, a god if you will, in contradistinction to the Nikaya belief that the Buddha was simply a man. In the Mahayana tradition there thus arose a whole new range of doctrines built on the deified conceptualization of emptiness including a whole new pantheon of Celestial Buddhas and Savior Bodhisattvas who could intercede in human affairs through prayer.[76] The form of Mahayana Buddhism most clearly reflecting this new idea is the Pure Land tradition focused on the Buddha Amitabha, who saves his devotees from the cycle of samsara by having them be reborn in his Western Paradise of Sukhavati.

But the idea of emptiness developed not only outward into a world of supplication and grace, but also inward as evidenced in *satori*, the sudden enlightenment of Zen meditation, which was a new development, because in the early tradition the experience of enlightenment was never sudden.[77] Rather, it was understood to be the culmination of an exceedingly long and arduous ordeal. Yet if enlightenment is not the quest to fathom the reality of no-self, but to experience one's own Buddhanature, then perhaps all that is needed is a good *koan*, or riddle, to rattle one's conventional mind thereby exposing the hidden, ultimate truth.

Of course, the appearance of Chan meditation in China and its later development in Japanese Zen were far away from the rise of the Mahayana and its development in India during the first centuries of the Common Era. How the Mahayana actually arose in relation to the social, economic, and political environment of India at this time, though, is not fully under-stood.[78] Even so, based on the rise of large monasteries and their extensive landholdings granted by the monied Buddhist elite, it is clear that the Dharma was profiting from the general economic expansion of the Gupta period.[79] Whether this benefited specifically either the Mahayana or Nikaya is hard to gauge, especially since in this early period monks of different schools could live in one monastery as long as they followed the same monastic code.

Regardless of such difficulties, scholars have nevertheless tried to link the changing socioeconomic realities of India at this time with the rise of the Mahayana. Liu, for example, has observed that the rise of emptiness and its rhetorical claims of the meaninglessness of material realities, includ-ing money, coincide ironically with the enormous wealth of monasteries.[80] Moreover, she has furthered this theological-economic link by arguing that the appearance of the "Seven Jewels" (gold, silver, lapis lazuli, crystal, pearl, red coral, agate) in Mahayana literature coincided with the rise of new consumption patterns and a tandem increase in Sino-Indian trade in these luxury commodities.[81] Yet, while there was certainly both an increase in trade and a deep Buddhist impact on Chinese material culture at this time,[82] it is unlikely that luxury goods were the bulk of this trade. Rather, the majority of trade was actually in nonreligious and bulk items, such as tin from Southeast Asia.[83]

Nevertheless, another angle through which to approach the issue is to wonder whether the Mahayana better captured the anxieties of the changing socioeconomic situation. In particular, was the Mahayana's "reliance on grace and saviors" a move away from the critical thinking and "open market" of early Buddhism and actually a reification of the "patronage and hierarchy" of Gupta society?[84] Perhaps, but there were presumably many other reasons why both monastics and the laity would adopt the ideas espoused by the Mahayana during this period of time. Even so, much as the Nikaya was to survive only in South and Southeast Asia, the Mahayana was to be transmitted during the Gupta period to East Asia where it would develop in new and interesting ways.

In India itself, however, the Mahayana would largely be eclipsed by the rise of tantra. One reason for this was intellectual.

In the Hindu case, the metaphysical categories or cosmic principles (*tattvas*) of Sākhya were deified, early on, in the form of the twenty-five faces of Mahāsadāśiva. Because it was an "exploded" metaphysics that denied any primal essence, absolute or universal, Buddhism resisted the Samkhyan model for several centuries; but here too, yogic experience eventually prevailed. Already in Aśvaghosa's (A.D. 80) theory of "suchness" (*tathāta*), the unbridgeable gap that the Buddha taught between existence (*samsāra*) and its cessation (*nirvāṇa*) was beginning to yield to the irresistible force of yogic experience. A few centuries later, it would collapse completely with the Mahāyāna notion of the Dharmakāya—the "Buddha body" composed of the body of the Buddha's teachings—as an absolute or universal soul, a Buddhist equivalent of the Vedantin's *bráhman*, with which the practitioner entered into mystic union. Once the inviolate gap between *samsāra* and *nirvāṇa* had been breached, the familiar corresponding hierarchies of the Indian cosmos came rushing in through the back door, as it were. Thus, while logicians like Śantideva and Diṅnāga were devising hairsplitting arguments by which to interpret the world as a void entity, Buddhist tāntrikas were deifying and hypostasizing the Buddha into five emanated

Buddhas or Tathāgatas: Amitabhā, Vairocana, Amoghasiddhi, Ratnasambhava, and Akṣobhya. These five primal Buddhas were subsequently equated with the five elements, the basic concept being that cosmic expansion, the multiplication of the absolute into fundamental forces, could be represented by lineages of gods just as easily as by metaphysical categories. Thus, each of the five primal Buddhas presided over five lineages of five bodhisattvas which, added to the transcendent Dharmakāya, generated a total of twenty-five divine beings, the same as the number of Samkhyan categories. Thus we read in the *Jñānasiddhi*: "Since they have the nature of the five Buddhas, the five constituents of the human personality are called *jīnas* (conquerors): and the five *dhātus* (elements) correspond to the Buddha's *śaktis*. . . . Therefore our body is a Buddha body."[85]

Such radical doctrinal developments, however, did not happen in a vacuum. The development of tantra was intimately connected with the social and political breakdown of post-Gupta India (map 5).[86]

The origin of tantra has been much debated. Nevertheless, it appears to have originated among a distinct subculture of yogis whose meditative and ritual practices focused on the acquisition of power "that often involved the transgression of social mores and rules of purity."[87] It is precisely because of these practices, most notably the ritual use of the forbidden "five M's" (meat [*mamsa*], fish [*matsya*], wine [*madya*], parched grain [*mudra*], and sexual intercourse [*maithuna*]), that tantra has been deemed through the ages as an outrageous abomination.[88] Practitioners of tantra have thus been labeled as "the Hell's Angels of medieval India."[89] But unlike Sonny Barger and his acolytes, the tantrikas were actually welcomed at the royal courts of India since they had something to offer: power.

As Davidson has convincingly shown, the mandala, the central religious paradigm of tantric practice, was a perfect metaphor for the changing environment of medieval India, which was witnessing not only agrarian expansion and the intensification of regional economies, but also political fragmentation and increased military confrontation. The cosmic map of the mandala, with the god-king at the center, thus became a perfect religio-political model with which to conceptualize and organize the horizontal consolidation of new regional dynasties.[90]

Here, it is important to note that the mandala was, in its origins, directly related to royal power. Indeed, "mandala" was simply a

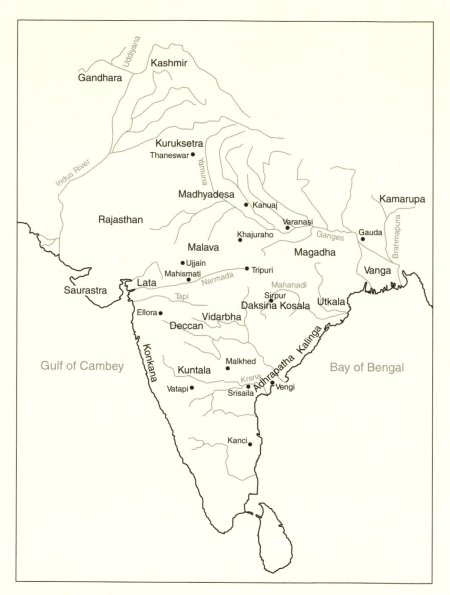

Map 5. Post-Gupta India.

term for an administrative unit or county in ancient India and has
continued to bear that meaning since at least the sixth century c.e.
in the expression "Nepāla-Maṇḍala" for the Kathmandu Valley and
its surrounding territory.

The concept of the king as *cakravartin*—as both he who turns
(*vartayati*) the wheel (*cakra*) of his kingdom or empire from its center and he whose chariot wheel has rolled its perimeter without
obstruction—is one that goes back to the late Vedic period. Central
to this construction of kingship is the notion that the king, standing
at the center of his kingdom (from which he also rules over the
periphery), mirrors the godhead at the center of its realm, its divine
or celestial kingdom. However, whereas the godhead's supermun-
dane realm is unchanging and eternal, the terrestrial ruler's kingdom is made so through the "utopia" of the mandala. As such, the
idealized "constructed kingdom" of the mandala is the mesocosmic
template between real landscapes, both geographical and political,
and the heavenly kingdom of the godhead, with the person of the
king as god on earth constituting the idealized microcosm.[91]

In many ways, it was precisely on account of this connection between spiritual and political power that the antinomian tantric practices originating in
cemeteries were able to move into the center of India's religious life and
remain there for almost four centuries.

But the rise of tantra did not go unchallenged. Other Buddhists saw the
tantrikas' access to the halls of power and the inevitable shift of economic
resources to tantric institutions as a threat. In fact they were particularly
disturbed when tantra came to be taught at the leading Buddhist institution
of Nalanda.[92] Some Buddhists even took things into their own hands. One
group of Nikaya monks from northwest India and Sri Lanka, for example,
was so enraged at the sight of the Vajrasena temple in Bodhgaya that they
burned the tantric texts preserved there and smashed the temple's silver
statue of Hevajra. These Nikaya monks furthermore purportedly asserted,
"That which is called the Mahayana is only a source of livelihood for those
who follow the wrong view. Therefore keep clear of those so-called preach-
ers of the True Doctrine."[93]

The historicity of this episode is certainly open to doubt; however, it
does powerfully capture the tensions, in particular the financial ones, which
arose between these competing Buddhist traditions. Yet, the fact of the mat-

ter is that such concerns seem to have been largely unfounded. Schools of both Nikaya and Tantric Buddhism were to subsequently flourish and expand enormously in the coming centuries. Tantra would develop not only in Cambodia and Indonesia, but it would also be adopted in Tibet, wherefrom it would have a profound impact on the history of both Inner and East Asia. Similarly, Nikaya Buddhism would come to be an integral part of the religious world of Southeast Asia.

To understand both of these developments, especially in relation to the simultaneous appearance of Islam in northwest India, it is important to recall the larger historical context. In particular, we need to recall that after the initial chaos of the post-Gupta period, wherein tantra was forged, the economic and political situation in India actually started to improve. By the middle of the eighth century the economic and political fragmentation of the post-Gupta period had largely come to an end and been replaced by three powerful empires: the Gurjara-Pratiharas in the north, the Palas in the east, and the Rastrakutas in the south (map 6).

Much of the credit for this rapid turnaround can be attributed to the expansion of Islam into northwest India, though not in the sense that the appearance of Islam rallied these Indian dynasties to somehow "defend the homeland." In this early period there were in fact rarely any battles between Muslims and India proper.[94] Rather, the impact of Islam was economic. In particular, the incorporation of India within the explosive world of global trade made possible by the Caliphate made the situation better both economically and politically. Thus as the Indian economy revived so too did the political structures that maintained the flow of commodities. In turn these states also used their new resources in order to finance religious institutions.

In this regard only the Pala dynasty was expressly Buddhist. The other two, especially the Gurjura-Pratiharas, actively promoted Hinduization. As noted above the support of Hinduism, with its caste and purity laws, might once again have enabled the Buddhist merchant elite to monopolize the expanding market of post-Gupta India. But that did not happen. At this time not only did local Hindus, such as the famous traders of Gujarat, challenge the Buddhists but Muslims who had direct access to the resources and institutions of the Islamic world also challenged them. Thus, as many of the factors that had made Buddhism such a dynamic force in the economic world of South Asia came to be usurped by those of other traditions the influence of the Dharma began to wane in India.

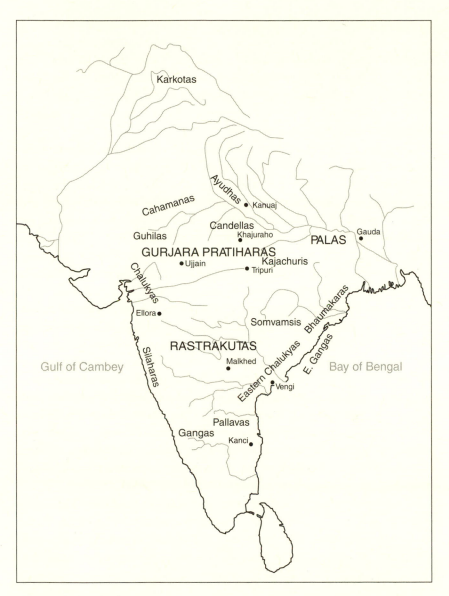

Map 6. Three Kingdoms.

The weakening of Buddhist economic power, however, occurred not only in India as Hindu groups "successfully represented themselves as the successors to the original Buddhist initiatives,"[95] but also in Central Asia. As we have seen, Buddhism had earlier moved into this area in tandem with the expansion of trade in Sogdiana. However, one of the curious aspects of Central Asian history is that although the Sogdians were famous Buddhist missionaries in China and elsewhere, they never actually supported the Dharma in their homeland.[96] Thus while Buddhism did become institutionalized in Central Asia, it seems that in many ways it also remained a marginal tradition in relation to the range of local Iranian religions that continued to be practiced in the area. In fact, when the first Muslim armies arrived in Central Asia in the late seventh century, it appears as if Buddhism had already lost the support of the merchant community and had largely disappeared.[97]

One religion that had taken its place was Manichaeism, which was founded by the third century C.E. Iranian prophet Mani and actually mirrored Buddhism in many doctrinal and institutional aspects. In particular, Manichaeism had strong affinities to the world of commerce.[98] Yet, unlike Buddhism, it was never able to receive the patronage necessary in order to fully establish itself as a "world religion." At one point, however, it seemed as if that dream might have come true when upon the counsel of his Sogdian advisors the ruler of the Uygurs adopted Manichaeism as the state religion in 762. It is unknown why Bügü Khan, who at the time ruled a wide swath of Inner Asia, took this step (map 7), though on one level adopting Manichaeism presumably brought the Sogdian Manicheans and their unrivalled economic power and technologies into his good graces. It also differentiated the Uygur Empire from the Buddhist empire of the Tibetans and simultaneously avoided stirring up problems with the anti-Buddhist tendencies of the Chinese Tang dynasty. Bügü Khan, of course, could also have believed in the teachings of Mani.[99] Regardless, his conversion was to radically alter the standing of Buddhism within the Inner Asian world. It was not the end, but it certainly signaled the diminishing stature of the Dharma.

Buddhist traders must have seen the writing on the wall. Thus, as had been the case previously, they moved on. But instead of going either north or south they went east. Some of them moved to Kashmir, just in time to offer their knowledge and resources for the rise of the Karkota dynasty of Lalitaditya (ca. 724–60 C.E.), who conquered most of north and central

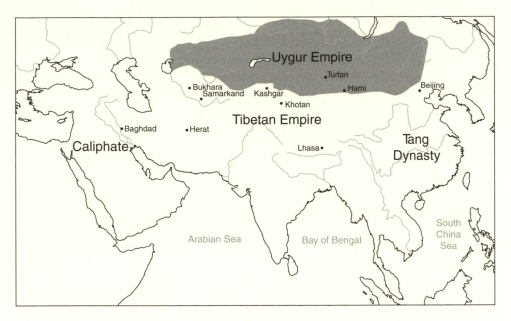

Map 7. Uygur Empire.

India, paving the way for the subsequent rise of the Gurjara-Pratiharas, Rastrakuta, and Pala dynasties. And in this way Kashmir was to become and remain a vital region of tantric Buddhism until the fourteenth century.[100]

The center of the Buddhist world, however, moved further east toward the domains of the Pala dynasty and the Bhaumakara of Orissa (750–950 C.E.).[101] Moreover, it was from this area that Buddhist merchants and missionaries were not only to connect with the Tibetan world, but also to fan out across the Bay of Bengal creating what one scholar has called a "Buddhist Mediterranean."[102] Thus during these centuries the interconnections between urbanization, Buddhist thought, international trade, and Buddhist institutions enabled the Dharma to once again blossom in new territories that coincidentally were far away from where Islam first made its appearance.

The Arrival of Islam

The flowering of Buddhism around the Bay of Bengal and in Inner Asia from the eighth to eleventh centuries was occurring at the same time that

Islam was making inroads on the other side of the subcontinent—in north-west India and Central Asia. And from the above description one may very well imagine that by this time Buddhist traders and their religious institu-tions had largely disappeared from this area where Buddhism had tradition-ally been strongest. Moreover, whatever may have remained in Central Asia, for example, was duly challenged when Muslim armies invaded this area and fifty thousand Arab families were transported from Iraq's Basra in order to bring Central Asia and its wealth firmly within the orbit of the Umayyad caliphate (661–750 C.E.).[103] Yet Buddhists had not entirely retreated from this strategic area, situated as it was on the valuable trade routes. The Chinese pilgrim Xuanzang who, just decades before the Muslim conquests passed through taking meticulous notes, recorded an extensive Buddhist presence in several areas. By his reckoning Bamiyan in Afghani-stan had 10,000 monks, the area of Sind had 460 monasteries,[104] and the coastal region toward Iran had 180 monasteries with 11,000 monks.[105] It was in these areas where Buddhism and Islam first came into contact in the early eighth century.

Before looking at what this encounter entailed specifically, one should perhaps return to the issue of why Muslims went into this area in the first place. As noted above, the primary reason was economic. A secondary rea-son was to hunt down heretics. Either way, however, it is vital to recognize that Muslims did not go there to spread the faith because in this early period only Arabs could be Muslim. The question of non-Arab converts, the so-called mawāli, was in fact a central problem for early Islam and played a key role in the internecine violence that plagued the formation of the early Muslim community. Thus the Arabs who marched into northwest India were not necessarily seeking to convert the Buddhists from their mis-guided ways. Rather, it is far more likely that they were chasing after Khari-jites, the first Islamic heretics who, perhaps unsurprisingly, drew much of their support from non-Arab Muslims. Even so, chasing down and killing heretics is not how Muslim historians came to remember the Islamic advance into India. There was instead to develop a far more glamorous tale involving pirates and damsels in distress.

Before exploring this story, however, it is important to note that our knowledge of Islam's appearance and the subsequent Muslim conquest in this area is hindered by the lack of contemporary sources. In the case of northwest India the problem is especially acute since the major source for this history, the Chachnama, is preserved only in a thirteenth-century Persian translation. Yet since earlier authors do cite passages from this work it must be assumed that the *Chachnama* is not simply a later fabrication, but in fact a later Persian redaction of an earlier Arabic history.[106] Nevertheless, it is on the basis of this source and a few others that we learn about the pirates of Daybul and the refusal of the local Hindu ruler to take action against them. It was this event that became the *casus belli* setting in motion the Muslim invasion.

Regardless of the historicity of this specific event this story does well capture contemporary historical realities. Notably it accurately reflects the Hindu dynasties, such as the Rai (489–632 C.E.), Brahma (632–724 C.E.), and Sahi (865–1026 C.E.), who had moved into the area south of the Hindu Kush during the chaotic period of the preceding centuries and claimed to be the rightful rulers of northwest India. But as evidenced in the lack of Hinduization carried out under their auspices, their rule was a light one. In accord with the many rulers both before and after themselves, these Hindu kings were less interested in meddling in the cultural and religious affairs of their subjects than in profiting from the established trade of the region. And not only had this trade remained in the hands of Buddhist traders, but it had also apparently survived through the centuries. In fact, just before the Muslim invasion the economy had expanded in tandem with the late Harsha's (r. ca. 606–647) unification of north India from the Punjab to Bengal during the first half of the seventh century (map 8).

Although Harsha's empire collapsed upon his death in 647 C.E. the impact of his reign was to be far-reaching. Much of this had to do with the revival of the economy. Harsha's capital city of Kanauj became not only the nodal point of the trade routes for the entire subcontinent, but it also drew into its orbit northwest India and parts of Central Asia. Harsha's vision, however, was even larger. He sent envoys to China, and the rulers of the newly formed Tang dynasty (618–907 C.E.) were very interested in becoming involved with the burgeoning trade of India and Central Asia and thus they sent envoys to India.[107] So was Songtsen Gampo (r. 614–50 C.E.), the ruler of the Tibetan Empire, as was the Khan of the Turks. All three saw the inherent value of controlling this area and as a result it devolved into a theatre of competing interests and proxy wars as local rulers in Central Asia and northern Afghanistan played these competing superpowers against each other.[108] In the end, none of these external powers ever really won and power simply reverted back to the local political structures with slight modifications; however, what did survive this tumultuous period was the

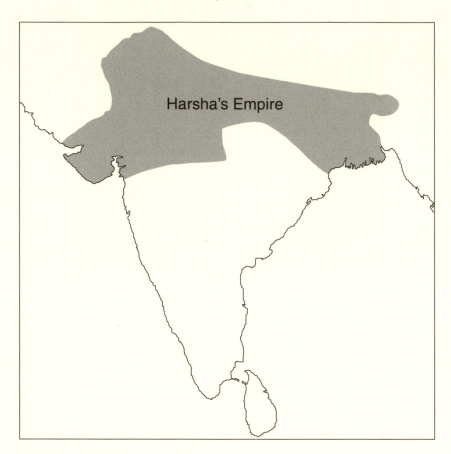

Map 8. Harsha's Empire.

economy. Moreover, it was these potential riches, as evidenced in al-
Qasim's seizure of forty thousand pounds of gold from a single house in
Multan that drew the Arab armies into northwest India.[109] The Arabs, however, did not simply want to plunder the economy. Rather, as is well captured in the story of the pirates, they aimed to be better guardians of the
trade networks than the current rulers.

According to the story, Muslim involvement in the area began when a
group of pirates operating out of the important coastal trading city of Daybul, located forty-five miles southeast of Karachi, seized the passengers and
merchandise of an Arab-trading vessel. In response Muslim authorities

wrote to the local Hindu ruler, Dahir bin Chach, to secure the release of both the prisoners and goods. The Hindu king, however, claimed that the pirates operated beyond his control and therefore nothing could be done. The Arabs refused to accept this claim since not only were the "pirates" resident in Daybul, of which the king's son was governor, but the Arab traders and their wives were also incarcerated in the city's prison.[110] To save their countrymen and the honor of their women the Arabs thus attacked Daybul. Twice they were repelled but on the third try they were successful. Conquering Daybul set the stage for their subsequent conquest of north-west India in its entirety.[111]

Whatever the historical accuracy of this episode, it is nevertheless a great story. It makes the Muslims into the liberators overthrowing a lying and corrupt ruler. Moreover, built into the narrative is the assumption that the Muslims will invariably be better stewards of the economy than the local Hindu despot. In addition, the Arabs claimed they were not interested in meddling with local affairs; rather, they simply wanted to bring in law and order so that the economy could expand, which would theoretically benefit everyone. Of course, how this shift in the economic regime was actually to disrupt local practices was an issue little discussed. Nevertheless, what is interesting about this story is how it plays upon a religio-economic para-digm. Namely, Dahir bin Chach is portrayed as a stereotypical Hindu ruler, one who does not like the city and looks down upon trade. In contradis-tinction, Muslim rule is presented as the one that favors the world of busi-ness. Muslims will even go to war in order to protect their financial interests. Arab rule was thus not aimed at conversion or the disruption of the status quo; rather, the Muslim state's fundamental goal was to enrich both itself and its subjects by overcoming any and all impediments to the circulation of commodities.

This was something Buddhists understood. And as evidenced in the Buddhist response to the episode of the Daybul pirates the Muslims were people with whom they could do business. The Buddhists thus sent envoys "in order to apologize for and dissociate themselves from the piracy at Daybul. They offered to remit a tribute in regular installments and received in return a written treaty from the governor in Iraq. It was these same Buddhists who, when the Arabs arrived in force a few years later, opened the gates of the city and 'bought and sold with the soldiers.'"[112]

Buddhists and Muslim Rule

The common view of Muslim rule is one of violence and persecution. Namely, non-Muslims were either threatened with the sword or else burdened with the loathsome *jizya*, the poll tax levied on those who did not accept Muhammad's revelation. While this certainly makes for a powerful story and still fires the imagination from Bosnia to India, as with so much else commonly said about Islam, it is wrong. As numerous scholars have shown, the fact of the matter is that early Muslim rulers were notably tolerant and there was little tension among the diverse religious groups under their rule.[113] One of the reasons for this was quite simply the fact that the Arabs were a tiny minority ruling a vast majority of non-Muslims, who were themselves not only grappling with the issue of conversion, but, as noted above, their conversion and status within the Muslim community was still a matter of great debate. And even when these issues were eventually settled in the eighth and ninth centuries and non-Arabs could readily become Muslim, the rate of conversion still remained markedly low. Even in the heartland of Muslim power, such as Iraq and Egypt, it was not until the tenth century that a majority of the population was actually Muslim.[114] On the fringes of the empire, in places like northwest India and Central Asia, the process of conversion may have been even slower. Bamiyan in Afghanistan, for example, continued as a functioning site of Buddhism well into the eleventh century.[115] In the area of Sind in what is today Pakistan, Buddhists were also erecting inscriptions recording their donations to the Buddhist community in the eleventh century.[116]

Be that as it may Buddhism still presented the early Muslims with a problem. One issue was quite simply what should be done with this religion, since unlike Christianity, Judaism, and even Zoroastrianism, the Dharma was wholly unknown to the Islamic tradition. This invariably raised a host of questions about how Buddhism could be both intellectually and legally categorized. In particular, how should Buddhists be understood and where should they be placed within the developing Muslim polity? Could Buddhists become one of the *dhimmi* communities, like Jews and Christians, who were allowed to live unmolested under a pact of protection within the Muslim state?[117]

Such questions were not isolated to the Buddhists, but were rather part and parcel of the inordinately complex issues facing the Islamic community in the wake of their remarkable conquests (map 9).[118] Not only did they

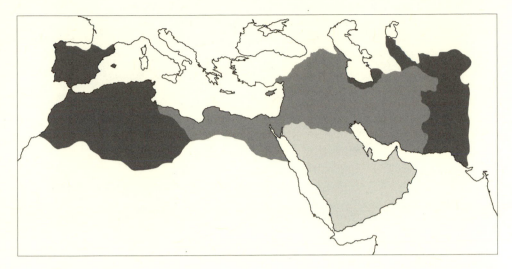

Map 9. Caliphate.

have to resolve the pressing internal issues of what it actually meant to be Muslim, but as their imperial expansion began to falter they also had to come to terms with how the Islamic community was to interact with not only those under their authority, but also those beyond their borders.

One step in this direction was the reinterpretation of *jihad*, meaning "to struggle," away from ideas of holy war. Thus not only was the final victory of Islam postponed from the contemporary historical moment to the mythic end times, but the struggle itself was also transformed from an external one of military conquest to that of an inner spiritual struggle,[119] the so-called "greater jihad," whereby one strives to live in accord with the teachings of Islam. Yet in seeking to address all of these problems in a more immediate and practical manner the Muslims also drew inspiration from Roman law and organized the world into three interdependent entities: the Abode of Islam, the Abode of War, and the Abode of Truce, those with whom the Abode of Islam had treaties.[120]

It was these new ideas and policies that came to shape early Buddhist-Muslim interaction. Most of northwest India, for example, was brought under Islamic control by treaty (*ṣulḥ*) rather than force (*ʿanwa*). Moreover, within this process the Buddhists were classified in relation to Zoroastrianism and thus given *dhimmi* status. As the ninth-century historian Baladhuri writes of the incorporation of the city of al-Rur: "He conquered the city by treaty (*sulḥ*) with the condition that he would not kill them nor enter their temple (*budd*). And he said, 'The Budd will be considered similar to the churches of Zoroastrianism (*majus*).' He imposed tribute (*kharaj*) on those in al-Rur and built a mosque."[121]

Thus, as with many other empires, the Muslims largely kept the local ruling elite in place and allowed them not only to practice their traditional religions, but also even to be confirmed as the local rulers of the Muslim state by means of traditional customs.[122] For example, "Kakah b. Kotok, the ruler of Budiyah, was confirmed as the hereditary sub-governor of the region for the Arabs in a ceremony which followed Buddhist (*samani*) customs of this family."[123] In fact, the early Muslim state even continued the policy of allotting three percent of tax revenues for non-Muslim religious mendicants. And when Buddhists petitioned the authorities in order to restore one of their temples, permission was granted.[124]

Before constructing too rosy a picture of early Muslim rule, however, it is important to recognize that all of these events and policies were carried out in the first decades of the eighth century. At this time Islam itself, to say nothing of its relations with other traditions, was in flux. Indeed, the ruling of al-Hajjaj, the governor of Iraq who allowed Buddhists to rebuild a temple, was in direct violation of the Pact of Umar (ca. 717 C.E.) and all subsequent Muslim law codes, which assert that non-Muslim religious structures cannot be restored, nor can new ones be built in Islamic territory.[125] Of course, how seriously Muslims took this policy differed widely from place to place throughout the centuries. Yet, how it came to shape Buddhist-Muslim relations in northwest India is unfortunately unknown, especially as this area moved further and further away from Abbasid control.

Indeed, when approaching the issue of early Buddhist-Muslim interaction it is important to keep in mind that Islamic control and the Muslim presence in this area was in a constant state of turmoil, and not only theologically, but also politically. The Caliphate could barely keep control of Central Asia even though it was vitally important on account of its location and economic resources. Thus when the Caliphate succumbed to fratricidal struggles upon the death of the Caliph Harun al-Rashid (763–809 C.E., r. 786–809 C.E.), the local Persian Tahirid dynasty (821–73 C.E.) was bequeathed control of Central Asia, who were in turn supplanted by the local Samanids (819–999 C.E.).[126] And the situation was the same in north-west India and Afghanistan.

Muslims did not in fact conquer parts of Afghanistan until the end of the ninth century during the rise of the Saffarid dynasty (861–1003 C.E.).[127] Moreover, in 871 the Caliphate completely renounced control of Sind. In turn this power vacuum was filled by the Isma'ilis, the third branch of the Islamic community beside the Sunni and Shi'a, who ruled Sind for the next 150 years (879–1025 C.E.). Moreover, being avowed enemies of the Sunni Caliphate in Baghdad the Isma'ilis shifted the trade networks of this pivotal economic region away from the Persian Gulf toward the Red Sea. In this way they bolstered the rise not only of their Shi'ite allies in Egypt, the Fatimid dynasty (909–1171 C.E.), but also the subsequent revival of the trading networks of the Mediterranean.[128] Nevertheless, all of these local Muslim dynasties of northwest India and Central Asia were ultimately to be swept away by the Turkic and Sunni ruler Mahmud of Ghazna.

As this cursory historical overview makes clear northwest India and Central Asia underwent a period of enormous political and religious turbulence during the first centuries of Buddhist-Muslim interaction. Yet remarkably, throughout all of these upheavals, or perhaps because of them, Buddhism survived. As confirmed by Arab geographers there were still many cities in these areas that had both "infidels" and "idolators" in the tenth and eleventh century.[129] The famous scholar al-Biruni, for example, whom Mahmud of Ghazna brought with him on his campaigns, recorded the existence of Buddhist monasteries in Central Asia in the early eleventh century: "Before the first establishment of their rites and the appearance of Budhasaf people were Σαμαναυιοι, inhabiting the eastern part of the world and worshipping idols. The remnants of them are at present in India, China, and among the *Taghazghar*; the people of Khurasan call them *Shamanan*. Their monuments, the *Baharas* (monasteries) of their idols, their *Farkharas* (monks) are still to be seen on the frontier countries between Khurasan and India."[130]

Moreover, Asadi Tusi described in his *Garshasp Name* of 1048 how Mahmud of Ghazna arrived at a Buddhist monastery outside of Kabul:

When he reached the Buddhist shrine [*bot-khane*] of the Subahar
He saw a house [*khane*] so fine that it was like the Spring.[131]

Indeed, the poet further informs us that the walls of this monastery were made of marble, the flooring of silver, and in the middle was a large golden

Buddha with a "face like the moon."[132] However, since the historical record is so spotty it is unclear how well, or for how long, this monastery, or any others, survived.

In approaching the history of Buddhist-Muslim interaction in this period we also need to keep in mind that, as with any encounter this meeting was not simply a one-sided affair. Even though we may not have sources offering us the Buddhist perspective on these developments we should not imagine the Buddhists as simply the hapless victims of Islamic rule. As we have seen with the Daybul affair, the Buddhists were very proactive. Some Buddhists, however, were not so welcoming and they instead decided to flee from Muslim domination. From copper-plate inscriptions we therefore know that Buddhists from this region moved into both the Rastrakuta and Pala domains.[133] Unfortunately, however, it is hard to know what those who remained behind were thinking since all we have are Muslim sources.

In using these sources it is nevertheless interesting to note how favorably the Muslims present the Buddhists. In a certain sense it is almost a precursor to the positive cachet Buddhism carries in contemporary popular culture. Of course, the early Muslim view is based on a different paradigm and the Dharma's goodness derives less from its own qualities than the Buddhists' willingness to accept Islamic rule. Indeed, as seen above, the Buddhists actually tried to work with the Arabs and apparently there was accommodation on both sides. In fact, in no Muslim source is there ever any mention of something like a "Buddhist revolt" against Islamic power. Rather, the Buddhists are flawlessly obsequious to Muslim authority. Whether this was actually the case is, of course, another issue entirely.

Either way, in thinking about these issues it is important to keep in mind that the Buddhists and Hindus we find in Muslim sources are less real historical figures than caricatures fulfilling the literary tropes of Islamic conquest literature. The Buddhists are thus the collaborators, the "good guys," while the Hindus are the resistance, or the "bad guys" (a trope that Hindu historiography invariably adopted in its own "anti-Muslim epics").[134] Of course, the historical fact that the Hindus were in power at the time and thus an obstacle to the Muslim advance surely played a role in this presentation. However, another and perhaps more interesting issue is the obvious parallelism between what Buddhism and Islam imagined themselves to be: a cosmopolitan religion of the merchant elite. Both religions were therefore speaking to the issues and concerns of the same audience; and while such a situation may not be by definition untenable, in this case it turned out to be so and ultimately the "Islamic international" beat out the "Buddhist international."

This is well known, but how or why is still open to debate.[135] When thinking about this development, however, one can begin with the case of the Buddhists who fled the Muslim conquest seeking refuge in India. Those who fled to the Rastrakuta domains would no doubt have been surprised to learn that the Dharma would survive two centuries longer under Muslim rule than in the domains of their own Hindu overlords. Indeed, from all the available evidence, including the account of an eighth-century Chinese prisoner of war from the Battle of Talas and the account of a Korean Buddhist pilgrim in Muslim-controlled Central Asia, it seems as if the Arabs largely allowed the Buddhists to continue with their religious observances.[136] Of course, the main reason for this policy was presumably that the Muslims recognized the central role the Buddhists played in the local economy. Indeed, it was largely along the same lines that Buddhists were presumably thinking about the Muslims who they hoped could potentially "reopen interregional trade routes, both maritime and overland, and hence benefit their class and, indirectly, their religion."[137] And presumably the Buddhist community did benefit as northwest India and Central Asia once again became the linchpin in the east-west trade under Muslim tutelage.[138]

The central question, however, is for how long this remained to be the case. As MacLean has convincingly shown, the early economic power and status of the Buddhist community eventually waned. "They could readily perceive the deterioration of their socio-economic position in religious terms as related to their belonging to the category of non-Muslim, since, as we have seen, the comparative reference group of urban, mercantile Muslims prospered during the same period."[139]

Islam was thus the first religion to be able to successfully challenge the entire support system that had sustained Buddhism for over a millennium. "This support system worked at several levels: at the ideological level it influenced the accumulation and reinvestment of wealth in trading ventures by lay devotees; at the social level, donations to Buddhist monasteries provided status to traders and other occupational groups; at the economic level, Buddhist monasteries were repositories of information and essential skills such as those of writing; and at the community level, participation in the fortnightly *uposatha* ceremony instilled an identity among the lay worshippers."[140]

Islam with its prosperity theology, its mosques, and the larger networks of the Islamic community within the Caliphate clearly offered a viable alternative to all four of these structural components. Yet at what point did these alternatives and the "spiritual capital" of Islam—namely, "the power, influence, knowledge, and dispositions created by participation in a particular religious tradition"[141]—finally overwhelm the support system of the Buddhist international?

On a personal level what would make a Buddhist merchant one day go to the mosque and profess the *shahāda*, the witness of faith, "There is no God but Allah, and Muhammad is His messenger"? Was it the demeaning non-Muslim poll tax that drove him to it? Or the more burdensome five-percent non-Muslim duty instituted by the Caliphate that cut into his trading profits? Or was it the realization of his family's shrinking social and economic standing in the community? Or when his child was sick were the skills of Muslim physicians better than those of the Buddhists?[142] Or was it simply the difficulties in finding a suitable husband for his daughter? Or did Islam simply make more sense than the Dharma? Was it all, or none of these?[143]

By putting these questions in terms of an individual one can readily see how difficult such questions are on a personal level; how much more so on an abstract, historical, and civilizational level? Of course, it is on that macro level that historians and scholars of religion often try to provide answers and thereby paint a convincing portrait of what "actually happened" through a logical chain of cause and effect. While such narratives are both admirable and necessary, at the same time we need to keep in mind that they also unfortunately often lead to simplistic and monolithic explanations that obscure precisely the complexities they are trying to explain.

Peter Brown, for example, has written, "I have long suspected that accounts of Christianization . . . are at their most misleading where they speak of the process as if it were a single block, capable of a single comprehensive description that, in turn, implies the possibility of a single, all-embracing explanation."[144] He goes on to note that this tendency for a simple, monolithic narrative results in a situation wherein "we are like little boys on the sea shore. We watch with fascinated delight as the tide sweeps in upon an intricate sandcastle. We note when each segment crumbles before the advancing waters."[145]

This image captures well the common story of the green wave of Islam crashing over the poor and defenseless Buddhists. Islamization, however, was a process no less complicated and drawn out than that of the West's

Christianization.[146] We therefore need to be wary of stories that simplify the inordinately complex dynamic that evolved between Buddhism and Islam over the centuries. And in this regard the realities of economic regimes and their linkages with religious ideologies is only one part of the equation; another is how individual Muslims and Buddhists actually tried to make sense of each other, which is the topic of the next chapter.

CHAPTER TWO

Understanding

I have read in the *Kitāb al-masālik* that the Buddhists form two parties: that which affirms that the Buddha was an apostle, and another which affirms that Buddha is the Creator who has manifested himself in this form.

—Mutahhar b. Tahir Maqdisi, *Kitāb al-bad' wa t-tārīkh*

Adam, Noah and Abraham; there are also five others endowed with an evil nature in the family of demons and snake: Moses, Jesus, the White-Clad One, Muhammad and the Mahdi—the eighth—who will belong to the darkness. The seventh will clearly be born in the city of Baghdad in the land of Mecca, where the mighty, ferocious idol of the barbarian, the demonic incarnation, lives in the world.

—*Kālacakratantra*

AT THE END of the eighth century a messenger from northwest India arrived in Baghdad and requested an audience with Caliph Harun al-Rashid. Since he believed that it would be valuable to display his magnanimity and magnificence to this poor vassal from the frontiers of the Islamic Empire the Caliph agreed. Yet when the man was finally brought before him in the glorious palace in the center of Baghdad, the Caliph was shocked to hear the message that this minion was sent to convey: "I have been told that you have no proof of the truth of your religion but the sword. If you are sure of the veracity of your faith, send some scholar from your place to discuss religious matters with a pandit of mine."

The Caliph was so enraged that he almost had the messenger put to death on the spot; however, he was also intrigued by the audacity of this overture and thus decided to send one of his religious scholars to debate this pandit. Unfortunately, the debate did not go well. The pandit drew upon the deep tradition of Buddhist debate and logic in order to systematically attack the Muslim scholar's claims of the existence of a single, all-powerful God. When the pandit asked his penultimate question—"If your God is all-powerful, can He create an entity like Himself?"—the Islamic scholar was so befuddled he could only respond that he did not know the answer. The local ruler of Sind, who had arranged the debate, thus announced the Buddhist scholar the winner and sent the mullah back to the Caliph with the following message: "I had heard from my elders, and now that I have seen with my own eyes, I am sure that you have no proof of the truth of your faith."

At this turn of events the Caliph was incensed and he summoned together all of his leading scholars in order to address this Buddhist challenge. None, however, could come up with an adequate response until at last a young boy stood up and said, "O Prince of Believers, this objection is baseless; God is He who has been created by nobody. If God creates an entity like Himself, that entity will be in all cases God's creation. Then, again, that there can be an entity exactly like God is an insult to God and God will not countenance His own disparagement. This question is like such questions as: Can God be ignorant? Can He die? Can He eat? Can He drink? Can He sleep? Evidently He cannot do any of these things as they are all derogatory to his dignity."

Everyone was pleased with this answer and Harun al-Rashid wanted to send the boy to India in order to defend Islam and defeat the Buddhists in debate. But the other scholars at the court objected by saying he was too young, and although he could possibly answer this question, what about other ones? Harun al-Rashid was swayed by this argument and thus he sent an older famous scholar in order to defeat the Buddhists in a new debate.

By one account this scholar readily won the debate and the local ruler of Sind converted to Islam. Another account claims that the Buddhist pandit sent out a spy to see whether this Islamic scholar was a theologian, or else a scholar familiar with rationalism. When his informant told him that the mullah was indeed familiar with rational logic the pandit was afraid that he might lose the debate. In desperation he therefore paid someone to poison the Islamic scholar and he died before ever reaching northwest India.

Both of these stories about a supposed Buddhist-Muslim debate at the time of the famous Caliph Harun al-Rashid are only recorded in a Muslim history from the fifteenth century.[1] Whether they have any basis in historical fact is doubtful. Nevertheless, what these stories do inadvertently reveal is the reality of Buddhist-Muslim interaction and intellectual exchange. Indeed, rather than the standard story of simple destruction and alienation it is important to recognize that Buddhists and Muslims actually lived side by side for centuries. Arab geographers, for example, wrote about cities in northwest India that were populated with both Muslims and "idolaters" well into the eleventh century.[2] In some places the merchant elite of these two groups even wore the same clothes,[3] which may seem a minor point; however, if we recall the fundamental importance that clothes play as a marker of group identification it is a telling episode. Nevertheless, an even more intriguing fact is that in some Central Asian cities the Muslims from Iraq, who had been moved in after the conquest, had become so assimilated they lost their status as tax-exempt Arabs.[4] All of this evinces the fact that Buddhists and Muslims were not only living together, but were also apparently somehow getting along.

Yet even so, one can still wonder how Buddhists and Muslims actually understood each other. Was it all peace and harmony as the Arab geographers imply? Or were there tensions—and not only theological ones—as is so well captured in story of the Buddhist-Muslim debate at the time of Harun al-Rashid? What follows is an attempt to answer these questions not only by looking at how Muslims and Buddhists tried to understand each other, but also by investigating some of the material exchanges that occurred during these centuries of cohabitation and mutual interaction.

The Early Muslim View

As explored in the preceding chapter, the expansion of the Caliphate into northwest India and Central Asia was driven fundamentally by economic concerns: in particular, the desire to control the financial resources and trade routes spiraling out from this nodal point in the Eurasian trading system. And this goal was ultimately achieved as the various kingdoms controlling this area were defeated and brought into the orbit of the Caliphate. However, as reflected in the story above, these areas also remained a borderland far away from the center of Muslim political and intellectual life. Such was the case especially during the first Muslim dynasty of the Umayyads, who built their capital in Damascus and focused their attention almost exclusively toward the west.[5] Indeed, it was their armies that marched all the way across North Africa and conquered Spain. Yet this westward orientation was not only military, but also in regards to the theological and intellectual formation of Islam itself.

Much of this, of course, had to do with defining and differentiating the Muslim tradition from the other Abrahamic traditions. Muslim scholars were thus not only engaging with the multifarious Jewish and Christian traditions of the recently vanquished Byzantine and Sassanid empires, but also the profound legacy of Hellenism that permeated both of these religions. As a result, early Islam developed largely within a Western matrix, but that was not all. As scholars are now realizing, the Muslim tradition also developed in relation to the East. Early Islam was in fact profoundly influenced by the cosmopolitan culture of Central Asia as evidenced in borrowed artistic styles.[6] It is also reflected in the quintessentially "Muslim" slave system—whereby promising young boys were brought from the frontier to be trained as an elite guard corps and later as statesmen—which was a tradition that actually developed out of Central Asian precedents.[7]

Of course, the fact that Muslims emulated Central Asian traditions at this time should not be surprising if we recall the centrality of this region to both the world's economy and its cultural systems. Moreover, it is even less surprising that these influences increased during the period of the Abbasids, who from their base in Central Asia overthrew the Umayyads and forged "a Perso-Arab partnership in power."[8] Yet although the impact of the Abbasids on both Islam and world history was profound, one facet of this revolution that continues to be overlooked is its concurrent turn of the Muslim world toward "the East." That is, the Abbasids brought to power many people from Central Asia and thus they brought with them their "Eastern" orientation.[9] Indeed, the most poignant symbol of this shift toward Asia was the move of the Muslim capital from Damascus to Baghdad. But during the early Abbasid period not only did the capital move; so too did the entire orientation of Islam.

The main reason for this was largely the result of one family, the Barmakids, who provided the Abbasid caliph with viziers during the last half of the eighth century.[10] The Barmakids descended from a distinguished Buddhist family who controlled the famous Naw Bahar monastery in Balkh. The uncle of the first Barmakid vizier was in fact the abbot.[11] Yet, for whatever reason—political, economic, familial, or spiritual—one line of this family converted to Islam.[12] In turn they were to move up through the

ranks and ultimately establish themselves as key figures in the Abbasid revolution and its early rule of the Muslim world.[13] And even though this family
grew in prominence in the Caliphate, it appears as if the family in Balkh
remained Buddhist and even tried to maintain its control of Naw Bahar
and its numerous satellite monasteries in Central Asia.[14] Yet for how long
they did so, or whether it was even possible to do so with the increasing
power of the Abbasid caliphate, is unclear. Nevertheless, what is clear is
that as with many religious converts, the Barmakids had their feet in two
worlds—the Buddhist and the Muslim—and as they moved into the upper
echelons of the caliph's administration this dual orientation was to have a
profound impact on the entire trajectory of the dynasty. In particular, coming from Central Asia they were well aware of the broader Indic world
made available to them through the Buddhist international, and it was this
world and its systems of knowledge that they started to promote at the
Abbasid court.

It is important to recall in this regard that when the Arab conquest had
come to an end, and the Muslims began to accommodate themselves to
their new world, there were two major intellectual traditions with which
they came into contact: the Greek and Sanskrit worlds. While both were
clearly outside the divine lineage of the Abrahamic faiths, each had a rich
literary, scientific, and philosophical tradition that had something to offer.
To a certain extent the Muslim tradition could theoretically have gone
either way. Of course, this did not happen and Islam came to engage almost
exclusively the Hellenic tradition.[15] But this was not necessarily a foregone
conclusion. The Muslim tradition could in fact have developed in dialogue
with the world of Sanskrit and Indic knowledge, which is in fact the path
the Barmakids supported. To them the Hellenic world and the interminable
internecine squabbles of the Abrahamic traditions were wholly foreign.
They had instead been brought up in the broader Indic world made possible by the Buddhist international and it was this world they wanted to bring
to Baghdad.

This Indian phase of early Islam had begun already during the tenure
of the first Barmakid vizier, Khalid ibn Barmak (d. 781/782 c.e.), and it was
to continue until the fall of the family from the Caliph's graces in 803. Yet
before this fall the Barmakid viziers not only sent envoys to India to bring
back medicines, texts, and scholars, but they also promoted Islamic engagement with the East. To this end they supported the translation of Sanskrit
texts into Arabic so that this material would be accessible to Muslim schol-

ars. Within this project one early focus was Indian astronomical literature. Three major textual traditions are known to have been translated in the eighth century and these Indian traditions were subsequently to shape Muslim calendrical and astronomical sciences for centuries.[16] Muslim scholars were also interested in Indian medical knowledge, as evidenced in Ali ibn Sahl at-Tabari's mid-ninth-century compendium of medicine and natural philosophy, the *Paradise of Wisdom* (*Firdaws al-Ḥikma*), which includes material from several Sanskrit works including the *Carakasaṃhitā*, *Suśruta-saṃhitā*, and Vagbhata's *Compendium on the Heart of the Eight Branches* (*Aṣṭāṅgahṛdayasaṃhitā*).[17]

The intellectual transfer from India to the Muslim world would also come to include mathematics. It influenced, for example, Muhammad ibn Musa al-Khwarizmi (fl. 807–847 C.E.), who was principally responsible not only for the diffusion of Indian numerals in the West, including the zero,[18] but also the creation of algebra and algorithms.[19] There also appears to have been an Indic influence in the realm of metaphysics, especially regarding the theory of atomism that "had become firmly established in [Muslim] theological circles by the middle of the ninth century."[20] Yet the Muslim interest in things Indian went beyond the sciences and included literature as well.[21] Thus it is from this period that there appeared the famous collection of animal tales, the *Kalīla wa dimna*, based on the Indian *Pañcatantra*.

Of course, none of these translations or intellectual transfers is specifically Buddhist. Nevertheless, their importance lies in how they reveal the larger shift toward the East during the Barmakids. In particular it provides a frame within which to situate the trip to India of Yahya ibn Khalid, whom the Barmakids sent to collect pharmaceuticals and speak to doctors and scholars. Moreover, upon his return to Baghdad he was also asked to write a report about his travels and it is from him, an individual who actually traveled in India in the eighth century, that we have our first extensive account of Buddhism in a Muslim source.

The original report, however, is now lost. But before disappearing into the bowels of the Baghdad bureaucracy it was fortuitously copied by the polymath Ya'qub ibn Ishaq al-Kindi (ca. 801–873 C.E.). In turn this copy fell into the hands of Ibn al-Nadim (d. 998 C.E.), who was a famous book dealer in Baghdad specializing in procuring valuable manuscripts for the growing class of urban elite. But al-Nadim was not simply a peddler of books that soothed the status anxieties of Baghdad's nouveaux riches. He was also a scholar. Indeed, on account of his pivotal role in the Baghdad

book trade he had an unparalleled perch wherefrom to survey the entirety
of contemporary Muslim literature and he compiled all of this knowledge
into his monumental *Kitāb al-Fihrist*. And one small part of this work is
Yahya ibn Khalid's account of his travels in India.

Since the version of his account recorded by al-Nadim is a late copy of
a copy it is difficult to say much about ibn Khalid's original work. Namely,
we do not know if his report was originally an imperial reconnaissance
report, or something like a personal ethnography written exclusively for the
Barmakid vizier. If the former, then we can conjecture that the presentation
would be more formulaic and not stray too far from standard Muslim conceptions of the day. But if it was written solely for the Barmakids, whose
proclivities to the East the author well knew, then he may perhaps have felt
freer in describing India and its culture. Unfortunately, however, we simply
do not know for whom, or for what specific reason, ibn Khalid wrote his
work, much less his exposé of Buddhism. Nevertheless, as it would turn
out, his work is not simply the earliest Muslim attempt to understand the
Dharma; it is also one of the best.

As preserved in the *Fihrist* the work of ibn Khalid begins *in media res*
with a description of a Hindu temple in central India, in the area of what
is today Hyderabad. It then goes on to describe the inordinate wealth of
this kingdom: the king's sixty thousand elephants, the temple with twenty
thousand jewel-encrusted golden statues, and the human sacrifices that
these idols demanded. The author then suddenly shifts from Hyderabad to
northwest India and describes the famous Hindu sun temple at Multan,
which drew pilgrims from as far away as Southeast Asia. And after noting
that the road from Balkh, the Barmakid's ancestral home, is not far from
Multan, and that the road is straight, the author begins his discussion of
Buddhism, ironically enough, with the Buddha statues of Bamiyan (which
were originally painted white and gold):

> They have two idols, one of which is called Jun-bukt [Gold-red
> Buddha] and the other Zun-bukt [White Buddha]. Their forms are
> carved out of the sides of the great valley, cut from the rock of the
> mountain. The height of each one of them is eighty cubits, so that
> they can be seen from a great distance.
> He [al-Kindi] said: "The people of India go on pilgrimages to
> these two [idols], bearing with them offerings, incense, and fragrant
> woods. If the eye should fall upon them from a distance, a man

would be obliged to lower his eyes, overawed by them. If he is lacking in attention or careless when he sees them, it is necessary for
him to return to a place from which he cannot view them and then
to approach them, seeking them as the object of this attention with
reverence for them."[22]

This description captures well both the importance of Bamiyan and the
centrality of pilgrimage as a means of acquiring merit and other blessings
in the Buddhist tradition.[23]

In the next passage, however, the author's astute observations seem to
go askew. "A man who has been an eyewitness to them told me that the
amount of blood which is shed beside them is not small in quantity. He
asserted that it might happen that perhaps fifty thousand or more might
offer themselves, but it is Allah who knows."[24] What are we to make of this
claim of human sacrifice at the Bamiyan Buddhas? At first we should note
that the author himself did not claim to have witnessed this ritual. Instead
he attributes it to someone else. Does this somehow cast doubt upon the
story? Most likely not, as in this age before empiricism and the idea of
"seeing is believing," the spoken or written words of others had just as
much validity as one's own.[25] For the Muslim author and reader this was
therefore something that had happened. But what was happening? One
scholar has suggested that it was something like a linguistic confusion arising out of the practice of entering the Buddhist monastery whereby one
leaves one's family and "gives up one's life" in order to practice the
Dharma. The fifty thousand who "offer themselves" are thus not sacrificial
victims, but rather those who have become monks. While this explanation
is certainly possible, one can also conjecture that these "sacrificial victims"
may actually refer to the bones of deceased Buddhists and may thus actually
reflect some aspect of Buddhist funerary practice.

Unfortunately, however, at this point we simply do not what ibn Khalid
was describing. Nevertheless, it is likely that the idea of human sacrifice at
both Bamiyan and at the Hindu temple in Hyderabad reflects a broader
component of contemporary Islamic discourse surrounding the issue of
idols and idolatry. In particular, it is well known that early Islam defined
itself as the very antithesis of idolatry, not only in relation to pre-Islamic
Arab religion, but also in relation to other monotheistic religions of the day,
such as Christianity and Manichaeism, which were in theological polemics
invariably identified as idolatrous.[26] In this overheated environment of

claims and counterclaims of idolatry among the "Western" traditions, the very real "idol worship" found in the East therefore became the defining feature of both Hinduism and Buddhism in the Muslim mind regardless of how they themselves understood their own practices. Thus much like the pre-Islamic Arabs, who had prayed to the Ka'ba and its idols for various reasons, it was assumed by Muslims that Hindus and Buddhists continued to do so toward their own statues.

Indeed, of the enormous range of practices and beliefs that both Hindus and Buddhists maintained at this time, the one defining characteristic that all Muslim sources invariably label them with is "idolatry." The reason for this, however, was not necessarily the result of actual Hindu or Buddhist practice, but rather internal Muslim understandings of Islam, which was largely defined as the religion of anti-idolatry. Thus regardless of their own theological specificities Hinduism and Buddhism were defined over and against Islam solely in terms of idolatry. In fact this circular logic would over time develop to the point where India came to be understood in Muslim thought as the very origin of all idolatry. Later Muslim scholars would thus claim that the idol worship of the pre-Islamic Arabs had actually been imported from India. When Muhammad threw down the idols from the roof of the Ka'ba, as it came to be represented in later Islamic art, he therefore threw down idols that looked like Hindu and Buddhist statues that actually represented Arab pagan gods and the earlier prophets (figure 4).[27]

Of course, the idea of India as the fount of all idolatry is a later development in the Islamic tradition and it is not found expressly in ibn Khalid's work. Nevertheless, this subsequent development is presented here as evidence of how Islamic thought developed on the basis of internal theological debates with little regard to realities on the ground.

It is therefore in this manner that one should approach the Muslim claims of human sacrifice in India. It is less a confirmation of actual Hindu or Buddhist practice than a commentary on Muslim dynamics of self-identification. On account of idolatry being perceived as so evil in Muslim thought it does not seem too farfetched to imagine that they made manifest this rejection of Allah by projecting upon "idolaters" the most egregious form of "idol worship": human sacrifice. Indeed, the same phenomenon took place when Europeans ventured forth and supposedly came across all kinds of monstrous practices around the world from human sacrifice to cannibalism. Yet as with the earlier claims of Buddhist human sacrifice

Figure 4. Muhammad and Ali destroying the idols of the Ka'ba, from a copy of *Rawdat aṣ-Ṣafā* (The Garden of Purity), Shiraz 1003 A.H./1595 C.E. (Per. 254.83). © The Trustees of the Chester Beatty Library, Dublin.

most of these later European claims were less a reflection of reality than a component of Christian theological polemic.

Regardless of this detour ibn Khalid's narrative does eventually return to more verifiable events and practices.

> They have a building at Bamiyan on the frontiers of India, where it borders on Sijistan. Ya'qub ibn al-Layth reached this locality when he sought to invade India. The idols which were sent to the City of Peace [Baghdad] from that locality of Bamiyan were transported at the time of its invasion. Ascetics and devotees occupy this great building. In it there are idols of gold adorned with precious stones, the number of which is unknown and to which no praise or description can do justice. The people of India go there on pilgrimages by land and sea from the furthest towns (regions) of their country.
>
> At Faraj [Multan] there is the House of Gold, a building about which there is a difference of opinion. Some say that it is a stone building, containing idols, and that is called the "House of Gold" because the Arabs took a hundred *buhar* of gold from it when they invaded this place during the days of al-Hajjaj.[28]

While this last passage is about the conquest and confirms the argument made previously about the financial dimension of the Muslim advance into northwest India, what is of greater interest here is the author's description of religious practice, in particular, the performance of pilgrimage. Since it is a fundamental element of the Buddhist tradition it certainly makes sense that ibn Khalid notes pilgrimage; however, one can also wonder whether this one practice is described because it is the one ritual similar to the Islamic tradition. Indeed, can we speculate whether the author was trying to draw a parallel between Buddhist pilgrimage and the Muslim Hajj? Or was he simply noting a readily observable Buddhist practice?

Unfortunately, we simply do not know. However, we do know that later Muslim geographers did make this connection. The thirteenth-century scholar Yaqut al-Hamawi, for example, who based his study on the earlier work of Ibn al-Faqih, makes a direct connection between Buddhist worship and the Ka'ba in his description of rituals at the monastery of the Barmakid family: "they took the house of the Nawbahar as the equivalent of the Holy House of God (i.e. the Ka'ba), erected idols around the building, decorated it with brocades and silks and hung precious jewels upon it."[29] Thus clearly a connection was made between Buddhist and Islamic pilgrimage in Muslim literature; however, whether this same idea inspired ibn Khalid is unclear.

Nevertheless, Yahya ibn Khalid's description of the Muslim attack on what is now Afghanistan and the subsequent conquest of Kabul rings true. Gold and statues were indeed sent back to Baghdad and even displayed in Mecca as reported by Saʿid b. Yahya:

"A king from among the kings of Tibet [i.e., Kabul] became a Muslim. He had an idol of gold that he worshipped, which was in the shape of a man. On the head of the idol was a crown of gold bedecked with chains of jewelry and rubies and green corundum and chrysolite. It was on a square throne, raised above the ground on legs, and the throne was of silver. On the throne was a cushion of brocade; on the fringe of the cushion were tassels of gold and silver hanging down, and the tassels were as . . . draperies on the face of the throne." Al-Maʾmūn sent it to Mecca as a trophy to be stored in the treasury of the Kaʿba. In Mecca it was first displayed in the Square of ʿUmar b. al-Khattab for three days, with a silver tablet on which was written: "In the name of God, the Merciful, the Compassionate. This is the throne of so-and-so, son of so-and-so, king of Tibet. He became a Muslim and sent this throne as a gift to the Kaʿba; so praise God who guided him to Islam."[30]

The fact of the matter is that the practice of sending back Hindu and Buddhist statues continued throughout the centuries. When the Saffarid ruler Ya'qub finally conquered Zabul in 870, for example, he sent fifty gold and silver idols to Caliph Al-Muʿtamid "who dispatched them to Mecca. Another set of idols, lavishly decorated with jewels and silver, sent by ʿAmr in 896 from Sakawand . . . caused a sensation in Baghdad on account of their strangeness."[31]

The strangeness of India, however, was manifested not only in its idols. In the Muslim world there also came into circulation a whole array of stories about the "magical and mysterious East." The same phenomenon, of course, was to happen centuries later in the West. Nevertheless, the account of India we find in Ibn al-Nadim's *Fihrist* was apparently one part of this trend since it added fuel to Muslim visions of the strange and spiritual East through its inclusion of two anecdotes about a magical floating monastery and a temple with talking statues.

> Abu Dulaf al-Yanbu'i, a traveler, told me that the building which is known as the House of Gold is not this one. The building is in the wild parts of India, in the territories of Makran and Qandahar. Nobody reaches it except the devotees and ascetics of India. It is built of gold. Its length is seven cubits and its width the same. Its height is twelve cubits and it is adorned with varieties of precious stones. In it there are idols made of red rubies and other marvelous precious stones, and it is adorned with glorious pearls, each one of which is like a bird's egg or even larger. He [Abu Dulaf] asserted that reliable authorities from among the people of India told him that the rain draws away from the top of this building, as well as from the right and left [sides], so that it does not strike it. In the same way the stream in flood avoids it, flowing to the right and left. He said, "One of the Indians said that if anyone sick with any disease whatsoever, sees it, Allah, may His name be glorified, cures him." He also said, "When I examined this matter, there was disagreement about it. Some of the Brahmans stated to me that it is hanging between Heaven and earth without support or suspension.
>
> Abu Dulaf said to me, "The Indians have a temple at Qimar. Its walls are made of gold and its roofs with beams of Indian lumber, the length of each timber being fifty cubits or more. Its idols, niches, and its parts faced in worship have been adorned with glorious pearls and precious stones." He said, "A reliable person told me that in the city of al-Sanf they have a temple other than this one. It is an ancient temple in which all of its idols speak with the worshippers, answering everything about which they are questioned." Abu Dulaf [also] said, "At the time when I was in India, the king of the government of al-Sanf was named Lajin." The Najrani [Nestorian] monk told me that the king at the present time is a monarch known as King Luqin, who desired al-Sanf. He devastated it and became ruler over its people.[32]

To put this story into context we need to recall that Abu Dulaf, who is cited as the source for these stories, had never actually travelled to the East. Instead he wrote two travel accounts that were wholly fictitious.[33] But they still had a great impact in the Muslim world precisely because the world of Islam and the East were at this time growing apart, and real knowledge was in short supply.

Yet even so the story of Abu Dulaf is not simply a fanciful form of Muslim "orientalism" about the mysterious East. The final episode about the temple at Qimar actually reflects an astute awareness of geopolitical realities on the other side of the world. Qimar, namely, is a transcription of Khmer and refers to the Cambodian kingdom that flourished at the time when Ibn al-Nadim was writing the *Fihrist*. Moreover, Lajin reflects the common phonological L ➡ R shift and refers to Rajen, or Rajendravarman, the Khmer king who conquered the Vietnamese Champa kingdom, here called Al-Saif, in 944–952 C.E. In addition, Luqin probably refers to Lung-pien, which lies southeast of Hanoi near the mouth of the Song-koi River, and was the kingdom that conquered Champa at the end of the tenth century.[34]

While this material confirms Muslims' awareness of developments in tenth-century Southeast Asia, we must also recognize that these events were not recorded in the initial eighth-century report of Yahya ibn Khalid. Rather, the inclusion of these later events reveals the palimpsest nature of the received version of the text. The comments of Abu Dulaf about Qimar and the Nestorian monk about King Luqin are clearly later additions by Ibn al-Nadim. So too is the previous episode about the floating monastery attributed to Abu Dulaf. In fact, it is most likely the case that this whole section about the magical East was not really part of ibn Khalid's report. In fact, it seems to be the work of later authors in its entirety. If one compares the no-nonsense and level-headed presentation of India that actually does seem to come from ibn Khalid's pen, then these episodes truly seem out of place. In particular, they seem less appropriate to a time when the Muslim world was actually engaging with India as was the case in the eighth century, than a time when the two had grown apart and India was seen as being far away and thus readily imagined as a land of snake-charming gurus and floating monasteries. In fact it is important to recall that this vision of India as a land of special wisdom dispensed by "naked philosophers" had been an integral part of the Greek and Roman view of the East,[35] and thus it is possible that this later Muslim view was actually shaped by these earlier Western views precisely when the worlds of Islam and India were growing apart.

And it was, of course, during this later period that Ibn al-Nadim wrote the *Fihrist*. But before exploring the disconnect between India and the Muslim world in the post-Barmakid period, let us turn back to the work of ibn Khalid and explore how he, in the eighth century, understood Indian Buddhism: "The people of India disagree about this [subject]. One party asserted that he [Buddha] was the likeness of the Creator, may His greatness be exalted. Another group said that he was the likeness of his apostle [sent] to them. Then they disagreed at this point. One sect (party) said that the apostle was one of the angels. Another sect stated that the apostle was a man among the people. Then a group said that he was a demon among the demons, while [another] sect stated that he was a likeness of the Budasaf, the wise, who came to them from Allah, may His name be glorified."[36]

This is a dense and confusing description of Indian Buddhism; however, it well captures the debates that tore asunder the Buddhist community. Indeed, it was in part on account of such debates that the Nikaya tradition broke into sixteen different schools. Moreover, it was the deification of the Buddha in the Mahayana tradition that ultimately shattered the community into two incompatible factions.

It is these debates that ibn Khalid is trying to present in the above passage, though unfortunately none of his descriptions can be identified with a particular Nikaya school. Nevertheless, what is perhaps more important in this presentation is how ibn Khalid seems to be trying to make sense of this foreign tradition by drawing upon categories within his own tradition. Thus rather than presenting Buddhism as wholly other or simply another form of idolatry he actually attempts to convey Buddhist ideas. Moreover, he does so by using terms and ideas familiar to any Muslim, such as the Creator and angels and demons. These terms may not have been applicable to Buddhism itself; however, it reveals a valiant attempt at trying to understand something wholly other by means of one's own mental framework.

Indeed, we should note at the outset that such intellectual engagement with "the other" was by no means always to be the case. Readily dismissing Buddhism by means of the all-encompassing derogatory label "idolatry" was much easier and less threatening. And as we will see below, later Muslim thinkers—especially theologians such as Shahrastani—did not try to understand the Dharma in the same way as ibn Khalid. Instead, as with the issue of idolatry, and even human sacrifice, they used Buddhism as a vehicle to drive forward their own theological agenda. Thus rather than trying to understand or engage with Buddhist thought they simply used the Dharma as an example of heresy within their larger project of legitimating their own theological interpretation. Some of these Muslim theologians even went so far as to use their own misconceptualizations of the Dharma in order to attack other schools of Islam that purportedly followed the same ideas. One egregious example of such an approach is evidenced in the case of Muslim theologians who, contrary to all the evidence, claimed that Buddhists did not believe in reason.

> Since the real Buddhists, as is well known, did not reject reason-
> ing at all, we have an example here of a basic mechanism which we
> also meet in other cases. In scholastic theology (*kalām*), a particular
> metaphysical position that is refuted as being contrary to Islam is
> often projected upon a specific, lesser known group of non-
> Muslims. This was done not because they were known to hold this
> doctrine in reality (real knowledge was lacking) but *simply in order
> to ascribe a heretical doctrine to a particular group of outsiders*. In this
> way the *mu'aṭṭila* were called the Sumaniyya [i.e., Buddhists] of
> Islam. This particular way of locating wrong doctrines implies a par-
> ticular way of "judging" non-Muslims without seeking to know
> them. After all, the real doctrine of the Sumaniyya was very different
> from that of the Muslim *mu'aṭṭila*.[37]

Indeed, the issue of not knowing the other was a central component of this whole enterprise, and it is an issue we will return to below. Nevertheless, such ignorance and the theological use of the other is not what we find in the case of ibn Khalid. He actually tried to present the different positions held by the Buddhists. Moreover, he put these ideas in Muslim terms not in order to level a critique, but to actually make the Dharma comprehensi- ble. And in this regard an interesting facet of ibn Khalid's work is his use of the term *Budasaf* without much ado.

The word is from the Sanskrit Bodhisattva, but ibn Khalid does not offer any explanation for this very technical Buddhist term. Why is this? Did he assume the reader already knew what such a thing was? Of course, he does provide something like a definition in that a *Budasaf* is a "wise" one sent to humanity by Allah, which is a somewhat valid interpretation of the bodhisattva figure, albeit one firmly situated within the framework of the Abrahamic tradition.[38] Yet in addition to this intellectual move on ibn Khalid's part, what is interesting is simply the fact that the term *Budasaf* seems to be a part of the Muslim lexicon, much as today there is a whole array of obscure Sanskrit terms that are part of everyday English.[39] How did this happen? In the case of English the explanation can be found in the Western fascination with Asian religions. But what about the case of Buddhist terms in early Arabic? Did Muslim youth of the eighth century, especially the idle wealthy sons of the merchant elite, also look to the spiritual East for answers?

While we know there was a long-running interest in the philosophical speculations of Manichaeism among the Muslim elite,[40] whether they were also drawn to Buddhism during the Barmakid period is unclear. Indeed, it is precisely because of such uncertainty that ideas of crypto-Buddhist influences in early Islam continue to circulate. Thus some scholars want to draw connections between Buddhism and Sufism, or mystical Islam. Some, for example, continue to claim that the early Sufi Ibrahim b. Adham (d. ca. 778) was born into the royal Buddhist family of Balkh, even though this tradition has long been discredited.[41] Others like to point out that the teacher of another one of the earliest Sufis, Abu Yazid al-Bistami (d. 875 c.e.), was Abu Ali al-Sindi. The implication being that this man from Sind had links with the Buddhist traditions still practiced there.[42] And when one looks at the central Sufi concept of *fana*, or "annihilation" of the ego in order to experience God, it is easy to parallel it with Buddhism's no-self and Nirvana and claim some kind of genealogical link. Yet no matter how enticing this possibility may be, there is actually no solid evidence for such a transmission.

This does not mean, however, that Muslims were unaware or uninterested in the East and the Buddha. Indeed, much as the life story of the Buddha has become a part of Western lore through films and novels like Hermann Hesse's *Siddhartha*, in the early Muslim world there was also the famous story of Bilawar and Budasaf, which was simply a retelling of the Buddha's life. The story had initially been translated into Arabic from Pahlavi, or medieval Persian, during the Barmakid period when interest in the East ran high. And the story apparently spread like wildfire.[43] One measure of this popularity is in fact revealed in ibn Khalid's use of the term Budasaf in the eighth century without much concern for its elaboration. Presumably it was on account of the Bilawar and Budasaf story that the term was well known. And this would in fact continue to be the case through the centuries. The noted Shi'ite scholar Ibn Tawus (d. 1266 c.e.), for example, used an episode from the Bilawar and Budasaf story in order to illustrate a particular point in a treatise on astronomy.[44] And he too felt no need to explain or elaborate the story—it was simply part of the Muslim cultural repertoire.

On account of its popularity in the Islamic world it is not surprising that the Bilawar and Budasaf story also eventually spread to Christian Europe. In the West, however, the story of Barlaam and Josephat became completely dislodged from its moorings. While the story retained the narrative structure of the life of the Buddha, it was completely reconfigured as a Christian story. Josephat is thus an Indian prince whose father, King Abenner, persecutes the Christian church that had been founded by the Apostle Thomas. Moreover, because a prophecy is given that his son will become a great Christian, the king locks him up in the castle. But Josephat eventually escapes, sees the three evils and then studies with Barlaam, a monk who introduces him to Christianity. For their efforts the Catholic Church declared Barlaam and Josephat martyrs and saints in the sixteenth century. Yet it was not only in the Christian West that the story of the Buddha took on a life of its own. It also continued to be part of the Muslim tradition, especially among the Shi'a and Isma'ili communities, who appreciated the story's theme of being gradually initiated into wisdom. In addition, the idea of internal and external wisdom coincided neatly with their own understandings of Islam.[45]

Even so, the Muslim familiarity with Buddhist literature went beyond the story of Bilawar and Budasaf. The "Story of the King's Grey Hair" told by the tenth-century Shi'ite theologian Ibn Babuya, for example, was apparently based on Buddhist stories about the *devadutta*, "messengers of death," as found in several *jataka* stories about the Buddha's previous lives.[46] Moreover, the circulation of Buddhist stories in the Muslim world is also evidenced in the Buddhist parable of the blind men trying to describe an elephant that became a famous part of Sufi lore.[47] How such transmissions actually occurred, though, is largely unknown. Indeed, one can wonder whether such stories were originally shared among the merchants at caravanserais on the fabled Silk Road. Or were they actually read in translation? The fact that Ibn al-Nadim listed a title similar to the "King's Grey Hair" in his *Fihrist* confirms that at least this story was eventually translated into Arabic and circulated in the Muslim community.[48] Of course, this fact raises further questions: How and when was such a project undertaken? In what kind of context did such a translation take shape? Moreover, did Buddhists and Muslims work together on such a translation?

Unfortunately, we do not know the answers to these questions. Indeed, virtually nothing is known about the actual day-to-day and person-to-person interactions that may or may not have taken place between Buddhists and Muslims in this period. As a result, how these stories moved from one community to the other is obscure. Nevertheless, from scattered sources we do get a glimpse of the two groups actually meeting. The twelfth-century Sufi Shaqiq al-Balkki, for example, briefly describes his visit to a Buddhist monastery among the Turks: "I went one day to a Buddhist temple, and saw one of their servants whom they call *toyin* in the language of China (Khitai) and *sthavira* in India. He had shaven his whole head and wore clothes of purple."[49] One can only wonder whether they sat down and drank a cup of tea and talked. And if so, what would they have talked about?

As is invariably the case the world over, part of their conversation would probably have been about other people. And this possibility is in fact confirmed in the case of the Muslim interpretation of the Ramanandis, the Hindu worshippers of Rama, which is from a decidedly Buddhist perspective. In fact, what was to become the "standard" Muslim presentation of Rama worship is fundamentally wrong from a Hindu perspective. "The Ramaniya (are the adepts of) Raman (Rama) who was a tyrannous king and exceeded the measure of oppression. He pretended to be [God's?] envoy and ordered his people to worship him, saying that it was conducive to the Creator's pleasure, and much other nonsense. The Ravaniya (adepts of Ravana) say that by Ravan's intermediary they seek the guidance of the Creator who accepted (Ravan's) repentance and gave him a lance. So they made Ravan their prophet."[50]

In this presentation Rama is evil and the righteous god is Ravana, which is actually the reverse of the *Rāmāyaṇa* wherein Ravana is the demon king, who abducts Rama's wife Sita, thereby setting in motion the mythological narrative of Rama and his heroic deeds. But what is relevant to note here is that the positive evaluation of Ravana is found only in Buddhist and Jain sources: two traditions that were historical enemies of Hinduism. Thus the fact that this story made it into Muslim sources seems to confirm Buddhist-Muslim interaction; however, the extent of such engagement and for how long it took place is unknown.

But we have now strayed far from ibn Khalid and his mission to India in the eighth century. From the preceding discussion, however, one gets a sense of not only the world in which ibn Khalid was operating, but also the one he was helping to create, one in which the ideas and products of the

Buddhist tradition were increasingly becoming part of the Muslim milieu. Thus let us return to his observations:

> Each sect among them has a ritual for worshipping and exalting him. Some of their trustworthy people have said that each one of their communities has an image to which people go so as to worship and exalt it. Al-Budd [Buddha] is a generic term, while al-asnam (idols) signifies [different] "kinds." The description of the greatest Buddha is that of a man seated on a throne, with no hair on his face and with his chin and mouth sunk [close] together. He is not covered by a robe and he is as though smiling. With his hand he is stringing thirty-two [beads].
>
> A trustworthy person has said that there is an image of him in every house. These are made of all kinds of materials, according to the status of the individual. They are of gold adorned with different jewels, or of silver, brass, stone, or wood. They exalt him as he receives them, facing either from the east to west, or from west to east, but for the most part they turn his back to the east, so that they face themselves toward the east. It is said that they have this image with four faces, so fashioned by engineering and accurate craftsmanship that from whatever place they approach it, they see the full face and the profile perfectly, without any part of it hidden from them. It is said that this is the form of the idol that is at Multan.[51]

What first strikes one in this passage is how different ibn Khalid's description of Buddha statues and their worship is from Ibn al-Nadim's fantastical interpolation. There are no talking statues or human sacrifices. Instead there is a rather clear-eyed ethnographic description of Buddha statues and the different ways in which Buddhists interact with them. There is even a clear identification of a particular image, that of a Buddha on a throne, which probably does not in fact represent Siddhartha, but rather Maitreya, the future Buddha.[52]

In Buddhist cosmology there are numerous Buddhas. Each one comes into the world at a time when humans have completely forgotten the teachings of the preceding Buddha and he then teaches the Dharma anew. Whereupon the same cycle will happen again: humans will forget the Dharma, the world will decay into an age of ignorance and violence, and then another Buddha will appear to usher in a new golden age. On account of this mythological cycle and the attendant prophecy of decline Buddhist thinkers had a ready framework with which to interpret any calamitous age. It also provided them a context within which to ask the question: If these are the end times, now what should we as Buddhists do?[53] Such speculation not only fueled doctrinal innovation in the Buddhist tradition but also inspired a vast array of millenarian movements focusing on the coming of Maitreya. In China especially the idea of Maitreya and the end times was mobilized repeatedly to challenge the contemporary order.[54] Yet leaving aside the long history of revolution in Chinese history, what is of relevance here is ibn Khalid's description of a seated Buddha. As noted above, in Indian Buddhist iconography such a figure most often represents the Buddha Maitreya (figure 5).[55]

Of all the myriad images of the Buddha that ibn Khalid could possibly have seen, the fact that it was only Maitreya he highlighted raises numerous questions, such as whether there was a millenarian movement in Indian Buddhism at the time of his travels. Based on the powerful rise of Hinduism, the floundering of the Mahayana, the chaotic political and economic situation, and the concurrent coming-into-being of tantra, it is very possible to surmise that many Buddhists may have felt that the eighth century was something of an "end times." From the literary and artistic record, however, there does not seem to have been a corresponding Maitreya cult to explain ibn Khalid's focus on this particular Buddha image. Thus it might simply have been the case that he had seen an especially large or somehow distinctive Maitreya statue. Indeed, one can wonder if it was the same thirty-foot seated Maitreya carved in sandalwood that was described by the Chinese pilgrims Faxian and Xuanzang at Darel in the upper Indus Valley.[56] Either way, what is clear is that above and beyond the seated Maitreya figure ibn Khalid also noticed another kind of Buddha statue, one with four faces. This was something new, and as with all religious art such a development was not simply a new aesthetic, but was tied into doctrinal shifts.

The history of Buddha images is greatly debated.[57] In the early Buddhist tradition there were supposedly no images of the Buddha. He was instead represented by aniconic symbols, such as a Dharma wheel, a footprint, a throne, or a Bodhi tree (figure 6). Doctrinally this made sense since in the Nikaya traditions the Buddha was not a god, but a man, and thus was not to be an object of worship. Moreover, once the Buddha had attained

Figure 5. Maitreya Buddha. Mendut Temple (732 C.E.–929 C.E.), Jawa Tengah.
Photo: John C. Huntington, courtesy of Huntington Collection.

Figure 6. Buddhapada. Kushan period (first–second century C.E.). Photo: John C. Huntington, courtesy of Huntington Collection.

parinirvana he no longer existed in any tangible way and was thus inaccessible. In other words, there was nothing left—only his teaching—which came to be represented by various abstract symbols.

Over time, however, Buddhist doctrine changed, as did the culture and artistic environment in which it operated. Thus eventually images of the Buddha started to appear. Yet where and when they did so is still debated. Regardless of the specifics, however, in none of these earlier images was the Buddha ever presented as a multi-headed deity. Such a development was a later phenomenon arising within the mélange of Gupta-period temple Hinduism, later Mahayana doctrine, and the nascent tantric movement, wherein the notion and representation of multi-armed and multi-headed deities were coming into being.[58] Ibn Khalid had therefore apparently tapped into these developments. Indeed, it was this maelstrom of social, political, and religious forces that would ultimately coalesce into what we now identify as tantra, which was a form of religious practice and ideology that was to radically alter the Indian landscape.

At the time of ibn Khalid's peregrinations, however, the distinctive schools and texts of tantra had not yet fully formed. The multi-headed Buddha he describes is thus not part of a distinctive third way of the Dharma, tantric Buddhism, but something that was in the process of being created. Indeed, it was only in the ninth and tenth centuries that there actually began to appear works specifically identifying themselves as either Hindu or Buddhist tantras. Before that these new ideas were circulating largely amidst the Siddhas, "a pool of wizards and demigods, supermen and wonder-workers that all South Asians (and Tibetans) could draw on to slake the thirst of their religious imagination, [who] were the most syncretistic landmarks on the religious landscape of medieval India."[59] In fact it was this world of the Siddhas and this moment in time that ibn Khalid captures so well. He thus does not talk about "tantric Buddhism" because such a thing did not yet exist.

Nevertheless, in his description of the religious traditions of India ibn Khalid does describe one group, right after his investigation of Buddhism, which does seem to capture the practices of the Siddhas and early tantrikas. Indeed, his description reflects some of the main ideas that were subsequently to become essential aspects of Buddhist tantra. Ibn Khalid called this group the Mahakalayah, the worshippers of Mahakala:

They have an idol named Mahakal which has four hands and is sapphire in color, with a great deal of lank hair on its head. It bares its teeth, its stomach is exposed, and on its back is an elephant's skin dripping blood. The legs of an elephant's hide are tied in front of it. In one of its hands is a great serpent with its mouth open, in another is a rod, in the third there is a man's hand. It has the fourth hand uplifted. Two snakes are in its ears, like earrings, and two huge serpents, which have wrapped themselves around it, are on its body. On its head there is a crown made of skull bones, and it has a necklace also made of them. They claim that it is a demon from among the devils, meriting worship because of its great power and its possession of qualities which are praiseworthy and lovable, as well as despised and abhorred, and also because of its giving and refusing, doing good and committing evil. It is, moreover, their refuge during times of adversity.[60]

If one looks at how Mahakala was eventually to be represented in the Tibetan tradition (figure 7), one can readily see how ibn Khalid was describing a tradition that was soon to become part and parcel of Buddhist tantra. And what is especially noteworthy is that his description captures so well the binary or reverse logic of tantra, wherein opposites are the same and enlightenment can be achieved through unorthodox means as in the case of compassionate and wrathful deities. Ibn Khalid was thus not only an astute observer of tantra's formation, but he may in fact have been the first foreigner to document this new South Asian religious movement.[61] Curiously, however, in the Muslim world he would also be the last. Even though tantra was to eventually become the dominant Buddhist tradition in India as well as Inner Asia, Muslim knowledge of this powerful new religious and political technology virtually ceased with the work of ibn Khalid.

To explain this development one can possibly conjecture that as Buddhist tantra evolved it was no longer distinguishable in practice and theory from Hinduism. The famous fourteenth-century traveler Ibn Battuta, for example, apparently lacked any awareness of the difference between the two.[62] Indeed, the idea that Buddhism eventually dissipated within the ever-amorphous category of Hinduism as a result of tantra is one of the most common explanations for the eventual disappearance of Buddhism in India. It may thus be possible that later Muslims who came into contact with Buddhist tantra saw nothing that distinguished it from Hinduism and thus both were readily cordoned off within the catch-all category of "idola-

Figure 7. Mahakala, Shadbhuja. Mongolia, nineteenth century. Ground mineral pigment, black background on cotton (C2006.66.279 [HAR 637]). Courtesy of Rubin Museum of Art.

try." Such may indeed have been the case. However, another important factor that needs to be taken into consideration regarding this confusion is the above-mentioned split between the Buddhist and Muslim worlds.

The Buddhist-Muslim Split

In the beginning of the ninth century the Barmakid family fell into disgrace and Islam's "India age" came to an end.[63] The possibilities of a Sanskritic Islam were replaced with a Muslim world solely engaged with the legacy of Hellenism. This turn to the West was to have profound consequences, including the subsequent transmission of the Hellenic tradition to Europe that laid the foundation for the Renaissance. Yet before that epoch-making shift in world history, another transformation took place in Eurasia: namely, rather than growing together on account of increased trade, the Muslim and Buddhist worlds actually grew apart.

In order to begin to understand this Buddhist-Muslim split we need to recall what happened during the course of the ninth century. Most notably, during this period northwest India and parts of Central Asia broke away from the Caliphate and were ruled by several local dynasties. While the rise of the Samanid and Saffarid dynasties had numerous consequences the one that needs to be noted here is its relationship with the tandem Muslim turn to the West. That is, even though some of these local Central Asian dynasties came to outshine the Caliphate in various ways—especially financially and technologically—in the larger scheme of things Central Asia became more and more marginal in the Muslim imagination. Thus instead of being part of the broader Muslim world this area became instead a sort of buffer zone between the Islamic heartland and India, which itself came to be seen as impossibly distant.[64] Thus unlike the Barmakid period when India was the land of science and mathematics and a place one could readily visit, India became instead a fantastical land far away, one, moreover, filled not with valuable knowledge but blasphemous gurus, magical mantras, and talking statues. Thus unlike the Barmakid period when India was within the Muslim orbit, in this later period India came instead to be seen as wholly other.[65]

It is within this environment that we witness the escalating tendency to project images of magic and mystery on India as seen in the work of Ibn al-Nadim. Thus contrary to the earlier clear-eyed reporting of ibn Khalid there instead arose an array of fantastical tales about India.[66] One of the more curious examples of such fantasies is found in the mid-ninth-century travelogue attributed to Sulayman the Sailor, who reports about the "courtesans of the Buddha," girls offered by their mothers to Buddhist monasteries to serve as prostitutes in order to gain merit and raise money for the temple.[67] Of course, to make sense of this simultaneous fascination and repulsion we need to recognize that it was fueled by extenuating political and economic concerns. Indeed, Sulayman was a merchant and thus his work reflects the growing Muslim interest in the Indian market and, as has been repeatedly witnessed in history, economic interest has nothing necessarily to do with intellectual curiosity or cultural engagement.[68] In fact there is often an almost inverse relation between interests in economic integration and cultural understanding. Thus it is not surprising that even as Muslim interest and involvement in the Indian economy increased exponentially, there was also a simultaneous decrease in actual awareness and interest in Indian religion and culture.

One of the more curious examples of these intertwined phenomena was the Muslim recognition of Sri Lanka as the Garden of Eden.[69] The development of this legend captures well the fruitful intersection of economic interest and religious imagination. Sri Lanka was, of course, the central transit hub in east-west maritime trade and thus claiming it was "Muslim" territory was of paramount importance in order to control the trade routes. At the same time, however, it also reflects the growing disconnect between the real India, or in this case Sri Lanka, and the "India" of the Muslim imagination. Yet it is important to recognize that this development not only occurred on account of economic interests, but was also tied into the larger cultural and intellectual shift of the Muslim world away from the East and toward the West. As a result, the previous interest and engagement with the East seen during the Barmakid era came to an end during this period. In its place there developed not only fantastical tales of India's riches, but also of its strangeness, which was clearly the perfect environment to foster the idea of Sri Lanka as being the Garden of Eden. And this development signaled not only the expansive economic reach of the Caliphate, but also the end of real Muslim intellectual engagement with the East.

On account of this shift it is not surprising that Muslim knowledge of Buddhism did not advance either. While some of this certainly had to do with the forces noted above, there were also others, and in fact at this time a real divide, or geographical gap, was developing between the Buddhist

and Muslim worlds. Some of this, of course, had to do with the gradual
conversion of Buddhist families in northwest India and Central Asia to
both Islam and Hinduism. This development over the centuries had
resulted in there quite simply being fewer and fewer Buddhists with whom
Muslims could actually interact, which was a phenomenon well captured
in the work of al-Biruni, who in the eleventh century lamented the fact that
he could not find any Buddhists to actually explain the Dharma to him.[70]
The Buddhists had therefore apparently disappeared, yet where had they
gone? As we have seen many Buddhists had simply moved away from where
Muslims were operating. Moreover, it is important to recall that the center
of the Buddhist world had long since moved away from northwest India.
In fact, during the consolidation of Muslim power in this region the Buddhist world had developed into two new religio-economic units. One was
noted earlier, the "Buddhist Mediterranean" around the Bay of Bengal. Yet
with the rise of tantra and its development in Tibet and its spread across
Inner Asia there also arose another Buddhist trade network, which can be
called the "Tantric Bloc" (map 10).

Although the Buddhist revival in Tibet in the eleventh century is well

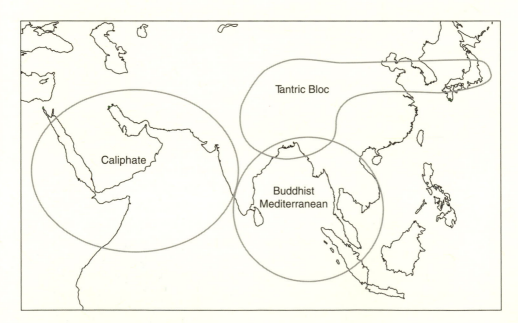

Map 10. Three Economic Zones.

documented little attention is paid to its economic dimension.[71] Yet in many ways one cannot understand the development of Buddhism in Tibet—its monasteries, its doctrines and rituals, its artistic traditions, etc.— without linking it to the integration of the Tibetan economy within the trading networks of Eurasia. Indeed, the rise of Tibet and the spread of tantric Buddhism across Asia was part and parcel of the development of this new Tantric Bloc that linked the Pala dynasty in India with Tibet, the Tangut kingdom (1038–1227 C.E.) in Central Asia, and the Khitan Liao dynasty (907–1125 C.E.) in north China, all of whom were Buddhist.[72] Of course, the financial well-being of the Tantric Bloc and perhaps even the whole Eurasian economy was intimately tied to the economic miracle of the Song dynasty (960–1279) in China proper.[73] Indeed, the importance of the Song economy and the explosion of maritime trade at this time are well known.[74] Yet it is perhaps on account of this focus on China and the Islamic world, as well as on the sea, that what was happening in Inner Asia is generally overlooked. Not that the simultaneous economic boom of this period among the Tanguts or the Khitan Liao has escaped observation, but rather the integration that it entailed has been less explored. Indeed, all too often these pieces are studied in isolation and thus their intertwined nature is overlooked.

Recent research, however, is revealing just how connected the Tantric Bloc actually was.[75] One notable piece of evidence in this regard is the famous Byodoin Amitabha temple in Kyoto, Japan. Built by Fujiwara Yorimichi in 1053 C.E., it has long been held up as a classic example of Japaneseness. The fact of the matter, however, is that the temple is less a monument of Japaneseness and more a confirmation of Eurasian integration since the architecture and style of the Byodoin temple is actually based upon Liao dynasty precedent. Moreover, some artistic elements in the Byodoin temple can even be traced back to Tibetan artistic elements found at Dunhuang in Inner Asia.[76] The Byodoin temple is thus less an example of Japanese uniqueness than a monument to the interconnectedness of the Tantric Bloc in the eleventh and twelfth centuries.

The case of the Byodoin temple also provides a further piece in the puzzle of why Buddhist-Muslim interaction seemed to decrease at this time. In many ways the map above captures the reason rather well visually: the Buddhist and Muslim worlds had grown apart economically. This is not to say that the Islamic world, the Buddhist Mediterranean and the Tantric Bloc were exclusive economic zones. In fact we know that at this time there

was an escalation in trade between India and China, which was invariably
mediated through these Buddhist zones.[77] However, while there was an
apparent increase in trade and movement among these various Asian economic zones, and even with the Muslim world by means of maritime trade,
it resulted in there actually being fewer possibilities for Muslims and Buddhists to interact. Buddhists were quite simply no longer living and con-
ducting business in areas close to those of Muslim dominance. It is
therefore not surprising that al-Biruni could not find a Buddhist when he
wanted one.[78]

Yet it was not only the rise of these different economic zones that fostered the growing divide between Buddhists and Muslims. A further development, which was tied into the rise of these zones, was the expansion of
maritime trade around 1000 C.E. on account of advances in nautical technology, such as innovations in ship building and mapping, as well as the
use of the compass.[79] This shift in transportation methods had a profound
impact on the traditional overland routes through Inner Asia, which were
no longer a cost-effective means of transporting commodities. Yet the shift
from land to sea also had less-tangible consequences, in particular, a growing disconnect between cultures. Maritime trade, that is, does not require
the intense social engagement that overland trade requires, and thus even
though the volume of trade may have increased on account of maritime
trade, this did not mean there was a simultaneous increase in cultural interaction. In fact, as noted above, it is quite often the opposite.

Such a dynamic was in fact described by one of Ibn al-Nadim's informers, a Nestorian Christian who had been in China. According to him the
rise of maritime travel had actually resulted in a decrease in the Muslim
world's knowledge of Asia. "Sea voyages have changed and sea travel degen-
erated, so that the person who understand these things are few in number.
Accidents have made their appearance, with fear and with islands to bar the
voyages, so that only a person willing to brave dangers undertakes travel."[80]
Indeed, by the eleventh century the links between the Islamic world and
China had become so frayed that when the Khitan Liao dynasty sent an
embassy to Mahmud of Ghazna in order to reestablish trade links, he dis-
missed it as impossible.[81]

Such ignorance of the possibilities of overland trade across Inner Asia,
much less the historical realities of such trade, reveals how far apart the
Muslim and Buddhist worlds had grown by the eleventh century. And as
noted by the Nestorian monk, the knowledge gap between these two worlds

only grew wider as time went on. The fact of the matter is that Muslim knowledge of the East largely froze in the eighth century. After that time the same ideas were repeated over and over again through the centuries even though the realities of Asia had changed in the interim. Muslim authors thus still talked about the Tibetan and Turk Empires in the twelfth century even though both had collapsed centuries earlier. And as one can well imagine in this "dark age," Muslim knowledge of Buddhism did not expand either. Instead the same cursory ideas about the Dharma came to be repeated through the centuries as witnessed in the brief summation of the Dharma that is the epigraph to this chapter. Namely, after pointing out that Buddhists are "theologically deficient [mu'aṭṭila]," the tenth-century polymath Mutahhar b. Tahir Maqdisi notes simply the difference between the Nikaya and Mahayana interpretations of the Buddha: "they form two parties: that which affirms that He was a prophet commissioned as an apostle, and another which affirms that the Buddha is the Creator Himself."[82]

This, however, is not to say that Muslim intellectuals ignored entirely the East or the Dharma. Even on the other side of the Muslim world, in Toledo, Abu'l-Qasim Qadi Sa'id al-Andalusi wrote about Indian religions in his Ṭabaqāt al-'Umam of 1068.[83] Yet what they wrote was nothing new. Moreover, this curiosity about the East was more a reflection of the above-noted turn to the fantastic than any real critical engagement. Thus if later authors dealt with Buddhism at all they simply repeated what the few earlier authors, such as Ibn Khurdadhbih, Jayhani, Zurqan, and Iranshahri (whose works are now lost), had written. Thus even though there may have been a little bit more information about Buddhism in these later works, none of them reflects any firsthand knowledge of contemporary Buddhism.

Gardizi's mid-eleventh-century Zayn al-akhbār, for example, notes the Buddha's focus on reason and the importance of meditation, but not the rise of tantra or even the varieties of Mahayana: "[Buddhists:] Those who believe in the Creator and in rewards and punishments, but reject prophets, say that God called upon his creatures wishing them to have no need of anybody else, because he has placed in their minds inclination to Good and hatred of Evil, (and he taught them) not to accept anything from another person which would be unacceptable to Reason, and to oppose the nature of their bodies. (As) God has no need of his creatures, or of their worship, they say that Paradise can be reached (only) through mental exertions and through opposition to the nature of the body, for this is a matter difficult to attain and especially to persevere in till the goal is reached."[84]

The same phenomenon is also found in Shahrastani's *Kitāb al-milal wa-n-nihal* of 1125 C.E.[85] His work has the longest description of Buddhism in any Muslim source, but as seen in the lengthy excerpt below, it does not contain anything new or an awareness of developments in the Buddhist tradition from the eighth century.

> The Buddha, in their opinion, means a person who is not born, who never marries nor eats food nor drinks nor grows old nor dies. The first Buddha appearing in the world was named *Shakaman*, which means "the noble master." Five thousand years elapsed from the time of his appearance to the time of the *hijra* (622). They assert that below the rank of the Buddha is the rank of the Budisa'iya, the latter term meaning "the one who seeks the way of truth." Indeed, one arrives at this rank only by (following certain measures for attaining moral discipline): (a) patience and alms-giving; (b) seeking after that which ought to be sought; (c) abstinence and withdrawal from the world, and aloofness from its desires and pleasures; (d) abstinence from what is forbidden; (e) compassion for all created beings; (f) avoidance of the ten offenses, which are: 1. to kill any living creature; 2. to consider it lawful (to seize) human property; 3. to commit adultery; 4. to lie; 5. to utter calumnies; 6. to use obscene language; 7. to vilify; 8. to slander; 9. to say a stupid word; 10. to deny reward (and punishment) in the after life; and (g) adherence to the ten virtues, which are:
>
> 1. to demonstrate goodness and generosity
> 2. to pardon those who offend and to overcome anger through patience
> 3. to abstain from worldly desires
> 4. to meditate on the deliverance of the soul from this transitory world to that eternal world
> 5. to exercise the intellect through knowledge and culture and much thought about the consequences of worldly things
> 6. to exert control over the direction of the soul, that it may seek after higher things
> 7. to be soft-spoken and courteous in speaking with everyone
> 8. to be kind in dealing with other men, so that their wishes become more important than one's own

9. to turn away totally from created beings and turn totally toward the truth

10. to dedicate the soul to seeking and attaining the truth.

This group maintains that the Buddhas came to them according to the number (of branches) of the Kil River, bringing them knowledge of the sciences and appearing to them in different kinds and as different individuals. Further, on account of the nobility of their substances, the Buddhas appeared only in the families of kings. They claim that there is no difference among the Buddhas with respect to what has been reported of them about the eternity of the world and about their assertion concerning reward already noted. The appearance of the Buddhas has been limited to India, however, due both to the wide variety of its creatures and climates and also to the many Indians who are intent on spiritual exercises and exertion. There is no one comparable to Buddha as they have described him—if they are right in that—except al-Khidr, whom Muslims recognize.[86]

Thus even though this work may have the most extensive study of the Dharma since ibn Khalid, it reflects neither an up-to-date engagement, nor an attempt at understanding.

Shahrastani was in fact a theologian who was presenting a catalogue of the world's heresies. Buddhism was simply one of them. Thus unlike ibn Khalid, who presented accurate descriptions of contemporary Buddhism, Shahrastani's work "juxtaposes accurate observations with gawky errors."[87] Moreover, unlike ibn Khalid, who compared Muslim ideas and practices with Buddhism in order to make sense of the Dharma, Shahrastani simply lists the few elements of the Dharma that he is aware of in order to ultimately dismiss them as false. The only curious exception to this theological strategy, however, is found in the final line of Shahrastani's description, where he parallels the Buddhist veneration of the Buddha with the Muslim veneration of al-Khidr, a saint famous for his quest for mystical enlightenment.[88] Yet although this comparison seems to reflect an attempt at religious comparison, the way it is phrased actually dismisses both of these practices as misguided since veneration of someone other than Allah goes against Muslim orthodoxy as Shahrastani imagines it.

But ultimately what is most remarkable about these later Muslim accounts is their complete ignorance of contemporary lived Buddhism in all its multifarious forms. And this ignorance is not only in terms of doctrinal differences, but also in regard to ritual practices that anyone actually traveling in Buddhist areas would readily come across, such as "idol worshipping" and pilgrimage. While ibn Khalid readily described both of these practices, in later sources they simply disappear. Indeed, this shrinking awareness of the Dharma is perhaps epitomized in Marvazi's *Tabī'iat al-Ḥayawān* (*The Natural Property of Animals*) from the beginning of twelfth century wherein the Buddhist tradition in its entirety is boiled down to one sentence: "They have many tales about Buddha and the Bodhisattvas on which they meditate. Most of them believe in metempsychosis [reincarnation]."[89]

Yet even reincarnation does not gain much attention in Muslim sources, which is notable because at the time there was a rather intense debate in Muslim intellectual circles about metempsychosis.[90] The reason was that Muslim scholars wanted to incorporate Neo-Platonism into Islam but the Greek philosophers, especially Plato,[91] believed in reincarnation and this presented a problem because it challenged their own belief in bodily resurrection. For Muslims to fully incorporate Neo-Platonic thought this contradiction had to be resolved. Yet in doing so the debate became wholly framed within a Western context. Never is the Buddhist view on the subject mentioned, much less engaged, and only rarely the Hindu. Indeed, the fact that Muslim scholars could so readily ignore Indian theories of reincarnation within this debate is symptomatic of how far apart the two worlds had grown. By the tenth, eleventh, and twelfth centuries Muslim thinkers had neither contact with, nor interest in, the East. In fact India and the broader Asian world was no longer a place that had something to offer. It was simply a wealthy fantasy land far far away.

Other Muslims, Other Buddhists

The growing divide between the economic and religious zones outlined above were not immutable. Muslims clearly encountered and observed Buddhists not only in South Asia, but also in places such as Tibet and China. Indeed, as noted in the introduction, the history of Buddhist-Muslim interaction is too often focused on India even though neither Buddhists nor Muslims were restricted to the subcontinent. Indeed, as part of their drive to expand the economic power of the Caliphate Muslim merchants ventured forth across the Asian littoral. Moving from south India to

Sri Lanka and through Southeast Asia, Muslim traders eventually moved up the coast of China.[92] By the eighth century some had reportedly already made it to Korea. And by most accounts these were not minor expeditions, but a concerted effort to establish a Muslim trading network that could exploit the riches of the East.

The extent of this economic advance is well captured in the claim that there were 100,000 Muslims in ninth-century Canton. Although they were expelled during the Huang Chao rebellion of 879 c.e.,[93] this number of 100,000 merchants, even if exaggerated, amply reflects the power and scope of the Muslim trading network at this time. And in this regard it is important to recognize that Muslim traders were not only plying the southern sea-lanes, but also going across the traditional trade routes of Inner Asia.[94] Tibet, for example, was an important region in the expanding Muslim trading network on account of its legendary deer musk, which, according to the Arab geographer Ibn Haugal, was "superior in both quality and price to all the varieties of musk."[95]

With all of these Muslim merchants working and traveling in both China and Tibet one would therefore imagine that there were ample opportunities for Buddhist-Muslim interaction. And there certainly were, as evidenced in an event recounted by the Japanese monk Ennin (793–864 c.e.), who traveled in China in 838–847 c.e. During his sojourn in Yangzhou he describes a monastery that needed to raise ten thousand strings of cash in order to restore the Balcony of Auspicious Images. To this end the monks arranged a lecture series on the *Diamond Sutra* over a two-month period in order to raise the required money. As it turned out a group of local Persian merchants gave one thousand strings of cash for this reconstruction project. Some other men from Champa in Vietnam gave two hundred strings of cash, while the Japanese themselves gave only fifty.[96] From this episode one gets a sense of the possibilities of Buddhist-Muslim interaction, which could have been close and intimate in various times and places.

But even so, based on the available sources from this period it seems as if the Muslim view of Buddhism in both China and Tibet remained cursory.[97] In fact, for centuries Muslim historians continued to believe that the Tibetan kings were actually of Yemenite origin.[98] In trying to make sense of such erroneous views it is possible to attribute them to the commercial environment in which information was gathered. Regardless, however, Muslim knowledge of Buddhism in Tibet was minimal. The anonymous Persian geography of 982 c.e., the *Ḥudūd al-ʿĀlam*, for example, describes

Tibetan religion in its entirety by noting simply that "all the people are idolaters." The author makes no specific connection with Buddhism, much less the tantric tradition.[99] In fact the entirety of Tibet's Buddhist tradition is described as follows: "Lhasa, a small town with numerous idol temples and one Muslim mosque. In it live few Muslims . . . K.rsang (usang) belongs to Tibet. In it large idol temples are found. The locality is called Great Farkhar."[100]

The *Hudud al-'alam* in fact does not offer much more about Tibet than these scant observations. Moreover, what it does offer is again more of the fantastical, which in turn became staple features in the Muslim representation of Tibet. One of these fantastical representations is the idea that Tibet is home to an enormous "poisonous mountain" (*Jabal al-samm*), a "fact" that is even repeated by al-Biruni.[101] Another fantastical element is even more curious: "A particular feature of their country is that whoever enters it becomes ever gay and smiling without knowing the reason for it, and never a sad (face) is seen in it."[102] Whether this vision set the tone for the subsequent Western view of Tibet as Shangri-La is unknown; nevertheless, it certainly set the tone for Tibet as a wonderful and carefree place. Regardless, what these fantastical representations of Tibet do reveal is that the Muslim engagement with Tibet, much less tantric Buddhism, was never serious, much less critical.

At the same time, of course, what now appears to be an age of ignorance may simply be a lack of sources from the period. Thus perhaps rather than seeing Ennin's description of Buddhist-Muslim interaction in ninth-century China as unique, or an anomaly, perhaps such exchanges were far more common than our sources allow us to reconstruct. Indeed, one small piece pointing in this direction is found in relation to Tibet. In Arabic, namely, there developed a peculiar term for Buddhists: *mahmarah*. The word means "wearer of red clothes," and must refer to the maroon robes that monks wear in accord with later Buddhist texts like the *Kālacakratantra*.[103] Thus clearly Muslims were in contact with Tibetan Buddhists, but unfortunately much of what happened in these exchanges has now been lost.

The situation is much the same in the case of China. While Islamic sources provide a wealth of material on Chinese customs, from burial rites to sodomy,[104] the Buddhist tradition gets short shrift even though Muslim writers do recognize that Chinese pray to "idols" and have "Indian teachers."[105] But at some point there developed the misconception in the Muslim world that all Chinese were Manicheans, and this mistake was maintained in Muslim sources for centuries.[106] Even so, as in the case of Tibet, there are also glimmers of a greater awareness of Chinese religious life. The Nestorian monk who had returned to Iraq after a failed missionary trip to China and became an informant for Ibn al-Nadim, for example, explains at length Chinese practices focusing on the family, the emperor, and the state, which today would conventionally be labeled as Confucianism.[107] At the same time, he also explains that "most of them are dualists and Shamaniyah." And in this regard al-Nadim cites another informer who also asserts that "among the ordinances of China are exaltation and worship of kings. This holds true for most of the common people, but the doctrines of the kings and important people are dualism and the Shaminiyah [faith]." In both of these cases, dualism and Shamaniyah (from the Sanskrit *sramana*) refer to Daoism and Buddhism, both of which were prevalent in Tang dynasty China (618–907 c.e.).[108]

Muslims were therefore rather astute observers of Chinese religious life. Indeed, they accurately captured the fluid nature wherein all three of the religious traditions—Buddhism, Confucianism, and Daoism—were practiced simultaneously for various ends, an idea that has in fact only been "rediscovered" by Western scholars in recent years.[109] Yet such astute observations by these early Muslim travelers did not necessarily lead to further explorations of Buddhism in China, much less an exposition of Chinese Buddhism by scholars and theologians in the Muslim heartland, who presumably imagined the Dharma in China was the same as that found in India. The only exception to this general pattern, however, is a curious comment found in Marvazi's twelfth-century *Taba'i' al-hayawan*, which contains the following description of China: "Most of their crops are cereals. Whenever the rains have been scanty, prices rise, and when the inhabitants have suffered from scarcity the king sends (his men) to the idol-temples to seize the shamans, to imprison them, to put them in irons and to threaten them with death if it does not rain, and they keep using them roughly till it does rain."[110] In this case the *shamans* in the idol temples are again the Shamaniyah, or Buddhist monks, who ever since the famous fourth-century thaumaturge Fotucheng of the Northern Wei dynasty (386–534 c.e.),[111] had been famous in China for their rainmaking abilities.[112] This small observation therefore reveals again an intimate Muslim knowledge of real Buddhist practices in China.

Yet even so, no Muslim source from this later period is as coherent or systematic as ibn Khalid's description from the eighth century. Indeed, none of them reflect the openness and attempts at understanding that were the hallmark of his work. In fact as time wore on and the political and economic scene changed, Muslim interest in and perhaps even tolerance toward the Dharma began to wane. This phenomenon is best captured in the Muslim representation of Khotan, the famed and wealthy Iranian Buddhist city-state on the Silk Road that was not only strategically located on the east-west trade route, but also sat on top of a treasure trove of jade. In recognition of this wealth and its attendant power the tenth-century *Ḥudūd al-ʿĀlam*, for example, claimed that "the king of Khotan lives in great state and calls himself 'Lord of the Turks and Tibetans.'"[113] In this regard the author of the *Ḥudūd al-ʿĀlam* was not simply repeating outdated historical realities. In the tenth century the Khotanese king had in fact sent six embassies to China, and also married his daughter into the powerful Cao family that had recently taken over Dunhuang.[114] Khotan was therefore a powerful city-state at the time of the *Ḥudūd al-ʿĀlam*'s composition. Yet, more importantly, it was also one of the last Buddhist kingdoms in the frontier zone between the Caliphate and the Tantric Bloc of Inner Asia.[115]

It is therefore not surprising that Muslim sources also contain information about the Dharma in Khotan. The *Ḥudūd al-ʿĀlam* notes, for example, that the area of Khotan "possesses many idol-temples."[116] But as in the case of both Tibet and China the author also reveals a deeper knowledge of the Dharma. In fact, it is only in regard to Khotan that a Muslim source describes the important Buddhist practice of relic worship:[117] "It is a pleasant place situated close to the mountains. In it there is a certain dead body (*yaki murda*) venerated by the inhabitants."[118] But at the same time that the author provides us with this important observation of lived Buddhist practice, he also makes the claim that the Khotanese, or people living within Khotan's borders, are cannibals.[119]

How can one reconcile these two incongruous descriptions? We may never know the answer to this question, though one can begin by noting that as in the case of Tibet and China, the Muslim awareness of Buddhist relic worship confirms that there was a greater knowledge of the Dharma than the extant sources seem to reveal. And as with the claim of human sacrifice in ibn Khalid's description of Bamiyan, it is possible to conjecture that the accusation of cannibalism was part of a larger religiopolitical discourse. Namely, Khotan was a place that not only continued to thrive economically, but also steadfastly refused to accept Islam. Claiming they were cannibals was thus a convenient way of dehumanizing them. They were thus not only Buddhists, but beyond the pale of humanity. Whether this interpretation is correct or not, the author of the *Ḥudūd al-ʿĀlam* need not have been so worried. Twenty-six years after this work was finished Khotan fell to the forces of the Muslim Qarakhanid dynasty.[120] The conquest was in turn immortalized in a short poem:

> We came down on them like a flood,
> We went out among their cities,
> We tore down the idol-temples,
> We shat on the Buddha's head![121]

The Buddhist Response

If we are to begin to fathom both the Buddhist response to Islam and the continuity of the Dharma in places like Khotan and Kashmir we need to return to the above map of the three economic zones. In doing so it becomes clear that Kashmir and Khotan were located precisely at the frontier of both the Muslim and Buddhist worlds and their respective networks of commodity and cultural exchange. Being thus situated had both its benefits and dangers. While the Khotanese and Kashmiris could act as important intermediaries between these two worlds, they were also far removed from the new centers of the Buddhist world—the Buddhist Mediterranean and the Tantric Bloc. Khotan and Kashmir were thus increasingly isolated and within this context it is perhaps not surprising that there arose among their inhabitants a certain sense of doom.

One factor generating this feeling of despair among the Khotanese and Kashmiris was clearly the expansion of Islam. Another factor, however, and perhaps one even more pressing in the Buddhist mind was the growth of Hinduism. As noted above, many later commentators have argued that Buddhism largely melded into Hinduism on account of tantra. Yet, while one can readily see similarities between Buddhist and Hindu tantra, it is also important to recognize that both the Hindu and Buddhist tantric traditions tried valiantly to differentiate themselves from each other. Indeed, as one scholar has noted, the problem faced by Buddhists was less about the two traditions merging into one another than the increasingly esoteric nature of tantric Buddhism itself, which made it "incomprehensible to India's masses and [thus] held few answers to their human concerns and aspirations."[122] In fact, the direct result of this Buddhist obscurantism was that the various forms of Hindu devotionalism became a far more valid alternative for the majority of people.

The shift away from Buddhism toward Hinduism is in fact a stock story in both Buddhist and Hindu sources.[123] One such example is found in the Tibetan historian Taranatha's early seventeenth-century *History of Buddhism in India*: "There is no doubt that many siddhas and sadhakas lived at this period. But since the karma of the people in general was unalterable, all these could not be prevented. At that time, most of the yogi followers of Gauraksa were fools and, driven by the greed for money and honour offered by the tirthika kings, became followers of Isvara [Siva]. They used to say, 'We are not opposed even to the Turuksas [Turks].' Only a few of them belonging to the Natesvari-varga remained insiders [Buddhists]."[124] Even though Taranatha's work is admittedly from a much later period, it does poignantly capture the anger and confusion of this earlier period when Buddhism was being challenged by both Islam and Hinduism. Besides lamenting, however, it is another issue entirely what Buddhists actually did about this deteriorating situation. Some, as we have seen, moved to other areas where they could continue to practice the Dharma. Others converted. And some apparently used tantric magic in order to defeat their enemies. Lilavajra, for example, having "heard the rumor of an impending Turk invasion defeated their soldiers by drawing the Yamari-cakra. After reaching Magadha, the soldiers became dumb and inactive and remained so for a long time. Thus they turned away."[125] An even more frightening use of such magic is found in the biography of Kamalaraksita:

> He once thought of holding a gana-cakra in the crematorium of Vikrama. Along with many Tantrika disciples, he brought there the materials for sadhana carried by the yoginis. On the way they encountered the minister of the Turk king of Karna of the west, who was then proceeding to invade Magadha with 500 Turks. They plundered the materials for sadhana. When, however, they came near the acarya and his attendants, the acarya became angry and threw at them an earthen pitcher full of charmed water. Immediately was generated a terrible storm and black men were seen emerging from it and striking the Turks with daggers in hand. The minister himself vomited blood and died and the others were afflicted with various diseases. Excepting one, none of them

returned to their country. This made both the [Hindus] and Turks terror-stricken.[126]

Another Buddhist response to Islam for which there is more evidence than tantric war magic was to turn to the well-established myths of the Dharma's decline.

One of the first of these myths appeared in Khotan, and it specifically prophesied the end of the Dharma at the hands of barbarian Persians and Turks.[127] Of course, knowing as we now do that Khotan would ultimately be conquered by the Qarakhanids in 1008 c.e., it is possible to read this prophecy as an astute and prescient commentary on the contemporary situation. But it was not only in Khotan that Islam would make a violent appearance in the eleventh century. The most famous Muslim advance at this time was Mahmud of Ghazna's conquest of northwest India, which would leave a wake of destruction in its path. And as pointed out by al-Biruni, it was precisely this slash-and-burn approach that generated so much hatred among the Indians toward Muslims and Islam in general: "Mahmud utterly ruined the prosperity of the country and performed there wonderful exploits, by which the [Indians] became like atoms of dust scattered in all directions, and like a tale told of old in the mouth of the people. Their scattered remains cherish, of course, the most inveterate aversion towards all Muslims. This is the reason, too, why [Indian] sciences have retired far away from those parts of the country conquered by us, and have fled to places which our hand cannot yet reach, to Kashmir, Benares, and other places. And there the antagonism between them and all foreigners receives more and more nourishment from both political and religious sources."[128] It is therefore within this context of real and impending disaster in the Buddhist borderlands that we need to situate our first extensive Buddhist response to Islam.

There had been a few earlier Buddhist notices of Islam,[129] such as in the eighth-century Korean pilgrim Ou-'kong's claim that out of fear he avoided the Islamic areas of Afghanistan.[130] But nothing compares to the extensive material found in the *Kālacakratantra* and its various commentaries. Moreover, having been compiled in the early eleventh century at a time and in a place where Buddhism was readily on the decline, it is unsurprising that a sense of doom and desperation permeates the work.[131] In fact, the teaching of this particular tantra is expressly claimed to be a hedge against the advance of Islam.[132] Indeed, it is the very possibility of Islam taking over the world as found in the earlier Khotanese prophecy that shapes both the eschatology and soteriology of the *Kālacakratanta*.

This vision is most eloquently encapsulated in the apocalyptic myth of Shambhala. It prophesies a future in which Islam takes over the world. At this point the Buddhist savior, Kalkin Raudra Cakrin, will ride forth with his army from the hidden Inner Asian kingdom of Shambhala and annihilate the Muslims thereby ushering in a new golden age of pure Buddhism.[133] Even though this vision was clearly a response to contemporary realities in northwest India, later commentators explained that this apocalyptic vision was not an external battle, but rather an internal battle within one's own mind[134]—an interpretation that curiously parallels in reverse the development of the theories about the "greater" and "lesser" jihad.

Be that as it may, the *Kālacakratantra* contains not only this vision of Islam's destruction, but also offers us the earliest Buddhist interpretation of Muslim thought and practice. Unfortunately, however, the precise Muslim school that the author(s) of the *Kālacakra* corpus had direct familiarity with is unclear. It is possible that the Buddhists were most familiar with the Ismaʻilis or the Mubayyida ("White Clad") followers of Abu Muslim (d. 755 C.E.) and his disciple al-Muqannaʻ (d. 779 C.E.). Yet even these conjectures are unlikely since the list of eight prophets found in the *Kālacakratantra*—Adam, Noah, Abraham, Moses, Jesus, the White-Clad One, Muhammad, and the Mahdi—does not accord with any known Muslim school. Indeed, it is perhaps the case that the authors of the *Kālacakra* were, like their Muslim colleagues, largely unfamiliar with Islam and thus were actually presenting a tradition that was no longer extant, such as the Mubayyida. Or else it may have been the case that they were most familiar with a heterodox school of Islam, of which we know nothing, since many of these unorthodox groups were fleeing Sunni persecution at this time and seeking refuge in north India. Yet, even so, which one of these groups, or if any of them, believed in the eight prophets, is unknown. Regardless, it seems unlikely the authors of the *Kālacakra* were engaging with Sunni Muslims, and to a certain extent this makes sense if we recall that the Ismaʻilis had ruled northwest India for the two centuries prior to the *Kālacakratantra*'s appearance.

Regardless of the specific Muslim tradition that the *Kālacakratantra* author(s) were trying to represent, however, they do have a rather coherent understanding of the general parameters of Islam. They recognize Muhammad as the founder of the tradition and that "ar-Rahman"—the common epithet for Allah meaning "the compassionate"—is the omnipotent creator of the world. Moreover, it is a person's duty to follow God's command and one will either be rewarded with heaven or punished with hell. The Buddhists also knew that Muslims did not believe in reincarnation, but in bodily resurrection in the afterlife. They were also cognizant of Muslim ritual practices, such as fasting during Ramadan. They also knew about the five daily prayers, during which they first wash, then kneel down and "draw in their limbs like a tortoise." Yet for the Buddhists the most bizarre Muslim custom was circumcision: "[they] cut the skin from the tips of their penises as cause for happiness in Heaven."[135]

Above and beyond these practices, the one Muslim ritual that receives the lengthiest and most vitriolic Buddhist attack is animal sacrifice. The Buddhists namely misconstrued the preparation of *ḥalāl* meat, during which an animal's throat is cut with the prayer *Bismillah*, as an actual blood offering to Allah. Although their understanding of this ritual was flawed from the beginning the author(s) of the *Kālacakra* spend a great deal of energy in condemning this practice. And in their misguided attack they parallel this Muslim practice with Vedic sacrifice, which Buddhists had long critiqued,[136] and thereby in a curious manner linked the two enemies of the Dharma—Islam and Hinduism—into one. In fact, since the two practices are so similar the Buddhists believed that the Hindus would invariably convert to Islam and thus further the prediction of worldwide Islamic domination.

[Sūryaratha, you and the other Brahman sages must be initiated into the Kālacakra, and eat, drink, and form marriage relations with the *vajra* family of the Vajrayāna.] Otherwise, after eight hundred years have elapsed your descendants will engage in the barbarian dharma and will teach the barbarian dharma in the ninety-six great lands of Shambhala and so forth. Using the mantra of the barbarian deity Bismillāh, they will slit the throats of animals with cleavers. Then they will prescribe eating the flesh of those beasts killed with the mantra of their own deity, and will prohibit eating the flesh of those that die due to their own karma. That the very dharma is authoritative for you [Brahman sages] because of the statement in the *smṛti*: "Beasts are created for sacrifice" (*Manusmṛti* 5.39a). With regard to killing there is no difference between the barbarian dharma and the Vedic dharma.

Therefore, your descendants will see the valor of those barbarians and the incarnation of their death deity (*māradevatāvatārum*)
in battle, and in the future, after eight hundred years have elapsed,
they will become barbarians. Once they have become barbarians,
everyone dwelling in the nine-hundred-and-sixty million villages,
the four castes and so forth, will also become barbarians. For the
brahman sages say: "Where the great man goes, that is the path"
(*Mahābharata* 3.297; appendix p. 1089, l. 68).

In the barbarian dharma as well as in the Vedic dharma one
must kill for the sake of the deities and the ancestors, and the same
is true in the dharma of the kshatriyas. For the brahman sages say:
"Having satisfied the ancestors and the gods, there is no fault in
eating flesh" (*Yājñavalkyasmṛti* 1.5.178cd); and likewise: "I see no
fault in one who would do ill to a vicious [beast]" [quotation
unidentified]

Thus, holding the Vedic dharma to be authoritative, they will
adopt the barbarian dharma. For this reason, so that in the future
you will not enter the barbarian dharma, I give you this precept.
Therefore, you venerable sirs must obey my command [to take initiation into the *Kālacakra*].[137]

On account of this entire conceptual edifice being constructed on a misun-
derstanding there arises the important question of how well informed the
Buddhists actually were about Islam. Indeed, a glaring omission in the Buddhist exploration of Islam is the fundamental practice of the Hajj, or pilgrimage to Mecca. While we recognize that this absence may have arisen
quite simply on account of the fact that Buddhists would have been especially unlikely to have seen the Hajj firsthand, it is nevertheless still surprising that according to the *Kālacakratantra*, Mecca is identified as the country
where Muhammad was born in the city of Baghdad.

Such confusion should certainly raise questions about the *Kālacakratantra* author's or authors' knowledge of Islam. But at the same time there are
sections of the tantra that display a far more sophisticated response to Islam
than such errors would suggest. This is seen, for example, in the following
philosophical refutation of Muslim doctrine.

The barbarians observe the demonic dharma; they are proponents
of a Creator, a soul, and are free of casteism. The barbarians have

two dogmas: the dogma of [the body being] an aggregation of particles, and the dogma of an epiphenomenal person (*upapattayaṅgika-
pudgala*) dwelling within the physical body that is composed of an
aggregation of particles, then who takes up another body when the
body consisting of an aggregation of particles is destroyed? Thus,
there is a spontaneously generated person (*upapāduka-pudgala*).
That proves that the heavenly reward is the reward of nirvana—
there is no so-called "nirvana other than the heavenly reward."

When [the barbarians] ask about reality, the Bhagavan [Buddha]
who knows reality, knowing their own beliefs, says [in the *Bhāra-
hāra-sūtra*]: "There is a person who bears the burden; I do not say
it is permanent, I do not say it is impermanent." That is indeed
true, because it is the statement of the Bhagavan; one who is unable
to say that the person [who is a product of] mental propensities in
the dream state is impermanent or permanent. Due to this statement of the Tathāgata, [the barbarians] abandon the barbarian
dharma and become Buddhist Vaibhāṣikas. Furthermore, some hear
the transcendental Dharma being taught to the bodhisattvas, abandon the dogma of a person, and resort to the path of the true, perfect Buddha.[138]

This critique of Islam and the wistful hope that it will sway Muslims to the
Dharma reveals that Buddhists were not only rather well informed about
Islam, but also actively involved in defending their beliefs at the same time
as they refuted those of Islam.

But such exchanges were not simply a one-sided affair as the following
passage reveals. In this case the Buddhists are defending the theory of karma
and reincarnation in reaction to a Muslim critique based on the belief in
bodily resurrection.

Now, "A living being," etc., states a [Muslim] refutation [of the
doctrine that one] experiences [the results of] previous karma [in
the present life] and accumulates present karma [for the future]:

Śrī Kālacakra 2.168
[Buddhists claim:] A living being experiences previously created karmas [in the present life], and [the karmas created]

in the present in another life. [The Muslims reply:] If this
were so, men could not destroy karma because of [their]
repeated other lives. There would be no exit from samsara,
and no entrance to liberation, because of their limitless existences. The rejection of other lives is indeed the belief of the
Muslims.

[The Muslim] believe that [the Buddhist doctrine that] a living
being experiences previously created karmas [in this life], and [the
karma] created in this life in another life [is false]. If such were the
case, [they say,] men could not destroy karma because they would
experience the results of karma in repeated other lives. Thus there
would be no exit from samsara, and no entrance to liberation,
because of limitless existences. That is indeed the belief of the [Mus-
lim]. However, [the *tantra*] says, "the rejection of other lives." The
barbarian Muslims believe that a dead man experiences happiness
or suffering in heaven or hell with that human body in accordance
with ar-Rahman's law. Thus, the rejection of other lives is [their]
precept.[139]

What is interesting about this passage is not whether either the Buddhists
or Muslims won this theological debate, but that it reveals a critical engagement in the tradition of the other by both parties. Indeed, it even makes it
seem as if there actually may have been Buddhist-Muslim debates.

Of course, the author(s) of the *Kālacakratantra* and its commentary the
Vimalaprabhā, where this debate is found, could easily have fabricated this
exchange in order to defend the correctness of their own views vis-à-vis
Islam, much as the later fifteenth-century Muslim historian imagined a
Buddhist-Muslim debate at the time of Caliph Harun al-Rashid being won
by the defenders of Islam. Yet there is in fact further evidence, as witnessed
in the case of the Ramanandis, that lends credence to the idea that such
intense Buddhist-Muslim exchange was not simply a figment of the imagination.

The most explicit evidence for such interaction is revealed in the *Kālacakratantra*'s astrological system, which was actually created in reaction to the
growing influence of Muslim science in tenth-century India. In particular,
Indian astronomy at this time had begun to adopt certain aspects of Islamic
Ptolemaic theory.[140] Buddhist scholars saw this importation of Western sci-

ence as a "corruption" of ancient Indian wisdom and therefore created the *Kālacakratantra* system as a direct refutation of Greek and Muslim influence.[141] But in doing so they actually created a new astrological system that was indebted to the very tradition it was rejecting. The *Kālacakratantra* thus not only uses Islamo-Ptolemaic methods for reckoning position, but also in its orientation of the heavens it abandons the Indian focus on the Pleiades and adopts instead the "Western" first point of Aries.[142] Thus in more ways than one the *Kālacakratantra*, which was to shape the Buddhist tradition for the next millennium, was very much a product of Buddhist-Muslim interaction.

What is surprising in this regard is that although much of the *Kālacakratantra* is clearly anti-Muslim it also contains positive evaluations of Islam. In particular, the Buddhists praise the Muslim doctrine of equality and its complete rejection of the caste system. Muslims are also respected for their ferocity and heroism in battle, as well as their monogamy and their attention to hygiene. Moreover, in accord with both the Buddhist and Muslim links to the world of business and trade the *Kālacakratantra* also notes approvingly that Muslims respect each other's property.

All of this material therefore leads one to conclude that there was more Buddhist-Muslim interaction than the common story and the available sources would lead us to believe. And the fact is that such exchange is reflected not only in the intellectual engagements outlined above, but also in terms of material exchange. The most well-known example of this phenomenon is the borrowing of the Buddhist monastery as a model in the development of the Islamic madrasa, which itself became the basis of the university in the Christian West.[143] Unfortunately, however, the full dynamics of this transmission are not fully understood—and indeed they are still debated—yet even so, there are other less dramatic examples of material exchange that shed light on Buddhist-Muslim interaction.

One such exchange that scholars have explored in depth is the Buddhist influence on Muslim art. "Geometrical and vegetal patterns, lions and mythical creatures which decorate Buddhist ivory panels and stone carvings reappear in later Islamic art, either faithfully copied, or in somewhat modified forms. However, the impact of Buddhism is perhaps most strongly manifested in early Islamic metalwork. Surprisingly not only the decorative designs were borrowed from Buddhist art, but more explicitly, Islamic metalworkers copied the forms of Buddhist monuments, first of all the shape of the stupas."[144]

Yet such transfers between the Buddhist and Islamic worlds were not unidirectional, nor were they exclusively in the realm of material products. There were also intellectual exchanges as evidenced in the transmission of Greek medical knowledge into Tibet,[145] which involved not only the theoretical conceptualizations of Galen, but also practical applications such as the Muslim methods of urine analysis and healing head wounds, both of which became a part of the Tibetan medical tradition.[146]

Of course, the transmission of the healing arts is a common feature of cross-cultural contact since such sciences often operate beyond the bounds of political and religious orthodoxy. As in the case in India, for example, where there is "good evidence that Hindu physicians and alchemists were welcomed into the courts of Muslim princes whose thirst for immortality, increased virility, and the philosopher's stone would have been stronger than their religious fervor. [And] we know that Muslim physicians, alchemists, and mystics were avid for the wisdom of their Indian counterparts."[147] Thus it is not surprising that it is within the realms of healing and magic that we also find exchange between Asia and the Muslim world.

The most well-known example of such a transmission is found in the case of the "magic squares" that were used for divination (figures 8 and 9).[148] Yet a further example of such east-west exchange is found in the blockprinted Arabic amulets that seem to have a Buddhist origin (figure 10).[149]

The first reason one can make such a conjecture is that Buddhists not only invented printing in the early eighth century,[150] but also were integral in transmitting papermaking technology across Eurasia.[151] Moreover, Buddhists had been using both of these technologies in order to make amulets for centuries.[152] Thus the fact that a similar practice would suddenly appear in the Muslim world, especially when East-West exchange was reviving during the twelfth-century, does not seem to be simply a coincidence.[153] Indeed, further evidence for such a transmission is borne out by the similarity of the Arabic amulets to Chinese and Tibetan prototypes. For example, the lotus in the square (figures 11 and 12) and the grid of squares (figures 13 and 14) found on several Arabic amulets is similar to many Tibetan amulets.[154]

Yet what is most intriguing about the Arabic amulets is that they do not follow the standard codex format of traditional Muslim books, rather the majority are in the distinctive long and narrow *pustaka* style of Indic and Tibetan texts that are based on palm leave manuscripts (figures 15 and 16).

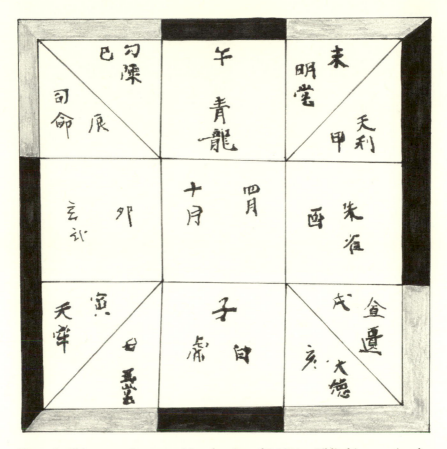

Figure 8. Chinese magic square. Line drawing of P 2964 r, Bibliothèque nationale de France. After Marc Kalinowski, *Divination et société dans la Chine médiévale: Études des manuscrits de Dunhuang de la Bibliothèque nationale de France et de la British Library* (Paris: Bibliothèque nationale de France, 2003), 298, ill. 22.

Indeed, based simply on these external features of the Arabic amulets it seems as if Muslims simply adopted the most prevalent form of paper in Buddhist Inner Asia, which was the *pustaka*. And while on one level this may not appear to be the best format for Arabic script, much less carving it into blocks, it is important to recall that other Aramaic-derived scripts used in Buddhist Inner Asia, such as Sogdian and Uygur, were also printed in the *pustaka* format. Of course, under the influence of Chinese these scripts were eventually read top-to-bottom rather than right-to-left, yet

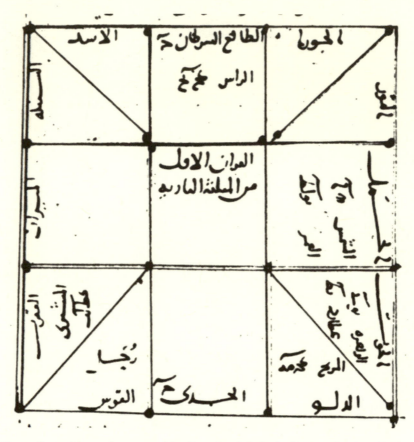

Figure 9. Arabic magic square. After Fuat Sezgin's facsimile reproduction *Al-Mughnī fī aḥkām al-nujūm* (1987): vol. 2, p. 435.

such a difference would make no difference in the carving of such blocks, and the resulting text could clearly be turned any which way in order to make it legible (figures 17 and 18).

Moreover, a further piece of evidence to support the Buddhist origin of this technology is that the Indo-Tibetan folio format apparently became so popular in the Muslim world that it was subsequently used in the preparation of manuscript Qur'ans, as seen in exemplars from twelfth-century Afghanistan.[155] As a result, it seems very likely that Muslims developed the tradition of blockprinting amulets through their relations with Buddhists in Inner Asia.[156]

Figure 10. Arabic amulet. Eleventh–twelfth century. Ink and colors on paper. Ht.
7 ½ in. (16.6 cm) W. 6 ½ in. (19.1 cm) 6 1/8 x 1 ½ in. (15.6 x 3.8 cm). The
Metropolitan Museum of Art, Gift of Richard Ettinghausen, 1975 (1975.192.21).
Image © The Metropolitan Museum of Art.

Yet my suggestion that Buddhists and Muslims exchanged ideas and
technologies regarding amulets is based not only on the value both traditions placed on such practices and the above inferences, but also on an
historical episode that reveals the Buddho-Muslim world in which such a
technological transfer could have taken place: in 1295 the Mongol ruler of

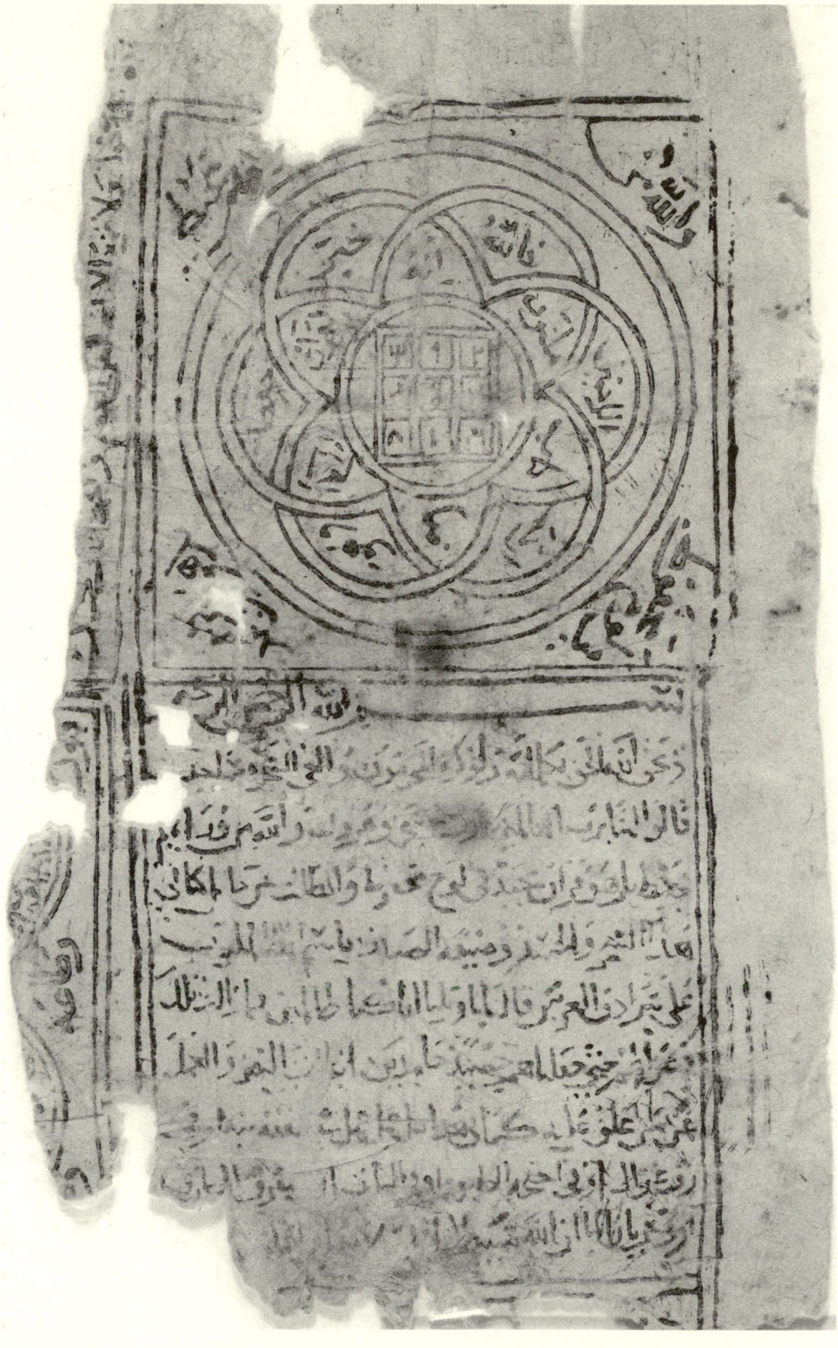

Figure 11. Arabic amulet. Michaelides (charta) E 33. Courtesy of Cambridge University Library.

Figure 12. Tibetan amulet, from Drepung Monastery, Tibet. Collection of author.

Figure 13. Arabic amulet. The Madina Collection of Islamic Art, gift of Camilla Chandler Frost (M.2002.1.371). Courtesy of the Los Angeles County Museum of Art.

Figure 14. Tibetan amulet, from Drepung Monastery, Tibet. Collection of author.

Figure 15. Arabic amulet. 11th–12th century. Ink on paper. 6 1/8 x 1 ½ in. (15.6 x 3.8 cm). The Metropolitan Musuem of Art, Gift of Richard Ettinghausen, 1975 (1975.192.20). Image © The Metropolitan Museum of Art.

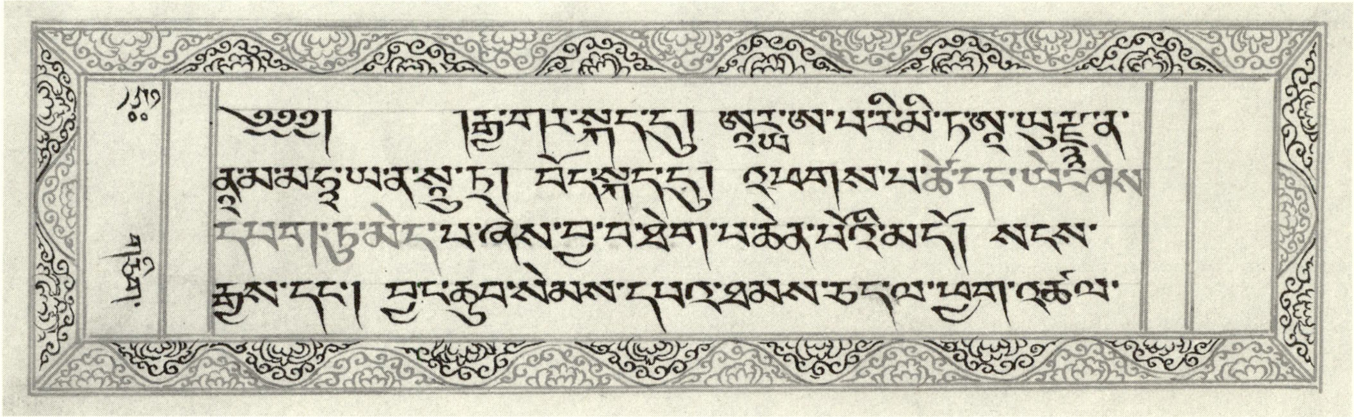

Figure 16. Tibetan text ('phags-pa tshe dang ye shes dpag tu med pa zhes bya ba theg pa chen po'i mdo). Collection of author.

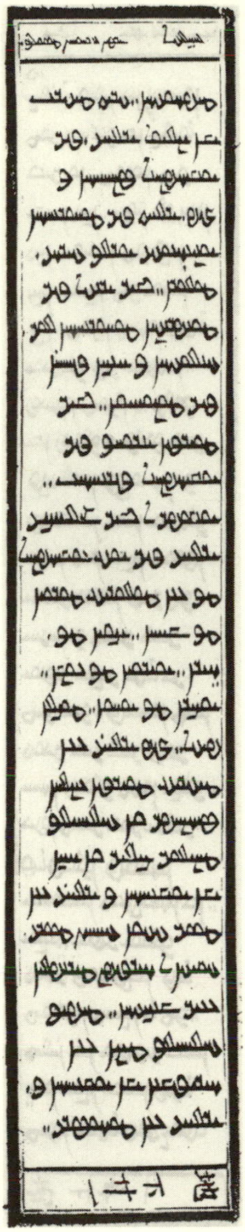

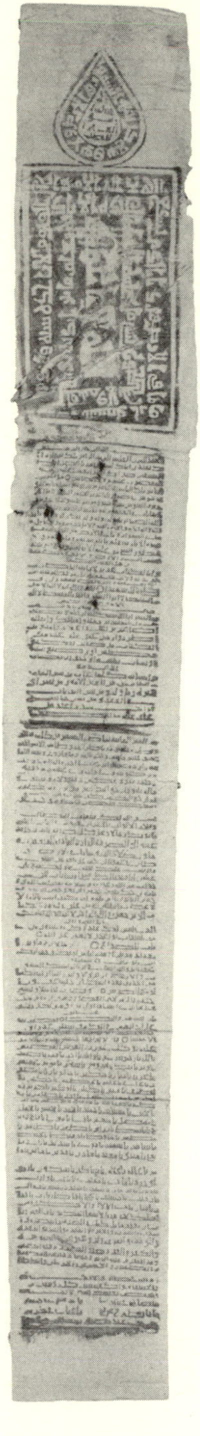

Figure 17. Mongol
blockprint, from Mergen
Gegen's *Sungbum*.
Collection of author.
Figure 18. Arabic amulet.
Papyrus 705b. Courtesy of
the Rare Book and
Manuscript Library,
Columbia University.

Iran, a Buddhist, converted to Islam, and what is interesting is that an amulet played a key role.

I sent him a robe which he put on, and he also wore a woolen cloak. He went to the palace where we joined him; he was standing. The people gathered round from all sides, (including) the army and the royal women. It was a great affair. I stayed at his side, and Nauruz was with me too; I had a talisman with me, in which (were written) some of the prayers of the Shaikh and his words and epitomes. He (Ghazan) saw it and asked about it. Nauruz explained what it was, giving some information about my father, and told him some of his miracles and traditions. I took out the talisman and presented it to him; he looked at it and gave it back to me. I put it in its pouch and handed it over to him. He took it and slung it over his right side. I suggested that he put it on the left side, as was customary, which he did. He was overcome with bashfulness and embarrassment, being only a youth not yet thirty years old and of fair complexion. He left the baths and shyness overcame him, so that his blush deepened.

Then Nauruz talked to him about Islam, and the king said, "I have given my promise on this, and now is the time, with this son of the Shaikh present." (Sadr al-Din said), Then he looked at me, and asked, "How should I say it?" I told him, raising up my finger: "I bear witness that there is no God but God," which he pronounced. Then I said, "and I bear witness that Muhammad is the Messenger of God." Then he talked with Nauruz in Turkish and said, "(should) I bear witness once more?" (Nauruz) said yes, and he pronounced it (again).

When he had finished, one and all thronged round where he was sitting, and it was impossible to restrain anyone (approaching) and scattering gold and silver and pearls over him. The people began picking him up, and kissing the king's hands and feet and asking his blessing. They became vociferous and the delight intensified. It was impossible to restrain anyone, and no-one was diffident about approaching the king. He sat on a throne and the people remained below him, carrying on their antics and their rejoicing, while he was looking at them and laughing.[157]

The conversion of Ghazan Khan therefore not only reveals the importance of amulets in both the Buddhist and Muslim traditions, but also affords us a glimpse of the Buddho-Muslim world wherein a valuable technology such as blockprinting could possibly be transmitted from east to west.

Yet, even though the actual history and mechanics of such a technology transfer are unclear, what all of these artistic and material exchanges confirm is that the meeting between the Buddhist and Muslim worlds at this time was not only one of confrontation as the *Kālacakratantra* and the writings of someone like Shahrastani would lead us to believe. Rather, by coming into contact both traditions had to assimilate new ideas and products, as well as respond to them as they best saw fit. And in this regard Muslim authors became over time more and more blasé and dismissive of the Dharma. Buddhists, on the other hand, responded frantically to Islam by creating entirely new mythologies and astrological systems.

These differing responses can be explained not only by the growing divide between the Buddhist and Muslim worlds, but also on the unlevel playing field that the two traditions imagined themselves to be upon. On account of the Islamic world's power and prosperity the Muslims clearly felt self-assured and confident—they were the future. And as is often the case in such a situation, the value of knowing or caring about others retreats before one's own sense of superiority. On the other hand, Buddhists, especially those in the frontier zone, had to not only understand its "enemy," but also come up with an appropriate manner in which to respond. The Khotanese prophecy of decline and the *Kālacakratantra* were two such responses.

But what would happen if the tables were to suddenly turn? What if the economic power of the Islamic world was somehow to falter, and Buddhism were to once again rise up? Indeed, contrary to the dire situation of the Buddhist borderlands captured in the *Kālacakratantra,* the fact of the matter is that the Dharma was flourishing. All along the Buddhist Mediterranean and across the Tantric Bloc of Inner Asia the Dharma had never waned. It was in fact experiencing a renaissance. Thus what would happen if this Buddhist world were to become harnessed to the most powerful military force the world had ever seen? One consequence would be that the Mongol ruler Hülegü, a Buddhist and brother of Khubilai Khan, would sack Baghdad in 1258 c.e. and kill the Caliph.[158] Moreover, on account of the Mongol conquest the earlier tripartite religio-economic zones of the medieval period would be shattered and Eurasia would be entirely reconfigured. How Buddhists and Muslims responded to these momentous events are the focus of the next chapter.

CHAPTER THREE

Idolatry

Allah's Apostle returned from a journey when I ['Aisha] had placed a
curtain of mine having pictures over (the door of) a chamber of mine.
When Allah's Apostle saw it, he tore it and said, "The people who will
receive the severest punishment on the Day of Resurrection will be those
who try to make the like of Allah's creations." So we turned it (i.e. the
curtain) into one or two cushions.

—*Ḥadīth of al-Bukhārī*, No. 838

May all of the states of knowledge achieved by the Blessed
One—analytical insight, perseverance, the four perfect confidences, the
forty paths—a total of seventy-seven different properties—be invested in
this image. May the boundless concentration and the body-of-liberation
of the Buddha be invested in this image for 5,000 years during the
lifetime of the religion. May all of the miracles performed by the Buddha
after his enlightenment in order to dispel the doubts of all humans and
gods be invested in this image for all time. . . . May all the gods, together
with Indra, Brahma, Mara, and all people protect this Buddha image, as
well as the relics and the religion for 5,000 years for the welfare of all
human beings and gods.

—*Buddha Abhiseka*

IN THE BEGINNING of the tenth century a man from Nishapur was
arrested and jailed for denouncing Islam. One of the day's leading
scholars, however, was intrigued by his materialist critique of Allah's
attributes and he thus asked the Amir if he could take custody of this heretic
in order to engage him in debate. The Amir agreed and the prisoner was

moved to the scholar's house in Bukhara and kept under lock and key. But one evening by means of a clever ruse he escaped. Fleeing the Amir's troops he traveled in disguise across the Silk Road all the way to the China. There he came to meet the emperor who, being impressed with his knowledge, made him an official. In this capacity the fugitive told the emperor about the situation in the Muslim world: it was weak, fractured, and could easily be conquered. The emperor therefore sent a letter to the Samanid ruler Nasr b. Ahmad demanding that he pay tribute and recognize Chinese suzerainty. If he refused the emperor promised he would unleash an army "whose vanguard, when they were on the march, would be in [Central Asia] whilst the rearguard was still in Chinese territory!"[1]

Shortly after this threat of Chinese "shock and awe" the emperor sent out four envoys to validate Muslim compliance. They arrived in Ferghana in 939 c.e. and the governor sent a letter to the Amir in Bukhara informing him that they had arrived. In response to this news the Amir put his plan into action. He had his governors send all their troops, able-bodied men, and slaves, young and old, to the village of Ashrufans on the outskirts of Bukhara. All of these men, totaling forty thousand, were then outfitted with new armor, weapons, silk robes, and banners, and arrayed on an open plain along the route the Chinese envoys were traveling. Thus when they came over a ridge "the envoys saw what looked like the expanse of the whole world ablaze with the glint of steel, the sun having caught those cuirasses and helmets. Their wits almost left them, and they gazed on a tremendous sight."[2] As the envoys continued further into Bukharan territory the displays of military power and wealth became even more grandiose. The Chinese envoys started to be impressed, even overwhelmed, especially when they were informed that what the Amir had was simply a pittance compared to the power and magnificence of the Caliph. "They exclaimed, 'By God, that scoundrel who came to China from here has completely deceived us. If our emperor had only known that within the whole world of Islam, there was just one army like this of yours, he would never have dared to mention the very name of Islam; but that scoundrel who came amongst us from here tricked us!' "[3]

The culmination of the Amir's plan, however, took place in Bukhara, where all the stops were pulled out. Thus when the Chinese envoys arrived not only was the city decked out in thousands of flags and banners, but they were greeted by forty of the Amir's generals, each of whom was accompanied by ten Turkish slaves with golden swords and maces, as well as a thousand soldiers wearing satin brocade kaftans and sable fur hats. And as the envoys walked toward the Amir's palace the roads were lined with hundreds of soldiers wearing black and holding gleaming white silver swords. In addition, there was a contingent of the Amir's "commanders of the wild beasts," who each held five trained cats with gilded collars and anklets. After passing through this awe-inspiring cacophony of sights and sounds the Chinese envoys finally reached the palace, where the Amir was seated on a gilded throne, encrusted with jewels, and covering him was a "quilted coverlet made from the plumes of pheasants, which had an exterior covering of black silk stiffened with gold thread. And from beneath this quilt, two of the wild beasts, in crouching position, peeped out. Every effort was made to overawe the Chinese envoys as they made their way between the ranks of panoplied warriors and fearsome beasts; the military commanders were successively made to appear, in all their splendour, as if they were the Amir himself, and the beasts were made to roar and howl behind them as they passed. As a result, they were brought to an extremity of fear and almost took leave of their senses. Unable in this state to present their communication to the Amir or to receive his reply, they had to retire. They were lodged in the official residence for ambassadors and only ventured to have an audience with the Amir forty days later."[4]

Having thus humbled the Chinese envoys the Amir felt confident to mock the emperor's demands. He had plenty of troops and weapons; in fact, the only thing holding him back from marching east was the Caliph's command, which he had to respect. After this dressing down the Amir then hosted the Chinese envoys at a sumptuous feast and shortly thereafter they departed. Upon their return the envoys relayed all they had seen and the emperor was so impressed that he himself became a Muslim.

Of course, no Chinese emperor ever actually converted to Islam.[5] In fact, as with the story of the Buddhist-Muslim debate at the court of Harun al-Rashid, the episode of the Chinese envoys contains little historical truth. This, however, does not mean that it is meaningless from a historical perspective. Rather, this story provides evidence of three interlocking factors that will provide the historical framework for our exploration of the development of a distinctive Mongol visual culture, which famously allowed for the portraiture of Muhammad for the first time ever.

The first of these elements is the political fragmentation of the Muslim world in the late Abbasid period, which as we will see was to have important cultural implications. Yet to appreciate these developments it is also important to recall not only the fractured Eurasian world captured in the above story, but also the East-West divide explored in the previous chapter, since it was this state of affairs that was to come to an end with the Mongol conquests of the thirteenth century. And while the Mongol conquest was to usher in many changes, the one relevant to us is the fact that it brought together Buddhists and Muslims under one regime. How this development influenced not only Muslim understanding of the Dharma, but also Islamic art is the focus of what follows.

Historical Background

Very little is known about Qadi ibn az-Zubair, the man who recorded for posterity the story of the Chinese embassy to Bukhara. Even so, his biography provides us with a good starting point from where to begin an exploration of the turbulent centuries of Eurasian history prior to the formation of the Mongol empire. Ibn az-Zubair was a Shi'a Muslim who began his career in Iraq under the Buyid dynasty (934–1055 C.E.). Yet when the Seljuk Turks conquered Baghdad in 1055, thereby expelling the Buyids and restoring Sunni control of the Abbasid caliphate, ibn az-Zubair fled to Egypt, which was at the time ruled by the Shi'a Fatimid dynasty (909–1171 C.E.). And it was in their domains that ibn az-Zubair wrote his history in 1071 C.E.

The life of ibn az-Zubair thus poignantly captures the fractured state of the Muslim world at this time, riven not only by the perennial Shi'a-Sunni schism, but also along cultural and linguistic lines—e.g., African, Arab, Berber, Persian, and Turk. In addition there were competing economic and environmental regimes such as nomadic pastoralism vs. agriculture and urbanism, and international trade vs. local manufacturing. Moreover, all of these tensions came to a boil as the power of the Abbasid Caliphate waned in the ninth century and local rulers began to take control. The most important and powerful of these new local dynasties was the Persian dynasty of the Samanids centered in Bukhara. At their height in the tenth century the Samanids ruled over the wealthiest and most advanced region of the Muslim world.

One consequence of this power was that the Turks in the surrounding steppe areas came to be impressed by the Samanids' power and gradually they too started to become Muslim. Islam for the first time thus began to move beyond the urban confines of Central Asia and acquire converts among the nomads of the steppe. Yet because the nomads always held a military advantage these conversions were a double-edged sword, especially as the Turkish slaves who made up the Samanid army began to challenge their masters. Indeed, although the practice of manning Muslim armies with Turkish slaves, acquired through raiding or the Inner Asian slave trade, was an age-old custom and had worked well for centuries, when the Turks themselves became Muslim the system began to break down. Fired up with the zeal of the newly converted, the Turks in fact not only started to challenge their erstwhile Persian rulers in Central Asia, but also moved into the heartland of the Muslim world itself.

The first group of Turks to do so were the military slaves of the Samanid dynasty, who established themselves as the Ghaznavid dynasty (994–1186 C.E.) in the area of what is now Afghanistan and Pakistan (map 11).[6] Shortly thereafter, however, another group of Turks known as the Qarakhanids,

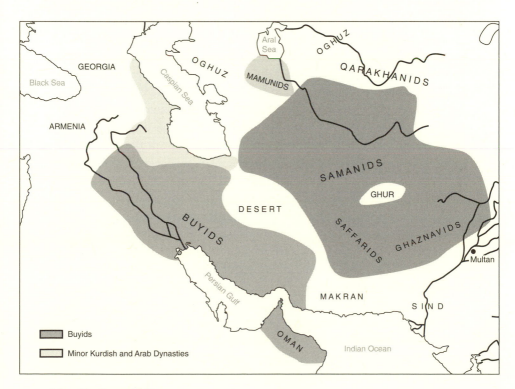

Map 11. Samanid Dynasty.

who ruled the eastern part of the Tarim Basin, took advantage of the Samanids' weakened state and conquered their remaining territory in Central Asia. Thus by the end of the tenth century all of Central Asia and northwest India was under the control of Sunni Turks. Yet there was no love lost between the Qarakhanids and the Ghaznavids. They fought endlessly and their feuding in part fostered the rise of the Seljuk Turks.

To fathom the rise of the Seljuks it is important to recognize that these events unfolding in Muslim Central Asia were not occurring in isolation. Rather in the ninth century the Eurasian system had largely collapsed when the great medieval empires came to an end—the Tang dynasty, the Tibetan and Turk empires, and the Abbasids—and as a result there was not only a worldwide economic collapse, but also a political power vacuum. When the Tang dynasty finally fell in 907 C.E., for example, it was followed by an anarchic fifty-year interlude known as the Five Dynasties and Ten Kingdoms period. Only with the rise of three new powerful states—the Chinese-ruled Song dynasty (960–1279 C.E.) in the south; the Khitan-ruled Liao dynasty (907–1125 C.E.) in the north; and the Tangut-ruled Xixia dynasty (1038–1227 C.E.) in the Gansu corridor between Mongolia and Tibet—did things settle down on the eastern periphery of Eurasia. Similarly, in Central Asia when the power of the Samanids collapsed in tandem with the fall of the Abbasids the Turks took advantage of the situation and invaded.

Yet, as noted above, events across Eurasia were intertwined and thus these two events did not unfold in isolation. Rather the two areas were connected through both trade and geography. As a result the upheavals in China had ripple effects across the continent. In particular, as the Khitans of the Liao dynasty advanced beyond north China and conquered the Mongolian plateau in the tenth century, and the Tanguts took over the Gansu corridor, these events forced the elites of various nomadic Turkic groups living in these areas to move westward. And in billiard ball fashion this in turn caused other Turkic groups to move as well.[7] One of these groups set in motion by both the events in China and Inner Asia were the Seljuk Turks. They were originally one of the Turkic Oghuz tribes inhabiting the area between the Aral and Caspian Seas, but on account of the tenth-century migrations they ended up moving south.[8] And as they came into contact with the Samanids they too became Muslim. Moreover, much like the Ghaznavid and Qarakhanids before them the Seljuk Turks also went on the offensive. In 1040 they defeated the Ghaznavids near Merv; however, rather than stay in Central Asia they kept marching west, conquering Baghdad in 1055.[9] After proclaiming themselves a Sultanate, they marched further west and took Anatolia from the Byzantine Empire in 1071.[10] Yet when they realized they could not defeat Byzantium, a feat only the Ottoman Turks would achieve four centuries later, the Seljuks returned to Central Asia.

Before continuing with this history, however, let us pause here a moment and recall that 1071 was the year that ibn az-Zubair wrote about the Chinese embassy coming to Bukhara. Having fled the Seljuk onslaught he knew that they had completely exterminated his Shi'a patrons, the Buyid, and were now in fact the real power behind the Abbasid Caliph. He also presumably knew about the Ghaznavids and the Qarakhanids. He himself had fled all of these Sunni Turkic states and sought refuge in the Arab Shi'a dynasty of the Fatimids in Egypt. In sum, ibn az-Zubair knew firsthand that the situation in the Muslim world was fractious and precarious,[11] which was, of course, exactly what the heretic from Nishapur had told the Chinese emperor. And what is interesting is that ibn az-Zubair makes no attempt to disavow this fact. Rather the whole point of his story—the Samanid Amir's Potemkin-village approach to international diplomacy—confirms the fact that the Muslim world was weak and broken and the only way to hold off a Chinese assault was through trickery. Ibn az-Zubair was therefore saying openly what any educated Muslim of the eleventh century would have known: the Caliph had no clothes.

This is not to suggest, however, that ibn az-Zubair simply made up this story out of whole cloth as a commentary on the contemporary situation. The fact of the matter is that the story actually has at its core a historically verifiable episode, albeit one that had become horribly distorted by the time it was written down a century and a half later. Namely, in the late 930s an embassy from the "King of China Qalin b. Shakir" arrived in Bukhara seeking a marriage alliance between his family and the Samanids. Unfortunately, we do not know the identity of Qalin b. Shakir, though it most likely refers to Cao Yijin (r. 914–935), who had recently taken over Dunhuang. In fact, it was his family that had arranged the marriage alliance with the king of Khotan noted in the preceding chapter. Yet be that as it may, the Samanid ruler Nasr b. Ahmad forbade his daughter to marry an infidel; however, he would accept a foreign princess marrying his son. The marriage thus took place when she arrived in Bukhara a few years later.

Of course, how and why this marriage alliance transformed into the story recounted above is another issue entirely, one, moreover, that is unlikely ever to be fully explained. Nevertheless, the actual wedding between the Samanid prince and the Dunhuang princess in the mid-tenth century points to a changed dynamic. In particular it seems to reveal an opening up of exchange between the formerly disconnected political and economic zones of the Caliphate and the Tantric Bloc of Inner Asia. Moreover, this marriage was not the only event reflecting such a shift. There was also the joint Khitan-Uygur attempt to reestablish trade ties with the Ghaznavids in 1027. Yet, as noted above, this attempt failed because Mahmud of Ghazna refused to open trade relations. Even so, these events seem to reflect a shift toward greater interaction between these disconnected entities.

Another piece that points in this direction is found in Tha'alibi's *Book of Curious and Entertaining Information* (*Laṭā'if al-ma'ārif*), which was composed in Nishapur in 1038 and describes China in a manner that seems to indicate an influx of new knowledge of the East. Tha'alibi, for example, reports about new technological developments in China such as napkins made of asbestos "for wiping away fat or grease, which, when dirty, can be thrown into the fire and made clean, without getting at all burnt."[12] Moreover, instead of praising Chinese painters for their skill, which was by this point a cliché in the Muslim world, Tha'alibi writes about Chinese sculpture. Most notably he expresses his admiration for the Chinese skill in representing human figures, "leaving out absolutely nothing except the man's soul." Tha'alibi then goes on to describe how these sculptors can "differentiate between the laugh of a man laughing derisively and one laughing out of confusion; or between a man smiling and one wondering in amazement; or between a laugh expressing pure joy and one expressing scorn."[13]

Tha'alibi's paean to Chinese sculpture is notable for many reasons. First, it seems to confirm renewed exchanges between China and the Muslim world. A second, and perhaps more intriguing factor, however, is quite simply that Tha'alibi praises sculpture at all, as Islam had historically not placed a premium on the three-dimensional representation of the human form. Rather, as captured in the famous hadith used as an epigraph to this chapter, Islam had a long tradition of forbidding the representation of Allah's creations. As a result, Islamic art had through the centuries focused its creative energies on abstraction, ornamentation, and calligraphy. Tha'alibi's praise of Chinese sculpture thus seems to contradict entirely this aesthetic sensibility.

Yet the fact of the matter is that Tha'alibi's appreciation of representational art was not necessarily a confirmation of renewed East-West interaction, but rather a reflection of an aesthetic shift in the Muslim world. At this time, namely, there had occurred a sea-change in Muslim aesthetics and representational art was suddenly widely popular. While this development will be explored in more detail below, it is important to note here that Tha'alibi's praise of Chinese sculpture was one aspect of this artistic revolution. Another confirmation of this aesthetic shift was the sudden Muslim appreciation of Buddha statues as objects of art. At this time, for example, Ghaznavid poets, who most often praised only jihad and the destruction of idols,[14] actually began using the imagery of Buddha statues in their poems.

> The new spring has come, bringing roses and jasmine.
> The park is like Tibet and the sloping hill like Eden.
> The garden, you'd think, has become like the Buddha of the shrine.
> The little birds are like the monk and the little rose bushes like idols.
> On the sole of its foot the monk kissed the idol.
> When will the idol kiss the monk on the sole of his foot?[15]

Tha'alibi's appreciation of sculpture was thus a part of this new aesthetic sensibility.

Even so, however, one can duly wonder how Tha'alibi actually came to be familiar with Chinese works of art. While we know there was a biannual market in Bukhara where "every day more than 50,000 *dirhams* were exchanged (for the idols),"[16] it is unlikely these were statues imported from China. In fact it is more likely that the statues sold in Bukhara were local "decommissioned" statues, as evidenced in the Central Asian Buddha statue that was traded westward along the Silk Road and ultimately ended up on an island off the coast of Sweden.[17] Yet at the same time it may be possible that this burgeoning Islamic interest in sculpture would have inspired Muslim merchants to actually bring back statues from China. There was certainly ample opportunity to do so since not only was there extensive maritime trade with the Song dynasty,[18] but the Qarakhanids in Central Asia were also sending two tribute missions every year to China along the Silk Road. Either one of these trading networks could potentially have provided Chinese statues for the Muslim market.

Regardless of the details, however, what both Tha'alibi's description of Chinese sculpture and the Samanid-Dunhuang marriage seem to confirm is a new phase of Eurasian economic integration. As we have seen, however,

increased economic exchange does not by itself translate into greater cultural interaction, much less increased awareness of the other. In the case of
maritime trade, in particular, it has actually been shown that knowledge
and cultural awareness often diminish as trade increases. Moreover, the
Muslim appreciation of Buddha statues does not necessarily reflect a new
Muslim appreciation of the Dharma, but more likely its opposite. Indeed,
it was precisely because there was no real interaction with Buddhists that
the statues had lost their power as symbols of "idolatry." Once actual Buddhists were gone their statues were therefore no longer manifestations of a
threatening and lived idolatry that needed to be destroyed. Instead, all that
remained were their statues, and being disembodied from their religious
and ritual context they no longer were emblematic of the feared other,
but were simply objects that could be appreciated as art. Thus rather than
reflecting an actual increase in Buddhist-Muslim interaction, the Islamic
fascination with Buddhist sculpture actually confirms the opposite: the continued separation of these two worlds.

The most remarkable example of this continued divide between the
Buddhist and Muslim worlds is revealed in the case of the Western Liao,
who used Muslim ignorance of China in order to legitimate their rule in
Muslim Inner Asia. To make sense of these intertwined developments, however, it is necessary to return to the historical narrative broken off above in
the year 1071, which was the year the Seljuk Turks conquered Anatolia and
then turned back toward the east. Arriving in Central Asia they in short
order defeated and expelled the Qarakhanids, though one group of these
Turks continued to rule the area further to the east in the area now com-
prising Xinjiang province of China. Yet the Seljuks eventually defeated them
as well in 1103. But as was often the case with nomadic Inner Asian
empires, the death of the great Seljuk Sultan Malikshah resulted in family
feuds and competing claims to the throne.[19] Thus even though Malikshah's
son was eventually able to take control the Seljuk state had been weakened
by this infighting. The Qarakhanids saw this as an opportunity and
revolted. Sultan Sanjar was able to suppress this uprising, yet at great cost,
and it was in this weakened state that he came up against and lost to the
Western Liao at the famous Battle of Qatwan on September 9, 1141.

In this long litany of conquests and uprisings over the centuries one
may wonder why this one battle deserves the moniker "famous." The reason lies less in the fact that this battle ushered in the reign of the Western
Liao in Central Asia, and more in the fact that it spurred on the develop-

ment of another disingenuous story: the legend of Prester John, the purported Christian king from the East who would finally annihilate all the
Muslims.[20] At this time Western Christendom had just launched its Crusade
to reclaim the Holy Land from the infidel Seljuk Turk. It was in 1095 at the
Council of Clermont that Pope Urban II called upon all Christians to join
the holy war, promising that those who died in the endeavor would receive
immediate remission of their sin.[21] In this context, when the news arrived
that the Seljuk Sultan had been defeated, visions of Prester John coming
from the East fired the Western imagination. Of course, the Western Liao
were not the Christian saviors from the East and thus the real importance
of the Battle of Qatwan was that it laid the foundation for Khitan dominance of Central Asia.

The Khitan were a Mongolic people who had adopted numerous Chinese customs during their rule of north China as the Liao dynasty (907–
1125 c.e.). Yet they had also maintained their nomadic traditions and thus
when they were conquered by the Jurchen—who founded the Jin dynasty
in north China (1115–1234 c.e.)—the Khitans fled to the Mongolian
plateau. There they regrouped and after acquiring numerous Turkic and
Mongol followers the Khitans—now renamed Qara Khitai ("Black Chinese")—moved into the area of Eastern Turkestan. From there the Western
Liao started to project their power westward, finally wresting control of
Central Asia from the Seljuk Turks. Thus for the first time ever Muslims
found themselves under the rule of the nomadic Sino-Mongol Qara Khitai.

Such a situation could have been problematic on numerous levels; however, the Western Liao used both their nomadic and Chinese backgrounds
to great advantage. Most notably they were able to leverage these two factors and thereby avoid converting to Islam.[22] "This was possible because
their dual identity as Chinese and nomads, combined with the broad religious tolerance they gave their subjects, enabled them to gain legitimacy
among their Muslim subjects despite their "infidelity." Furthermore, unim-
pressed by Muslim military power, which they were able to overcome, and
less impressed by Muslim material culture because of their close familiarity
with Chinese culture, the Qara Khitai themselves were not eager to embrace
Islam. This was also because Chinese tradition fulfilled for the Qara Khitai
the same functions Islamic tradition rendered for other nomads: communal
identity, means of statehood and, as mentioned above, legitimization."[23] In
order to understand how the Khitans converted their "Chineseness" into

legitimacy among the Muslims of Central Asia we need to recall how little the Islamic world actually knew about China.

As we have seen Muslim interaction with China had been minimal for centuries and as a result real knowledge of China was essentially frozen in the time of the Tang dynasty. Moreover, this lack of genuine first-hand knowledge had resulted in China developing into something of a fantasy-land. Yet unlike India, which became the spiritual land of talking idols and magical mantras in the Muslim imagination, China became the rational materialist utopia. It was thus the land of bureaucratic order, education, sumptuous wealth, and technological wizardry.[24] Indeed, the common view of China was so favorable that Central Asian Muslims even remembered wistfully their time as subjects of the Tang dynasty.[25] For example, they believed it was then that the Chinese introduced to them papermaking technology, which fit into the larger Muslim view of China as an unparalleled realm of sophistication and power. It was precisely this vision that fed into the Qara Khitai's project of legitimating themselves. Indeed, the fact that it was the "Chinese" who were their rulers even helped blunt criticism among their Islamic subjects about the Qara Khitai not being Muslim.

In many ways, however, the main reason the Muslims of Central Asia were thankful for the Qara Khitai was that they not only brought back order, but also reinvigorated the Inner Asian economy. In fact it was precisely because they were able to do so that Muslim jurists were able to claim that the Western Liao, although infidels, were nevertheless a righteous government. One of the main reasons such an argument was feasible was that since the eleventh century Muslim political theory had been based on the principle of justice. Indeed, the importance of justice above all else came to be encapsulated in a famous phrase—"A just infidel is preferable to an unjust Muslim ruler"—that was remarkably attributed to the Prophet Muhammad.[26] For a people who had suffered nearly a century of continuous political and economic upheaval at the hands of various ineffectual Muslim rulers, righteous infidel rule was no doubt a blessing.

Muslim scholars, however, did not only recognize the Qara Khitai as just rulers, but also depicted them "as a mighty wall or dam that protected Islam from its eastern enemies."[27] A valid question, of course, is: who were these enemies in the context of the twelfth century? The Chinese? The Turks? In many ways the image was simply figurative, based as it was on the Alexander Romance and the wall the famous Macedonian general had built in Inner Asia to keep out the evil forces of Gog and Magog. Moreover, the fact of the matter is that the Western Liao were not a wall at all. Rather, what made their rule so effective was precisely the porousness of their borders that enabled the east-west trade to once again revive across Inner Asia. And Muslim traders were heavily involved in this revived economy, especially with the nomads of the Mongolian plateau.[28] As a result, the claim of the Western Liao as being a bulwark against the infidel hordes of the east was largely a literary trope, but it was an image that burnished the Khitan's reputation and fostered their claims of legitimacy in the Muslim world.

Even so, what is surprising about this renewal of east-west interaction under Qara Khitai tutelage is that it did not really foster any increased knowledge of "the East." In fact, throughout this period Muslim scholars continued to draw upon the old tropes of the Tang dynasty and Tibetan empire, seemingly blissfully unaware of how horribly out of date they were. And this situation was clearly the same in relation to the Dharma, where there was a particularly acute knowledge gap. This to a certain extent is surprising because the Khitan had ostensibly been Buddhist when they ruled north China. However, from all the available material it is now clear that the Qara Khitai scrupulously avoided the promotion of Buddhism when they ruled Central Asia.[29] As a result, one unintended consequence was that the Western Liao actually did function like a wall, one that kept the Buddhist and Muslim worlds apart (map 12).

On account of their Sino-nomadic legitimization policies the Qara Khitai state therefore functioned as a perfect buffer between the Muslim world and the Tantric Bloc. In large measure the Muslim and Buddhist worlds would therefore remain separate during the Western Liao. The coming of the Mongols, however, was to change this dynamic completely. Yet before turning to the impact of the Mongol conquest it is important to leave the Muslim world and outline the developments in the Buddhist world. Indeed, to avoid the common mistake of ignoring the interconnectedness of Eurasian history we need to keep in mind that developments in the Buddhist world were intimately related to events unfolding in Muslim Central Asia. In fact, the very creation of the Tantric Bloc, with Tibet as its spiritual core, was very much related to the course of events described above.

The most important element in this regard was clearly the revival of Buddhism in Tibet. After the Tibetan Empire collapsed in the ninth century so too had Buddhism on the Tibetan plateau. Yet on account of the Muslim advance into the Buddhist frontier zone Buddhist masters from places like Kashmir and Khotan started to seek refuge in the Guge kingdom of western

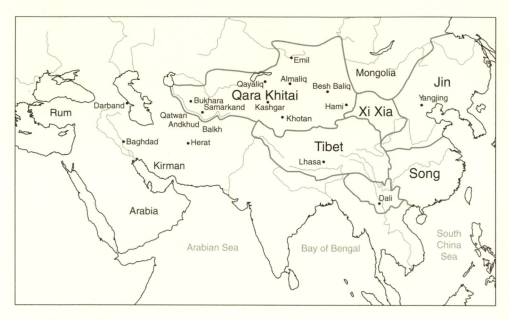

Map 12. Western Liao.

Tibet.[30] And as news spread of this Buddhist revival in Tibet ever more
Buddhist masters from South Asia made their way across the Himalayas. In
turn, as these teachers acquired disciples and the support of the ruling
Tibetan families, Buddhism became more and more intertwined with all
aspects of Tibetan society, including its culture and its political structures.
Yet this development was to not only radically impact the subsequent
course of Tibetan history, but also the very development of Tantric Buddhism itself. Most notably, once the Muslim armies of the Ghurid dynasty
marched across north India, the exodus of Dharma masters intensified and
as a result the very center of the Buddhist world shifted.

The Ghurids were eastern Persians, or Tajiks, from the mountainous
heartland of what is now northwest Afghanistan, who under the guidance
of Muhammad Ghuri (1162–1206 C.E.) overthrew the Ghaznavid dynasty.
Shortly thereafter he started to invade India. Muhammad Ghuri was in fact
the first Central Asian ruler who projected Muslim power beyond the Punjab. And by 1206 his forces had marched all the way across north India and
even attempted an invasion of Tibet by following the Brahmaputra River
up through the Himalayas.[31] While this particular expedition failed spectac-

ularly, by the early thirteenth century India from the Khyber Pass to Bengal was under the control of the Ghurids. And in order to secure their hold on power they followed the age-old Muslim custom of temple destruction. Although it is now known that the claims of such destruction are vastly inflated in Muslim conquest literature as well as in Hindu and Buddhist histories, we do know that at least eighty temples were destroyed during this period.[32]

Two of these destroyed temples were Buddhist.[33] While this may not seem like a great deal it was actually a devastating blow to the Buddhist community since that was basically all they had left. Not only had they lost ground to the Hindus over the previous centuries, but also as we have seen many Buddhists had simply moved further and further east and north. Thus when the Ghurids arrived, India was far from being a Buddhist country. Nevertheless, with the support of an ever-dwindling pool of Buddhist merchant elite the tantric tradition had been kept alive in the few remaining Dharma institutions, such as the monasteries of Nalanda, Odantapuri, and Vikramasila. When the Ghurids sacked these institutions it was therefore a devastating blow to the Dharma in India. At the same time, however, it was also a boon to the burgeoning Buddhist movement in Tibet, where many Tantric masters sought refuge.

On one level the diaspora of these Khotanese, Kashmiri, and Indian Buddhists into Tibet could have ended as with the Nestorian Christians in Central Asia: as an historical oddity of little concern to anyone. Yet that was not to be the case. As we all know Tibet and its Tantric Buddhism continues to exert a profound influence on the world stage. Why and how this happened is far beyond the scope of this study; nevertheless, one thing is clear: the Indian masters and their Tibetan disciples turned the obtuse antinomianism of Tantric Buddhism into gold. The alchemical transformation of Indian tantra and its fusion with Buddhist thought from Inner Asia and China into what was to become "Tibetan Buddhism" was a long and complicated process; however, it resulted in Tibet and its Tantric Buddhism becoming a major player on the Eurasian stage.

The reasons for this are many, though one important factor in this development was, oddly enough, the Muslim invasion of India. It was this event that set in motion the brain drain of tantric masters that ushered in both the withering of Buddhism in India and the simultaneous growth of the Dharma in Tibet. Essential to this growth were, of course, the Indian masters themselves, their teachings, and their texts, but there was also a further factor that played a fundamental role in forging the future of Tibetan religious power. And one central factor in this regard was the decision of these tantric masters to not cling to India as the Holy Land and clamoring for a *reconquista*. Rather these Indian and Tibetan Buddhist masters used the central component of tantric practice—the mandala—in order to reconceptualize Tibet as the new center of the Buddhist world (map 13).[34]

Indeed, the importance of India as an actual place to visit, much less one needing to be reconquered, is well borne by the fact that the number of Tibetans who actually visited India at this time can be counted on the

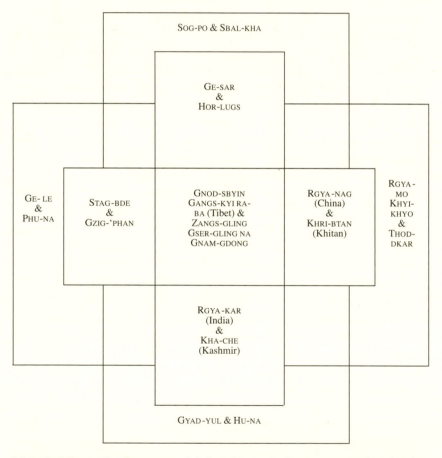

Map 13. Tibet at the Center. Mandala based on textual sources, reproduced with the permission of Dan Martin.

finger of one hand.[35] By the middle of thirteenth century Tibet had therefore become the new Holy Land, the center of the Buddhist universe, and
in very short order Tibet was to become the very fount of Buddhism in the
minds of many. As a result, Tibetan tantric masters with their numerous
rituals concentrating on power and its projection were welcomed at imperial courts across Asia.

Mongols, Buddhism, and Islam

On account of these developments, when Muslims once again came into
direct contact with Buddhists in the thirteenth century, they were most
often tantric Buddhists. Or at least that was the case in Inner Asia and
certainly within the ruling circles of the Mongol elite, who after a brief
dalliance with Chinese Chan Buddhism, had opted instead for the pag-
eantry of Tibetan Tantra.[36] Other Muslims, especially those living and
working in China and Southeast Asia, no doubt came upon other Buddhists
as well; however, the record of this encounter is sadly lost.[37] Moreover, in
other cases we simply do not know what type of Buddhism was involved,
as in the case Güchlüg Khan (d. 1218 C.E.), who can in many ways be
credited with reintroducing the Buddhist and Muslim worlds.

Based on the reporting of later Muslim historians the term "reintroducing" is, however, perhaps not the best way to describe what happened. They
claim Güchlüg Khan, who converted from Christianity to Buddhism on the
recommendation of his wife, launched a genocidal Buddhist pogrom
against Islam. To make sense of this Muslim claim, however, it is necessary
to recall the contemporary Inner Asian context, which was rapidly changing
in tandem with the rise of Chinggis Khan (1160–1227 C.E.). In particular,
it was his dynamic process of power consolidation among the various Turkic and Mongolic peoples of the Mongolian plateau that had forced Güchlüg Khan to flee to the safety of Western Liao territory. Güchlüg had tried
to resist Chinggis Khan but failed and therefore sought refuge with the
Qara Khitai. On account of the Western Liao's weakness at this time, however, Güchlüg eventually took over as ruler (r. 1211–1218). In doing so he
also very publicly converted to Buddhism,[38] which was a dramatic change
from the Qara Khitai policy of studiously avoiding any identification with
the Dharma and promoting instead something like religious tolerance.

The Muslim response to this shift, as well as the deteriorating geopolitical and economic situation under Güchlüg's reign, was inevitable. They

prayed for infidel rule to come to an end. And their prayers were shortly answered when Chinggis Khan launched his first campaign to the west. He did so, however, not to save the Muslims. Chinggis Khan was himself an infidel. Rather he had the more narrow aim of exterminating the threat Güchlüg Khan posed to his own claims of dominance on the Mongolian plateau. Nevertheless, the fact that Chinggis Khan had put an end to the openly Buddhist and infidel rule of Güchlüg Khan was perfect fodder for later Muslim historians who worked for the Mongols: it allowed them to portray the Mongols as the liberators of the Muslim world.[39]

To this end it is very likely that authors like Juvaini and Rashid al-Din, both of whom were employed by the Mongol Il-Khanid court in Iran, also vastly exaggerated the supposed Buddhist persecution of Muslims.[40] Moreover, Muslim historians who took the opposing view of the Mongols, seeing them not as liberators but as the coming of the apocalypse, added fuel to the fire by presenting fabricated stories of Buddhist persecution. One such author was Juzjani, a Muslim historian writing in India, who told a story of how a miracle saved the Muslim world from the scheming Buddhists.

A fraternity of recluses and devotees of the infidels of Chin, and idol-worshippers of Tingit and Tamghaj, whom they style by the name of Tunian [toyin], acquired ascendancy over Güyük. That faction constantly used to study persecuting Musulmans, and were wont to promote means of afflicting the people of Islam continually, in order that, mayhap, they might entirely uproot them, extirpate them completely, and eradicate both name and sign of the true believers from the pages of that country.

One of those [monks], who had a name and reputation in China and Turkestan, presented himself before Güyük and said: "If thou desirest that the sovereignty and throne of the Mughals should remain unto thee, of two things do one—either massacre the whole of the Musalmans, or put a stop to their generating and propagating." . . . On account of the numerousness of the Musalmans in the countries of China, Turkestan, and Tingit, to massacre them would not be feasible, they therefore [the monks] came to this conclusion that it would be right that a mandate should be issued by Güyük, that all Musulmans should be emasculated and made eunuchs of, in order that their race might become extinct, and the empire of the Mughals be safe from their rebellion and sedition.

When such [like] tyranny and barbarity took root in the mind of Güyük, and his decision in this course was to, he commanded that a mandate should be issued, to this effect, throughout all parts of the Mughal dominions. . . . Accordingly he delivered this mandate to [one of] those Mughal [monks], saying: "Do ye transmit this mandate into all parts of the empire, and use the utmost efforts in so doing."

When that accursed base one, who held that tyrannical mandate in his hand, was issuing from the place of audience in great glee and confidence, there was a dog which they used constantly to keep there, and which was wont to be near the throne, at the sides, and in the precincts of the dais, and the sovereign's exclusive seat; and on the animal's collar, studded with precious stones, was impressed a brand denoting its being royal property. It was a dog, which, in courage and fierceness, greatly exceeded and far surpassed a thousand roaring lions and howling tigers. This dog was in Güyük's place of audience, and, like unto a wolf upon a sheep, or fire among wild rue seeds, it seized hold of that impious monk, flung him to the ground, and then, with its teeth tore out that base creature's genitals from the roots; and by the Heavenly power and Divine help, at once, killed him, and the imprecation, according to the *hadith*, which Mustafa—on whom be peace!—had pronounced upon the son of Abu Lahb: "O God! Let one of thy dogs defile him!" was fulfilled upon that accursed wretch of a priest.

Such a miracle as this was vouchsafed in order that, under the shadow of the protection of the Most High God, the faith of Islam, the felicity of the Hanafi creed, the happiness of the Ahmadi belief, the prestige of the followers of the orthodox Muhammadi institutes, might continue safe from the malevolence of these accursed one. . . . Praise be to God for the triumph of Islam and the overthrow of idolatry![41]

Although this is a wonderful story that well captures the possibilities of Buddhist-Muslim conflict, it is not true. The reality is that Güyük (r. 1246–1248) favored Christianity, not Buddhism.[42] Juzjani's story, nevertheless, does reveal the tensions that boiled to the surface as the Mongol conquests brought the Muslim and Buddhist worlds back together again for the first time after centuries of separation.

Further confirmation of such tension is also revealed in a story recounted by the Persian historian Juvaini about another purported Buddhist massacre of Muslims. This episode took place among the Uygurs, who upon the collapse of their empire on the Mongolian plateau had taken over the cities on the eastern end of the Tarim Basin, where they came to establish a thriving cosmopolitan Buddhist culture.[43] Initially the Uygurs had drawn largely upon Indian and Chinese traditions, including both Nikaya and Mahayana Buddhism, but by the time of the Mongols they too had adopted Tantric Buddhism.[44] As a result, when they submitted to Chinggis Khan in 1209 the Uygurs became one vehicle through which the Mongols became familiar with tantra (another was the Tangut Xixia state where Tibetan Buddhist masters were also active).[45]

Nevertheless, regardless of their origins or doctrinal orientations, these Uygur, Tibetan, and Tangut Buddhists were successful in obtaining the support of Mongol rulers. Ögedei Khan, for example, had ordered the building of Buddhist monuments in 1235.[46] That this meant that the Mongols were Buddhists in the exclusive modern sense, however, is not likely. Rather, Mongol policy was not to sanction one tradition, but rather allow all religions to flourish as long as they were subservient to Mongol imperial power.[47] Invariably such an open policy led to much jockeying between religious traditions and in many cases these feuds became further intertwined with the internal political struggles of the empire.[48] As was the case with the anti-Muslim Uygur Buddhist conspiracy that Juvaini claimed took place during the reign of Möngke Khan (r. 1251–1259), which was less about Buddhist-Muslim hostilities than a question of the khan's ascension and his exercise of power.

Nevertheless, the framing of the story within a Buddhist uprising that aimed to exterminate all the Muslims in Uygur territory offered Juvaini an unparalleled opportunity to simultaneously condemn the Dharma, glorify Islam, and praise Möngke Khan.

> When confessions had been obtained from them all [by torture] and had been submitted to the firm judgment of the Monarch of the Face of the Earth, he gave orders that the *idi-qut* [the Uygur king] and his accomplices should be sent back to Besh-Baligh together with the messengers. And on a Friday, the day on which they had thought to attack the true believers, the common people, both monotheists [Muslims] and idolaters [Buddhists], were brought out

on to the plain and the command of the mighty World-Emperor
was put into execution. Ögünch, the brother of the *idi-qut*, with his
own hand severed his head; and his two accomplices Bilge Quti and
Idkech were sawn in half. And thus was this country cleansed of the
mark of the guile of these wicked infidels and of the impurity of
their religion. "*And the uttermost part of that impious people was cut
off. All praise be to God, the Lord of the Worlds!*" [Qur'an 6:45] The
faithful were exalted and the idolaters downtrodden by the grace of
God Almighty.[49]

The trifecta noted above—condemning the Dharma, glorifying Islam, and
praising Möngke Khan—was probably not simply an element of Juvaini's
historiographical approach. Rather, it presumably also captures some of the
actual feelings and tensions that did arise among Muslims when they came
into contact with the Buddhist world for the first time, especially since
many of them had been forcibly moved into Buddhist areas as part of the
Mongols' policy of population transfers. One Muslim source, for example,
records that by the mid-thirteenth century fifty thousand Muslims had
been moved to Besh-Baliq, the Uygur Buddhist capital.[50] How did they feel?
Moreover, how did the Uygur Buddhists feel to be inundated with Central
Asian Muslims?

As evidenced in the material presented above the tensions between the
two groups were rather raw. Juvaini, in fact, claims that "none [are] more
bigoted than the idolaters of the East, and none more hostile to Islam," and
as if to confirm this he offers a harrowing account of how Güchlüg Khan
had an imam in Khotan crucified to the door of his own madrasa.[51]
Although there is no corroborating evidence to confirm this event, the tension between Buddhists and Muslims was also noted by the Franciscan friar
William of Rubruck, who claimed that Muslims "shun them [Buddhists]
to the point that they are unwilling even to talk about them. Consequently,
whenever I asked the Saracens about these people's religion they were scan-
dalized."[52] And although such tensions clearly existed it is also the case that
some dialogue must have occurred since Juvaini offers us the first informed
Muslim description of Buddhism in centuries.

The *toyins* [= noble monks] call a reading from their [holy] book
nom.[53] Now the *nom* contains their theological speculations and
consists of idle stories and traditions; but excellent homilies are like-

wise to be found in it such as are consonant with the law and faith of every prophet, urging men to avoid injury and oppression and the like, to return to good for evil and to refrain from the injuring of animals, etc. Their dogmas and doctrines are manifold; the most typical is that of reincarnation. They say that the people to-day existed several thousand years ago: the souls of those that wrought good deeds and engaged in worship attained a degree in accordance with their actions, such as that of king, or prince, or peasant, or beggar; while the souls of those that had engaged in debauchery, libertinism, murder, slander, and injury to their fellow creatures descended into vermin, beasts of prey and other animals; and so they are punished for their deeds.[54]

While this is not an elaborate exploration of the Dharma it nevertheless reveals that Buddhist-Muslim interaction was not quite as hostile as the material above would lead us to believe. Some form of dialogue was not only possible, but actually took place.

Indeed, the fact of the matter is that the Mongols, even though they supported the Dharma, also realized from the very beginning that Muslim scholars, soldiers, scientists, engineers, and merchants had much to offer in helping them run their expanding domains. Chinggis Khan, for example, employed Muslims as advisors during his campaigns into Central Asia and eventually appointed Mahmud Yalavach to rule there as his representative.[55] His successor Ögedei (r. 1229–1241) followed suit by introducing tax-farming to north China upon the recommendation of his Muslim advisers.[56] And on account of such actions Ögedei subsequently came to be presented in Muslim sources as a staunch defender of Islam.

In one story, for example, he angrily interrupted the performance of a Chinese theatre troupe when they began to openly mock Islam. He then gave a demonstration about how superior Muslims are to the Chinese during which he claimed the Han were no better than donkeys.[57] In another story Ögedei supposedly came to the aid of a Muslim man who could not repay his loan to the Uygur Buddhist ruler. Unless he did so the ruler claimed the man had to not only convert to Buddhism, but also receive one hundred bastinado lashings in the town square. After pleading his case Ögedei Khan was outraged. He not only gave the man money, a Uygur wife and a house, but also ordered the Uygur ruler to be lashed a hundred times.[58] In a final story about Ögedei, which is recorded both by Juvaini and Juzjani, an Arab apostate tells Ögedei about his dream wherein Ching-gis Khan orders him to kill all the Muslims. In response Ögedei asks him whether he knows Mongolian. "'No,' said the man. 'Neither am I in any doubt,' said the Qa'an, 'but that Chingiz-Khan knew no language save Mongolian. It is clear therefore that what thou sayest is nothing but lies.' And he ordered the man to be put to death."[59]

Of course, whether this event ever happened is another issue entirely. In fact, one can wonder whether this Muslim portrait of Ögedei corresponded at all with reality. Was he really a defender of Islam? Perhaps, but it is also evident that he was simultaneously promoting Buddhism. Indeed, over time numerous religious traditions came to claim the Mongols as their patrons even though the fact was that the Mongols simply accepted all religions and supported none exclusively. Such an attitude invariably confounded Christians like William of Rubruck; however, recognizing and allowing the practice of all religious traditions was an important aspect of Mongol statecraft.[60] It was precisely when this policy changed and Mongol rulers began supporting one particular tradition, such as Islam in the West and Buddhism in the East, that problems really began.[61]

But during the thirteenth century Mongol rulers followed an open religious policy and thus Buddhism and Islam both received support. Möngke Khan, for example, both entertained the Tibetan lama Karma Pakshi and respected Islamic practices.[62] Khubilai Khan (r. 1260–1294 C.E.) received tantric initiation from his personal guru Pakpa Lama,[63] and actively supported not only the promotion of Muslim administrators in China, but also the importation of people and ideas from the Islamic world.[64] To this end he also established numerous institutes for the Islamic intellectual elite in Yuan dynasty China (1272–1368 C.E.), such as the Muslim Medical Office (established in 1270), a Directorate of Muslim Astronomy[65] (1271), and a Muslim School for the Sons of the State that taught Persian (1289). And it was the same in the Muslim world, as evidenced in the case of Hülegü, the founder of the Il-khans in Iran.

Just like his brother Khubilai, he was both a devotee of Tibetan lamas and an avid supporter of Muslim science. Yet while Hülegü's relation with Nasir al-Din Tusi and his building of a state-of-the-art observatory near present-day Tabriz is well known,[66] his affiliation with Buddhism has often been downplayed. But as is evident in the contemporary account of the Armenian Christian Kirakos Ganjakec'i (1203–1271 C.E.), it is clear that Hülegü took the Dharma seriously.

He also built a huge dwelling for enormous idols, having mustered there all sorts of skilled workmen: for masonry, for carpentry, and for painting. There is a lineage among them, the so-called *toyins*. These [*toyins*]—sorcerers and wizards, by their magical art compel horses and camels, corpses and felt images to speak. They are all priests, and shave the hair and beard, wear yellow vestments on the breast, and worship everything, but most of all Sakmoni (Sakyamuni) and Madrin (Maitreya).

They deceived him (= Hülegü), promising him immortality, and he lived, moved, and mounted a horse at their bidding, entirely having given himself over to their will. Many times a day he bowed and kissed the ground in front of their leader, and was fed [food] which was consecrated in their heathen temple, and extolled him more than all the rest. And therefore, he had intended to build a temple of their idols in particular magnificence.[67]

Hülegü in fact built three Buddhist temples: one at his summer pastures in the mountains of Armenia and two in Iran at Khoy and Maragha. Three of his successors—Abagha (r. 1265–1282 c.e.), Arghun (r. 1284–1291), and Gaikhatu (r. 1291–1295)—also supported the Dharma.[68] Gaikhatu's investiture ceremony, for example, included a tantric initiation; and Arghun held debates at his court that pitted Indian, Tibetan, and Uygur Buddhists against local Muslim scholars such as 'Ala' ad-Dawla as-Simnani.[69] Arghun, moreover, wanted his son, the future Ghazan Khan, to be trained in the faith.

Let it not remain concealed from the people of the world that when the Padishah of Islam was in his infancy, his grandfather Abaqa Khan kept him near and reared him. Over him as attendants and teachers he set idolatrous *bakshis*, and by that means that practice became firmly rooted in his soul, particularly since his fathers had believed in that sect and practiced that way. The practice of idolatry, which had been completely eliminated throughout the region from the beginning of Islam, reappeared during their time, and that group had become powerful. All sorts of *bakshis* were brought with all honor and respect from India, Kashmir, Cathay, and Uyghur lands. Temples were built in every place, and vast sums were spent on them. This sect had risen to the apex of power, as was apparent to all. The Padishah of Islam was constantly in the company of the *bakshis* in the temple observing their rites. Day by day his inclination to that sect increased, and his belief became firmer. When Abaqa Khan passed away and [Ghazan's] father Arghun Khan sent him to Khurasan as governor and commander of the army, he built major temples in Khabushan, and he spent most of his time conversing, eating, and drinking with the *bakshis* in those temples. The belief he had for that sect and the worship he performed of the idols were beyond description.[70]

These purportedly idyllic days of Ghazan's Buddhist youth, however, eventually came to an end. As we saw in the previous chapter Ghazan Khan converted to Islam in June 1295.

The common scholarly consensus as to why he did so is politics.[71] The economy was in tatters, local powerful Muslim rulers were rebelling, and most of his leading Mongol and Turk generals had already converted. He therefore simply had to become a Muslim. Ghazan also had to prove his zeal and thus he issued an order to destroy all Buddhist monasteries and shrines and convert all Buddhists to Islam.[72] Yet there is some debate as to whether this action was actually carried out. Issuing such an order and claiming one killed Buddhist infidels is a standard component of Islamic conversion stories and does not by itself mean that it actually took place.[73] Moreover, the same history that tells us of these anti-Buddhist actions also reveals that Buddhists continued to be active in Iran for years after this purported purge. As a result, whether Ghazan really launched a scorched-earth campaign against the Dharma is unclear. In fact, it is very likely that Ghazan's attack against Buddhism was based more on financial considerations than religious ones. The Il-khanids, namely, were in dire straits after the profligacy of Gaikhatu and something had to be done.[74] Thus as had happened repeatedly throughout history, Buddhist temples were ransacked for their wealth in order to fix the economy.[75] Yet, as had happened in China and Burma, once the Buddhists had been divested of their assets it is clear that they were allowed to practice their faith as apparently also happened in Il-khanid Iran.

In fact, we know that some of the surviving Buddhists tried to convert Ghazan's successor, Öljeitü Khan (r. 1305–1316 c.e.), back to the Dharma.[76] Although the attempt failed it does reveal that Buddhists were active in the Il-khanid domains for more than fifty years. Moreover, for nearly four decades of that time the Buddhists had not simply been active in this area, but had received the support and largesse of the Mongol court. And as we have seen such a policy was unprecedented in the history of Islam and thus before proceeding we need to explore not only how the Muslims responded to the Mongols, but also to the Dharma.

The orgy of violence Hülegü unleashed upon Baghdad after its fall still resonates in Muslim memory today.[77] Although it is now often held up as one of Islam's darkest hours the establishment of Mongol rule was at the time met with ambivalence. For one, infidel rule was not new and Hülegü and his Muslim advisors wasted no time in promoting the idea of a just infidel being preferable to an unjust Muslim ruler. Juvaini, the newly appointed governor of Baghdad, was one individual who lent his voice to this argument.[78]

It is the *yasa* and custom of the Mongols that whoever yields and submits to them is safe and free from the terror and disgrace of their severity. Moreover, they [i.e., the Mongols] oppose no faith or religion—how can one speak of opposition?—rather than encourage them; the proof of which assertion is the saying of Mohammed (*upon whom be peace!*): "*Verily, God shall assert this religion through a people that have no share of good fortune.*" They have exempted and dispensed the most learned of every religion from every kind of occasional tax ('*avāriẓāt*) and from the inconvenience of contributions (*mu'an*); their pious foundations and bequests for the public use and their husbandmen and ploughmen have also been recognized as immune; and none may speak amiss of them, particularly the imams of the faith of Mohammed, and especially now in the reign of the Emperor Mengü Qa'an, when there are several princes of the family (*urugh*) of Chingiz-Khan, his children and grandchildren, in whom the dignity of Islam hath been joined to worldly power. . . . In view of the foregoing it is necessary on the grounds of reason, now that the Piebald Horse of the Days [i.e., the world] is tame between the thighs of their command, that men should comply with the commandment of the Lord: "*And if they lean to peace, lean thou also to it*" [Qur'an 6:63], and should yield and submit; and desist from rebellion and forwardness in accordance with the words of the Lord of the Shari'at: "*Let the Turks be as long as they let you be, for they are endued with terrible prowess*"; and place their lives and property in the stronghold of immunity and the asylum of security—"*for God guideth whom He pleaseth into the straight path*" [Qur'an 2:209].[79]

How this argument played among the masses is hard to gauge; however, one factor that did play into the hands of the Mongols was the age-old animosities within Islam that helped foster divided loyalties. Thus while Sunnis bemoaned the death of the Caliph, they also greeted Hülegü's destruction of the Shi'a Assassins with joy.[80] On the other hand, the Shi'a, especially those in southern Iraq, looked favorably upon the Mongols precisely for their destruction of the Sunni caliphate.[81]

Yet even more important than these mutual antagonisms were the rulings of Islamic scholars that decoupled the idea of justice from Islam, thereby making it possible for a non-Muslim state to be defined as just.[82] Of course, once the Mongols converted to Islam these rulings were subsequently reevaluated and the linkage between justice and Muslim rule reaffirmed. Even so, not all Muslims were satisfied with Ghazan Khan's conversion to Islam, much less Mongol rule as being just. Imami Shi'a scholars, for example, rejected the argument of Mongol rule being just since Ghazan Khan did not recognize the Imam. In fact, they came to support Mongol rule only when Ghazan's successor, Öljeitü, actually became a Twelver Shi'a.[83] But it was not only the Shi'a who questioned the Mongol adoption of Islam.

Ibn Taymiyya, the reformist Sunni theologian from Syria, leveled the most famous critique against the Mongols.[84] He saw their continued adherence to not only non-Islamic Mongol rituals,[85] but also Mongol laws that contradicted the *shari'a*,[86] as evidence of their impiety. As they were less than true believers ibn Taymiyya therefore claimed the Mongols could be killed. Famously, and more controversially, he also asserted that anyone who had dealings with the Mongols, even if they were Muslim, could also be killed.[87] All Muslims, of course, did not agree with ibn Taymiyya, and not only about his justifying the killing of innocents.[88] Many also opposed ibn Taymiyya's other hardliner interpretations of Islam, such as his rejection of music, dancing, and relic worship.[89] Thus when Ibn Taymiyya tried to stop the worship of Muhammad's footprint in Damascus in 1304 he was driven away by an enraged mob who accused him of impiety.[90]

The Muslim response to the Mongols was therefore not only ambivalent, but also diverse on account of many extenuating factors such as religious, economic, and political concerns. And this reality is made evident in the response of the Persian elite to the Mongol conquest.[91] For them, religion was not the sole driving force in their decision to work with the new rulers. In fact, some of them were more concerned about staying in power and increasing their financial well-being than adherence to Islam. If that required learning Mongolian and working with the infidels so be it.[92] It was therefore by downplaying Islam that the Persian elite remained in power during Mongol rule. Yet this is not to suggest that they completely abandoned Islam. When possible they also promoted a return to Islamic principles as during the two-year reign of Ahmad Khan (1282–1284). But when his successor, the anti-Muslim Arghun, overturned these policies, the elite fell in line again.[93] From afar it is very easy to see such actions on the part of the Persian elite as opportunism, or else a sophisticated manner in which to promote both their political and religious agendas. Either way, however, the point here is not to dredge up the inordinately complex issues surrounding the relations that develop between native elites and any new imperial power, but rather to highlight the complexity of the Muslim response to the coming of the Mongols. Indeed, the key point to be kept in mind is that Islam is never monolithic and rarely is there a uniform "Muslim" response. Thus while some Persian elites may have minimized the role of the religion at certain times, others like ibn Taymiyya clearly did not.

Curiously, however, those who did mobilize Islam against the Mongols never specifically focused on their adherence to Buddhism. Rather, the main charge leveled against them by thinkers like ibn Taymiyya and the Imami Shiʻa was that the Mongols were not Muslim enough, or that they were the wrong kind of Muslim. Even in the earlier Islamic debates about justice and Mongol rule the question never focused on Buddhism in particular, but revolved instead around the general issue of infidel rule and more specifically the issue of stability and the use of coercive power needed to maintain it. Indeed, it was largely along these same lines that Juvaini championed the Mongols, and he too, for obvious reasons, did not broadcast their support of the Dharma. He highlighted instead their attitude of religious freedom, as well as their lack of "fanaticism" of any kind.

But even though the Dharma is absent in these works we should not assume, as has so often been the case, that Il-khanid Buddhism did not leave a trace in the Muslim world. Rather, we need to recognize that the bringing together of Buddhists and Muslims within the Il-khanid domains for a period of almost a half-century resulted not only in a new intellectual engagement between the two traditions, but also in the creation of a whole new visual culture—one that even allowed the representation of Muhammad (figure 19).

Portraying Muhammad had never occurred in the Muslim world before the Il-khanid period. Moreover, it would not continue long after the end of Mongol rule. In fact, if Muhammad were portrayed in the later period he would come to be veiled (figure 20).

Yet before exploring the Buddhist role in the aesthetic revolution encapsulated in the appearance of images of Muhammad, let us first turn to the issue of intellectual engagement and the role it played in laying the groundwork for such artistic works to be created.

Rashid al-Din and the Dharma

Rashid al-Din, the son of a Jewish pharmacist, was born in 1247 in the town of Hamadan. When he was thirty he converted to Islam and joined the court of Abagha Khan as a doctor. After the economic crisis that ensued when the Il-khans tried to introduce Chinese paper money in Iran,[94] Rashid al-Din was brought into the Il-khanid administration as an associate of the new vizier Sa'd al-Din Savaji. In this capacity Rashid al-Din performed extraordinarily well and thus he not only went on military campaigns with Ghazan Khan against the Mamluks and arranged peace negotiations in Syria, but also resolved long-standing financial problems. Yet Rashid al-Din's remarkable rise to power was soon to be challenged.

Upon the death of his associate Sa'd al-Din Savaji, he was accused of poisoning Ghazan Khan. Although he was able to prove his innocence Rashid al-Din continued to clash with his new associate, the vizier Taj al-Din Ali-Shah. To resolve this feud Öljeitü Khan divided control of the Il-khanid territories between the two men, but tensions between them persisted and came to a head when Öljeitü died under Rashid al-Din's medical care. Ali-Shah used this event to convince Öljeitü's successor, Abu Sa'id, that Rashid al-Din had poisoned his father. The young khan agreed and Rashid al-Din, who had faithfully served both his father and grandfather, was executed in 1318. His decapitated head was paraded around Tabriz for days accompanied with the chant, "This is the head of the Jew who abused the name of God: may God's curse be upon him!" The enraged mob then ransacked his house and destroyed the legendary workshop that bore his name, the Rab'i Rashidi.[95] And to add insult to injury Miran Shah, the "crazy" son of Tam-

Figure 19. Muhammad mounted on Buraq and escorted by angels passing over the Ka'ba, from the *Khamsa* of Nizami, Herat, Afghanistan, 1494–1495. © British Library Board. All Rights Reserved (Or. 6810, f.5v).

Figure 20. Muhammad's ascent into heaven, from the *Khamsa* of Nizami, Tabriz, Iran, 1539–1543. © British Library Board. All Rights Reserved (Or. MS 2265, f. 195).

erlane, had Rashid al-Din's body exhumed from his mausoleum and reburied in the Jewish cemetery.[96]

Prior to his tumultuous fall from grace, however, Rashid al-Din had been commissioned with a delicate task of the utmost importance: Ghazan Khan had asked him to write a history of the Mongols and their rise to power. The reason Ghazan gave for launching this undertaking was so that the recently converted Mongols would not forget their glorious pre-Islamic past; however, there were clearly other motives behind this endeavor.[97] Indeed, being composed in Persian and then translated into Arabic, this history of the Mongols was clearly aimed at a much broader audience. Moreover, its narrative aim was probably less an act of remembering than a project of legitimating Mongol rule. Yet be that as it may, to compose his history Ghazan Khan made it possible for Rashid al-Din to have unprecedented access to Mongol sources. He was not only allowed to interview important members of the Mongol elite, but was also given access to the secret archives of the Mongol chancellery. As a result, Rashid al-Din was able to produce a history of the early Mongols that was remarkably rich in details and unparalleled in its scope.

On account of this success Ghazan Khan's brother and successor, Öljeitü, asked Rashid al-Din to expand his history beyond the Mongols. He wanted Rashid al-Din to not only include the earlier Hebrew, Persian, and Islamic dynasties, but also chronicle the histories of India, China, and Europe. To this end Rashid al-Din brought in a whole team of foreign experts to help him write what was to become the first-ever world history, the *Jami' al-tawarikh*, or *Compendium of Chronicles*. It was a monumental work and also a stunning success. Upon its completion Rashid al-Din was reportedly paid a million gold *dinars* as a reward. Moreover, since the project was deemed so important to the Il-khanid court they ordered that an illustrated copy in Persian and Arabic be prepared annually so that it could be disseminated across the empire.

In order to fulfill this command Rashid al-Din hired the best calligraphers and painters from Iran and China and put them to work in the Rab'i Rashidi.[98] On account of his subsequent fall from grace, however, only four illustrated copies of this history survive today. Yet on the basis of these remaining fragmentary copies one can get a glimpse of the cosmopolitan culture within which Rashid al-Din produced the *Compendium of Chronicles*. The paintings, for example, draw influences not only from Central Asian Buddhist and Chinese sources, but also from contemporary Italian (especially Sienese) paintings as well as Byzantine icons.[99] The nature of this distinctive Mongol visual culture will be explored in more detail below.

Let us begin instead with Rashid al-Din's presentation of the Dharma. His presentation of Buddhism comprises twenty chapters and is the most extensive and well-informed presentation of Buddhism in any Muslim source.[100] The main reason Rashid al-Din was able to present such a rich exploration of the Dharma was quite simply that unlike all of his Muslim predecessors he had access to actual Buddhists. As we have seen above, the Il-khanid court had actively supported the Dharma for nearly half a century and thus Iran was filled with a vast array of Buddhists from across Asia. The Dharma was therefore not something far away and little understood; it was a lived reality. During his life Rashid al-Din could thus readily have visited Buddhist temples, seen Buddha statues, witnessed Buddhist rituals, and like as-Simnani, he could also have actually talked with Buddhists. These were possibilities simply unavailable to earlier Muslim scholars such as al-Biruni, who lamented his not being able to find a single Buddhist with whom he could discuss the Dharma.

Rashid al-Din, on the other hand, readily acknowledges that he had three Buddhist informants: the Kashmiri monk Kamalaśrī, and two Chinese collaborators named Litaji and Kamsun.[101] Since the Buddhism practiced in Kashmir and China were two very different things, however, a preliminary question to consider is how these different informants shaped Rashid al-Din's presentation. Indeed, this question feeds into the larger issue of what kind of Buddhism was actually being practiced in Il-khanid Iran. On one level, of course, the answer to this question is already known: the Mongols in Iran followed the lead of Khubilai Khan and adopted the Tantric Buddhism espoused by Tibetan lamas. Yet unlike Khubilai, who had allied himself with Sakya order of central Tibet,[102] Hülegü had established connections with the Kagyü suborders of the Drigungpa and Pakmo Drukpa. Beginning already in the mid-1250s he had started to financially support the monasteries of both these orders in western Tibet,[103] and throughout the thirteenth century the Il-khanid court maintained these relations by having an official stationed in western Tibet.[104] Thus it is very likely that when Gaikhatu Khan received the Tibetan name Rinchen Dorjé during his tantric initiation ceremony in 1291 it was presumably monks of the Drigungpa and Pakmo Drukpa orders who performed this ritual.

The Tibetan influence among the Il-khans is also borne out in the *Com-*

pendium of Chronicles as evidenced in its doxography, which presents tantric Buddhism as the supreme form of the Dharma.

> The followers of Sakyamuni fall into three groups; the first is known as Sravakas [i.e., Nikaya] and consist of the lowest class, the disciples; they seek only self-cultivation on account of the rigour of the Way shown to them by Sakyamuni. The second group are the Pratyekabuddhas [i.e., Mahayana], the middle group, who maintain that they liberate people from evil and help them. The third group, known as Samyaksambuddhas, claim to have attained the highest degree of perfection. They give right guidance to all creatures and perfect the imperfect souls: they raise people from the stage of animals and devils to the degree of the angels and holy spirits. They know and understand the secrets, commands, wisdom, arguments and revelations of Sakyamuni.[105]

In another section of the text the superiority of tantra is also made evident in the Buddha's response to a question about "what doctor and what medicine liberate people from all pain and torment?" To which the Buddha replies, "the doctor and also the medicine which cures all diseases is the perfect human being, who is called by Indian sages *Samyaksam-buddha*."[106] In this case, as in the passage above, *Samyaksambuddha* refers to tantric practitioners. Moreover, as Rashid al-Din explains elsewhere in the text these tantric masters come specifically from Tibet, as well as from among the Uygur and Tangut.[107]

As noted above, it was through these three groups that the Mongols initially came into contact with Tantric Buddhism and thus their presence in Iran makes sense. Unfortunately, however, while we have no evidence of Tangut Buddhists there is ample evidence of Uygur involvement at the Ilkhanid court. In fact, they are recorded as being active all over the Mongol empire in an array of administrative and religious capacities. Toqtogha Khan (r. 1290–1312 C.E.) of the Golden Horde of southern Russia, for example, supported Uygur Buddhists, and in the Chaghatai realm in Inner Asia the Uygurs were promoting the Dharma well into the fourteenth century as evidenced in a Sino-Uygur inscription from 1326 recording the restoration of a Maitreya temple.[108] Yet although we know Uygurs were widely influential among the Mongols, it is little understood how they actually impacted or influenced the Buddhism being practiced among the Mongols. Thus while it is well known that the Uygurs were involved in the early translation of Buddhist texts,[109] and also the development of the Buddhist canon,[110] it is little understood how the Uygurs actually shaped or defined the Buddhism of the Il-khanid court. Indeed, over time the Tibetans and their tantric Buddhism would come to dominate the Buddhism practiced by the Mongols so much so that the earlier role of the Uygurs and the Chinese, not to mention the Tanguts, would largely be forgotten.

Rashid al-Din, however, presents a different picture. His work reveals that there were numerous streams shaping Il-khanid Buddhism. Thus even though the *Compendium* lauds Tantric Buddhism as the supreme teaching it contains nothing that can be specifically identified as "tantric," much less "Tibetan." Rather, in presenting the Dharma Rashid al-Din and his informers draw almost exclusively on Sanskrit Nikaya and Chinese Buddhist texts. Yet before investigating the implications of this choice, we should begin by summarizing the general overview of the Dharma as presented in the *Compendium of Chronicles*, which has three main foci: the biography of the Buddha, the Wheel of Life, and the worship of Maitreya.

The Mongol veneration of Maitreya was already noted above in the description of Il-khanid religious life by the Armenian Christian Kirakos Ganjakec'i, and thus it is not surprising that it is also found in the *Compendium*. In fact, the chapter on Maitreya is the longest one of all those focusing on the Dharma. Even so, it presents us with nothing out of the ordinary in terms of the Buddhist worship of Maitreya since it is based entirely on a Sanskrit Nikaya text, the *Maitreyavya-karana*.[111] The same can be said of Rashid al-Din's presentation of the Buddha biography and the Wheel of Life. Namely, both are faithful reproductions of Buddhist doctrine.[112] The only exception is Rashid al-Din's unorthodox presentation of the Buddha's death, in particular, the claim of the Buddha being encased in a crystal tomb.[113] While the origin of this story is unclear, on account of its inclusion in Rashid al-Din's work it was to become a subsequent part of Muslim understandings of the Dharma. Thus, for example, in an illustrated version of Hafiz-i Abru's *Collection of Chronicles* (*Majma' al-tawarikh*), written for the Timurid ruler Shahrukh Khan in 1425, the manuscript illustrator actually represented the Buddha in a crystal mausoleum.[114]

Yet, besides this oddity, Rashid al-Din's presentation of the Buddha's biography is rather straightforward. In fact, his narrative deviates from the conventional narrative only when stories about the Buddha's previous lives are inserted in order to enhance the basic teachings about reincarnation and morality as represented in the Wheel of Life (figure 21).[115]

The Wheel of Life has been a part of the Buddhist tradition almost from the very beginning.[116] It was during his enlightenment experience that the Buddha visited the six realms of existence and came to learn not only about karma and how it causes one to be reborn into each of these realms, but also that all these realms, even heaven, involve some degree of suffering. As a result, the ultimate quest should be to break out of the cycle completely and not be born at all, which is, of course, Nirvana. On a more mundane level, however, the Wheel of Life is a foundational element in the Buddhist system of teaching about ethics. It explains how one's actions have karmic consequences resulting in particular rebirths, and it is this facet that takes up the bulk of Rashid al-Din's exploration of the Dharma. Chapters 8 and 15, for example, explore the increasingly better attributes of the numerous Buddhist heavens. Chapter 11, on the other hand, outlines *in extenso* the increasingly worse punishments one suffers in the eight levels of hell, while Chapter 12 has a long list of the actions that lead one to be reborn as a "hungry ghost." For example, those who exploit children will be reborn as ghosts who consume nothing but menstrual blood. Chapter 13 briefly lists the actions that lead one to be reborn as an animal, such as those of men who love their wives to excess and cannot be separated from them. They will be reborn as a tick on the teat of a milk cow. And finally, Chapter 14 describes the possibilities of achieving the highest birth, which is a human birth, since only then does one have the possibility to both change one's karma and practice the Dharma. To this end Rashid al-Din informs us that those who are generous and kind will be reborn into distinguished and rich families, while those who give to charity will not only be reborn noble and wealthy, but also have a long life and be loved by all. The builders of temples will be born with beautiful, healthy bodies and will be rich. Those who ridicule and slander others will be born blind, weak, lame, small, and full of infirmities.[117] And as for gender, men who are devoted husbands will always be reborn as men, while a philanderer will be reborn a thousand times as a woman.

Whether Rashid al-Din included all of this material on Buddhist notions of reward and punishment because it related somehow to Muslim notions of divine retribution is not known. Similarly, it is unclear whether the extensive focus on heaven and hell was on account of its coinciding neatly with the Islamic tradition.[118] Indeed, in this regard one can actually

Figure 21. Wheel of Life. Simtokha Dzong, Bhutan. Photo: Johan Elverskog.

wonder whether it resonated with Muhammad's famous journey to these realms during his night flight to Jerusalem, which was to subsequently become a favorite topic of Islamic painting as seen in the famous 1436 *Miraj Name* from Herat, Afghanistan (figure 22).

In looking at this image one can only but wonder about the possible parallels between Muslim and Buddhist visions of heaven and hell. Moreover, in the case of this particular painting one must also wonder about not only possible mythological similarities, but also very real Buddhist influences. Yet even though it is most likely the case that this painting of a multi-headed angel was based on Tantric Buddhist precedents, it is actually very difficult to tease out the possible linkages.[119] And it is the same with Rashid al-Din's focus on heaven and hell. Was it an attempt at making a link between the Dharma and Islam, or was it just presenting a fundamental aspect of Buddhism that is too often overlooked in the modern West?[120]

Either way, what is clear from the entirety of Rashid al-Din's presentation of the Dharma is that he was earnestly trying to make the Dharma comprehensible, and possibly even palatable, to a Muslim audience. One piece of evidence in this regard is how the Sanskrit sources used by the author(s) are translated. In general it is a rather direct and simple translation, but when there is a difficult Buddhist term its meaning is fully explained.[121] Moreover, in order to foster commonalities Muslim terms are often used in relation to Buddhist terms.[122] Thus the Buddhist demon Mara is called "Iblis." Similarly, when Mara/Iblis sends down his daughters to tempt the Buddha they are called *huris*, the beautiful maidens of Islamic lore. Similarly, in describing the Buddhist world the author(s) transpose common Muslim elements, such as when a hell realm is described as being for those who destroy madrasas or rabats. Or when the famous Jetavana grove of Buddhist lore is said to contain not only a "madrasa, khanaqah, sauma'a and a hospital," but also to be open to all "Sufis, Bakshis, and Dervishes."[123] Rashid al-Din also describes a Buddhist heaven in terms of the Garden of Eden, and in the best example of this sort of comparison he also explains the experience of Nirvana in relation to Sufi conceptualizations.[124]

Rashid al-Din and his informers were therefore trying hard to parallel the two traditions. And the most remarkable example of this endeavor is the attempt in Chapter 1 to present the Buddha as a prophet with a book, just like Muhammad and the Qur'an.[125] The question of whether a religious group had a prophet and/or a holy book had always been a part of earlier

Figure 22. Muhammad and the angel with seventy heads, from the *Miraj Name*, Herat, Afghanistan, 1436. (Manuscrit Supplément Turc 190, f. 19v). Reproduced by permission from Bibliothèque nationale de France.

Muslim taxonomies of Indian religions, and in this regard Buddhism had always come up lacking. In the hands of Rashid al-Din and his informants, however, a wholly new narrative of Indian religious history is presented. In this vision there is the same evolutionary prophetic progression as in Islam, albeit with Sakyamuni being the sixth and final prophet. The earlier prophets are Siva, Vishnu, and Brahma, each of whom created a religion named after themselves. The fourth prophet is called "Arhanta," but clearly refers to the Ajivakas, and the fifth is the materialist school of the Nastikas. Yet these were all false prophets. "Sakyamuni has called these gods devils, because of their arrogance, their self-exaltation and egotism."[126] The Seal of the Prophets in the Indian tradition is thus the Buddha, who possesses a book called the *Abhidharma*.

The *Abhidharma* is, however, not a book. Nor is it the teaching of the Buddha. In fact, of the three parts of the traditional Buddhist canon—the Buddha's Teachings (*Sutra*), the Monastic Code (*Vinaya*), and the Higher Teachings (*Abhidharma*)—the later is the only section that is expressly understood as not being the word of the Buddha. The *Abhidharma* is instead the collected works of the Buddhist exegetes who tried to make sense of the Buddha's teaching. Thus it is certainly odd that the *Abhidharma* is presented as the Prophet Sakyamuni's "Holy Book." Indeed, it would have made more sense to pronounce the Sutras as the Buddha's revealed scripture. Yet be that as it may, the issue of *Abhidharma* or *Sutra* was clearly secondary; more important was the attempt to draw parallels and links between Buddhism and Islam, which was done most ingeniously in Rashid al-Din's reconceptualization of Indian religious history within an Islamic framework.

Yet Rashid al-Din does not only present Buddhism within this new historical frame; he also tries to accurately portray Buddhist practice. Thus rather than using the Dharma as a vehicle to advance a theological agenda, or else simply repeating earlier observations in an encyclopedic fashion, Rashid al-Din offers us a view of the Dharma not seen in a Muslim source since the eighth-century work of ibn Khalid. Indeed, one of the more striking examples of this objective or "ethnographic" approach is found in his description of the consecration and worship of Buddha statues: "Sakyamuni said that the Exalted Creator had commanded temples to be built and images of Sakyamuni to be placed in them. At the times of prayer candles should be lit (before the images), perfumes burnt and the people should (come to) pray there. 'For verily, I must then appear there. Therefore make gifts to charitable institutions and give alms freely, for I will receive them all! And it is seemly that only pure gifts should be brought there by those who have severed themselves from their connections (with the world), so that I may appear there, may hear their invocations and grant their prayers. And of each one who prays in these temples I know the extent of his meritorious participation in it. Verily it can neither be calculated nor measured.'"[127] Unlike with Tha'alibi and the earlier fad for Buddha statues this passage reveals a new level of appreciation and understanding of Buddhist practice. Indeed, unlike in the earlier period when Buddha statues had been disassociated from their ritual context and thus approached solely as objets d'art, in this case Rashid al-Din presents an accurate and sympathetic awareness of Buddhist ritual.[128]

With this in mind we can return to the question raised above about what Rashid al-Din's work tells us about Il-khanid Buddhism as a whole. Indeed, based on his presentation of the Dharma and the sources he uses, what can we know about the nature of the Buddhism practiced in Iran? While we have already noted Rashid al-Din's connection with Tibetan Buddhists, and his use of Sanskrit Nikaya texts, it is also important to note that one of the most pronounced elements in the *Compendium* is actually Chinese Buddhism. Indeed, Rashid al-Din not only discusses three distinctively Chinese Buddhist practices, but also identifies their textual tradition. One of these is the worship of the Buddha Amitabha,[129] which is explained in terms of one of the key Chinese Pure Land texts, the *Guanwu liang shou jing*:[130] "And it is said that every man who recites the *Book of Amitayur* daily, dons a clean garment of white muslin and performs the daily ablutions, will live long and, when he dies, will be taken to Amitabha Buddha in the Paradise of Sukhavati. And every one who hears what is recited from this Book will also go to Paradise when he dies."[131]

The second Chinese element found in the *Compendium of Chronicles* is the worship of Guanyin, the Bodhisattva of Compassion,[132] which is based on the *Kārandavyūha Sūtra*, which was "translated by T'ien-hsi-tsai in 1000, [and] represents the height of Kuan-yin glorification."[133] "In this book it is said that Sakyamuni, when he became a prophet, sent [Guanyin] to hell, commanding him to purge it of those who were there. And he purged Hell of its inhabitants. And on his way there each part of the Hell-fire which he touched with his foot changed into roses and flowers. And when the inhabitants of Hell saw his face, they were all freed from the pains of Hell and entered into Paradise. And the guardians of Hell went to their chief and told him that someone had come to them who had redeemed Hell and who was able to take them to Paradise. When the chief guardians of Hell entered Hell and saw Guanyin they threw themselves before him and joyfully obeyed his commands."[134] Yet the most striking evidence of Chinese influence is borne out by an elaboration of the Buddho-Daoist worship of the Big Dipper. "It is said that he who recites this book and with lights and candles implores the stars, which he zealously worships, for help, will speedily have his wish fulfilled, whether it concerns a person or a thing, and that future trials and misfortunes will be spared him through the goodness of Allah the Exalted."[135] Although the worship of the Big Dipper had become an important part of the religious life of Yuan-dynasty China,[136] it is another question how and why it came to be present in Iran. Moreover, returning again to the question raised above, what does this Chinese influence tell us about Il-khanid Buddhism?

Let us begin with the first question. In doing so one can point out that the ties between the Il-khans and the Yuan dynasty were particularly strong and that there was much interaction between the two,[137] and as noted above Rashid al-Din had two Chinese informants.[138] Yet we should also recall that Rashid al-Din was himself very interested in the Chinese tradition,[139] and he himself had even translated a Chinese treatise on medicine into Persian, the *Tansuq Name* (figures 23 and 24). Rashid al-Din also had numerous Chinese artists working for him at the Rab'i Rashidi. Thus clearly there were numerous ways in which Rashid al-Din could familiarize himself with Chinese Buddhism in Iran.

Yet at the same time why should we assume these particular practices were Chinese? While today it is common to identify Pure Land Buddhism, the worship of Guanyin, and the worship of the Big Dipper with China, why should we do so in regard to the Mongol period? The Uygurs, for example, not only engaged in all these practices, but also had Turkic translations of the relevant texts.[140] In fact, by the mid-fourteenth century even the Tibetans had a translation of the pseudo-Daoist ritual text for worshipping the Big Dipper.[141] As a result, it is very possible that these "Chinese" practices were not only being performed by non-Chinese, but also from texts in languages other than Chinese. And one small piece of evidence that supports this idea is found in one of the stories about the Buddha's previous lives recounted by Rashid al-Din. Namely, in an earlier birth the Buddha was a merchant traveling by ship, and when a sea monster seized the hull he prayed, "*Namo buddhayah*." Upon hearing this phrase the sea monster

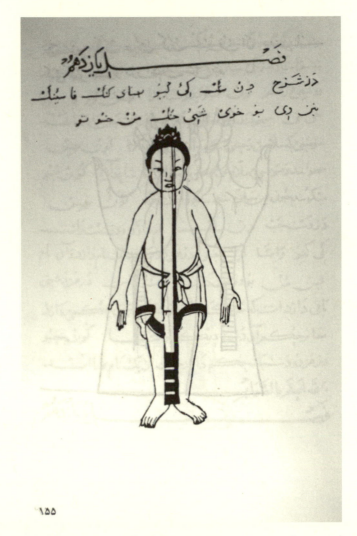

Figure 23. Body meridians in Rashid al-Din's *Tansuq Name*. After Mujtaba Minuvi's facsimile reproduction *Tanksūqnāmah yā Ṭibb-i Khatā* (Tehran, 1971).

remembered his previous human birth and how he had said the same prayer, thus he came to be filled with compassion and let the ship go.[142] While this story confirms again the link between the Dharma and the world of trade, what is of relevance here is the prayer, *Namo buddhayah*, which is a distinctive phrase found only in Central Asian Buddhism.[143] Of course,

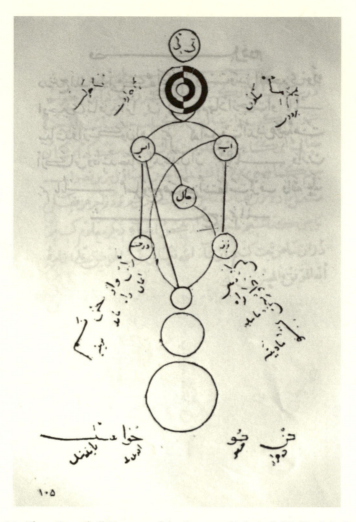

Figure 24. Zhou Dunyi's "Diagram of the Supreme Polarity" (*Taiji tu*) in Rashid al-Din's *Tansuq Name*. After Mujtaba Minuvi's facsimile reproduction *Tanksūqnāmah yā Ṭibb-i Khatā* (Tehran, 1971).

on one level this may seem like an insignificant piece of evidence and perhaps even a minor or irrelevant point; however, it is precisely such evidence that affords us a better picture of Il-khanid Buddhism.[144]

Moreover, the issue of Rashid al-Din's Buddhist influences also feeds into the larger historiographical problem of identifying the Dharma in relation to modern ethnonational units without much consideration of its implications.[145] Indeed, it is vital to recognize that Buddhist doctrines and practices were never tied to one "ethnicity" or "nation" and thus labeling them as such is inherently problematic. In the case of Il-khanid Buddhism, for example, evidence of tantra does not by definition mean a Tibetan presence. As Rashid al-Din makes clear it can mean Tanguts, or Uygurs, or Kashmiris; and the same is true of the "Chinese" practices of worshipping Guanyin and the Big Dipper. As we have seen these practices could just as well have been done by Uygurs and Tibetans, not to mention Mongols.

That said, however, there are two elements in the *Compendium* that can be attributed only to a specific Buddhist group. The first is the promotion of vegetarianism: "Concerning that which is allowed and that which is forbidden, he [the Buddha] said furthermore: 'Drink no wine, kill no animal for the sake of food and make not your stomach the grave of living creatures; neither kill harmful animals, insects and reptiles, for had they not been hurt in a previous form of existence, they would not do the same in this present existence.' "[146]Although vegetarianism is often linked with Buddhism in the modern imagination, the fact is that the Buddha never advocated it.[147] The prohibition against eating meat only appeared in late Mahayana texts and the idea was only fully adopted and put into practice in China and in the Buddhist cultures that followed its lead, such as Korea and Japan.[148] Nowhere else, however, is vegetarianism a part of Buddhist culture. The inclusion of this pro-vegetarian mandate in the *Compendium of Chronicles* thus actually confirms that there were Chinese Buddhists in Il-khanid Iran.

The second distinctive element in the *Compendium of Chronicles* confirms, on the other hand, a specifically Tibetan presence in Iran. Rashid al-Din, namely, concludes his description of Buddhism by claiming that the teachings of the Buddha are collected in a volume called the *Kanjur*,[149] which is a term that derives from the Tibetan *bka' 'gyur*—the "collected" (*'gyur*) "word" (*bka'*) of the Buddha. Since Rashid al-Din uses this term in reference to the Buddhist canon we must assume it came from a Tibetan source, via a Uygur or Mongol intermediary. At the same time, however, his use of this term is really not that simple since the *bka' 'gyur* itself was only then being created. In fact, the idea for creating a Tibetan Buddhist canon was only fully realized in the late thirteenth century as Tibetans became heavily involved with the Mongol court in China.[150]

The appearance of the term *Kanjur* in an early fourteenth century Persian history is thus surprising. For one, the fact that an idea just germinating in Beijing and Lhasa was already known in Tabriz gives one a sense of just how interconnected the eastern half of the Eurasian continent was during this period of time. Indeed, Rashid al-Din's awareness of a Tibetan Buddhist canon encapsulates the world of Buddhist-Muslim exchange ushered in by the *pax Mongolica*. Yet the Mongol empire brought together not only the Buddhist and Muslim worlds; it also brought together for the first time Buddhists of many different cultural backgrounds and religious affiliations. Thus in theory a Tibetan lama could talk with a Chinese Zen master as well as a Uygur devotee of Amitabha, which had never really been the case previously. As a result, when trying to answer the question raised above about the nature of Il-khanid Buddhism, the answer seems to reside in something like such a conversation. And it is precisely this rich Buddhist diversity of Il-khanid Iran that the *Compendium of Chronicles* captures. Unfortunately, it is precisely this complexity that is too often obscured when modern scholars try to make distinctions based on narrow definitions of either doctrinal affiliation or modern ethnonational identifications. Neither of these ideas were relevant to the Buddhists of Il-khanid Iran. Rather, the *Compendium* offers us a valuable perspective into the multifaceted complexity of the Buddhist community in Mongol Iran, and in doing so Rashid al-Din's work also reveals the interactions between Buddhists and Muslims that were possible on account of the *pax Mongolica*.

Mongol Visual Culture

The development of Persian miniature painting during the Il-khanid period is now well known and amply documented.[151] Perhaps less well known, however, is that for all its legendary importance in the history of Islamic art there is actually very little extant material from this period. In fact, there are only four groups of Il-khanid illuminated manuscripts.[152] The first comprises the early illustrated texts of the *Manafi' al-Hayawan* (*On the Usefulness of Animals*) from about 1290 and the 1307/1308 copy of al-Biruni's *Athar al-Baqiya* (*Chronology of Ancient Nations*).[153] The second group is Rashid al-Din's *Compendium of Chronicles*, pieces of which are now housed in various collections around the world.[154] The third group comprises four manuscripts of Firdausi's *Shahname* (*Book of Kings*), the so-called "little *Shahname*," that were produced in Baghdad around 1300.[155] The fourth and final group consists of an illustrated version of the *Miraj*

Name, Muhammad's journey through heaven and hell, and the later version of Firdausi's *Book of Kings*, better known as the Demotte or "Great Shahname."[156] Of course, there was a great deal more art produced during the Il-khanid period than these illuminated manuscripts;[157] however, since these works capture the essence of the changes that Islamic art underwent during this period they will be the focus of what follows.

In order to begin to unravel what these changes were and the possible role Buddhism may have played in them it is necessary to provide a starting point, and in this regard it is important to begin by pointing out that these Il-khanid paintings were not created out of whole cloth. As we have seen above there was already in fact a rather well-developed Islamic painting tradition when the Mongols arrived. Moreover, the famous Islamic prohibition against the representation of living beings had come under juridical scrutiny for more than a century. Scholars, for example, had observed that the Qur'an only forbids "idols," and since idols are presumably three-dimensional images it raised the question whether representations that did not cast a shadow were permissible.[158] While Muslim scholars disagreed on this point it was precisely such speculations that opened the door for the development of two-dimensional representational Islamic art in the twelfth century.

This was a momentous development because the Islamic prohibition against such art had largely been upheld since it was first instituted in the middle of the eighth century in relation to Jewish and Byzantine iconoclasm.[159] Indeed, it was because of these events that so much Islamic art came to focus on calligraphy or abstract ornamentalism rather than the representation of the animate world. As a result, an important question is why this radical shift happened when it did. Why in the second half of the twelfth century did the eastern half of the Islamic world undergo a "radical revolution in taste that affected all manufactured goods from books to buildings"?[160] One explanation can be found in the disunity of the Muslim world described above, which created an "equilibrium" that Marshall Hodgson has called "the victory of Sunni internationalism."[161] Namely, the "new territories of Anatolia and India had been conquered, the Crusades had been almost entirely repulsed, heterodox groups had weakened or were being incorporated into new political and intellectual syntheses, mysticism and orthodoxy were developing a symbiotic relationship, and, in spite of considerable bickering and fighting among various dynasties, the Ayyubids, Seljuqs of Rum or Kirman, Ghorids, Khorezmshahs, Kara-Khitays, and other locally based feudal kingdoms had settled into a certain equilibrium. The long rule of the caliph al-Nasir (1180–1225), the only imaginative and powerful 'Abbasid to reign after the second half of the tenth century, in many ways symbolizes what seemed a reasonable and satisfied state within the Muslim body politic."[162]

It was therefore within this particular moment in Muslim history on the eve of the Mongol conquests that a cultural explosion took place.[163] Representational art was thus not only being produced, but it was also suddenly fashionable and the urban bourgeoisie were sponsoring and buying such objects in order to confirm both their taste and status.[164] Indeed, the Islamic fascination with Buddha statues described above was one part of this phenomenon.

Yet Muslims did not only begin to appreciate and collect "idols" at this time; there was also a broader shift in Islamic artistic culture away from abstraction toward representation. Representational art was thus suddenly all over the Muslim world. It was in mosques, on tapestries, silks, ceramics, and in glass and metalwork. It was also in books, such as illustrated versions of the animal tales in the *Kalīla wa Dimna*,[165] and the Persian love story of Waraq and Gulshah.[166] Painting and representational art were also used to enhance the understandability of works on science like the *Book of Herbs* by Dioscorides and the *Book of Antidotes to Poison* by Pseudo-Galen.[167] Yet perhaps the most famous illustrated book from the pre-Mongol thirteenth century is Hariri's *Maqamat*, which drew its artistic inspiration wholly in both form and style from earlier and contemporary Byzantine art.[168] On account of this earlier explosion of Islamic representational art one can well wonder what the Mongols added to the mix. They cannot be credited with creating the Persian miniature since it had a long pedigree before they arrived. Nevertheless, one thing that the Mongols and the *pax Mongolica* offered were new influences far beyond neighboring Byzantium. Because of the huge expanse of the Mongol empire and the possibilities of travel that it fostered Il-khanid art came to include influences from places as far away as China and Italy. Indeed, it is precisely this Eurasian mix that makes Il-khanid art unique and it is for this same reason that it can rightfully be labeled as a distinctive Mongol visual culture.

Nevertheless, within the cosmopolitan crosscurrents of Il-khanid Iran, the Chinese influence was probably the greatest.[169] Yet as with the case of "Chinese" Buddhism one needs to be careful when tracing the Chinese influences in Islamic art because the actual number of Chinese in cities like

Tabriz was actually rather small. The Chinese influence was thus less the result of actual Chinese painters than local artisans adopting the new fashions that developed in Yuan-dynasty China, with which they became familiar through imported goods such as silk tapestries.[170] And within this dynamic of cultural and aesthetic appropriation and emulation the greatest lesson learnt was how to represent landscapes. Thus as Grabar has noted, "there are, for example, great artificial rocks framing spaces that are of different tonalities, oblique traces vaguely indicating folds in the terrain and suggesting separate planes within the space, small white clouds, tortuous and richly knotted trunks of trees; for the representation of certain animals, one notes the precision of drawing, done with a pen, variable tonalities in the modeling of bodies, and elegant movements" (figure 25).[171] Yet Muslim artists did not only emulate Chinese garden painting during this period, they also adopted another brand-new Chinese technique: the creation of continuous space.[172]

Of course, within this largely "Chinese" matrix of influences one can readily wonder what role Buddhism played. In trying to answer this question one can begin by looking for identifiable artistic traces. In doing so, however, it becomes quickly evident that the Buddhist influence is minimal. Moreover, none of the famous Il-khanid paintings described above is actually from the "Buddhist period" before Ghazan Khan's conversion in 1295. In fact, only one pre-1295 painting seems to represent a Buddhist, that of a monk partaking in an enthronement ceremony.[173] Even more problematic, though, is the fact that evidence of direct Buddhist artistic influence is limited—for example, the flaming halo and the similarity between the representation of Muslim angels and Buddhist apsaras.[174]

While such parallelism is by itself important and clearly confirms the presence of Buddhist influence on Islamic art, at the same time one can certainly wonder whether that was all.[175] Indeed, if that is all then the Buddhist influence does not seem to add up to much. Yet although this may be the case, it also seems as if it is approaching the question from the wrong angle. In fact, perhaps the question should not simply be about how many stylistic elements went from East to West or vice versa; rather, one should wonder about the particular environment that the Mongols fostered in which such new art forms could develop. And in this regard the role of Buddhism cannot be discounted, especially since it is such a profoundly visual tradition.[176] Thus even though the Muslim tradition had already moved in the direction of representational art this tendency was exponen-

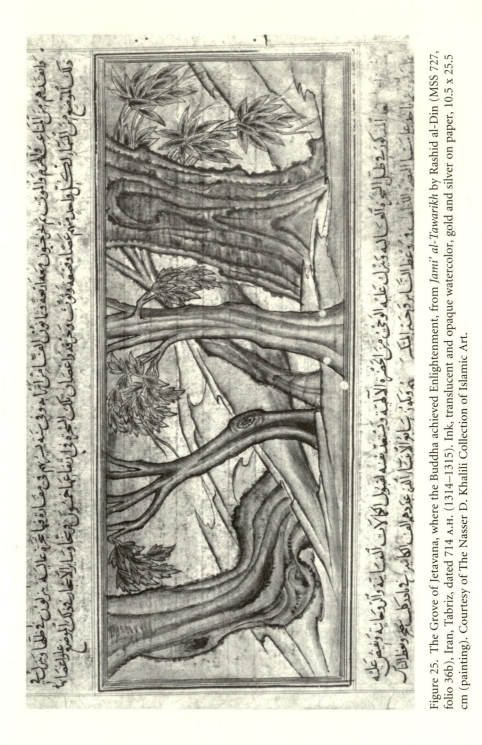

Figure 25. The Grove of Jetavana, where the Buddha achieved Enlightenment, from *Jami' al-Tawarikh* by Rashid al-Din (MSS 727, folio 36b), Iran, Tabriz, dated 714 A.H. (1314–1315). Ink, translucent and opaque watercolor, gold and silver on paper, 10.5 x 25.5 cm (painting). Courtesy of The Nasser D. Khalili Collection of Islamic Art.

tially enhanced when the Mongols arrived. And without a doubt the most profound development in this regard was the representation of the Prophet Muhammad, which had never been done in the Islamic world.[177] Moreover, after the heydays of the Il-khans and their Timurid successors it would never happen again. Rather, in fits of pious rage later Muslims would even deface the representational art of their ancestors (figure 26).[178]

The representation of Muhammad must therefore be seen as a distinctive element of Mongol visual culture, and a fundamental question is: How did it develop? In trying to answer this question the noted Islamic art historian Robert Hillenbrand has pointed out the Mongols' Buddhist background, which, in his words, "had accustomed them to religious images, and thus they had none of the traditional inhibitions of Muslims on this score. Indeed, they might well have wished to celebrate, indeed broadcast, their recent conversion by honoring the Prophet and singling him out in this way."[179] In his view it was therefore precisely the Buddhist context that fostered the development of Muhammad's representation, since Buddhists have no aversion to representing the Buddha in a range of formats. In Hillenbrand's view it was precisely the climate of visuality generated by the Buddhists in Il-khanid Iran that enabled Muslim artisans to finally breach the ultimate taboo: representing Muhammad. Yet while Hillenbrand's interpretation is certainly true I think we need to go one step further in order to fully appreciate the Buddhist influence on this development.

The main reason for doing so is that the portraits of Muhammad are not simply generic images arising out of Il-khanid Iran's Buddhist context, but rather they serve a particular purpose. In particular, all of the early Muhammad portraits represent specific Sunni or Shi'a interpretations of Islamic history.[180] Never before in the Islamic world had representational art been used in order to promote one's theology, yet that is precisely what happened in Il-khanid Iran. Competing Sunni and Shi'a groups actually used the visual medium in their efforts to promote their respective faith among the Mongols.

The central question is therefore: From where did they acquire this idea, or what did they use as a model? To answer this question we need to recall that the Buddhist tradition had long used visual culture as a means of propagating the faith. In particular, the Buddha had advocated the use of the Wheel of Life as a medium for teaching the Dharma.[181] The Buddha had in fact told his disciples to teach the Dharma using visual aids.

Figure 26. Princely feast, from the *Khamsa* of Nizami, Iran 1574–1575, with later iconoclastic alterations. © British Library Board. All Rights Reserved (IO Islamic 1129, fol. 29).

"I command all monks to paint a wheel of rebirth and death beneath the room at the gate of the temple."

At that time the various monks did not know how to paint one. The World-Honored told them: "Being careful of the proportions, draw an image of a circle. Place the hub in the middle and then place five spokes to represent the five paths. Beneath the hub paint hell, and on its two sides paint animals and hungry ghosts. . . . In the hub make a white circle and paint an image of the Buddha in the center. In front of the Buddha image paint three symbols. First make a pigeon to symbolize greed. Next make a snake to symbolize hatred. Last make a pig to symbolize delusion. . . . All around this you should then paint the Twelve Conditions and the signs of life and the extinction of life, which means ignorance, dispositions, and so on, up to old age and death. . . . Above the wheel make the Great Demon of Impermanence with disheveled hair and a gaping mouth. In his outstretched arms he holds the wheel of life and death. . . . Next, above the Great Demon of Impermanence, you should make a round, white altar, in order to symbolize the perfection and purity of nirvana. [Thus] as I have instructed, you should make a wheel of birth and death beneath the room at the gate. . . . You should [also] station a monk beneath the room at the gate and have him point out the reasons for the turning of the wheel of birth and death to all visitors and Brahmins. [Thus] as I have instructed, you should order someone to offer an explanation."[182]

On account of such directives the teaching and spread of Buddhism came to be intimately tied to visual culture and especially the Wheel of Life. Indeed, it is very likely that such techniques were used in Iran and one can even conjecture that it was precisely on account of such pedagogical techniques that Rashid al-Din came to use the Wheel of Life in his own presentation of the Dharma. While it is unfortunately unknown whether Rashid al-Din actually learned the Dharma by means of visual images of the Wheel of Life, it is certainly the case that the Buddhists in Iran promoted the linkage between visuality and theological explication during the Mongol period. And it was precisely this Buddhist technique that competing Shi'a and Sunni groups not only came into contact with in Il-khanid Iran, but also emulated. The appearance of the Muhammad portraits was thus not only a consequence of the Dharma's general acceptance of visual

representation, but also a Muslim adaptation of Buddhist visuality in order
to promote Islam.

It is also the case, however, that the development of the Muhammad
images was not simply a case of borrowing whereby one can easily trace the
arrows going from point A to point B. Rather, as is often the case in any
cultural encounter, it is far more complicated. Indeed, at about the same
time as the portraits of Muhammad were developing in Iran there also
arose a tradition of portraiture in the Buddhist painting of Tibet.[183] This
was something wholly new in Tibet and why it happened is still something
of a mystery. One possible explanation is that portraiture arose in tandem
with the explosion of competing Buddhist lineages in Tibet. Namely, portraiture was an effective means to visually differentiate different tantric traditions by means of painted genealogies. Thus the iconic but generic lamas
of earlier lineage paintings came to be replaced with actual portraits of the
teachers to facilitate recognition among the faithful. This development was,
of course, very similar to what was happening in Il-khanid Iran where both
Sunni and Shi'a were using distinctive representations of Muhammad in
order to both visualize and promote their competing theologies.

The simultaneous development of these two traditions invariably makes
one wonder if there were any influences. Moreover, in what direction were
they going, especially since the tradition of portraiture developed in the
west of Tibet, closer to the Muslim world?[184] Moreover, we should also
recall that the very reason Buddhism was developing in this border area
was because Buddhists were fleeing Islam. Yet as we have seen in the previous chapter this did not mean that all ties were severed. As a result, one
can certainly speculate whether there were artistic exchanges taking place
between Buddhist Tibet and the Muslim world at this time. Indeed, one
can wonder if the twelfth-century artistic explosion of the Sunni renaissance possibly influenced Tibetan art as well. Or was the artistic influence
going the other way? Was Muslim art of the period influenced by Tibetan
and Indian art?

While these are all important questions we do not at this point have the
answers. In fact, tracing such connections is often problematic as evidenced
in the two following paintings (figures 27 and 28). At first glance these
two paintings seem similar, and one can certainly wonder about possible
influences or borrowings. But in which direction, and how, and when? The
first one is from a mid-sixteenth-century *Falname* (*Book of Divination*)
and portrays the Shi'ite sanctuary consecrated to the footprint of 'Ali.[185]

Figure 27. Sanctuary for Ali's Footprints, attributed to Aqa Mirak, from a *Book of Divination*, 1550–1560 (1971–107/35a). Image © Musée d'art et d'histoire, Ville de Genève.

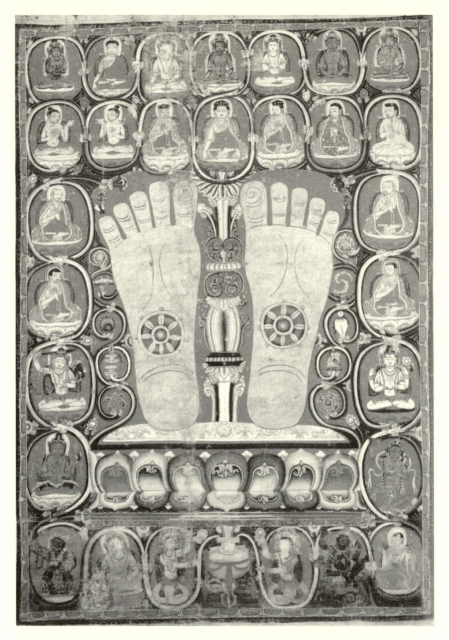

Figure 28. Thangka of the Footprints of Rangjung Dorjé. Private Collection,
Courtesy of Doris Wiener.

The second one is from the fourteenth century and portrays the feet of the Third Karmapa Rangjung Dorjé (d. 1339).[186]

Whether they influenced each other, however, is not the point to be addressed here.[187] Rather, the point of introducing them is to highlight the problem with some of the art-historical fixation on origins and borrowings. This is not to dismiss such transmissions as being unimportant. Clearly knowing that Muhammad's birth scene in the *Compendium of Chronicles* is based on Christian originals is vital to our understanding of Mongol visual culture.[188] But what needs to be further explored is the larger historical and cultural context in which such borrowings actually took place. Indeed, why in Il-khanid Iran was it suddenly possible for Muslim artisans to draw upon the Christian nativity scene to represent the birth of Muhammad?

The answer that numerous scholars and art historians have readily provided is simply the Mongols and the remarkable cross-cultural exchange made possible by the *pax Mongolica*. Yet scant attention has been paid to the role Buddhism played in these developments. Some of this oversight can no doubt be explained by the general absence of any mention of Buddhists in Muslim sources, which lead a generation of scholars to generally dismiss the possibility of any Buddhist impact on Il-khanid Iran. However, as one scholar has astutely observed, the fact is that Muslim scholars were actually "mortified into silence" by the overwhelming presence of Buddhists in the Muslim heartland.[189] Indeed, the reality was that the Buddhist presence in Iran was formidable even though evidence for it continues to be surprisingly sparse. Art historians, for example, seem to find more influence from Simone Martini and Lorenzetti in Il-khanid art than they do from Buddhism.[190] But in a certain sense looking exclusively at such Italian traces seems to be like looking at Mongol visual culture through the wrong end of a telescope. We need to turn the telescope around and realize that the whole glorious richness of Il-khanid art is largely the result of the Buddhist culture of early Mongol rule. Moreover, it was precisely this fact that the Mongols and everyone else wanted to forget as soon as they converted to Islam.

Yet if one is to truly understand Mongol visual culture one needs to go back to the earlier Buddhist context of Il-khanid Iran. This was a world where Mongol khans and the Persian and Turkic elite rubbed shoulders with Tibetan lamas and Sufi sheikhs, a world in which Sufi masters like 'Ala' ad-Dawla as-Simnani could declare the Dharma as being the same as Islam.[191] It was a world in which a charismatic Sufi like Baraq Baba could draw upon the new Tibetan Buddhist idea of incarnations and proclaim Öljeitü Khan to be a manifestation of ʿAli.[192] Indeed, it was in precisely such a world of Buddhist-Muslim interaction that Rashid al-Din was able to write a study of Buddhism that would be unmatched until the European discovery of the Dharma in the Age of Empire. In sum, it was precisely within the cosmopolitan Buddhist world of Il-khanid Iran that the distinctive Mongol visual culture developed that for the first time allowed the representation of the Prophet Muhammad.

This, however, is not to give all the credit to the Dharma. As with any complicated cultural encounter there were numerous factors involved and it would be a mistake to try to explain it all by means of one single factor. Rather, the aim here has been an attempt to bring the Dharma back into the equation in order to better understand what made Il-khanid art so distinctive. And in this regard one cannot solely blame modern scholars for minimizing the Buddhist role in the development of this Islamic visual culture. It was a fact that the recently converted Mongols, as well as their Muslim subjects, wanted to quickly forget, which they did. And to a certain extent this may in fact have been a good thing, because it subsequently allowed this artistic tradition to continue. Only when it was thoroughly dissociated from Buddhism could this new representational art live on among the Il-khanid's numerous successors, the Timurids, Safavids, Mughals, and Ottomans.[193] Of course, by then the Dharma and the roots of the tradition had long been forgotten,[194] and in its place there had arisen a new world where Buddhist-Muslim exchange was more often drowned out by calls for jihad. It is to this post-Mongol world to which we now turn.

CHAPTER FOUR

Jihad

Fight against such as those who have been given the Scripture as believe
not in Allah nor the Last Day, and forbid not that which Allah hath
forbidden by His messenger, and follow not the religion of truth, until
they pay the tribute readily, being brought low.

—Qur'an 9:29

As the living being (*sattva*) does not exist, the sin of murder does not
exist; and since there is no sin of murder, there is no regulation to forbid
it. . . . We commit no fault by killing the five aggregates that characterize
emptiness and are similar to dreamlike visions or mirror reflections.

—*Mahāprajñāpāramitopadeśa*

MUCH LIKE HIS Mongol ancestors the Sultan Sa'id Khan had a
drinking problem,[1] but even so he was a firm believer in jihad.
He "was always on the look-out to participate himself in holy
war, and his thirst and hunger were never assuaged by sending out military
expeditions every year to acquire heavenly reward."[2] Thus after becoming
sober in 1532 he launched a Muslim holy war against the infidels of Tibet.
Although this was not the first Muslim invasion of the roof of the world,
no one had envisioned as grandiose an invasion as Sultan Sa'id Khan,[3] who
wanted to march all the way to Lhasa and destroy its holy temple because
he believed it was the *qibla*, the direction of prayer, for all the Buddhists of
China and Tibet.[4] In his mind, taking the fight to Lhasa would greatly
advance the cause of Islam.

To this end the sultan began amassing his troops in late summer.
Although this was not the best of time year to launch a campaign onto the

high Tibetan plateau, his commanders and troops were ready and willing. For them nothing could have been greater. Having been forged in the ideology of jihad these battle-hardened soldiers cherished the idea of assaulting the Mecca of the infidels, as is well captured in the inspiring words of the commander who was to lead the jihad against Lhasa, Mirza Haydar—first cousin of Babur (1483–1530), Mughal ruler of India.

> Among the pillars and precepts of Islam, the chief pillar and firm basis is holy war. The Koran is eloquent in the excellence and necessity of holy war, and the sayings of the Prophet confirm this. Any act of worship that has the good quality of training the self and in which the self is exposed to death is necessarily beyond comparison with any other. In addition, for preserving the religion and spreading the community, under which holy war is subsumed, no other act of worship can be compared. Another good quality is that holy war is peculiar to the [Muslim] nation, and if it existed among the nations and communities of the past it was not of this sort. If occasionally others were commanded to undertake holy war, the only thing belonging to the infidels that was licit to them was their blood. Self-sacrificing lovers of the court of eternity and those allowed in honorable proximity to the court of the One always hope to attain the felicity of martyrdom in holy war.
>
> *If one could buy union with the beloved with the cash of the soul,*
> *everyone who possesses a soul would be searching for union with you.*[5]

Perhaps on account of these motivational words the invasion started out well. As Mirza Haydar and his three thousand troops moved into Ladakh in western Tibet they met little resistance. On September 2, 1532, they sent out a blanket invitation for everyone to convert: "*There is a general invitation to Muhammad's religion: happy the lot of him who enters it.*" Supposedly some locals complied; other "wretches," however, tried to resist. They were all put to the sword. Yet this initial success came to a halt as the winter started setting in. Moreover, word came that Sultan Sa'id Khan, who was leading two thousand troops into Tibet from Khotan, was suffering severe altitude sickness. He had been unconscious for days but still refused to give up the fight, declaring, "While there is yet life in me, take me to the field of war so that there may be a victory in my intention to carry out holy war."

When he heard this news Mirza Haydar had already been thinking about the coming winter, especially the lack of food and fodder for his troops and horses. Thus even though the khan's determination was inspiring, the decision to retreat was finally made. As they left Tibet and moved into lower climes the sultan recovered, and he then took his forces and invaded Baltistan. Mirza Haydar, on the other hand, led his army into Kashmir, which over the course of the winter he largely subdued. But when spring came and the mountain passes cleared Mirza Haydar and his army went back into Tibet. As before, their advance was met with both compassion and scorn. In one village the Muslim soldiers were given gifts. In another area, with particularly steep valley walls, they were attacked.

> Several times they threw stones from above and sent the forces of Islam tumbling down, but the Muslims tucked their shirts of valor into their belts of endeavor and kept their steadfast footholds on the mountain of holy war. In the end the breeze of Islam blew away the infidels' foundation, which had been like a mountain, and cast it to the winds like straw. Most were put to death, and the rest flight. Everything they possessed, animate and inanimate, fell to the Muslims.
>
> Thereafter unlimited fear and trembling fell into the hearts of the infidels of Tibet, and they offered all they had to save their own lives and of their children. All of the tribute from the Province of Purik, one of the major provinces of Tibet, was collected and divided among the soldiers. A few valuable items were selected for the Khan, and we set out for the Maryul [Ladakh] fortress.[6]

On the way to the fortress Mirza Haydar and his forces reconnoitered with Sultan Sa'id Khan, who had successfully conquered Baltistan, yet being at high altitude again the khan was feeling weak. He knew he could not make it to Lhasa and thus asked Mirza Haydar to continue the jihad without him.

> You will realize that I have always spoken sincerely and with purity of intent to conduct a holy war myself and to discharge honorably this thing, which is a duty upon all people of Islam, and to destroy the idol temple at Utsang [Ü and Tsang are the two main provinces that comprise central Tibet], which is the direction of prayer of all of Cathay. It has never been possible for any Muslim ruler to do

this, and no Muslim has ever reached that place. Moreover, my constitution will not now allow it. As much holy war as has been carried out in Tibet has been effected, even though I have constantly felt great illness within myself. Now, on my behalf, you must tuck the shirt of endeavor into the belt of holy war and proceed with the destruction. I shall return to my homeland, and I delegate to you the overall supervision of state matters. Leave me and your uncle, who are both old, in a corner of worship where we will be comfortable, and take the glory yourself. We will help you by praying for your welfare, and you will help me by doing a charitable deed.[7]

Thus on July 4, 1533, after having celebrated the Feast of the Sacrifice, Mirza Haydar took his horse's reins and set out toward Lhasa.

For twenty days he and his army saw no Tibetans. He presumed they were hiding in the forts they passed. But Mirza Haydar thought it best to not even try assaulting them since these forts situated on hills and cliffs seemed impregnable. Instead he decided to ride ahead with a small contingent to check the terrain. By the end of August Mirza Haydar had reached Purang where there was a large camp of nomads. Mirza Haydar and his forces attacked and seized 300,000 head of sheep, horses, and yaks as well as other valuable items. Then they settled down and waited for the rest of their forces to catch up. They never did. Mirza Haydar's other troops had tried to attack one of the forts. In response the Tibetans had requested help from an Indian raja, who had speedily sent three thousand Hindu infantrymen. As a result, the Muslim force was outnumbered. Yet inspired by the ideals of jihad the Muslims went into the fray undaunted. They were slaughtered to a man, including Mirza Haydar's beloved brother, Abdullah Mirza.

> The wine of the honey of martyrdom went down his throat.
> May it be licit, for he has gulped it down.
> There was I in the world with my dear brother,
> The matchless pearl on the string.[8]

Mirza Haydar wrote this verse upon hearing of his brother's death. But rather than wallowing in grief he decided to soldier on in his effort to bring the holy war to Lhasa.

Yet it was not to be. Shortly thereafter almost all his horses died from altitude sickness. Moreover, it was October, the winter was coming, and Mirza Haydar was far away from central Tibet. He therefore decided to retreat. By January his forces had made it to Guge and after being helped by the locals the Muslims pushed on. Nevertheless, by the time they reached Ladakh they had all suffered severe frostbite. Once again the locals helped them, even putting them up in a nearby fort for some time. Other Ladakhis, however, were not so welcoming, so after some of his men were killed Mirza Haydar therefore decided to move onto Zanskar in northern India, where word finally came that Sultan Sa'id Khan had passed away and that his successor Rashid Khan wanted the Tibet campaign to come to an end.

The Great Lhasa Jihad thus drew to a close with none of its stated goals having been achieved.[9] Even so, the entire episode captures well the tenor of the times and reveals how much had changed since the Mongol Empire period when Buddhists and Muslims had been interacting in a less hostile fashion from the steppes of southern Russia all the way to China. Indeed, with the collapse of the Mongol Empire the cosmopolitan world and the early modern form of globalization it had created had come to an end. In its place arose a very different world, one defined by an array of new political actors, states, and social groupings as well as new religious communities and reorganized economic networks.[10] Within all of these enormous changes, however, the one most relevant here was the development of a new divide between the Buddhist and Muslim worlds of Inner Asia—a world split into a Turkic-speaking Muslim half and a Tibeto-Mongol Buddhist half—which more often than not stared at each other with hostility across an ever-expanding gulf of incomprehensibility.

It was within this world that the Great Lhasa Jihad took place. Yet an important question is why this actually happened. In particular, why was the theory of jihad suddenly mobilized in the sixteenth century? At the outset it is important to recognize that this was something new. For more than half a millennium Buddhists and Muslims had been interacting and never had the idea of holy war been so actively deployed. Rather, as we have seen, Muslims had through the centuries approached the Buddhists in various ways but very rarely in terms of jihad. A fundamental question is therefore why did this change? What follows is an attempt to answer this question by looking at the larger political, economic, and social forces within which the religious ideology of jihad was forged and mobilized in post-Mongol Inner Asia.

Six Pieces of a Puzzle

Nearly every religion justifies violence to some extent. Most religious traditions have some form of "just-war theory," be it in self-defense or as a
legitimate means for spreading the faith. But at the same time very few
religions, if any, are always in a state of war. Rather, at some point there
invariably develops a certain level of equilibrium in which the existence of
other religions is not only recognized, but also made theologically acceptable. Thus, as we have seen, in the case of Islam the theory of jihad transformed as the expansion of the Arab Empire drew to a close, and thus not
only was the external battle against the infidels transformed into an internal
struggle, but also the final victory of Islam was postponed from the contemporary historical moment to the mythic end times. And as we have seen,
the main reason for this transformation was the changing historical situation within which Islam was operating. In particular, the end of Muslim
expansion required that the theory of jihad be reconceptualized.

In order to unravel the reappearance of jihad in the post-Mongol period
we need to elucidate the six major forces shaping this particular period in
terms of how they defined post-Mongol Inner Asian history: the appearance
of jihad rhetoric, the Chinggisid principle, political fragmentation, Islamization, urbanization, and Naqshbandi revivalism. Yet in addition to identifying the six elements shaping this period, we also need to choose a starting
point.[11] In this regard, let us begin with a place: the city of Turfan, an oasis
not only in the middle of Eurasia, but also one on the frontlines of Buddhist-Muslim interaction.

The city of Turfan and its environs had been taken over in the ninth
century by the Uygurs.[12] When they arrived, Turfan was inhabited by a mix
of people (Tocharians, Qarluq Turks, Chinese), practicing a mix of religions, but especially Buddhism and Nestorian Christianity.[13] The Uygurs
themselves were primarily Manichaean, but over time, as they settled into
the region, they too started to dabble with the local religions and ultimately
they came to favor Buddhism.[14] Concurrent with this religious transformation the Uygurs also changed their political structure. They abandoned the
idea of their leader being a "khan" and instead reimagined him anew with
the title "Idiqut," the Sacred One. Moreover, when the Qara Khitai established themselves in Central Asia the Idiqut submitted to the Western Liao.

In the beginning of the thirteenth century, however, when the power of
the Western Liao was collapsing, the Uygurs changed their allegiance. They

saw a promising future in a young leader named Chinggis Khan and submitted to him in 1209. The Uygurs were the first to willingly do so and
thus began their long career as the "steppe intelligentsia" of the Mongol
empire.[15] And on account of these strong connections between the Uygurs
and Mongols it is not surprising that the Uygurs' hometown of Turfan
became an important battleground of control between competing Mongol
rulers. And this competition had many consequences, including the collapse of the economy in the area, yet even so Turfan remained a strategic
asset.[16] And thus eventually the Mongol court in China decided that the
city should be included within the jurisdiction of the ruler of Dunhuang,
the so-called Prince of Xining, a key post in the empire that was always
filled by a member of the Mongol royal family.

In 1330 this position was given to Sulayman, who would later rule Iran
between 1339 and 1343. Before then, however, he was the Prince of Xining.
In that capacity he invariably had close relations with the Buddhist Uygurs,
and as the following poem reveals they praised him.

On Prince Sulayman who is respectful, wise, and of heavy merit,
On his special statements, which cannot be found in other people,
And his superior works, which make in peace more than all words
Let us tell more or less, just little by little.

Guarding his ancestor's rules extremely skillfully
Understanding the rules of other countries in detail
One who keeps respecting all nations
One did not exist before like this prince who is special and holy.

Loathing drinking too much alcohol (and considering it) as poison
And drinking a little in order to accomplish others' advantages
One who never neglects beneficial deeds at all times
Never existed one like this prince who is special and holy.[17]

Although this poem is fragmentary it captures well the nature of the *pax
Mongolica* as described in the previous chapter. In many ways it encapsulates the essence of that age in which Buddhists and Muslims met openly
with one another, interacted with each other, and also learned from one
another.

Of course, this may be reading too much into this poem. Nevertheless, the nature of Buddhist-Muslim interaction at this time is also reflected in another Uygur poem, which, in praising the Buddha, notes that even Muslims can generate good karma:

(Dharma is) in the power of meritorious deeds,
In these words of the former masters,
In the reward for previous good deeds,
Even if they were the work of Muslim Tajiks.[18]

The Buddhist Uygurs were thus well aware of Islam; however, at the time this did not by definition mean confrontation.[19] Indeed, the possibilities of Buddhist-Muslim interaction during the *pax Mongolica* is well captured in the further history of Sulayman's family. Namely, one of his descendants, Prince Asudag, sponsored the translation into Uygur of a Tibetan Buddhist *Book of the Dead*.[20] The reality of a Muslim prince requesting a Turkic translation of a Tibetan tantric text perhaps captures best the possibilities of Buddhist-Muslim relations during the Mongol empire.

Another example of such interaction, though one going in the opposite direction, is the Arabic astronomical handbook (*zij*) prepared in 1366 for Prince Radna by Khwaja Ghazi al-Sanjufini from Samarkand. At the time Prince Radna was the Mongol viceroy of Tibet resident in Hezhou in Gansu province. And although a Buddhist he was—like Khubilai and Hülegü before him—also interested in Islamic science. Thus in order to better understand al-Sanjufini's work he had parts of it translated into Mongolian and even glossed in Chinese and Tibetan.[21] Such linguistic dexterity captures well another component of the *pax Mongolica* that is often overlooked: the art of translation. Indeed, the remarkable transmission of goods and ideas during this period could hardly have been possible if people could not communicate with each other. Thus it is not surprising that in order to facilitate communication numerous dictionaries were prepared during the empire period.[22] And surely the most remarkable of these was the six-language dictionary (Arabic, Persian, Turkic, Mongol, Greek, Armenian) prepared in 1360 by order of Sultan al-Afdal al-Abbas, the ruler of the Rasulid dynasty of Yemen. At the time Yemen was a key hub in the Eurasian maritime trade network and thus the 1,200-word *Rasulid Hexaglot* was less about the possibilities of translating tantric Buddhist texts into Arabic or Islamic scientific tracts into Mongolian and more about easing linguistic confusion in order to foster international commerce. Even so, it is still important to recognize that all of these endeavors were part of a whole: namely, interest in the languages and ideas of others, as well as the possibility of actually engaging with them in any meaningful way, was part and parcel of the economic boom made possible by the integration of Eurasia under the *pax Mongolica*.

Of course, this is not to suggest that there is a simple connection between political consolidation, economic prosperity, and intellectual and cultural openness. Or that one should simply take the next logical step and assume that everyone should have loved the Mongols and appreciated them for what they made possible. Invariably, as with any empire, many people chafed under the "Mongol yoke" regardless of what benefits they may have accrued at the time,[23] or what we can look back on and deem in hindsight as having been good for them. My point here, however, is not to defend or critique the dynamics of empire; my aim is more limited. It is simply to highlight the fact that such interaction as we have seen in Il-khanid Iran or in the area around Turfan in the mid-fourteenth century was all very much a part of the Mongol imperial world, and more to the point, it was this world that was rapidly coming to a close.

The collapse of the Mongol empire and its numerous consequences, from political fragmentation to economic contraction and increased religious friction, is a rather well-worn story.[24] Nevertheless, it is obviously a vital one if we are to understand the development of Buddhist-Muslim relations in the post-Mongol period. To this end let us return to Ghazan Khan's conversion to Islam in 1295, which above and beyond its obvious religious implications was also to have profound political consequences. In particular, once he was proclaimed as the Padishah-i Islam, the world ruler of Islam, questions invariably arose about the arrangement whereby the Il-khan, the "subordinate khan," was to serve under the "Great Khan" ruling in Mongolia and China. This arrangement, whereby several lesser khans ruled domains across Eurasia while simultaneously being subservient to the "Great Khan" in the East, was how the Mongol empire was supposed to function. And invariably the origin of this system—as with everything else Mongol—was traced back to Chinggis Khan, who had reportedly imagined such a family-based system when he divided the world among his four sons into the so-called Four Ulus. Jochi, the eldest, was given southern Russia; Ögedei inherited China; Chaghatai received Central Asia; and Tolui, the youngest, was, according to Mongol inheritance custom, given "the hearth," or Mongolia.[25] Yet Chinggis Khan's purported division of the world among his heirs was in a reality a grandiose fiction since he had not conquered all of this territory by the time of this death (map 14).

Indeed, the "Mongol Empire" as it is commonly understood was actually formed during the campaigns of conquest carried out by Chinggis Khan's successors, especially Ögedei and Möngke (map 15). Moreover, it was only in the wake of these conquests that the idea of the Four Ulus was put into practice in tandem with the notion that the three rulers of all the "lesser" Ulus were subordinate to the "Great Mongol" ruler in China. In many ways, however, this system was just as much of a fantasy as the original story of Chinggis Khan divvying up the world and bequeathing it to his heirs. Indeed, the common idea of the Mongol Empire as the "world's largest land empire in history" and readily represented on world maps as a contiguous entity stretching from Korea to Poland is something of a misconceptualization since the "empire" was never as unified as such a vision would lead us to believe.

The Jochid Ulus, or Golden Horde, in southern Russia, for example, had virtually no relations with the "Great Khan" throughout its history. The tone between these two realms was in fact set when the Jochid ruler

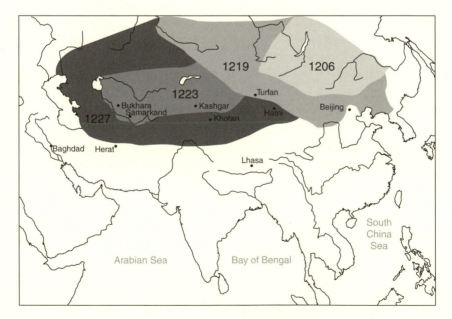

Map 14. Chinggis Khan's conquests.

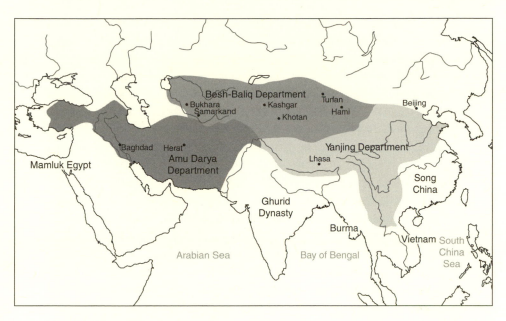

Map 15. Mongol Empire in 1250.

Batu Khan (ca. 1205–1255) refused to return to Mongolia in order to attend the *quriltai* in 1229 that elected Ögedei as Great Khan. Moreover, the Jochids were the first Mongols to convert to Islam.[26] Over time the Jochids therefore moved further away from the Mongols in the East as they came to be drawn more and more into the orbit of the Islamic world, a development that was greatly spurred on by the Golden Horde's involvement with the slave trade that supplied soldiers to the Mamluks of Egypt.[27] As a result, the connections between the Jochid Ulus and "the East" became ever more tenuous.

Yet even more pressing was the fact that the Golden Horde's extensive financial dealings with the Mamluks also put them increasingly at odds with the Il-khans, who were for decades fighting the Mamluks over control of Syria and the Holy Land.[28] The fighting that thus eventually erupted between the Il-khans and the Jochids was the opening salvo in the ultimate disintegration of the Mongol Empire into wholly separate entities. Yet besides its foreshadowing of the political fissures to come, what is of particular relevance about this episode is how it was framed within the discourse of jihad.

In the previous chapter we already came across one of the most famous exponents of jihad, Ibn Taymiyya, and in this regard we should recall that his *fatwa*s legitimating the killing of both Muslims and innocents in the name of Islamic Holy War were issued specifically in reaction to Il-khanid incursions into Syria. But Ibn Taymiyya was not the first to advocate jihad within the context of these conflagrations in the Levant. Much earlier the Mamluk ruler Baybars al-Bunduqdari (1260–1270) had tried to mobilize Muslim resistance against the Mongol advance into his domains by calling for a Holy War against the Buddhist Il-khans. Moreover, after the Jochid ruler Berke Khan had converted to Islam the Mamluks called upon the Golden Horde to join them in jihad against the infidel Hülegü, who the Muslims mistakenly thought was a Christian.[29] Whether this confusion arose on account of the Il-khan's overtures to the pope, and their hope that the Christians would join them in a "Crusade" against the hated Mamluks, is unclear.[30] Nevertheless, while Berke Khan was probably better informed about Hülegü's Buddhist proclivities, in his letters to the Mamluk court the question of religion was never really his concern. For him, a more pressing issue was the fact that both he and Hülegü were Mongols. They were both direct descendants of Chinggis Khan and the idea of Mongol unity still loomed large. As he lamented upon seeing the carnage after the Il-khan's defeat in Syria, "Mongols are killed by Mongol swords. If we were united, then we would have conquered all of the world."[31]

Two years later, however, the Golden Horde abandoned any notion of Mongol unity and adopted instead the rhetoric of jihad. How religiously motivated this decision was, though, can be debated. What seemed more pressing for the leaders of the Golden Horde were financial concerns. Namely, the Il-khans wanted the Jochids to stop the slave trade with Egypt since Turkish slaves directly supported the Mamluks' military power. Complying with this Il-khanid request, however, would have put an end to the Golden Horde's main engine of economic growth. Thus they refused. To make matters worse, the Jochids were also furious about Il-khanid claims to the territory of northern Iran and its economic resource base. On account of both these factors the Jochids' earlier vision of Mongol brotherhood eventually fell by the wayside and in its place arose a Muslim–non-Muslim divide.

That Muslim identity came to trump Mongol identity in these wars, especially with its rhetoric of jihad, is thus the first piece in our puzzle of explaining the fractious religiopolitical landscape that defined post-Mongol

Inner Asia. The second piece, while related to the first, is, however, something entirely different: the so-called "Chinggisid principle." This idea held
that a ruler—especially one who took the title khan—had to be a direct
descendant of Chinggis Khan. While this principle was to become a particularly sensitive issue for subsequent Mongol and Turkic leaders who arose
in the wake of the Mongol empire, for the immediate Mongol generations
after Chinggis Khan a more pressing concern was who could rightfully
claim the title "Great Khan," and thus hold supreme power. As is well
known Chinggis Khan wanted his third son Ögedei to succeed him. His
eldest son was out of the question because he was not his own. During
Chinggis's rise to power his wife had been kidnapped and raped, and Jochi,
which means "guest" in Mongolian, was the result. Chinggis Khan's second
son was his own, but he was erratic and a drunk to boot. Tolui was too
young and thus Ögedei was the chosen one. And in many ways it was a
good choice; however, his reign was short and when he died with no clear
successor family feuds erupted. After years of dissension, with powerful
Mongol women working behind the scenes to push their children or husbands into the top position, Möngke finally became Khan. He was the eldest
son of Tolui. In other words, the lineage of Tolui had out-maneuvered the
lineage of Ögedei and thereby set the "Chinggisid Principle" on a slippery
slope.

After Möngke's death the Toluid claim to the title of Great Khan did
not go unchallenged. Qaidu (1230–1301), the grandson of Ögedei, in particular, carried out a thirty-year war against the Toluids in order to restore
the lineages of both Ögedei and Chaghatai.[32] Unfortunately, he had formidable adversaries in Tolui's other two children—Khubilai and Hülegü—
founders respectively of the Yuan dynasty in China and the Il-khans in
Iran. Thus while Qaidu may have lost the war he was able to carve out for
his descendants a territory in Central Asia, which was to become known as
the Chaghatai Ulus. And along with the three other Ulus—the Yuan
dynasty, the Il-khanids, and the Golden Horde—these four groups compose what we now know as the Mongol Empire (map 16).

Yet as has been made clear by this brief historical sketch, the very creation of these Ulus was not one of imperial unification.[33] Rather, the very
creation of the Mongol Empire was one of conflict and separation. Indeed,
at no point did there exist a massive unified empire that was then conve-
niently divided up among the descendants of Chinggis Khan as the map
above and later histories would lead us to believe. Instead, the formation of

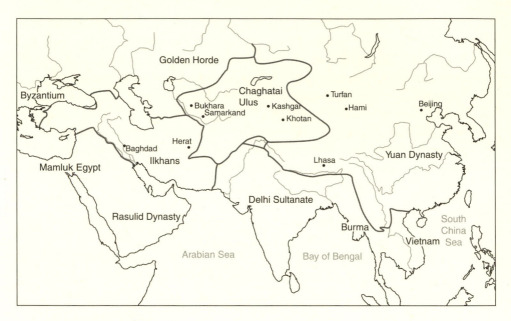

Map 16. Four Ulus.

the empire was always one of conflict and the forces of disintegration. As a result, one can almost say that the Mongol Empire as it is often conceived is largely imaginary. This, however, is not to suggest that there was no Mongol conquest or *pax Mongolica*;[34] or that ambassadors and taxes never moved between the Ulus as if the empire was unified;[35] or that the Mongols did not have a theory about a unified realm under Mongol power.[36] These things happened and the Mongols did have a theory of empire. But theory is not practice and thus we need to recognize that the very creation of the Mongol Empire as manifested in the Four Ulus was one of confrontation and disunity. And the reason this needs to be stressed is because it is the third piece of the puzzle. Namely, not only had theories of jihad against non-Muslim Mongols already been mobilized in the late thirteenth century, but also the coming political fissures of the post-Mongol world, and its relation to the Chinggisid principle, were built into the very structure of the Mongol Empire itself.

With that in mind let us turn to the fourth piece of the puzzle: Islamization. In particular, the conversion of the Chaghatai Ulus, since it was the area sandwiched between the Islamic West of the Golden Horde and Ilkhanids, and the non-Islamic East of the Yuan dynasty. Of course, nowadays the area of the Chaghatai Ulus is largely Muslim, but that was not the case in the fourteenth century. The rulers of the Chaghatai Ulus in fact continued to support the Dharma for several decades after Ghazan Khan's conversion of 1295. In 1339, for example, the Chaghatai ruler Yisün Temür issued a decree for the protection of the Yogacari Buddhist monastery.[37] Yet why the Chaghataids continued to support the Dharma is little understood; however, there were certainly several valid reasons to do so. One was quite simply the Chaghataids' desire to differentiate themselves from the Mongol Muslims of the West. Such a strategy may also have helped in restoring their frayed relations with the Yuan dynasty after Qaidu's thirty-year war. Indeed, with the Yuan dynasty becoming the most powerful player in Eurasia, it probably made sense to stay aligned with them.

Beyond such immediate political and economic concerns the Chaghataid rulers also had to contend with the legacy of their own lineage. In particular, they had to answer the question of what it meant to be a Chaghataid—a descendant of Chaghatai. What defined them, or set them apart from, the other Chinggisid lineages and their distinctive realms?[38] The answer the Chaghataids came up with was that they were the last, true Mongols. They had not become Muslim like the Golden Horde or Il-khans, nor had they become sinified like the Yuan Mongols. Instead they continued to follow Chinggis Khan's law code, the *jasaq*, not the *shariʿa* or Chinese law. The implications of this decision were clearly numerous, but one that needs special mention here is the Chaghataids' focus on Chinggis Khan's declaration that he ruled "the people of the felt-walled tents,"[39] which resulted in the Chaghataids refusing to give up their nomadic ways and adopt urban life as had their Mongol brethren in both China and Iran.

In sum, it was this claim that they were the last true nomadic Mongols that came to define the Chaghataids. Moreover, as one would expect they came to see all of these particular attributes in the life of their ancestor Chaghatai, who had famously been the staunchest supporter of Chinggis Khan's law code, which had in many ways come to define "Mongolness," much as the *shariʿa* defined what it meant to be Muslim. And in this regard, Chaghatai had not only upheld the *jasaq*, but in doing so he had also repeatedly persecuted Muslims since the *shariʿa* contradicted Mongol law.[40] As a result, if Chaghatai was known for anything in the Mongol historical imagination it was for being anti-Muslim.[41] Thus once Chaghatai came to symbolize "Mongolness," and a rejection of Islam, for the Chaghataid rulers it was clearly difficult to turn around and embrace the Muslim faith.

In addition to this ideological problem the Chaghataid khans also had to deal with two further issues. The first and most pressing was quite simply their own weakness. After the death of Qaidu Khan the Chaghataid Ulus was led by a series of weak and ineffectual rulers. Indeed, this legacy was to plague the Chaghatai Ulus over the coming centuries. Local rulers therefore continually challenged central authority and fratricidal wars invariably erupted after the death of a khan; and during the first decades of the fourteenth century the situation was particularly acute. Thus even if one of the earlier Chaghataid Khans had wanted to convert to Islam, he would have had to have first dealt not only with the issues noted above, but also an entrenched Buddhist order on the local level. For example, the Buddhist Uygurs in Turfan had enormous power not only locally, but also at the highest levels of power in both the Yuan dynasty and among the Il-khans.

It was an account of all these factors that the Chaghataid Khans continued to support the Dharma well into the fourteenth century. In 1331, however, a recent Muslim convert named Dharmashri took the Chaghataid throne.[42] Why he converted is somewhat of mystery, though again it is very likely that political and economic reasons played a role. Dharmashri, for example, recognized that adopting Islam would bolster his support among the Central Asian Muslims within his realm and thereby strengthen his power as khan. Being Muslim would also open up trade relations with the Islamic world, which if the economy improved would also bolster his political standing. And in fact we know that Muslim merchants from Syria, Egypt, and the Delhi Sultanate visited the Chaghatai Ulus once Dharmashri was khan.

Even so, Dharmashri's reign was a complete failure. Three years later he was killed while trying to flee to India. What went wrong? The gravest mistake Dharmashri committed was that he openly favored *shari'a* over the law code of Chinggis Khan. The problem of reconciling these two legal systems had always been a thorny issue for Mongol converts, and most often the solution had been to create some form of balance, or accommodation between the two.[43] Of course, not everyone agreed with such compromises. Ibn Taymiyya, for example, accused the Mongols of being false Muslims precisely because of such accommodations. Dharmashri, on the other hand, was accused by his Chaghataid brethren of forsaking the sacred Chinggisid code.

Yet Dharmashri was run out of town not only on account of this violation of the Chaghataid order. Another issue was that his pandering to Islam did not sit well with all of his constituents. While it may have played well in the Central Asian western half of the Chaghataid Ulus—in Bukhara and Samarkand—his avid promotion of Islam met with resistance in the non-Muslim eastern half of his realm, which remained staunchly Buddhist into the late fourteenth century.⁴⁴ And they were the ones who deposed Dharmashri. Moreover, after his death those Chaghataids of the eastern half of the realm put on the throne one of their own, Jankeshi (r. 1335–1338), who, according to Muslim sources, was not only a devout Buddhist who built temples, but also had Buddha statues put into mosques.⁴⁵ In other words, he turned mosques into Buddhist temples.

The case of Jankeshi Khan thus reveals not only the tenacity of the Dharma in Eastern Turkestan, but also the growing rift between the two halves of the Chaghatai Ulus. But the Buddhist-Muslim divide only partly explains this split. On a certain level the topography of the region naturally lends itself to such a division and thus it is perhaps unsurprising that political, economic, and religious networks developed that conformed to this landscape. Yet in the case of the eventual breakup of the Chaghatai Ulus into the Timurids in Central Asia, and the Moghuls in East Turkestan,⁴⁶ there is one further environmentally related factor that needs to be taken into account. By making nomadic pastoralism a defining feature of "Mongolness" the Chaghataids were not only bound to a region with suitable terrain, but they were also bound to resist urbanization. As we have seen in Chapter 1 the process of urbanization brings with it enormous social changes, and it was precisely these changes the Chaghataids wanted to resist. The Timurids, on the other hand, adopted wholeheartedly the urban culture of Islamic Central Asia, and these decisions invariably had consequences.⁴⁷ Indeed, it is for this reason that urbanization is the fifth piece of the puzzle.

The first consequence of these different approaches to urbanization inevitably caused the two halves of the Chaghatai Ulus to grow further and further apart not only politically, but also culturally and religiously. In particular, while the Timurids quickly became part of the cosmopolitan Islamic world of Central Asia and thereby created some of the greatest architectural monuments in history, the Moghuls—on account of their obstinate resistance to the lure of the city—avoided not only this urban cultural world, but also its religious world as well. Indeed, when the Moghul

khan Tughluq Temür (d. ca. 1363) finally adopted Islam in 1354 he did not
align himself with a famous Sufi sheik from Central Asia's urban world, but
rather Jalal al-Din and his son Arshad al-Din, local Sufi masters from the
town of Lop Katak.[48] Why Tughluq Temür did so is little understood, but
certainly one factor in this decision was precisely because the Kataki were
not prominent Central Asian Sufis and thus did not bring with them any
urbanizing demands. Instead, the Kataki, who descended from a prominent
family of Hanafi jurists from Bukhara that had been deported by Chinggis
Khan to Qaraqorum and then settled in Lop Katak, had over the centuries
lost their connection with Central Asia and its deep roots in urban Muslim
culture, and thus they had no doctrinal demands tied to the forces of
urbanization.[49] Indeed, they did not need madrasas, or the many other
institutional aspects of urbanized Islam, and this suited the Moghuls well.
As nomads they had no need for such things; indeed, if anything they saw
such things as a degeneration of their "Mongolness." As a result, the Kataki,
who allowed the Moghuls to practice a form of "nomadic Islam," were a
perfect fit for the descendants of Chaghatai.

Of course, making such an alliance with the Kataki and maintaining
their nomadic traditions had numerous intertwined political, economic,
and religious consequences. Most notably it further alienated the Moghuls
from the Timurids and their particular urban Sufi traditions. Moreover, the
Moghul practice of "nomadic Islam" also had an unintended consequence,
which was that it allowed Buddhism to continue to flourish under Moghul
rule. The reason this happened was that Buddhism and Islam were both
fundamentally urban religions, and thus it had historically been in cities
that they either interacted or else came into conflict. This common
dynamic, however, was altered on account of the Moghuls' "nomadic
Islam." Since they had no interest in cities the Buddhist urban centers of
the Silk Road were largely left alone as long as they paid their taxes to the
Moghul dynasty.

Thus the fact of the matter is that for two generations after the Moghuls
converted to Islam there was relative peace between the Muslims and Buddhists in Eastern Turkestan. One Muslim traveler, for example, who passed
through the area noted that Buddhist monasteries and mosques stood side
by side: "On the 21st of Rajab [August 2] they reached the town of Qamul
[Hami]. In this town Amir Fakhru'd-Din had had built a magnificent
mosque, facing which they had constructed a Buddhist temple of a very
huge size, inside which there was set up a large idol. On the left and right

sides of which there were considerable number of smaller idols. Just in front of the big idol there stood a copper image of a child of ten years of age of great artistic beauty and excellence. On the walls of the building there were frescoes of expert workmanship and exquisite colored paintings. At the gate of the temple there were statues of two demons which seemed ready to attack one another."[50] The same situation was also recorded in Luo Yuejiong's *Record of Tribute Guests* (*Xian bin lü*), which notes that "In Lükchün [in Eastern Turkestan] . . . live two kinds of people: Muslims and Buddhists."[51] This peaceful situation, however, was to come to an end.

The reason for this was the appearance of the Naqshbandi Sufi order, which was to ultimately displace the Kataki order among the Moghuls. And one of the reasons the impact of this new Sufi order in Inner Asia was so profound was that the Naqshbandiyya were from Central Asia, and thus brought with them religious practices that derived from an urban milieu. As a result, after a century of resistance the Moghuls eventually fell under the sway of urbanization and started settling down in the cities of the Tarim Basin during the fifteenth century. But the promotion of urbanization was not the only innovation that the Naqshbandiyya would bring to Inner Asia. In fact, they would profoundly influence the entire subsequent history of the region and thus they are the sixth and final piece of the puzzle.

The Calm Before the Storm

To connect all of these developments into a coherent whole let us step back and look again at the larger picture. In particular, we need to recognize that the Buddhist-Muslim détente of the late fourteenth and early fifteenth centuries cannot be explained solely by events unfolding within the borders of the Chaghatai Ulus. Two other factors shaping the situation in Inner Asia were the simultaneous collapse of the Yuan dynasty in China and the rise of Tamerlane (1336–1405), the founder of the Timurid dynasty (1405–1507), in Central Asia.[52]

The fall of the Mongols in China in 1368 should not have surprised anyone. The dynasty had in fact been wracked by political paralysis and economic malfeasance ever since the death of Khubilai Khan in 1294. At the root of many of these problems lay the same question faced by the Chaghataid Khans: should the Yuan rulers maintain their Mongol ways, or else adopt the imperial and cultural practices of China? On one side of this debate stood the powerful Turkic and Mongol military elite and on the

other the entrenched Chinese bureaucracy, and both of these forces operated behind the scenes promoting their competing agendas through a series
of young, incompetent, and politically beholden emperors.[53] The most ludi-
crous example of this dynamic was the six-year-old Rinchenbal, who in
1332 was accepted as a compromise candidate by the Turkic general El
Temür and the Empress Dowager Budashiri. After being put on the throne
he passed away fifty-three days later.[54]

Yet even before Rinchenbal's inglorious tenure Mongol rule was woefully unstable. In the previous twenty-five years six different emperors had
graced the Yuan throne, all promoting the competing agendas of their powerful political backers.[55] And this tradition continued apace as Rinchenbal's
successor, Toghan Temür—the last Mongol ruler of China—took the
throne in 1333. He was the grandson of Khaisan Khan (r. 1307–1311), who
had himself promoted a steppe-oriented policy. He had even ordered a new
capital, Zhongdu, to be built on the steppes north of Zhangjiakou on the
Mongolian plateau. But when he passed away his designated heir, Buyantu,
completely reversed these policies and promoted instead a Chinese agenda.
Most notably in 1313 Buyantu reinstated the Neo-Confucian–oriented civil
service exam. Moreover, he also ordered the codification of the Yuan
dynasty's laws based on Chinese precedent, which was completed in 1324
with the 2,400 legal documents of the *Da Yuan Tongzhi*.[56]

It was in the nexus of these competing Turko-Mongol and Chinese
forces that Toghan Temür had been perceived as a threat. At the age of ten
he had therefore been exiled to an island off the northwest coast of Korea.
He was then moved to Guangxi in the far south of China. Upon Rinchenbal's death, however, Toghan Temür's supporters outflanked El Temür and
put him on the throne. Since he was only thirteen, however, the real power
was in the hands of others and they set about promoting their "pro-China"
policy, which in turn was invariably challenged by the "pro-Mongol" side.
But Toghan Temür's reign was not only beset by these political and ideological feuds; the dynasty as a whole was also challenged by massive environmental problems, including famines resulting from the flooding of the
Yellow River and outbreaks of disease that killed enormous numbers of the
population in the 1350s. These disasters gravely impacted the economy as
whole, and in response the government tried to solve the problem by printing money, which invariably drove up inflation and only made the situation
worse. The inevitable response to this perfect storm of political paralysis,
environmental disaster, and economic collapse was revolution, and as was

often the case in China the revolution was framed in apocalyptic religious terms. Fired up with Buddhist messianic visions, groups like the Red Turbans rose up against the Yuan. Ultimately, however these various groups were eventually to merge with other rebel movements under the able leadership of Zhu Yuanzhang, a former Buddhist monk and devotee of Maitreya, who led these revolutionaries on a northward march to expel the Mongol rulers. On September 10, 1368, they were victorious and Zhu Yuanzhang (r. 1368–1398) was declared emperor of the Ming dynasty (1368–1644).

For their part, Toghan Temür and his Mongol followers fled north. Much to their surprise, however, the old Mongol capital of Qaraqorum was already occupied. Indeed, the entire Mongolian plateau, their ancestral "homeland," had been taken over by the Oirad. Believing it was not possible for his recently defeated army to wrest control away from the Oirad, Toghan Temür and the Mongols found themselves in limbo. Eventually they went south and established themselves in the no-man's land between the Great Wall and the Gobi Desert, which nowadays is the Inner Mongolian province of the People's Republic of China.[57] Two years after arriving as a refugee in this environmentally and politically marginal buffer zone Toghan Temür died of dysentery.

While his ignominious death symbolizes well the waning fortunes of the Mongols in the post-Yuan period, such was not the view from China.[58] Instead the Ming court continued to see the Mongols as a mortal threat to their very existence and they launched several campaigns against them. Yet much to the anger and consternation of the Ming court the Mongols continued to elude defeat.[59] Nevertheless, one unintended consequence of the continuing Mongol-Ming struggle was that it enabled the Oirad to become stronger. As noted above, the Oirad had taken over the Mongolian plateau during the later Yuan dynasty, though how this happened—as well as who the Oirad were, and where they came from—is somewhat obscure.[60] Nevertheless, by the fourteenth century the term Oirad was an overarching designation for four groups—the Oirad, Naiman, Kereid, and Barghud—that had taken control over the plateau as the Mongols had become more and more embroiled in the affairs of China during the Yuan dynasty.

Yet even though the Oirad controlled the "heartland" of the Mongolian plateau they were not a major power in the immediate post-Yuan period. In the west there was the powerful Moghul ruler Tughluq Temür Khan and in the south there were the Mongols, who although weakened were still a powerful force. And the power of both the Mongols and the Moghuls rested not only on their military might, but also in their economic position. In particular, they controlled the east-west trade, and most important, they controlled the trade in Central Asian horses, which were essential for both the Ming military and its larger economy. Without them the Ming would quite literally grind to a halt since Chinese soil lacks selenium, a vital mineral for the raising of strong horses,[61] and the immensity of this trade is reflected in the fact that annually the Ming bought nearly two million horses from the Mongols.[62] Thus even though the post-Yuan Mongols may have been battered and defeated they still had the Ming over a barrel.

For the Ming court this situation was clearly intolerable since in their view China's national security was in the fickle hands of their barbarian enemies. This vital issue therefore had to be dealt with, and the initial option as we have seen was invasion and conquest. But every campaign of both the Hongwu and Yongle emperor (r. 1402–1424) were resounding failures. The Mongols simply retreated into the steppe and once the supply lines were overextended the stranded Ming army was decimated. In response to these failures the Ming court adopted a two-prong strategy. The first was to find another source of horses, which they did by reestablishing the tea-for-horse trading network with Tibet.[63] And although this trade was to expand enormously—one single transaction in 1435, for example, involved 1,097,000 pounds of tea for 13,000 horses[64]—the Ming court still wanted to keep alive their trade with the Mongols and Moghuls. To this end, they therefore decided to normalize trade relations, but on their own terms. Their plan was thus to funnel all trade with the West through the small independent city-state of Hami, which in 1406 had been brought into the Ming system of frontier garrisons.[65]

The Mongol khan Gülichi (1402–1408), however, did not agree with these terms and he poisoned Engke Temür, the prince of Hami, who had initially made the deal with the Chinese. At this turn of events the Ming court was bewildered, but they still hoped to salvage the trade negotiations. Yet when their envoys were executed at the command of the new Mongol ruler Punyashri, the Ming court finally decided to circumvent the Mongols entirely. They therefore made contact with the Mongols' archrival, the Oirad. The Ming then not only bestowed titles and privileges upon the Oirad ruler, but they also opened up direct trade relations. To repay the favor the Oirad ruler Mahmud (d. 1416) launched an assault on the Mongols in 1412. After killing Punyashri, Mahmud put his own son Delbeg (r.

1412–1414) on the Mongol throne. Thus with the help of the Ming the age of the Oirad had arrived.

The Oirad ruler's name Mahmud is, of course, an Arabic name and there is every reason to believe that many of the Oirad elite were at this time Muslim. Indeed, having been frozen out of relations with both the Mongols and the Ming, the Oirad had inevitably turned their attention toward the Moghuls and Timurids in the West.[66] And while this turn to the West may have begun as an economic decision, it would also come to have religious implications. By aligning themselves with the West the Oirad were drawn into the Islamic fold, as happened simultaneously in Southeast Asia. Namely, when trade with China withered after the fall of the Yuan both the Oirad and the Southeast Asian kingdoms linked up with Islamic trade networks and this inevitably brought with it Islamization.[67] Yet unlike Southeast Asia, the Oirad's conversion to Islam was short-lived. Only a few decades later the Oirad would in fact become Buddhist.

The Oirad are therefore one of the few peoples in the history of Islam to have given up the faith. Moreover, unlike in Spain and the Balkans where the retreat of Islam was accompanied by the brutal use of force, the Buddhist conversion of the Muslim Oirads seems to have been a bloodless affair. Of course, some of this may be explained by the fact that the Oirad majority may not have been too devoted to Islam to begin with. In addition, once trade with China opened up the Oirad were no longer dependent on Islamic trade networks and thus being Muslim no longer had much value. In fact, being a Muslim was probably a hindrance in dealing with China at this time. Yet be that as it may, the Oirad ruler's decision to abandon the Sufi sheiks of his earlier Moghul and Timurid allies, and align himself with Tibetan lamas, was to have profound consequences. In many ways it was the historical hinge in the coming Buddhist-Muslim divide.

Before exploring the Oirad ruler's turn toward the Dharma in the mid-fifteenth century, however, let us return to the lull before the storm, in particular the first decades of the fifteenth century before the appearance of Naqshbandi Sufis and Tibetan lamas among the Moghuls and Oirads. It was during this short-lived era of peace that there was a final explosion of trade and communication across the Silk Road between the Timurids and the Ming dynasty.[68] And in a certain sense this trade and cultural exchange was the last gasp of the *pax Mongolica*. Yet since there was no unifying empire holding these regions together at the time it is perhaps more accurate to understand this particular moment in time—including its trade and

cultural openness—as another age of equilibrium, such as during the age
of "Sunni internationalism" just prior to the Mongol conquests. Indeed,
from about 1370 until 1430 a similar equilibrium developed across central
Eurasia among the Timurid, Moghul, Oirad, Mongol, and Ming dynasties
(map 17).

And we have already come across one famous monument from this
period that well captures the age: the passage cited above about a mosque
being built across the street from a Buddhist temple in Hami.

The author of this telling anecdote was the painter Ghiyath al-Din Naq-
qash, the official scribe of a Timurid embassy Shahrukh Khan sent to China
in 1419. Though what is even more interesting than his reporting of Buddhist-Muslim coexistence at this time is his fascination with Buddhist art
and sculpture. As noted in the previous chapter, the linkage between the
Dharma and the tradition of Persian miniature painting would largely be
forgotten. In the case of Ghiyath al-Din, however, we catch a glimpse of
the fascination and inspiration that Buddhist art held for Muslim artists at
this time. Upon seeing the murals in a temple housing a reclining Buddha
statue, for example, Ghiyath al-Din exclaims that the paintings are "of such

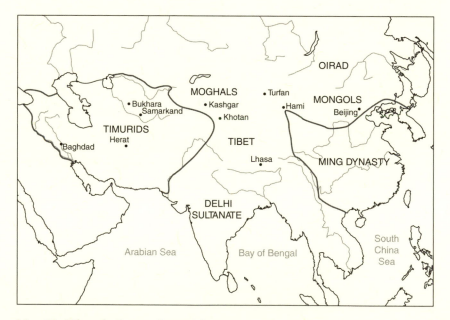

Map 17. Fifteenth-Century Inner Asia.

character that all painters of the world would be struck with wonder." Moreover, echoing Tha'alibi's much earlier description of Chinese artistic skills, Ghiyath al-Din claims that the statues of the Sixteen Arhats are "so vividly reproduced that one would think that these infidels were really alive."[69] And his enthusiasm for Buddhist art does not even wane in the face of an enormous statue of the Thousand-armed and Thousand-eyed Guanyin.

> Among others there was a big idol-temple of such character that in the midst of it there was erected an idol cast in bronze and so gilded over as to look like one made of solid gold, measuring fifty cubits in height. Its limbs were all made symmetrical in form. All over the limbs of this idol there were figures of hands set up and over the palm of every hand there was the image of eye. It is called the thousand-handed image and is celebrated throughout the whole of China. First of all a big solid plinth which was constructed out of finely cut stones is set up, on which this idol and the whole building rests, around the idol rise a large number of alcoves, verandahs and galleries, several flights of stairs running along the same in such a manner that the first stairway passes a little beyond the ankle of the idol, the second stairway does not come as high as its knee, the third stairway passes above the knee, while the fourth one reaches its breast and so on up to the head, the whole structure being executed with masterly elaboration. Thereafter the top of the building was surmounted by a conical dome and so covered up as to excite the wonder of men. The total number of stories being eight, around every one of which one could walk outside as well as inside the building. This idol is made in a standing position, its feet of which the length is about ten cubits each rest on a pedestal of cast metal. It has been estimated that at least one hundred thousand donkey-loads of brass must have been used in that work. Besides all round that big idol there were smaller idols of plaster which were colored and painted in gold. There were the paintings of hills, peaks, caves with the figures of Buddhist monks, priests and ascetics sitting in their cells doing religious penance. There were also pictures of rams, mountain goats, lions, leopards, dragons and trees all painted on plaster. The rest of the walls were so painted with frescoes as to call

forth the wonder of even skilled artists at their sight. Similar was the case with the surrounding buildings.[70]

In this paean to Chinese artistry Ghiyath al-Din captures well not only the dynamic in which Persian miniature painting was influenced by Buddhist and Chinese art, but also the calm in the early fifteenth century when Buddhists and Muslims lived side by side. Indeed, it was during this time that the Moghul ruler, a Muslim, not only allowed Buddhist monasteries to be built next to a mosque, but also exempted Buddhists from taxes.[71] Yet this state of affairs was the lull before the storm.

Esen Khan and the Buddhist Turn

A decade after Ghiyath al-Din had visited Turfan and written favorably about the Uygur Buddhists,[72] they would be fleeing Muslim persecution and seeking refuge in Ming-dynasty China. The times had clearly changed. A vital question is why? The six pieces of the puzzle noted above all played their role; however, much of the credit for this radical transformation can be attributed to the appearance of the Naqshbandi Sufis among the Moghuls in the fifteenth century. And of particular import in this regard was not only their promotion of urbanization among the Moghuls, but also their call for the implementation and enforcement of shari'a law.

The Naqshbandi fusion of mystical Islam and politicized shari'aism ("a pre-eminent emphasis on the strict observance of Islamic law")[73] was to a certain extent unique.[74] At the same time, however, it was in many ways a perfect union of the two major strands of Islam that had arisen in the wake of the Mongol conquests, both of which were dealing with the profound shock of the Mongol invasions.[75] From the destruction of the Caliphate to the introduction of bubonic plague, many Muslims must have wondered: What went wrong? Why did the world of Islam so easily collapse? Moreover, was it the fault of Islam itself, or had Muslims gone astray? As the feverish Christian responses to the Mongols and the Black Death readily attest, such questions were not unique to the Muslim world, nor were their responses.[76] In fact, many religious believers saw the Mongol conquests as either divine retribution or evidence that the proper path had been forsaken. Either way, the proper response invariably pivoted on the need to return to the origins of the true faith, however that may have been imagined.

As noted above there were two common responses in the Muslim world: mysticism and shari'aism. A representative of the latter was Ibn Taymiyya, whose response to the Mongol conquests was firmly grounded on the importance of the *shari'a*. In particular, if only Muslim law was instituted and a true Muslim state created then truth and justice would prevail. Other thinkers, however, felt that the turn to *shari'a* was misguided. For them the answer did not reside in external institutions that would force compliance with new doctrinal demands; instead, they saw the answer in the spiritual development of each one individually.[77] Indeed, the Sufi belief that the external world was simply illusory and but a shadow of the true glory of God clearly resonated in a world where all known institutions had been shattered. Moreover, for many it was precisely those same institutions that had led to the current disaster. The possibility of individual salvation promised by the Sufi brotherhoods therefore offered hope in a chaotic and disorienting world; and, indeed, as the *shari'a* movement floundered, the Sufi brotherhoods blossomed.

The Sufis were thus the great beneficiaries of the Mongol conquest. Thus although Sufism had spread rather widely in the Islamic world prior to the coming of the Mongols, especially on account of the work by Abu Hamid al-Ghazali (1058–1111), in the wake of the conquests the Sufi path came to be even more widely adopted, and indeed the prominence of Sufism in Central Asia and South Asia today can be traced directly to this period. And the Sufis even recognized this themselves—so much so that Sufi histories came to claim that it was their spiritual masters who had invited Chinggis Khan to invade and decimate the Muslim world.[78] In their view it was only by weeding out the old corrupt Muslim order that the true and righteous form of Sufi Islam could flourish.

In Central Asia the Sufi order that initially benefited most from this transformation in the religious landscape was the Kubraviyya, which had been founded by Najm ad-Din Kubra. But as one would expect, the power of the Kubraviyya was quickly challenged in the post-Mongol age as new Sufi masters and their followers—such as the Yasaviyya, who traced their tradition back to Ahmad Yasavi (d. ca. 1166)—entered the religious marketplace. And indeed in turn the power of the Yasaviyya was challenged by Baha ad-Din Naqshband (d. 1389), who rather ingeniously challenged the spiritual legitimacy of the Yasaviyya by claiming that he was restoring the mystical path of the Khwajagan ("Masters"), which was actually the real and secret lineage of Ahmad Yasavi's teacher, Abu Yusuf al-Hamadani (d.

1140).[79] And central to this claim, as it was to be later articulated by the Naqshbandi order, was a distinctive tradition of a secret initiation lineage that ran parallel to the conventional master-disciple transmission lineage (*silsila*) that define all schools of Sufism. Yet while this theological innovation came to define the Naqshbandiyya it is unlikely that it deserves much credit for their subsequent success. In fact, the key to the Naqshbandiyya's success lay in their decision to fuse together the two major strands of post-Mongol Islamic thought. Namely, by coupling Naqshband's original mystical teachings with calls for the reinstitution of the *shari'a*, the Naqshbandiyya created a potent cocktail that not only brought them to power, but would also spill over Central Asia with devastating consequences.

Of course, to understand the Naqshbandiyya's decision to adopt the rhetoric of shari'aism and its subsequent implications it is important to recall the religious and political situation; in particular, the Timurid dynasty's support of the Yasaviyya. Tamerlane, for example, had commissioned the building of the famous mausoleum of Ahmad Yasavi.[80] Yet that was not the only operative factor at play. As we have seen there was also the Mongol legacy, the Chinggisid principle, and Chinggis Khan's law code. For the Timurids these were all extremely sensitive issues because they were not actually Mongols: Tamerlane was a Turk from the Barlas clan. As a result, even though he was indisputably the most powerful ruler in the world at the time he could never proclaim himself "Khan." Doing so would have been too great a violation of the sacred Chinggisid principles. To circumvent this genealogical problem Tamerlane therefore married several Chaghataid princesses and declared himself the "Imperial Son-in-Law."

Tamerlane, moreover, also promoted himself as the great defender of Islam. Timurid legitimacy therefore came to rest on the twin pillars of the Mongol legacy and Islam.[81] The Timurid ruler Shahrukh, for example, would place a cenotaph over Tamerlane's burial site in 1420 that claimed not only that the legendary Mongol ancestor Alan Qoa was associated with the Virgin Mary and the Abrahamic Holy Spirit, but that Tamerlane was also a descendant of 'Ali, son-in-law of the Prophet Muhammad and first Shi'ite Imam.[82] In so doing Shahrukh was thus boldly proclaiming the legitimacy of the Timurid dynasty largely on the basis of this dual genealogy: the Chinggisid and Islamic. At the same time, of course, both of these genealogical claims were purely imaginary and thus capture well the urgency the Timurids faced in trying to legitimate their rule in the shadow of the Mongol legacy. Yet it also points to the timorous nature of Timurid claims to legitimacy, and it was largely on account of these weaknesses that the Naqshbandi critique of the Timurids was so devastating, as it struck at both of the pillars supporting the whole edifice.

In particular, by claiming the Timurids and their Yasaviyya enablers were not Muslim enough the Naqshbandiyya undermined their claims to be the upholders of Islam. Moreover, built into the very logic of shari'aism is the rejection of the entire Mongol legacy and its infidel customs, all of which must be abandoned in the project of creating a pure Muslim state. Thus having taken up the mantle of restoring Islamic law in the external world, the quiet and internal path of mystical introspection was no longer an option; instead jihad against the impious Timurids was in order. To this end the Naqshbandiyya started to look for political and military support among the nomads in the east, and they found a willing supporter in the Moghul ruler Uways Khan (r. 1417–1429).

To understand his decision to align himself with the Naqshbandiyya it is perhaps enough to simply recall that Tamerlane had taken over half of the Chaghataid Ulus and that the Moghuls and Timurids had been fighting ever since. Thus on one level joining the Naqshbandiyya's jihad against the Timurids simply made sense. But another important issue that must surely have been in the minds of both the Sufis and the Moghuls was the Mongol legacy, most notably the fact that the Moghuls, unlike the Timurids, were actual descendants of Chinggis Khan. Thus if the Moghuls rejected the local Kataki Sufis, whom they had been following ever since Tughluq Temür, and opted instead for the Naqshbandiyya—a prominent Central Asian Sufi order with a legendary pedigree—they would be both the heirs of the Mongol legacy and the true rulers of Islam. A Moghul-Naqshbandiyya alliance was thus a winning proposition on both sides. Yet not everyone won on account of this alliance.

Some of the first losers were the Buddhists. Being infidels they had to be expelled from the new Islamic utopia being forged within the Moghul domains under the guidance of Naqshbandi shari'aism since they specifically advocated for the "remov[al] of the evil customs of the strangers."[83] Thus, as we have seen above, by the 1430s the city of Turfan had essentially been purged of all its Buddhist inhabitants.[84] The same fate would befall Hami over the coming decades. The city where mosques and temples had stood side by side would be emptied of its Buddhist population by the 1480s. Yet such persecution was not the only consequence of the Moghul adoption of Naqshbandi Sufism.[85] Rather, much as had happened earlier in

India, it also inadvertently fostered a rebirth of the Dharma among the
Oirad. To fathom the Oirad ruler Esen Khan's turn toward the Dharma
and its implications for shaping subsequent Buddhist-Muslim history in
Inner Asia it is therefore important to return to the narrative of the Oirads
where we left off.

In 1412 Mahmud had just killed the Mongol khan and put his own son
on the throne. But this was not solely an Oirad-Mongol affair. Indeed, the
central player in these unfolding events was the Ming court, which had
approached the Oirad in order to undermine the recalcitrant Mongols for
what were, in Chinese eyes, unfair trading practices. Their hope was that
the Oirad would be more willing to do business, and they were. The Ming
therefore cut their relations with the Mongols and established direct economic ties with the Oirad. The immediate consequence of this was that any
power the Mongols had over the Ming simply evaporated and both their
wealth and power rapidly collapsed and in their place rose the Oirad. The
growing power of the Oirad, however, impacted not only the fortunes of
the Mongols. It also came to impinge upon the Moghuls. Uways Khan, for
example, fought the Oirad twenty-one times and lost every battle but one.
Uways Khan was even taken hostage three times and to ensure his release
he had to give the Oirad ruler his sister as a wife.[86] And the situation among
the Moghuls only grew worse after the death of Uways Khan in 1429. Part
of the difficulties that ensued certainly had to do with the succession struggle that erupted between his two sons, Yunus and Esen Buqa, but at the
root of the crisis was the collapsing Moghul economy.

In 1424 the Ming emperor had abolished the horse trade with Central
Asia. Yet even so such trade continued surreptitiously through the city of
Hami.[87] But this lifeline of the Moghul economy was cut when the Oirad
ruler Toghan (d. 1440) married into the Hami ruling family and took control over this last entrepôt of Muslim trade with China. The final blow to
Moghul trade, however, came when Esen moved the horse trade away from
Hami completely and established it in Datong near Beijing. At this turn of
events the economic situation became so dire that Muslims fled the Moghul
domains and became refugees in China.[88] It is therefore within this changing economic situation that we need to place not only the Naqshbandi
revival among the Moghuls, but also the rise of the Oirad. Moreover, it is
also on account of this economic shift that we should understand the Oirad's gradual move away from the orbit of the Islamic world and their return
to the Dharmic fold. Return, however, is perhaps not the right word as it is

very unlikely that any Oirad had ever been Buddhist before Esen. And it is precisely for this reason that Esen's engagement with Tibetan lamas in the 1450s is so important since it revived—or perhaps even created—the idea that was to shape Mongol conceptualizations of themselves, their ruler, and their state for the coming centuries.[89]

In particular, it was at this time that Mongol rule came to be envisioned as being wholly Buddhist. Although this had never been the case histori- cally, promoting such an idea was important for the legitimacy of the Oirad. Indeed, much like the Timurids they too had to contend with the Mongol legacy as non-Mongols. And thus much as the Timurids had come to iden- tify themselves with Islam, the Oirads came to focus on Buddhism and especially the relationship between Khubilai Khan and the Tibetan Pakpa Lama. Thus much as had happened in the Islamic world the Dharma was thereby superimposed on the traditional matrix of the Mongol legacy and the Chinggisid principle. In the case of Buddhism the theory that came to be articulated owed its origins to the writings of Pakpa Lama and his vision of "two realms": the sacred and the secular.[90] Proper Mongol Buddhist rule was therefore based on a symbiotic relation between the khan, who controls secular affairs, and a Tibetan lama, who controls spiritual affairs.

> Secular and spiritual salvation are something that all living beings try to obtain. Spiritual salvation consists in complete deliverance from suffering, and worldly welfare is secular salvation. Both depend on a dual order, the order of Religion and the order of the State, or worldly rule. Just as the religious order is based on the sutras and magic formulae (*dhāraṇī*), the secular order rests on peace and quietness. The order of Religion is presided over by the Lama, and the state by the Ruler. The priest has to teach religion, and the ruler has to guarantee a rule which enables everyone to live in peace. Religion and State are thus mutually dependent. The heads of reli- gion and state are equal, although each has different functions. The Lama corresponds to the Buddha, and thus the Ruler to the cakra- vartin.[91]

It was therefore this ideal that Esen revived in grappling with the Mongol legacy.

Yet why he chose the Dharma in particular is another question entirely. No other Oirad ruler, much less Mongol ruler, had done so. Indeed, after the fall of the Yuan dynasty the interest of the Mongol elite in tantric Buddhism waned. Tibetan lamas were still active among the Mongols,[92] as they were among the Ming elite,[93] but since Buddhism had never become a part of the Mongol legacy or the Chinggisid principle, the Dharma was not considered important by any post-Yuan Mongol ruler. Yet this was all to change profoundly with Esen Khan. But why did he do it?

At the time Esen was one the most powerful rulers in eastern Eurasia. In 1449 he had even captured the Yingzhong emperor at Tumu Fort, fifty miles northwest of Beijing.[94] But like Tamerlane before him Esen could not claim Chinggisid blood. Esen could therefore never be proclaimed khan; however, much like Tamerlane he could ameliorate his genealogical deficiencies by cloaking himself in the sanctifying garb of religion. Following in the footsteps of Tamerlane, or perhaps emulating the Moghul khans and their relationship with the Naqshbandi Sufis, Esen therefore established relations with Tibetan lamas. And in so doing he presented this new religio-political relationship as a restoration of the great Buddhist rule of Khubilai Khan.

Esen therefore claimed to be restoring the righteous Mongol rule that had been forsaken when the Dharma had been abandoned. Thus after having secured his Buddhist bona fides in the mold of Khubilai Khan, Esen actually proclaimed himself khan and the rightful ruler of all the Mongols in 1453. While the Ming court hesitantly approved this move, the Mongols saw this action as a gross violation of the Chinggisid principle and a bold usurpation of the Mongol throne. They therefore violently resisted, and after Esen's death in 1455, the power of the Oirad collapsed. Yet even so, Esen's Buddhist turn would live on as a means of becoming khan among the Mongols, especially for those of less than pure Chinggisid lineage such as Altan Khan, the Tümed ruler, who met with Sönam Gyatso in 1578 and famously gave him the title Dalai Lama.[95]

Interaction in the Trenches

The meeting between Altan Khan and Sönam Gyatso, which took place on the shores of Lake Kökenuur in the northern reaches of the Tibetan plateau, was to become an iconic moment in Eurasian history. Indeed, because the Mongols, Tibetans, and especially the Manchus took so much stock in this new Buddhist Chinggisid vision of rule, much of East Asia's subsequent history would flow out from this event. Yet to fathom the immense ripple effects of this obscure and at the time perhaps rather insignificant meeting between the ruler of the Tümed and a young monk of the Gelukpa order, it is important to yet again take a step back.

In particular, we need to recall that more than a century had elapsed between Esen Khan's Buddhist turn and the meeting between Altan Khan and Sönam Gyatso. During that time both the Oirad and Timurid Empires collapsed, the Mongols rose to power, the Ming dynasty floundered, and in short order all of China and Mongolia would be taken over by the Manchu Qing dynasty (1644–1911). Thus to point out that the world of Inner Asia was changing during the Mongols' conversion to Buddhism is perhaps an understatement. Unfortunately, however, whenever the well-worn story of the meeting between Altan Khan and the Dalai Lama is rehearsed this larger complex reality is very often ignored. In fact, because the meeting was to become so iconic in later Mongol, Tibetan, and Qing imaginings of themselves, their religion, and their state, this meeting came to be less a historical event than a powerful symbol. As such it was never questioned or contextualized and instead came to be presented as virtually having taken place outside the bounds of conventional history. Thus rather than being simply one episode in the broader context of Eurasian history, it came to be seen as the *summum bonum* of an inevitable Mongol Buddhist history. Yet clearly the meeting of Altan Khan and the Dalai Lama was not inevitable, nor did it happen in a vacuum.

The story in fact begins with the Mongols fighting their way back from the brink of extinction after Esen's failed attempt at claiming the Chinggisid mantle. How the Mongols were actually able to rally themselves at this particular point in time is little understood. One factor in their favor, however, was the environment. Chinese sources namely record that on account of poor climatic conditions north China suffered severe famine during the 1450s and 1460s.[96] The same conditions must clearly have affected both the Mongols and the Oirad, yet since the Oirad were on the Mongolian plateau, which has far greater weather extremes than "Inner Mongolia," it is very likely that they were far worse off during these decades than the Mongols. Moreover, being closer to China the Mongols could not only trade with the Chinese, but if need be they could also raid over the border.

A further factor that facilitated the rise of the Mongols, or least the weakening of the Oirad, was the changing situation among the Moghuls. During the Oirad's rise to prominence the Moghuls had been in disarray as a result of the succession struggle between the sons of Uways Khan and the weakening economy. When his son Yunus eventually became khan in 1468, however, many of these problems evaporated. Under the leadership of the charismatic Khoja Ahrar (d. 1490) the Naqshbandiyya became firmly established among the Moghuls and thus put an end to earlier religious squabbles.[97] But the unifying and urbanizing force of Naqshbandi Sufism even went beyond the confines of the Moghuls.[98] In fact, because Khoja Ahrar was so respected, most Central Asian rulers came to have one of his religious representatives at their courts, and through this Sufi network there actually developed a dialogue among all of these fractious groups.[99] Even the long alienated Timurid and Moghul rulers came into contact once again on account of Khoja Ahrar's dealings. The two even subsequently developed political and trade relations. Yet while this was good for the position of the Naqshbandiyya in Central Asia, and also improved the economic situation among the Moghuls, it was disastrous for the Oirad as it left them isolated between east and west. But the final blow was still to come.

In 1500 the Timurid dynasty was conquered and divided into two. The Uzbeks, who traced their origins back to the Golden Horde, took over Central Asia; and the Safavids, a local Persian dynasty, took over Persia and Iraq. One consequence of this event was that the earlier political, economic, and religious alliances that had recently developed on account of the Naqshbandiyya between the Timurids and Moghuls came to end. As a result, all of these relations had to be renegotiated with the Safavids and Uzbeks. Such a possibility, however, was made difficult when the Safavids declared Twelver Shi'ism as their state religion. Their decision to make a radical break with Turko-Mongol Sunni rule and mark their independence by becoming Shi'a did not endear them to either the Uzbeks or the Moghuls, much less the Naqshbandiyya. Nor was the situation ameliorated by the Safavids' invasion of Central Asia. Moreover, as these political tensions mounted whatever earlier economic networks had tied these regions together started to fray as well,[100] and this set in motion a downward spiral, since as east-west trade diminished in the sixteenth century the deteriorating financial crisis only added fuel to a worsening religiopolitical situation.

Even more fuel was added to the fire by the Naqshbandiyya. They had cut their teeth and risen to power in Central Asian politics within the rhetoric of shari'aism. The Safavid conversion to Shi'a Islam thus not only infuriated them, but also caused them to redouble their efforts as agents of both religious and political reform. Yet since the Safavids now acted as a buffer to the West the Naqshbandiyyas were forced to push further into the east.

One of Khoja Ahrar's disciples, Khoja Taj ad-Din (d. ca. 1533), for example, carried the Naqshbandi message all the way to China's Gansu province, where he found supporters not only among the nomads, but also in the cities.[101] But the Naqshbandiyya were not the only ones who were forced to move their operations to the east. With their political and economic options stymied in the west on account of the Safavids and Uzbeks, the Moghul khans also began pushing east. Mansur Khan (1485–1545), who was ruling the eastern half of the Moghul Ulus, attacked China's northwestern frontier in the hopes of accessing the riches of the Ming dynasty. Sultan Sa'id Khan, who ruled the western half of the Moghul Ulus, was on the other hand apparently more inspired by the Naqshbandi rhetoric of jihad, since it was he who launched the invasion of Tibet.

It is therefore within this context of Sufi revivalism, economic collapse, and the attendant Moghul push eastward that the final collapse of the Oirad needs to be situated. It is also in relation to these events that we need to locate the rise of the Mongols. As noted above the actual rise of the Mongols in the mid-fifteenth century is clouded in mystery.[102] Nevertheless, it is commonly held that after Molon Khan's death in 1466 the Mongol throne was empty for a decade and then Mandagul became khan and reigned briefly in the late 1470s. Upon his death, Bayan Möngke became khan and upon his death in 1484 his seven-year-old son was married to Mandagul Khan's widow, which enabled him (of rather suspect Chinggisid lineage) to be recognized as the rightful ruler of the Mongols. Yet once the fortunes of the Mongols began to turn under this young ruler's direction he came to be seen as truly upholding the Chinggisid legacy.[103]

Dayan Khan's meteoric rise to power began with his consolidation of the Mongols living in the eastern area of "Inner Mongolia" and his reorganization of them into the Three Eastern Tümen (Chakhar, Khalkha, and Uriyangkhan). Next came his greatest military achievement, the conquest of the Mongols of Ordos, who had taken advantage of the Tumu incident to occupy the area within the great bend of the Yellow River.[104] Having thus only recently moved into and taken over this territory the Ordos Mongols did not initially want to ally themselves with Dayan Khan. Instead they violently resisted Dayan Khan's project of unification.[105] Ultimately, however, Dayan was victorious and the Ordos Mongols were then organized into the Three Western Tümen (Ordos, Tümed, and Yüngshiyebü). And it was on account of this organizational reformulation of the Mongols into the Six Tümen under the authority of the Chinggisid ruler Dayan Khan that they were able to reassert their power against the Oirad. While military prowess, marriage alliances, and shrewd politics certainly held this new sociopolitical structure together, it was also ideologically reinforced through the concept of a return to proper Chinggisid rule and a reaffirmation of the Mongol legacy.

Unfortunately, however, this was not enough to hold the Mongols together after Dayan Khan's death. None of his children had either the iron fist or the political savvy to keep the fractious Mongols together and thus the political situation devolved into a virtual civil war. Within this infighting, however, one leader was to rise to the top: Altan Khan (1508–1582). He was the eldest child of Dayan Khan's third son and therefore had no legitimate claim to the Chinggisid throne. Instead he was simply the local ruler of the Tümed in the Ordos. But like Chinggis and Dayan Khan before him, he was ambitious, politically astute, and a military genius. Over the course of several decades he was therefore able to establish himself as the undisputed ruler of the Mongolian plateau.

In doing so his options were nevertheless limited to the realities on the ground. In particular, unlike his glorious ancestors he could not push westward since that area was occupied by the Moghuls, who, under the banner of Naqshbandi revivalism, were themselves pushing eastward away from the "heretical" Shi'a Safavids and toward the riches of China. In fact, like the Moghuls, Altan Khan recognized that the linchpin of his future success would be his relation with China and access to its markets. To this end he put all his military energy into consolidating control of "Inner Mongolia," which ran all along the Ming dynasty's northern border. In so doing he pushed the Mongols of the "Eastern Tümen" out of their traditional pastures, thereby setting in motion an important migration. Most notably the Khalkha Mongols moved into the territory formerly occupied by the weakened Oirad, which is now "Outer Mongolia." The Oirad in turn were pushed further west into the pastures north of the Tianshan mountains where they came upon the remnants of the Moghuls and other nomadic groups whose distinguishing features were that they were nomadic and non-Muslim. Recall, the Naqshbandi revival—with its focus on saint shrines and other religious institutions—had fostered the urbanization of the formerly nomadic Moghuls, and thus these remaining groups were those that had been left out of both these processes: Islamization and urbanization. In turn, it was these non-Muslim nomads with whom the Oirads would eventually forge the powerful nomadic Buddhist empire of the Zünghars. Yet even though the Zünghars' turn toward Tibetan lamas was itself inspired by Altan Khan, during his own rise to power Altan had absolutely no interest in Tibet.[106]

What concerned him was China, especially the normalization of trade relations. In particular, he wanted markets to be opened along the Sino-Mongol border where goods could be bought and sold. Such a free-market system, however, was not only potentially beyond the ever hyper-vigilant control of the Chinese state, but it was also antithetical to the traditional Chinese tribute system, whereby trade with foreign countries was never simply an economic transaction but instead an elaborate piece of the imperial ideology keeping alive the illusion of China as the center of the universe. All trade was therefore imagined as being tribute presented to the Chinese emperor by subjects from afar, and the Chinese goods sold in return were simply the magnanimous gift of the Chinese sovereign. Since the Chinese market was so valuable most foreign traders through history had been willing to put up with this charade. When the European imperial powers arrived, however, they were not willing to play the game and problems invariably ensued.[107] Altan Khan did not want to play the game either. He wanted open markets. But the Chinese refused. They wanted to control the trade and thereby limited Mongol "tribute" missions to the imperial capital to one every few years. In response Altan Khan launched continual raids into Ming territory, which invariably only further hardened Chinese resolve. Indeed, it was within this context that the Ming dynasty began in earnest to build the Great Wall, perhaps the world's greatest monument to xenophobia and trade protectionism ever built.[108]

Nevertheless, in 1550 the situation for Altan Khan was particularly dire. It had not rained for 155 days, the Mongols were facing a severe famine, and the Ming court still refused to talk. They had instead killed the Mongol trade representatives. Altan Khan thus launched an audacious invasion of China and by September he had surrounded Beijing and forced the Ming court to capitulate to his demands. The emperor agreed to the normalization of relations and he allotted 100,000 taels of silver to purchase goods at two border markets in Datong and Xuanfu. But after various problems arose, including security issues and cost overruns, the Ming emperor closed the markets two years later. This decision resulted in another twenty-year cycle of famine, disease, and violence that only came to end in 1571 when the Ming court and Altan Khan ratified a peace treaty.

In sum it was only in the wake of this momentous event that Altan

Khan made his very public embrace of the Dharma. However, in contradis-
tinction to how later histories would present the meeting of Altan Khan
and the Dalai Lama, this event was not a foregone conclusion. Indeed,
contrary to later Mongol and Tibetan historians it was not the inevitable
summation of history. Of course, for these historians it made sense to present it in this way since it legitimated their present, a world in which the
majority of Mongols were Gelukpa Buddhists on account of Altan Khan's
having met the Dalai Lama. During the reign of Altan Khan and his immediate successors, however, the Dalai Lama and his Gelukpa order had no
exclusive claim to the Mongols' hearts and minds. They were simply one of
a hodgepodge of religious specialists who provided their services at the
Mongol court. With the subsequent rise of the Gelukpa, however, this diffuse religiosity was to be readily forgotten. Instead, all that was to be
remembered was that Altan Khan met the Third Dalai Lama and thus the
Mongols supported the Gelukpa order. But the reality was rather different.
For example, a month before Altan Khan met Sönam Gyatso on the shores
of Lake Kökenuur he met with the head of the Taklung order. They had
been in contact for years and they even continued their relationship after
Altan's meeting with the Dalai Lama.

Yet Altan Khan was not only interested in various Tibetan traditions;
he had also been a great supporter of the Chinese White Lotus Buddhist
order, who had famously offered Altan Khan a "secret weapon." They
claimed to possess a mantra so powerful it could shatter the walls of a
Chinese city. But the White Lotus was not the only religious group that
offered the Mongol leader a technological edge in his never-ending feud
with the Ming court. The charismatic preacher and adept fortune teller Lü
He, who called himself the Patriarch of Mount Lu, not only acquired a
large following by preaching a messianic message that claimed a massive
Mongol invasion would result in the death of 70 percent of the Chinese
population, but he also claimed to have an elixir that enabled one to survive
without grain. Altan Khan was invariably greatly interested in such a
potion, but so was the Ming court. They knew that grain was the key commodity in Sino-Mongol trade relations and thus if this elixir worked they
would no longer have any leverage with Altan Khan. Thus when they captured Lü He in Beijing in 1564 he was summarily executed.[109]

The secret weapon of the White Lotus did not fare much better either.
When Altan Khan took the Chinese Buddhists out into the field their mantras had no effect. Thus when the Chinese fortifications still stood after two

days of chanting Altan Khan apparently gave up on the White Lotus. Their future among the Mongols was therefore sealed. The same kind of failure had also turned Altan Khan away from his shamans. They had advised him that 1547 was an auspicious year to inaugurate trade relations with the Ming and thus Altan had tried to present one black-headed white horse, seven camels, and three thousand geldings. He also provided intelligence to the Ming court about another Mongol ruler's impending attack on Liaodong. But the shamans were wrong. The Ming court still refused to open trade relations.[110]

It was at this time Altan turned to the White Lotus. But they too had failed and now Altan Khan faced another crisis. Namely, the increased Sino-Mongol intercourse ushered in by the 1571 peace accord had been a double-edged sword. While it had brought normalization in trade relations and improved the economic situation among the Mongols, it had also enabled the urban diseases of China, especially smallpox, to run rampant across the steppe with devastating consequences.[111] Indeed, it was these epidemics that not only put a halt to the rise of the Mongols at this time and enabled the Manchus to rise in their place, but also opened the door for Tibetan lamas and their vast repertoire of medical lore and tantric rituals to be invited back among the Mongols.[112]

Altan Khan's meeting with the Dalai Lama was therefore not inevitable. Nor was it definitive. Altan Khan's funeral in 1582, for example, took place on the southern side of a mountain according to "shamanic" practices and a Buddhist astrologer and Chinese fengshui master deduced his burial site. To make sense of such an event it is important to recognize that both Altan Khan's approach to religion and the empire he forged was very much in tune with the Mongol empire itself. All too often, however, this reality is lost because the history of Altan Khan and the Dalai Lama has so often been shoehorned in to promote various visions of ethnonational and religious exclusivism. Altan Khan, for example, is often presented as *purely* Mongol and he meets *only* with the Dalai Lama. Yet, as we have seen in the case of Sönam Gyatso, this was never the case. And it was not the case either when it comes to Altan Khan's Mongol purity. Fifty thousand Chinese settlers had in fact fled the Ming dynasty and established cities and farms within Altan Khan's domains. One of Altan Khan's many Chinese advisors even launched a campaign to recruit educated Chinese by posting the sign, "All graduate scholars of the second rank who kindly join the barbarians (*huchung*) will be treated very well." The response to this advertisement was reportedly so great that all the applicants had to be screened. While this "brain drain" was probably more symptomatic of the deteriorating state of the Ming dynasty and its growing class of overeducated and underemployed literati, it nevertheless captures well the complex nature of Altan Khan's reign, one in which Mongols, Tibetans, Chinese, "shamans," Buddhists of different lineages, Daoists, Confucians, farmers, nomads, aristocrats, and so on were all in contact. But within this pluralistic world, what about the Moghuls? What about Islam?

In the conventional narrative that was to develop there was invariably no interaction. In fact Altan Khan's conversion to tantric Buddhism has in many ways come to be seen as the moment when the Buddhist and Muslim worlds went their separate ways. His meeting with the Dalai Lama firmly established the Tibeto-Mongol Buddhist world on one side, and the Turkic-speaking Muslim world on the other. However, as with everything else that has come to be said about Altan Khan this was not exactly true either, since not only did he continue to have relations with the Muslim Moghuls, but they also had relations with him.

> 'Abd al-Karim Khan, the Lord of the Twelve Cities of the White
> Turbans,[113]
> Greatly revered his older brother, Altan Khan, and his messengers.
> He greatly rejoiced and said, "Let us unify our states!" and sent
> tribute worth granting.
> Including diamonds and jewels of many kinds, large and fine
> western horses, pure geldings and camels with flopped-over
> humps.[114]

As recorded in an early Mongol history this event took place in 1578, right after Altan Khan had met the Dalai Lama. Thus, in other words, 'Abd al-Karim Khan, the grandson of Sultan Sa'id Khan, the ruler who had led the Great Lhasa Jihad, submitted to the "Buddhist" Altan Khan.

Of course, as the passage above makes clear, the issue for 'Abd al-Karim Khan was not one of religion, but of blood and the Mongol legacy. Thus although he himself was a Muslim and Altan may have been a Buddhist, what mattered more was that Altan Khan was his "older brother" (aq-a), which was a term with a long pedigree.[115] Specifically, it was the term used during the empire period to define the relations between the Four Ulus. As noted above, the Mongol empire was a family affair, and the Great Khan was therefore the "older brother" whom the others were supposed to follow. Whether it worked like that in reality is, of course, another question entirely; nevertheless, this family model was the conceptual framework that defined the Mongol empire. And as evidenced in the following passage this same conceptualization continued well into the sixteenth century:

> Üijeng Jaisang, who was immeasurably knowledgeable in the ancient
>   stories, customs and legends,
> Was sent as a messenger [by Altan Khan] to Shah Khan of the White
>   Turbans.
> When he described the genealogy from Chaghatai to the present,
> [Shah Khan] was greatly pleased and gave as tribute fine western
>   horses and diamonds.[116]

Shah Khan's tribute and 'Abd al-Karim Khan's submission to Altan Khan therefore offers us a different picture of Buddhist-Muslim relations during this period than is often imagined. In particular, it reveals how on account of the Mongol legacy it was still possible for there to be Buddhist-Muslim interaction.

Such possibilities, however, were soon to come to an end. Whether this shift was a direct consequence of 'Abd al-Karim's recognition of infidel rule is unclear; however, what is certain is that the Naqshbandiyya, under the leadership of the firebrand preacher Ishaq Wali (d. 1599), ultimately deposed him. Ishaq Wali then put Muhammad Khan (d. 1609) on the throne. But Ishaq Wali then went one step further.

> Ishaq's influence over Muhammad Khan became so strong that the
> Ishaqiyya, rooted in both the trade guilds and the ruler's court at
> Yarkand, became the dominant network linking together Altishahr's
> various oases. The Ishaqiyya's masterstroke—which established the
> Naqshbandiyya from then on as Altishahr's principal mystical
> path—was to name Muhammad Khan grand master of the Ishaqi-
> yya at the end of this life, identifying him not only as Ishaq's succes-
> sor but also as *qutb* ("mystical axis" or "pole of the universe") and
> *ghwath* ("mystical helper of the age"). The fact that the ruler was
> not just a Naqshbandiyya but the grand master himself gave the
> path a special position in Altishahr from which no other mystical
> path ever displaced it. The combination of Chaghadayid royalty with

the grand mastership of the Naqshbandiyya probably contributed also, some decades later, to the Makhdumzada khojas' audacious seizure of the Moghal throne.[117]

By uniting religious and political power into one person Ishaq Wali had paved the way for a theocracy.

Such a religiopolitical structure had never before existed in Inner Asia. As we have seen in the case of the Buddhist model of rule there was always to be a separation of power between the spiritual and secular realms. Each was therefore represented by the lama and the khan, who specialized in their separate fields. The same structure had also been operative for centuries in the Muslim world, where balance was maintained between the Caliph and the Muslim clergy. By fusing these two entities into one Ishaq Wali's vision thereby shattered this separation of power. It also coincidentally ended the possibility of Mongol blood or the Mongol legacy transcending religious divisions since one's faith was now inalienably tied to one's lineage / group / tribe / ethnicity / nationality. And as can well be imagined the elevation of Muhammad Khan as Grand Master of the Naqshbandiyya did much to generate a sharp divide between the Buddhists and Muslims of Inner Asia. Yet it was not the only one. In Tibet the Great Fifth would promote a similar theocratic model as the Naqshbandiyya by fusing both religious and political authority within the institution of the Dalai Lama. Thus two theocracies would develop in seventeenth-century Inner Asia: one Buddhist, the other Muslim.

Religion, Politics, and Intolerance

The Dalai Lama's Gelukpa order was the youngest Buddhist lineage in Tibet. The Nyingma was the oldest and they traced their roots all the way back to the Tibetan empire period of the seventh and eighth century. The Kagyü, on the other hand, saw their origins in the revival of the eleventh and twelfth centuries when Indian masters fleeing the Muslim advance came to Tibet. The Sakya saw themselves as part of this era as well, though their heyday was during the Yuan dynasty when they ruled Tibet as representatives of Mongol imperial power. Nevertheless, in the eyes of Tsongkhapa (1357–1419), the founder of the Gelukpa, all three of these venerable orders had gone astray. In his view the situation could only be rectified through a puritanical return to the fundamentals, and in this sense Tsongkhapa was part of the reform movements that swept Eurasia in the wake of the Mongol conquests. Though unlike the Muslim world, Tibet had never suffered the full force of the Mongol onslaught and thus Tsongkhapa's revivalist message was at first met with skepticism. The early Gelukpa movement also had to face the problem of overcoming the long-established ties between Tibet's ruling families and the three other schools.

For these reasons the Gelukpa order could very well have disappeared, as was the fate of so many other religious schools throughout history. But the Gelukpa were blessed with Gedündup (1391–1475), posthumously recognized as the First Dalai Lama. He was Tsongkhapa's relative and successor. He was also both politically savvy and a particularly good missionary. In short order he therefore established good relations with the land-holding aristocracy of central Tibet and with their support founded Tashilhünpo monastery in 1447. After he passed away a boy born just north of Zhikatsé, Gedün Gyatso (1475–1542), was recognized as his incarnation and brought to the Gelukpa monastery of Drepung outside of Lhasa to receive his religious training. After finishing his studies in 1498, however, he was forced to flee because Lhasa was captured by the prince of Rinpung, who not only ruled central Tibet, but also favored the Karmapa, the leader of the Kagyü order. As a result, the Dalai Lama was able to return to Lhasa only twenty years later when Gongma Chenmo, the secular ruler of the Pakmo Drukpa order, expelled the Rinpung from Lhasa. And as a symbol of his return Gedün Gyatso had the Ganden Phodang palace built, which was to become the subsequent seat of the Dalai Lamas.

It was into this world of conflict, where powerful Tibetan families fought against each other with the backing of various Buddhist orders, that Sönam Gyatso was born (1543–1588). At two years of age he was recognized as an incarnation of Gedün Gyatso and brought to Drepung, where he was installed as abbot and began his studies. But in 1565 when the Rinpung rulers captured Zhikatsé and took control of south central Tibet Sönam Gyatso was forced to leave Lhasa and seek allies to save the Gelukpa. He found some along the Indian border but they and the Pakmo Drukpa were no match for the Rinpung. But as luck would have it, just as the Rinpung were about to capture Lhasa, Mongol envoys arrived and requested Sönam Gyatso to meet with Altan Khan on June 19, 1578, at Lake Kökenuur. He readily accepted and headed north ahead of the advancing Rinpung army. When the two met they followed the protocols of the Buddhist model of rule established by Esen Khan. Altan thus gave Sönam

Gyatso the title Dalai Lama (a title retroactively applied to his two previous incarnations, making him the Third Dalai Lama). He in turn gave Altan the title Brahma, Great, Powerful, Cakravartin King of the Dharma. A glorious title, but in truth the Dalai Lama was not really satisfied with Altan Khan. In his quest for powerful allies Sönam Gyatso therefore sent a letter introducing himself to the Ming emperor.

At the time the wisdom at the Ming court held that Buddhism would pacify the warlike nature of the Mongols and thus it should be promoted.[118] As a result, the Dalai Lama was seen as a perfect pawn in the Ming court's peace-through-Buddhism plan. Upon receiving the Dalai Lama's letter the Wanli emperor (r. 1572–1620) therefore sent him gifts and an imperial title. Then when the Dalai Lama came to Mongolia in order to officiate at Altan Khan's funeral in 1586 the Wanli emperor invited him to Beijing and presented him with an even grander title: National Teacher (*guoshi*), which was the title Khubilai Khan had given Pakpa Lama. Imagining the possibilities—the Gelukpa as powerful as the Sakya during the Yuan with the help of the Ming—the Dalai Lama anxiously headed off to Beijing. Yet the possibilities of this dream were dashed when he died en route. And another wrench was thrown into the religiopolitical machinations of both the Ming and Gelukpa when the Mongols declared Altan Khan's great-grandson as the incarnation of the Third Dalai Lama. The Tibetans were invariably skeptical, but they finally recognized Yontan Gyatso as the Fourth Dalai Lama (1589–1617). But then the Mongols would not let them take him back to Tibet. Eventually, however, the Mongols were swayed by the argument that the boy needed to receive both Buddhist training and tantric initiations that could only be provided in Tibet. But as had been the case with his predecessors his religious education quickly fell victim to politics, since his presence in Lhasa fanned the embers that had lain dormant since the Third Dalai Lama had fled twenty-five years earlier.

In 1605 the Pakmo Drukpa therefore attacked Lhasa, and in response the Mongols came to the aid of the Dalai Lama and attacked central Tibet. They were repelled by the Rinpung, who simultaneously crushed their old enemies the Pakmo Drukpa, yet during these mêlées the Dalai Lama fled Lhasa. But he was invited back by the Rinpung ruler Puntshog Namgyal, who wanted the Dalai Lama to give him a special tantric initiation. Upon the advice of his ministers the Dalai Lama refused and inevitably violence erupted. Shortly after fleeing Lhasa yet again the Fourth Dalai Lama died at the age of twenty-eight. Nevertheless, as evidenced by the Mongol invasion of Lhasa in 1607, the religious and political crisis in Tibet was quickly becoming an international issue.

But the Mongols were not only defending the Gelukpa. Indeed, after the death of Altan Khan his centralizing project had come to an end. Instead various local Mongol chieftains followed his lead and abandoned the Chinggisid principle of one Mongol ruler, and by allying themselves with a Tibetan lama they proclaimed themselves khan. This development set in motion not only a civil war among the Mongols themselves, but since these competing khans had allied themselves with different Buddhist orders, they were also drawn into competing sides in Tibet's civil war.[119] Chogtu Taiji of the Khalkha, for example, had allied himself with the Karmapa and launched an invasion of Tibet against the Gelukpa and their Tümed allies. On account of these competing religious and political alliances the situation in Inner Asia was quickly spinning out of control. But again, the crisis was not contained to this area. Indeed, much as the Ming dynasty's economic and political weakness in the mid-sixteenth century had played an important role in setting this whole crisis in motion,[120] it was the Ming that would suffer the ultimate fate of this Tibeto-Mongol Buddhist war. Namely, in 1644 the Ming would be annihilated by the Manchus, who before the invasion had coincidentally built a massive temple complex designed as a mandala to house the statue Khubilai Khan had given to Pakpa Lama.[121] History had apparently come full circle.

But the Ming were not the only victims of this Buddhist revival; so too were the Moghuls. Wedged as they were between their archrivals in the west, the Shi'a Safavids, and in the east by an escalating civil war fueled by Buddhist sectarianism, the Moghuls had nowhere to go. Moreover, since they had adopted urban life at the urging of the Naqshbandiyya they were now settled and thus could not easily migrate. Moreover, with the trade that had earlier sustained their urban economy at a standstill, Moghul power was quickly evaporating. And in their place arose the Oirad, who from their base in the area between the Altai and Tianshan mountains had remained true to their nomadic origins. In fact being mobile at this time was to their great advantage, as was their largely nonaligned position in the currently raging conflagrations.

Both of these factors enabled the Oirads to expand their area of control at the expense of the warring Mongols and Tibetans. During the early seventeenth century the Oirads thus developed into two powerful groups: the Zünghars in their "native" territory north of the Tarim Basin, and the

Upper Mongols, led by the Khoshuud, in the area around Lake Kökenuur, now Qinghai province (map 18).[122]

Yet even though Oirad power was rapidly increasing in Inner Asia they never took it upon themselves to claim control. They remembered better than anyone the fate of Esen when he proclaimed himself khan. The Oirad therefore presented themselves as a commoner dynasty. They called their ruler simply Khong Taiji, from the Chinese *huang taizi*, "crown prince, heir apparent."[123] But this situation and the balance of power in Inner Asia were quickly to shift with the appearance on stage of the next incarnation of the Dalai Lama.

The Fifth Dalai Lama, Ngawang Lobsang Gyatso (1617–1682), is often known simply as the Great Fifth, and rightfully so. He was without a doubt one of the towering figures of seventeenth-century history. He not only won the Tibeto-Mongol war and thereby made the Dalai Lama the supreme religiopolitical ruler of Tibet, but through his political alliances he also reformulated both the map and nature of Eurasian politics.[124] Indeed, so great was his stature that the Tibetan elite was so terrified of the potential political fallout from his death that they decided to keep it secret. They

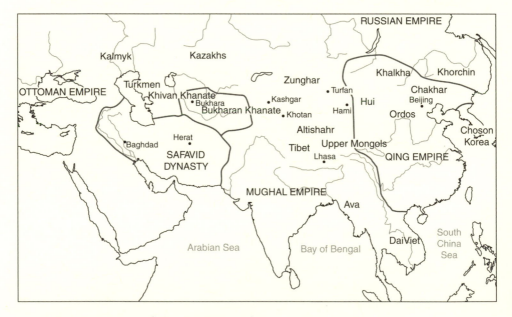

Map 18. Seventeenth-Century Inner Asia.

therefore claimed that he was in meditation retreat, and for a good fourteen years kept issuing decrees in his name. Of course, when the truth eventually leaked out no one was amused, least of all the Manchu emperors, who subsequently would become more and more involved in Tibet's political affairs. And in the wake of the Gurkha War in the early 1790s the Manchus would ultimately make Tibet an inalienable part of the Qing dynasty.[125] Yet the Manchu conquest of Tibet was more than 150 years into the future from the time when the Great Fifth began his remarkable rise to power.

To accomplish this goal the first issue he tackled was the Gelukpa's political and military weakness, since he knew that without powerful backers the Gelukpa could never challenge the power of the Karmapa and his Rinpung allies. He therefore set about establishing alliances with the day's political and military superpowers: the Zünghar and Manchus.[126] In particular, by utilizing the Buddhist model of rule he could bestow upon these dynasties with Chinggisid pretentions—but with no Mongol blood—the title of Khan. Having received this blessing and seal of approval these rulers could thus turn around and claim authority within the mold of the Mongol Buddhist legacy created by Esen Khan. The Dalai Lama's tantric initiations thus in essence whitewashed their non-Mongol past. The Dalai Lama's blessing gave both the Zünghars and Manchus not only Buddhist legitimacy, but also the ever-important legitimacy of the Mongol legacy. In many ways the Fifth Dalai Lama therefore became Inner Asia's ultimate "khan-fixer," which certainly burnished his image and gave the institution of the Dalai Lama a stature it had never had before. But if he wanted to consolidate his power in Tibet the Great Fifth needed more than respect and adulation; he needed weapons. He also needed soldiers willing to kill and maim in the name of the Dalai Lama.

He found what he was looking for in the Upper Mongols, who in many ways became his fundamentalist Gelukpa death squad. Leading these shock troops was the Khoshuud leader Güüshi Taiji, who had taken the throne in 1630. Four years later the Fifth Dalai Lama requested his help in defeating the Karmapa and his supporters the Rinpung as well as the Khalkha prince Chogtu Taiji.[127] By 1637 the Khoshuud had defeated Chogtu Taiji and taken over northern and eastern Tibet in the name of the Dalai Lama. Güüshi Taiji then went on to systematically crush all of the Fifth Dalai Lama's enemies, whereupon on April 13, 1642, the Great Fifth declared him khan of Tibet, a position Güüshi Khan held for thirteen years, whereupon his son Dayan succeeded him. But even though the relationship between the

Khoshuud Khans and the Dalai Lama was imagined in the classic model of Buddhist rule, with each controlling their own separate sphere, the reality was that the Great Fifth was more often than not simply using the Mongols to secure both his religious and political position in Tibetan society.[128]

Moreover, as with many powerful rulers the Great Fifth used fear and violence in order to secure his position. Recall this is how he told his shock troops to treat his enemies:

> [Of those in] the band of enemies who have despoiled the duties
>   entrusted to them:
> Make the male lines like trees that have had their roots cut;
> Make the female lines like brooks that have dried up in winter;
> Make the children and grandchildren like eggs smashed against
>   rocks;
> Make the servants and followers like heaps of grass consumed by
>   fire;
> Make their dominion like a lamp whose oil has been exhausted;
> In short, annihilate any traces of them, even their names.[129]

Indeed, it was with such tactics, including the execution of recalcitrant Tibetan aristocrats,[130] that the Great Fifth created the Tibetan theocratic state headed by the Dalai Lama. Yet since the Great Fifth was creating a Gelukpa theocracy, it was not only the aristocracy that felt his wrath, but also other Buddhist lineages. The Jonangpa school, for example, which the Great Fifth particularly loathed, was brutally suppressed.[131]

Another lineage the Great Fifth found troublesome was the Drukpa, another suborder of the Kagyü. Most galling in the Dalai Lama's view was the fact that the king of Ladakh supported the Drukpa and not his own Gelukpa order. The Great Fifth was also troubled by the fact that the Ladakhis not only controlled trade with the West, but that they were also rich on account of their abundant gold mines, and thus in 1680 he launched an invasion.[132] In response the Ladakhis requested help from the Moghuls; however, they were no match for the Dalai Lama's army, or his war magic.

> The lord and his ministers, courageous, valiant and violently angry,
> advanced fearlessly in the middle of the opposing army, which filled
> the place without opportunity [of deploying]. Of the enemies who
> had thrown away their weapons some were killed, others fled; and

even the powerful chargers called *tobcaq* [in Turkish] were taken as trophy. Then, since the Victorious Ones (the Buddha and their incarnations) can see without obscurities every point of the three times (past, present, and future), [there came] through a riding messenger a letter sent by the All-Knowing Dalai Lama, which said, "If the army of Kashmir arrives, let me know it", [and thus] he opened the door of good actions enabling [the Tibetan general] to put [his feet] on the head of the Nawab. The hopes of those bent on increasing the quantity of their merits without sparing their efforts, doubtlessly are easily realized. In a part of the night following that [of the battle], the powerful well-wishing protectors encompassed a magical trick, following which the Kashmiri troops, frightened without reason, uttering wails of terror, fled away. [And this] caused to be hoisted on the top of the world the white banner which was the heroic sign of complete victory over the warriors of that country together with their followers.[133]

The Dalai Lama's war magic was actually rather prosaic: the Tibetans bribed the Moghuls to retreat and it worked. Nevertheless, the point to be made here is that 150 years after the Great Lhasa Jihad another Muslim army had marched into Ladakh. But they did so not in the name of jihad; they did so in order to save one Buddhist kingdom from the depredation of another.

To understand this event, as well as the Great Fifth's campaign into Ladakh, we need to recall the central point raised at the beginning of this chapter: while all religious traditions sanction violence, such rhetoric is mobilized only within certain historical contexts. Thus if we are to understand such calls for "Holy War" and their attendant eruptions of religious violence it is vital to explore the larger political, economic, and social context wherein such rhetoric arises. For example, in trying to understand the Great Fifth's invasion of Ladakh we should focus not only on the rhetoric of Buddhist polemics, but also recognize the profound economic importance of Ladakh for both the Tibetans and the Moghuls. Thus while the war may have been framed in religious terms by both sides, there were clearly other contributing circumstances that enabled such rhetoric to be drawn upon at this particular juncture in Eurasian history.

In this regard one can readily point to the factors articulated above, such as political fragmentation and economic contraction, both of which invariably fostered the rise of the Buddhist and Muslim theocracies of the seventeenth century. Yet what is curious about these theocracies is that their establishment did not necessarily lead to greater confrontation. Indeed, what is perhaps most surprising about the history of post-Mongol Inner Asia is that most religious violence was not directed outward, such as Muslims against Buddhists or vice versa, but rather against internal enemies of the faith. Indeed, even though there were clearly tensions between Buddhists and Muslims at this time, for the most part they continued to interact since, rhetoric aside, religion was often secondary to other political, economic, and ideological concerns. Of course, to explain this development it is important to recognize that the same forces driving the breakdown of the Eurasian system that fostered the development of these theocracies also ensured that these newly formed religiopolitical entities were for the most part kept separate. Thus although the post-Mongol period came to be "the age of jihad," in both the Muslim and Buddhist worlds, the victim of most religious violence was not the "other," but rather members of one's own faith.

And this was not only the case in Tibet under the Great Fifth, but also among the Moghuls, where the call to jihad was directed more often than not against other Muslims. In the seventeenth century, for example, the Naqshbandiyya had broken into two competing lineages and were fighting each other for control of Eastern Turkestan.[134] While both of these lineages traced their origins back to Ahmad Kasani (1461–1542), the Makhdum-i A'zam ("Supreme Teacher"), they split in relation to his two sons. Ishaq Wali was of the younger son's lineage and had found success among the Moghuls. The lineage of the elder son, on the other hand, had remained in Central Asia and found support among the Uzbeks. But the Juybari Sufis soon eclipsed their power at the Uzbek court and as a result Ahmad Kasani's grandson, Khoja Muhammad Yusuf (d. 1653), left Bukhara and headed east to the territory of the Moghuls. While traveling to the oasis towns of Eastern Turkestan he quickly acquired a devout following largely because the Moghuls were becoming increasingly exasperated with the lineage of Ishaq Wali, the Ishaqiyya, and their meddling. But the Ishaqiyya were quick to grasp the implications of Yusuf's growing support and therefore they killed him by poisoning his food.

This opening salvo in the feud between these two lineages was followed shortly thereafter by the Moghul ruler Isma'il Khan's expulsion of Yusuf's son and successor, Khoja Afaq (d. 1694), from his stronghold in Kashgar. Fleeing for his life Khoja Afaq first went to Kashmir. Then the story goes that he went to Lhasa and met the Great Fifth, with whom he had a friendly competition to see whose magic was more powerful. According to Muslim sources Khoja Afaq's magic was more powerful and the Dalai Lama therefore converted to Islam![135] Regardless, what is more historically accurate is that in his feud with the Ishaqiyya, Khoja Afaq did eventually secure the support of Galdan (1644–1697), the ruler of the Zünghars, who had not only been a student of the Great Fifth, but had also been anointed khan by the Great Fifth in 1671.

The Zünghars living to the north of the Tianshan had first become Buddhist in 1615 and the spread of the Dharma among them was greatly advanced by the famous Oirad monk Zaya Pandita, himself a disciple of the Gelukpa.[136] Yet, even though they had become thoroughly Buddhist within the context of the Tibeto-Mongol Buddhist civil war, and the Great Fifth's theocratic project, the Zünghars maintained cordial relations with the Muslims of the Tarim Basin throughout the seventeenth century. Much of this had to do with the fact that the Muslims of the oasis cities handled their trade with both Tibet and China.[137] But such trade was hampered on account of the increasing tensions between the Ishaqiyya and Afaqiyya. In fact, it was only when the feud between these two Naqshbandi lineages began to impinge upon the Zünghar's financial situation that this familial theological struggle could no longer remain an internal affair. To bring it to an end the Zünghar ruler Galdan therefore conquered the Tarim Basin and appointed Khoja Afaq and his sons as the local rulers with the obvious hope that this would stabilize the economic situation.

While this was briefly the case, after Galdan passed away a succession struggle for the Zünghar throne erupted and the Muslims took the opportunity to reassert their authority and throw off the Zünghar yoke. The Ishaqiyya of Yarkand thus declared independence and installed a puppet ruler drawn from the deposed Moghul royal house. Yet a few years later when Tsewang-Rabten (r. 1694–1727) had finally secured his power among the Zünghars he reasserted control over the Muslims in the Tarim Basin, and to secure their compliance Tsewang-Rabten took hostage the leaders of both the Ishaqiyya and Afaqiyya. While this worked to a certain extent in controlling Eastern Turkestan, the Zünghars had a much larger problem to deal with and that was their escalating war with the Manchus.

The war between the Manchus and Zünghars was the last monumental struggle fought in the shadow of the Mongol legacy.[138] It pitted two of Eurasia's most powerful empires against each other, both of whose rulers had been recognized as khan in the Chinggisid mold through the graces of the Fifth Dalai Lama. Thus when the Manchus finally won this struggle in 1757, they not only defeated the Zünghars, but they also put an end to the Mongol legacy. Many of the driving factors that had shaped the preceding three hundred years were thus no more. Instead the Manchus created a whole new world—the Qing dynasty—with its own logic and political and economic structures. Moreover, within this brave new world the Buddhists and Muslims of Inner Asia were once again brought together under one regime. What happened as a result is the topic of the next chapter.

CHAPTER FIVE
_____

Halal

Forbidden to you is that which dies of itself, and blood, and flesh of
swine, and that on which any other name than that of Allah has been
invoked, and the strangled (animal) and that beaten to death, and that
killed by a fall and that killed by being smitten with the horn, and that
which wild beasts have eaten, except what you slaughter, and what is
sacrificed on stones set up (for idols) and that you divide by the arrows;
that is a transgression.

—Qur'an 5:3

On Tingyu [of the 12th moon of the 16th year of Zhiyuan (January 27,
1280)] the Bargu presented gerfalcons. When the Muslims came and
food was furnished, they refused to eat it. The people were troubled by
it. The emperor said, "They are my slaves. In the matter of food how
dare they presume not to follow the custom of our dynasty?"

—Yuan Shi

IN THE EARLY weeks of the year 1280 a group of Muslim merchants set
out across the frozen steppe toward the Mongol capital of Daidu. Their
goal was Khubilai Khan's court and their aim was to present him with
several birds of prey, which they hoped he would use while hunting. But
the journey was hard, and the only thing that kept them going was the
dream of seeing the legendary magnificence of Khanbaliq, the Khan's City.
When they arrived they were not disappointed, since the city that is now
Beijing was beautiful and filled with products and people from across the
world.[1] Walking through the bazaar these well-traveled merchants heard
languages wholly foreign to their ears, and saw goods beyond their wildest

dreams. It was therefore with great trepidation that they went toward the khan's palace in order to present their gift of a white eagle and several white-footed, red-beaked gerfalcons.

They need not have worried, however; the khan was exceedingly pleased with the birds and he asked numerous questions about them and as their conversation about new hunting techniques became more animated the khan invited them to join him for dinner. They all thus retired to another tent and continued their lively discussion. For those preparing the food just outside the tent all they heard was lively chatter punctuated with the khan's hearty laugh. They knew everything was going well, and since the drinks were flowing they held off on serving the main course. Yet when they heard a lull in the conversation a small army of servers dashed into the tent and arrayed a multitude of dishes. Then just as quickly they departed. Upon their return the cooks and servers were surprised, however, to hear that the party did not seem to resume where it had left off. Instead there was simply some muted discussion and a little scuffling of feet. Then to their utter consternation the khan was shouting. He was enraged, and shortly thereafter his guests came scurrying out of the tent. The cooks were shocked and then terrified. They did not know what to do, especially since they were unsure of what had happened. Shortly thereafter, though, they knew; indeed, everyone knew. The incident was the talk of the town. Even Marco Polo, who was in the city at the time, wrote about this event.[2]

Although the exact details were to be greatly debated afterward, all agreed that everything began when the Muslim merchants refused to eat the meat prepared for Khubilai Khan's banquet. They had refused because it was not halal, and it was this act that had so infuriated the khan. As a result he issued the following edict:

On the 24th day of the 12th Moon of the 16th year of Zhiyuan [January 27, 1280]:
Chinggis Khan was born and collected all the various countries from where the sun rises to where it sets and made them follow [Mongol] customs. Among these many diverse peoples only the Muslims [objected] saying, "We do not eat food [prepared in] Mongol [fashion]." [Chinggis Khan thus] asked, "Being protected by Heaven we conquered you. You are our slaves, but you refuse to eat our food, how is this right?" and then issued a decree saying, "Make them eat

it. If they slaughter sheep by slitting the throat, let them be held accountable!"

This decree was in effect from then until the time of Ögedei Khan. From the time of Güyük Khan, however, because we were not as strong as our ancestors, we were negligent. Thus [for example] in the region of Bukhara, because Tarabi, Baba Rasul and Sheikh Adi had evil intentions, not only were they executed, but they also involved many others in the disaster.

After that, because the Vizier Sayf al-Din, the astrologer Husam al-Din, and Majd al-Din had also harbored evil intentions, they were killed by Prince Hülegü. He not only made the many Muslims eat the food of our dynasty, but also had [his order] translated into Muslim writing for them.

At that time, if they had understood as they should have, it would have been fine. Because they did not understand, there was Parwanah [Mu'in al-Din Sulaiman] who also harbored evil intentions. He was executed by Prince Abugha. At that time they did not understand either.

Now, [on account of the] Muslims, who brought falcons from the region of Bargu in the north, saying "We do not eat what other people have slaughtered," and because they harassed the common people, it has been decreed: Muslims and Jews must eat meat regardless by whom, [or how] it is slaughtered. They are forbidden to kill sheep by slitting the throat. They are forbidden to perform circumcision. And because they are supposed to pray five times a day, if they do so twice and pray [ten times a day], then they will understand.

If, having violated this order, by slitting the throat of a sheep or performing circumcision, or if one marries a cousin, or if one forcibly takes a slave and has them circumcised, or if a slave denounces one [for these things], then he shall be taken away and made a freeman. The property, money, and everything else of the owner shall be given to that man. If anyone else denounces [him], it shall be decided to give [the property, money, and all else] in accord with this regulation.

Respect this.[3]

With how much zeal the Yuan authorities followed this decree is debated. At first, however, it seems as if it was enforced with draconian glee. Seeking

the freedom to practice their religion many Muslims therefore left the territory of the Yuan dynasty. In so doing they also took with them their businesses, and this hit the Mongol economy hard. When this unintended side
effect became apparent to the Yuan court they subsequently revoked the
anti-halal decree in the hope that Muslims would not only stay, but also
possibly return. But the damage had been done and in many ways this
decree set the tone for the remainder of the dynasty.

Khubilai Khan's decree captures in essence many of the issues explored
in the preceding chapter. In particular, it reveals the central tension that
arose between the laws of Chinggis Khan and the *shari'a*; indeed, how the
two were to be reconciled was continually debated. In this particular case
Khubilai Khan had decided to uphold Mongol law above Islamic law, but
then changed his mind when the economic fallout of his decision became
apparent. And it was precisely such a balancing act that shaped much of the
"accommodation" that was to develop between these two legal traditions in
the subsequent centuries. Namely, for those groups who tried to wed the
Mongol legacy with Islam, the *jasaq-shari'a* debate was an ongoing negotia-
tion fraught with multiple opportunities for politicization. At the same
time, however, this debate had no relevance for those outside these Mongol-Muslim communities. Indeed, as we have seen in the preceding chapter
such internalization was a basic feature of the post-Mongol period. In fact,
it was for this reason that religious violence was most often directed against
coreligionists and not at those of other faiths. And in many ways the question of halal was the same, since after the empire it was only those Turko-
Mongols who needed to balance the Chinggisid legacy with Islam who
needed to wrestle with this issue. How they resolved it was of absolutely no
concern to the Buddhists.

During the Qing dynasty (1644–1911), however, this was to change as
the Manchus dismantled and reformulated the religiopolitical and cultural
structures that had largely kept Buddhists and Muslims separate in the
post-Mongol period. Namely, rather than Buddhists and Muslims operating within their respective theocratic states, the Qing forged an empire that
brought them both together under one regime. As a result, Buddhists and
Muslims had to grapple with this new reality and reenvision not only their
recently forged theocracies, but also what it meant to be part of the Qing.
Both groups thus had to figure out what it meant to be Buddhist or Muslim
within a Sino-Manchu state. Moreover, they also had to reevaluate the

nature of Buddhist-Muslim interaction now that both were part of the Qing.

These were no doubt large and complex questions with many different answers. Nevertheless, within this process one issue that came to take on a defining role for the Mongol Buddhists was the question of halal. In fact, it became the pivot around which the questions raised above were answered. It became the node that defined the Buddhist-Muslim divide. Exploring the issue of halal therefore offers us a window into the final chapter of Buddhist-Muslim interaction in Inner Asia before the onslaught of modernity and the many new questions it threw into the mix.

Historical and Legal Precedent

To begin to unravel the revival of the halal issue during the Qing dynasty we need to return to the original incident of 1280. In doing so we can start by looking at the presentation of this event as recounted by Rashid al-Din in his *Compendium of Chronicles*.[4] In his view the entire episode was blown out of proportion and manipulated by Khubilai Khan's Christian advisors so that they could drive their anti-Muslim agenda forward. Thus according to Rashid al-Din, after this initial decree was issued, Khubilai's Christian advisors argued that the khan needed to be firmer. They claimed that showing any sign of weakness would only embolden the Muslims. They therefore argued that stripping the Muslims of their wealth was not enough; instead, they convinced the khan to issue a new edict that stipulated the death penalty for "whoever slaughtered a sheep in his house."[5]

It was the threat of the death penalty that caused many Muslims to abandon the Yuan. Yet not all Muslims had given up hope. Some of the Muslim elite petitioned Khubilai Khan to change his mind. "Thereupon most of the chief Muslims of those parts—Baha al-Din Qunduzi, Shadi Zo-Cheng, 'Umar Qirqizi, Nasir al-Din Malik Kashgari, Hindu Zo-Cheng and other notables—jointly offered many presents to the vizier, so that he made the following representation [to the Qa'an]: 'All the Muslim merchants have departed from hence and no merchants are coming from the Muslim countries; the *tamghas* are inadequate and they do not bring *tangsuqs*; and all this because for the past seven years they have not slaughtered sheep. If it be so commanded, the merchants will come and go and the *tamgha* will be collected in full.' Permission was given for the issue of a *yarligh* to this effect."[6]

At this turn of events the Christians, at least according to Rashid al-Din, tried another strategy in their quest to disenfranchise the Muslim community. They told the khan that there was a verse in the Qur'an that said, "Kill all of the Polytheists, all of them,"[7] and thereby made the argument to Khubilai Khan that all Muslims are inherently fanatical jihadis.

The Qa'an was annoyed and asked: "From whence do you know this?" He was told that a letter on this subject had arrived from [the Il-khanid] Abagha Khan. He sent for the letter and, summoning the Muslim scholars, asked the senior amongst them, Baha al-Din Baha'i: "Is there such a verse in your Qur'an?"

"Yes," he replied.

"Do you regard the Qur'an," asked the Qa'an, "as the word of God?"

"We do," he said.

"Since then," the Qa'an went on, "you have been commanded by God to kill the infidels, why do you not kill them?"

He replied, "The time has not yet come, and we have not the means."

The Qa'an fell into a rage and said: "I at least have the means." And he ordered him to be put to death. However, the Emir Ahmad the vizier, the Cadi Baha al-Din, who also had the rank of vizier, and the Emir Dashman prevented this on the pretext that they would ask others also. They sent for Maulana Hamid al-Din, formerly of Samarqand, and the same question was put to him. He said that there was such a verse.

"Why then," said the Qa'an, "do you not [kill these people]?"

He answered, "God Almighty has said: 'Kill the polytheists', but if the Qa'an will so instruct me, I will tell him what a polytheist is."

"Speak," said the Qa'an.

"Thou are not a polytheist," said Hamid al-Din, "since thou writest the name of the Great God at the head of thy *yarlighs*. Such a one is a polytheist who does not recognize God, and attributes companions to Him, and rejects the Great God." The Qa'an was extremely pleased and these words took firm root in his heart. He honored Hamid al-Din and showed favor to him; and at his suggestion the others were released.[8]

By slyly paralleling the Abrahamic God with the Great God of the Mongols, Hamid al-Din was thus able to put a stop to the anti-Muslim policies of Khubilai Khan's Christian advisors.[9] Even so, tensions between the Mongol court and the Muslim community in China continued.

Yet as we have seen it had not always been so. Khubilai Khan, in particular, had followed the lead of Chinggis, Ögedei, and Möngke and readily supported the Muslim community. He actively recruited Muslims to come and serve at the Mongol court. But as seen above the Muslims in China were prominent not only in the fields of science, but they were also key figures in the Yuan economy as both merchants and tax collectors.[10] And invariably, it was precisely on account of this success that Muslims were often vilified by others, especially the Chinese, and a ready scapegoat when things turned sour. And it was these tensions and contradictions that the Mongol court had to continually try to resolve.

The situation with the Muslims was therefore always tense. Indeed, no matter what decision was made it inevitably had both positive and negative consequences; nonetheless, when dealing with these issues Khubilai Khan seemed willing to err on the side of the Muslim community. He recognized their importance to the Yuan court, and so too did many of his successors. But things took a turn for the worse when Khubilai Khan's grandson Ananda, who had been raised in a Muslim household, converted 150,000 of his troops to Islam. Although Ananda's attempt to seize the throne in 1307 was thwarted, as a decisive signal to the Muslim community his family's appanage was abolished. Yet even after such troubles the Muslim influence in China continued.

The peak of Muslim influence in Yuan China came under Yisün-Temür (titled Taidingdi, 1323–1328), when the Muslims Dawlat-Shah (d. 1328) as left grand councilor and 'Ubaidullah (d. 1328) as manager (*pingzhang*) dominated the administration. Dawlat-Shah had good relations with the Christians and granted both them and Muslims exemption from corvée. Ananda's son Örüg-Temür was reinstated in northwest China, and payments to mostly Muslim *ortoq* merchants selling pearls reached extraordinary levels. The conspirators who overthrew Yisün-Temür's son in 1328 executed both Dawlat-Shah and 'Ubaidullah, abolished the position of cadi (Islamic judge) in the capital, Daidu (modern Beijing), and after first putting all religions on equal tax footing, later granted Buddhist

and Daoist monasteries special exemption from the commercial tax.
In 1332 Ananda's son Örüg-Temür was accused of treason and executed. Muslims never again achieved high office in the Yuan.[11]

The reasons for this fall from grace were numerous. They ranged from
increasing Buddhist influence at the Mongol court to the larger "pro-
China/pro-Mongol debate" described above—a debate that more often
than not excluded Muslims and thus put the Islamic community at a disad-
vantage.

Even so, Muslims were not simply at the mercy of events beyond their
control. As we have seen many took things into their own hands and simply
left Yuan territory. In making such a decision, however, Muslims were not
only responding to the worsening political and economic situation; they
were also propelled by further anti-Muslim legislation as evidenced in this
legal ruling from 1340.

Prohibition of Marriage Between Cousins
The Central Secretariat memorialized on the 5th day of the 11th
month of the 6th year of Zhiyuan [1340]: "The Censorate reported,
with an attached document dispatched from the Southern Branch
Censorate: 'During the time of Buyantu Emperor [1312–1320], it
was ordered to stop marriage between Muslim scholars, Muslims,
and Jews. Recently Muslim scholars, Muslims and Jews still marry
their cousins, so it is appropriate to prohibit it.' Because they sent
the document with this content, the Ministry of Punishment and
the Ministry of Rites discussed and concluded: 'Husband and wife
are the basis of human relations, and brothers are actually the rela-
tives of flesh and blood. While those who have the same family
name cannot marry, how can cousins be allowed to marry? From
now on, if there are people who marry in this way, they should be
regarded not only the same as a marriage of the same family name,
but also two more degrees should be added [as a penalty]. So each
of them should be hit 67 strokes and ordered to be separated. The
matchmakers should be hit 47 strokes. Let anybody who reports to
an office receive from the dowry ten *ding*s of Zhongtong cash as a
reward. And let this regulation be circulated and observed.' How is
it if we do as the [two] Ministries have discussed?"
Then we respectfully received an edict, saying 'Do it in that way!' "[12]

While the revival of such exclusionary laws certainly provided further incentive for Muslims to leave Yuan dynasty China, it is another question as to why such laws were originally implemented?

If we are to better understand the subsequent history of Buddhist-Muslim interaction in China, and the halal question, it is important to back up and ask why the Mongols were so averse to this practice. The common answer is Chinggis Khan. It was he who reportedly mandated the Mongol slaughtering technique whereby all the blood is retained within the carcass. In this method an animal's belly is cut open and then the aorta is pinched causing death (figure 29). Slaughtering according to the rules of halal, on the other hand, requires that an animal be butchered by having its neck severed, which drains all the blood. The two practices were clearly irreconcilable. By implementing such a law Chinggis Khan had therefore set him-

Figure 29. Mongols slaughtering a sheep. Photo: Cynthia Beall and Melvyn Goldstein.

self, and the Mongols, on a collision course with the Muslim world. Yet since Chinggis Khan had been allied with Muslims from early on, one can rightfully wonder why he would have instituted such a policy. Indeed, of all the possible social, religious, and cultural customs to uphold "Mongolness"; why this one? Moreover, why did he make everyone in the empire subject to this one Mongol custom when so many other laws and institutions were designed precisely to differentiate the Mongol ruling elite from everyone else? And even more to the point, could the Mongols, even at the height of their power, really have enforced this practice, much less outlawed Muslim butchering practices?

While this final question can readily be answered with a resounding no, the others are not so easy. Yet at the same time they may not in fact be the right questions. The first question should actually be whether Chinggis Khan ever issued such a decree. In answering this question we should begin by noting that the contemporary sources about Chinggis Khan are woefully scarce. Nearly everything we know about him is based on sources written long after his death.[13] In using these sources one therefore needs to be wary of the particular image of Chinggis Khan that the authors were trying to convey. The now-iconic image of Chinggis Khan leaving towering pyramids of skulls in his wake, for example, is less a reflection of reality than the negative image later Muslim historians wanted to convey about the Mongol conquests. Indeed, virtually everything written about Chinggis Khan needs to be balanced with regard to where, by whom, and why it was written.[14]

Such skepticism is also necessary when using the famous *Secret History of the Mongols*, our only Mongolian history of Chinggis Khan. And the main reason for this is that the *Secret History* was compiled in the early 1250s, and as such a central driving component of its narrative thrust was to legitimate Möngke Khan's Toluid lineage.[15] Recall that the Toluids had outmaneuvered the lineages of both Ögedei and Chaghatai. Yet even though the Toluids had power the two other lineages still saw this as usurpation, and thus the *Secret History* was used as a vehicle to promote the legitimacy of the Toluid lineage. And one element in this legitimating project was the presentation of Möngke Khan as the rightful heir because he supported the "pro-Muslim" tradition of Chinggis Khan. Chaghatai, of course, was famous for his anti-Muslim stance and thus by implication his heirs, especially Qaidu Khan, were not suitable rulers of the Mongol empire. In the hands of Toluid historians the reign of Möngke Khan was therefore presented as a legitimate continuation of Ögedei Khan's reign since he too had been pro-Muslim.[16] On account of this rhetoric it is therefore not surprising that the *Secret History* is in general rather pro-Muslim. More to the point, however, the *Secret History* never mentions Chinggis Khan's banning of halal.

The earliest mention of this regulation is actually found in the work of the Persian historian Juvaini.[17] He finished his history around 1260 while he was governor of Baghdad, and as many have pointed out his work is a sycophantic paean to the Mongols. In particular, he spends a great deal of time explaining why the Islamic community should support the Mongols even though they are non-Muslim. And as we have seen he does this by praising the Mongols' policy of "religious freedom" and stressing their avoidance of all forms of "fanaticism." His argument is thus essentially that even though the Mongols are not Muslim, they will not persecute Islam. Yet then there is Chinggis Khan's decree about slaughtering practices, which cannot be seen as anything other than a direct affront to Islam. However, that is not how Juvaini presents it. Rather, he uses this decree to reinforce the image of Mongol magnanimity and the viability of non-Muslim rule of Islamic lands.

To make this argument Juvaini follows the model of the *Secret History* and juxtaposes the rule of Ögedei and Chaghatai. Ögedei is thus the good Mongol ruler who follows the policy of religious freedom and thereby rejects implementing Chinggis Khan's anti-halal decree.[18] Chaghatai, on the other hand, is presented as the fanatic hardliner. He ruthlessly implements the law to such a degree that "Muslims were forced to eat carrion."[19] Whether this actually happened is beside the point; Juvaini's larger aim was to make it clear that Mongol rule was not by definition anti-Islam. Rather, much as was the case with Islamic law, the Mongols could in fact change their laws as they saw fit. Individual Mongol rulers like Ögedei could even reject the supposedly sacrosanct legal rulings of Chinggis Khan and establish his own legal precedent.[20]

Of course, conveying the actual mechanics of Mongol jurisprudence was not Juvaini's aim. Even so, his presentation does accord with the historical narrative of Khubilai Khan's edict quoted above, which also notes that the slaughtering law had largely been ignored for generations. Indeed, according to the logic of the edict it is precisely on account of this laxity that Mongol rule has had to deal with Muslim resistance. The clear implication is that if Chinggis Khan's initial edict had been maintained, then all of these problems would have been avoided. Khubilai Khan's legal solution is therefore to reinstitute not only this law, but also a marriage law that brings the *shari'a* in line with Mongol custom.

But Khubilai Khan's legal argument is in many ways dubious. In fact, all the incidences of Muslim unrest he cites are of specious value in the case of the Yuan dynasty, since none of them actually have to do with China. Tarabi, for example, who Khubilai notes stirred up a great deal of trouble and was therefore executed, was actually the leader of a new religious movement in Bukhara, who claimed he communicated with the spirit world and had magical powers.[21] Husam al-Din, whom Khubilai accuses of having "harbored evil intentions," had actually been appointed by Möngke Khan as Hülegü's court astronomer. But he got in trouble for trying to dissuade Hülegü from sacking Baghdad. Namely, he claimed that if the caliph came to a violent end there would be six natural disasters. Yet Husam al-Din's argument was discounted by Hülegü's other court astronomer, the Shi'ite Nasir al-Din Tusi, and the assault and subsequent murder of the Sunni caliph went ahead.[22] Of course, what any of these episodes have to do with events unfolding in China is an open question. Indeed, was Rashid al-Din correct in blaming the Christians for stirring up all of this anti-Muslim hysteria? Or was his own presentation of Christian meddling shaped more by the situation in Il-khanid Iran, where Christian-Muslim tensions did in fact run high? Although we cannot be certain, the point to be made here is the importance of the historical context in which these works were written.

Yet, the issue is not simply historiographical since there were clearly numerous factors that may have influenced Khubilai Khan's decision to use these little-understood and far-away incidences of Muslim unrest in order to portray Islam as subversive and dangerous. In particular, it is important to recall that Khubilai Khan issued this edict in the midst of growing Chinese resentment toward Muslims on account of their perceived control over the Yuan economy as ministers and tax collectors, and because of their powerful merchant associations. Indeed, precisely because of Khubilai's sustained support of Muslim officials and their policies, such as tax farming, Muslims had come to be associated in many Chinese minds with the worst financial abuses and outright economic exploitation. And this popular anger was galvanized in 1278 when a Chinese official accused Khubilai's chief financial minister, Ahmad, of corruption. The khan, however, refused to believe these accusations and therefore allowed him to keep his position, which was a decision that outraged many and resulted in a group of Chinese finally rising up and killing Ahmad in 1282.[23]

It is therefore within the midst of this growing Chinese animosity toward corrupt Muslim ministers and merchants that Khubilai's anti-edict of 1280 needs to be situated. Yet it is not the only one. It is also important to recall that this edict was issued only a few months after the Yuan had conquered the Southern Song dynasty. And thus at this particular juncture not only did the Mongol court have to appease the increasingly disaffected Chinese populace in the north, but also the entire heartland of Chinese civilization in the south.[24] Indeed, coming up with a plan of how to soothe Chinese anger as well as incorporate this new and enormous Chinese territory within the Mongol empire was probably of far more importance to the Yuan court at the time than whether some Muslim merchants ate the food offered at the khan's table.

At the same time, however, it also seems as if in their deliberations the Yuan court realized that the two issues were in a certain sense intertwined. The Muslim refusal to eat Mongol food directly challenged the much-touted magnanimity and authority of the state. Thus if such insubordination were not dealt with properly the wrong message would be sent not only to the northern Chinese, but also to the new subjects of the recently conquered Southern Song.[25] Moreover, by issuing such a decree the Yuan also made it clear to the Chinese that the power of the Muslims was not unchecked. Indeed, for the Yuan court this was probably the most pressing concern since within their deliberations on how to deal with the Song a central question was whether they could continue to use Muslim advisors and tax collectors in the political, cultural, and intellectual heartland of the Han Chinese. Khubilai Khan's anti-Muslim edict of early 1280 was thus very likely one small part of a deliberate strategy that was trying to balance the demands of a state that was suddenly overwhelmingly Chinese by sending the message that not only would the court not brook any dissent, but also letting the Chinese know that Muslim influence was not driving the Mongol state.

The intended, or unintended, consequence of this decision was that Muslim power and influence at the Yuan court invariably started to decline. Indeed, as the Song was gradually incorporated within the Yuan dynasty the power of the Muslim elite was gradually taken over by the Chinese political elite. Moreover, as we have seen, from this point onward the political debates at the Yuan court came to be defined largely by the intellectual and political struggles of the Sino-Confucian and the Turko-Mongol elite. Within this new context the era of Muslim dominance in China therefore started to draw to a close. Yet, even so, for some time Muslims continued to play a role in the fields of science and business. It was during this period, for example, that Muslim merchants created the famous blue-white porcelain that was to become the first "global brand."[26] But as time went on their power and influence continued to dissipate and with the collapse of the Yuan dynasty, and its replacement by the nativist Han Chinese dynasty of the Ming, this era of Muslim involvement in Chinese history came to a definitive end.

But Islam did not disappear from China. While many of the people who had defined this epoch—the Arabs, Persians, and Turks—had returned to their homelands, there still remained a large group of Chinese Muslims. Their origins, however, are wrapped in mystery. Some claim they are descendants of the original Arab and Persian merchants who arrived in China during the Tang dynasty. Others see their origins within the Muslim elite of the Yuan period.[27] Some, however, were probably part of the large number of Muslims that the Mongol court had moved into China during the thirteenth century.[28] Either way, however, during the political fragmentation and religious realignments of the post-Mongol period a large Chinese Muslim community came to establish itself in the border region of Gansu province, the traditional transit corridor of east-west trade in western China. Being thus situated—with the Muslim Moghals to the west, China to the east, Mongols and Oirads to the north, and Tibetans to the south— the Chinese Muslims were perfectly situated to function as a vital link among all of these regions. In fact, the Chinese Muslims used their hyphenated Sino-Islamic identity to its fullest advantage by then fanning out across China, Mongolia, and Tibet and establishing themselves in various niche businesses.[29] Many, for example, used their international connections in order to establish successful trading operations. Others used their outsider position in order to corner the market in specific jobs that the locals did not want to do. One such occupation was the butcher. In China, for example, there was a beef taboo and thus Chinese Muslims handled the slaughtering of oxen and buffalo.[30] Similarly, in Tibet, where the Buddhist theory of karma advocated no killing, the Chinese Muslims butchered the animals that the Tibetans ate.[31] In this way the Chinese Muslims, also known as the Hui, converted their outsider status into a means of integrating themselves within both of these cultures. Thus even though the Tibetans and Chinese might have abhorred the Muslims and their butchering practices, it receives scant attention in any of their written records. Even during periods of crisis when there was increased tension and actual violence between these groups the issue of slaughtering practices was never utilized as a vehicle to heap opprobrium on the Muslims.

But this was not the case among the Mongols. They, of course, had a long historical and legal tradition regarding the issue of halal. In fact, during the post-Mongol period the Mongol view of the matter was succinctly summarized in their own legal code: "When an animal is to be eaten, its feet must be tied, its belly ripped open and its heart squeezed in the hand until the animal dies; then its meat may be eaten, but if anyone slaughters an animal after the Muslim fashion, he is to be himself slaughtered."[32]

You Are What You Eat

Over the last several decades there has accumulated a veritable mountain of scholarly literature investigating the intersection of food and culture.[33] Much of it boils down to the old adage, "you are what you eat," but not in the sense meant by the 1930s American food-guru Victor Lindlahr, who popularized the phrase. While he was talking about nutrition, most scholars look at the heavy symbolic weight food carries as a vehicle of defining who we are. What we eat, namely, defines us in terms of religion, class, nationality, and so on. Food is therefore not only a means of nutrition; it is a powerful means of drawing boundaries.

While there are innumerable examples that can be given to confirm this idea, one can simply point out two well-known examples. The first is Ferdinand and Isabella's promotion of pork consumption in Spain after they conquered the last Muslims of Andalusia in 1492, a policy that clearly said Spain is now a Christian world. And indeed the pork and salami belt that stretches across southern Europe says much the same thing: Islam stops here.[34] The same linkage between military conquest, religious identity, and food consumption is also encapsulated in both the croissant and the bagel, both of which were supposedly created to commemorate the Christian victory over the Ottomans at the siege of Vienna in 1683.[35] Thus eating a buttery pastry in the shape of a crescent, the symbol of Islam, or a bagel—which legend has it represents the stirrup of the Polish king Jan Sobieski who helped drive off the Turks—captures well not only this particular moment in history, but also the role of food in marking historical and cultural boundaries.

Drawing such boundaries by means of food was, of course, not the sole preserve of the Christian West. Muslim sources also routinely focus on food, and as Ferdinand and Isabella well knew, the central focus is very often the question of pork.[36] The Timurid envoy Ghiyath al-Din, for example, who wrote so appreciatively of Chinese artistic skills, also notes with dismay the Chinese penchant for pork. He recoils, in particular, when he sees pork placed side by side with other meats in Chinese markets.[37] Ruy Gonzalez de Clavijo, the Portuguese envoy to the Timurid court, recorded another interesting example of how pork operated as a boundary marker between the Muslim world and "the East"[38] when he noted that Tamerlane called the Chinese emperor the "King Pig."[39] Indeed, when we recall that Tamerlane was planning on invading China this title captures well not only the Muslim aversion to pork, but also the role of food in conceptualizing one's world.[40]

Of course, creating such boundaries does not by definition mean that it leads to violence and persecution, as was to be the case in both reconquista Spain and Yuan-dynasty China. Indeed, as observed by another author from the early fifteenth century: if only foodways were respected then a harmonious society could be created.

> The king of the country is a Nan-k'un man; he is a firm believer in the Buddhist religion [i.e., Hinduism]; [and] he venerates the elephant and the ox. The population of the country includes five classes, the Muslim people, the Nan-k'un people, the Che-ti people, the Ko-ling people, and the Mu-kua people. The king of the country and the people of the country all refrain from eating the flesh of the ox. The great chiefs are Muslim people; [and] they all refrain from eating the flesh of the pig. Formerly there was a king who made a sworn compact with the Muslim people, [saying] "You do not eat the ox; I do not eat the pig; we will respectfully respect the taboo"; [and this compact] has been honoured right down to the present day.[41]

The writer of these words was the Chinese Muslim Ma Huan, who recorded for posterity the famous naval expeditions of Zheng He that went from China all the way to the Horn of Africa, and this observation about respecting foodways concerned a kingdom in southern India.

Yet unlike the Hindus of southern India the Mongols did not always respect Muslim foodways, and thus rather than harmony there was often tension. However, as noted above, such tension was prevalent only during the empire period, when Mongols and Muslims were engaging each other within a unified realm. When the empire collapsed and Muslims and non-Muslims went their separate ways the issue of halal was no longer of pressing concern. However, when Muslims and Mongols were brought together once again within the Qing dynasty this situation was to change.

Islam and the Qing Dynasty

The people who were to become the Manchus and found the Qing dynasty were originally farmers and fishermen inhabiting the forests northeast of China.[42] From such humble beginnings it is perhaps hard to imagine that they would one day rule the richest and most populous empire in the world. But that is what they did, and how they did so has exercised scholars ever since. Yet in thinking about this issue one can begin by noting simply that the Manchus happened to be in the right place at the right time. The Ming dynasty was politically paralyzed; its economy faltering, and most important, their army could barely maintain 100,000 regular mounts for its cavalry.[43] Moreover, the Mongols were occupied with the Tibeto-Mongol Buddhist civil war and thus they saw the Manchus not as a threat but as a potential ally. Many Mongol groups thus allied themselves with the Manchus hoping that they would join them in the fray, and the Manchus did join the fight. But they kept right on going until by the 1630s all the Mongols of Inner Mongolia were under their control. And this development not only increased the Manchus' military ranks, but also gave them unlimited access to horses. With these reinforcements the Manchus turned their attention southward and in short order they conquered Beijing and put an end to the Ming dynasty in 1644. While the conquest of the other surrounding realms and peoples took longer, by the end of the seventeenth century all of south China was under Manchu rule, as was the Mongolian plateau and the Chinese Muslims of Inner Asia.[44] During the next century the Manchus would double the size of their territory by conquering the Zünghars and the Muslims of Eastern Turkestan in the 1750s, and finally in the 1790s, Tibet.

Nevertheless, while the main reason the Manchu army marched into Tibet was to repulse an invasion by the Nepalese Gurkhas, the Qing court was also concerned about British influence in the area. Warren Hastings, the governor general of India, had already sent George Bogle to establish diplomatic relations with Tibet in the 1770s.[45] Yet the Qianlong emperor's interest in Tibet was not driven solely by realpolitik geostrategy. He was also a devout disciple of his Tibetan guru Rolpé Dorjé. Indeed, tantric Buddhism had been an integral component of Manchu rule from the very beginning and it was one of the things that helped forge such a successful bond between the Manchu state and its Mongol subjects.[46] At the same time, however, the Qing dynasty was never an exclusivist Buddhist empire. Rather, the Manchus envisioned their realm as a benevolent empire that would respect the cultural differences of its subject peoples. Indeed, as long as they served the interests of the Manchu emperor these various groups were allowed a certain degree of autonomy in maintaining their own traditions. Invariably over time the cultural practices of the subject peoples did change in conformity with Qing practices; however, at the same time each of these groups—Chinese, Mongols, Tibetans, Turks—was able to maintain a distinctive identity within the Qing dynasty. That the Manchu rulers were able to maintain this balance may explain in some measure how they were able to successfully rule such an enormously diverse empire for nearly three hundred years.

The case of Islam, however, reveals some of the problems that were to eventually shatter this carefully articulated Manchu vision of multiethnic harmony. In particular, it was the Chinese Muslims who presented the Qing authorities with a problem, because not only did they not accord with a recognizable "cultural bloc" like the Chinese, Mongols, and Tibetans, they also did not live in one contiguous territory. And this later issue particularly vexed the Qing court since they believed that tensions among their subject peoples could best be avoided by keeping them separate. The Manchu state thus maintained various mechanisms to keep these different groups away from one another. The Chinese Muslims, however, challenged this system since they were dispersed across the empire. Many officials therefore argued that the Manchu policy of "multiculturalism" was flawed in the case of Islam. They argued that while it made sense in the case of others, the Muslims had to be dealt with in a unique fashion. Yet the Kangxi emperor (r. 1661–1722) held firm to his belief that all subjects had to be treated equally and promoted this idea with the widely disseminated slogan, "Equal benevolence toward Chinese and Muslim."[47]

In the beginning of the eighteenth century, however, local Chinese officials began to question the wisdom of this policy. One of the first was the Shandong judge Chen Shiguan, who wrote to the court in 1724 arguing that

Muslims are inherently different and Islam should therefore be outlawed in the empire: "'It is a perverse doctrine that deceives the people and should be banned by law. Those who enter it do not respect Heaven and Earth and do not worship the gods, instead setting up their own cultic deity. . . . They aid the evil and harm the people. Please force them from their [perverse] teaching and destroy their mosques.'"[48]

In his reply the Yongzheng emperor (r. 1722–1735) agreed that Islam was foolish, but he felt it did not pose a threat. Three years later he reiterated his views in a letter to the Grand Secretariat:

> All over the direct [-rule] provinces, the Hui [Muslim] people, having resided there from old, are enumerated as part of the population and are all still children of our country. It follows that they cannot be regarded as separate. Over the years secret memorials have frequently been submitted arguing that the Hui [Muslim] people maintain their separate religion, speak a foreign tongue, wear strange clothes, and are fierce, perverse, and lawless, and demanding that they be strictly punished and placed under restraint. I deem, however, that the Hui [Muslim] have their religion because their ancestors bequeathed them their family habits and local customs. . . . As long as they peacefully keep their customs they are not to be compared with traitors, lawbreakers, or those who seek to delude and lead people astray. . . . Our court looks on them with the same benevolence as on all.[49]

When an official questioned this policy and argued that Muslims should be punished more severely than others the Yongzheng emperor removed him from office.

Several years later another Qing official, Chen Hongmou, promoted again the idea of harsher punishment being necessary to steer Muslims toward law and order.[50] In his 1751 *Covenant to Instruct and Admonish Muslims*, which he sent to the Board of Punishments, Chen took the earlier argument of Chen Shiguan even further by placing the responsibility for criminal behavior on Muslim leaders directly. The Board of Punishments, however, did not adopt Chen Hongmou's policy recommendation. But his argument set a precedent, and in 1762 the governor general of Shaanxi-Gansu actually put it into effect. He therefore not only had Muslim criminals punished more harshly than Chinese criminals, but he also made the imam of a mosque responsible for the actions of his congregants. Such a policy clearly went against the ethos of earlier Manchu policy, yet the Qianlong emperor (r. 1735–1796) endorsed it.

To understand his decision to overturn the policies of both his father and grandfather it is important to recognize that a similar sea change was taking place within the Chinese Muslim community. Most notably they were coming under the influence of the Naqshbandiyya, who had been moving toward the east for a century.[51] To appreciate fully the impact of this particular Sufi order on the Hui, however, it is vital to recognize that the Chinese Muslims had long since transformed their religious practices into a localized Sino-Islamic form.[52] Indeed, on account of the struggles between the Moghals, Oirad, Ming, and Mongols during the post-Mongol period the Hui had developed largely in isolation from the intellectual and religious currents of the broader Muslim world. Yet beginning with the Moghal and Naqshbandiyya push toward the east in the seventeenth century, this isolation came to an end. Muhammad Yusuf, for example, preached in Suzhou and supposedly won over the head of the Hui scholars to the Naqshbandiyya.

But it was to be Yusuf's son, Khoja Afaq, who would have the greatest impact among the Chinese Muslims.

> In 1671–1672 Khoja Afaq, who is spoken of in Chinese sources as "Hidayat Allah (*Hsi-ta-yeh-t'ung-la-hei*), the twenty-fifth generation descendant of Muhammad," visited the Kansu capital of Lanchou, Ti-tao Subprefecture (now in Lin-t'ao) in southern Kansu, Hsi-ning Guard in what is now the province of Tsinghai, and is said to have made a further appearance at Ho-chou, China's "Little Mecca" (*Makha 's-saghira*), now renamed Lin-hsia, in western central Kansu. Huis, Salars, northeastern Tibetan Muslims, and undoubtedly also Muslims of China's other ethnic groups came to hear the khoja preach. Among these Chinese Muslims, Khoja Afaq won the commitment (*inabat*) of the subsequent initiators of three Naqshabandi saintly lineages (*men-huan*) that came eventually to dominate Muslim religious life in the Chinese northwest.[53]

Of Khoja Afaq's three principal successors the initiation lineage of Maitai Baba (fl. ca. 1680–1690) was to become the most important, not necessarily on account of Baba himself, however, but because of his student Abu 'l-

'Futuh Ma Laichi (1673–1753), who was an ambitious and brilliant student. When he was only eighteen he had already completed his studies and been appointed imam at a local mosque. Maitai Baba then gave him his daughter in marriage and appointed Ma Laichi as his successor in the Naqshbandi lineage of Khoja Afaq.

Ma Laichi's greatest feat, however, was to reconnect the Hui with the Islamic heartland. He did this by traveling and studying with Muslim scholars in the West. He first studied for a year in Yemen and then studied Sufism in Bukhara. Thereupon he went on pilgrimage to Mecca, where the famous teacher Mawlana Makhdum accepted him as a student. As a result of his travels and studies Ma Laichi therefore had a rare status in the Chinese Muslim world: he had studied in the West. When he returned to China his views therefore carried great weight and thus he quickly became embroiled in the current religious debates raging in the Chinese Muslim community.

One such debate concerned how the Ramadan fast should be broken. One group, calling itself the "Fore-Breakers," argued that after the fast one should first eat and then go to the mosque and pray. The other group, the "After-Breakers," maintained that one must pray at the mosque first and only then eat. Ma Laichi, for his part, sided with the Fore-Breakers and thus won over the Turkic Salars and numerous Hui to his Naqshbandi lineage. But the dispute between the Fore-Breakers and After-Breakers persisted. Tensions eventually escalated to such a point that in 1731 these two factions brought their case to court. The Qing authorities, however, were wholly perplexed by the affair and asked them to simply resolve this internal theological dispute among themselves. But they were not able to do so. Moreover, the feud between the Fore-Breakers and After-Breakers was further compounded when another dispute about proper ritual practice erupted within the Chinese Muslim community.

In this instance the question revolved around the proper practice of *dhikr*, the Sufi ritual invocation of God. Ma Laichi had taught that dhikr should be performed silently (*khufi*). Another Sufi master, however, claimed it should be chanted aloud (*jahrī*). This teacher was Ma Mingxin, who like Ma Laichi had also studied in the West. The two had in fact crossed paths in Bukhara. But when Ma Laichi returned to China, Ma Mingxin had gone to Yemen, where he was to stay and study for twenty years. Most notably, he studied with the Zabid Naqshbandiyyas, who were teaching that dhikr should be recited aloud.[54] But that was not all Ma Ming-xin learned in Yemen.

He was also deeply influenced by the neo-orthodox thinking that was then sweeping the Middle East in response to European imperialism. Much like the Mongol conquests the rise of the post-enlightenment Christian West had invariably raised the same question: What went wrong? In trying to answer this question many Muslims once again made the argument that the proper response to this calamity was a return to the fundamentals of Islam. In their view it was only by returning to the true and original teachings that Islam could return to its former glory. One such thinker was Muhammad ibn 'Abd al-Wahhab (1703–1792), whose strict interpretation of Islam would be adopted by the Saud family in their struggles to dominate the Arabian Peninsula. Coincidentally, Ma Mingxin was studying in Yemen at this time and he came to be profoundly affected by this new *tajdīd*, or renewal movement, of the eighteenth century. And his politically charged revivalist vision was given added poignancy upon his return to China, since in his absence the infidel Qing dynasty had conquered all of Muslim Inner Asia.[55]

Upon his return, however, Ma Mingxin could not activate his broader vision of a political Islamic renewal. Rather, much like Ma Laichi before him, he became entangled within the internal theological debates of the Chinese Muslim community about ritual minutiae. In Ma Mingxin's case the central question was how dhikr should be performed, and as tensions mounted between the followers of Ma Mingxin and Ma Laichi over this issue of Islamic practice the two sides once again brought their case before the Qing court. In this case, however, the Qing court did not tell them to settle their dispute among themselves. In their deliberations the Qing authorities sided with the older of the two teachings and thus Ma Laichi's son and his Khafiyya (the "Silentists") were deemed orthodox, while Ma Mingxin's Jahriyya (the "Aloudists") were declared as heterodox.

Yet Ma Mingxin was not dissuaded by this imperial decree and he continued with his teaching, which invariably resulted in further legal confrontations with the Khafiyya. In response, the Qing authorities eventually forbade Ma Mingxin to teach in Xunhua district, and seven years later in 1769 he was ordered to leave Hezhou and return to his home village. Ma Mingxin moved instead to Guanchuan. From there he then traveled and acquired followers in the provinces of Xinjiang, Ningxia, and Shaanxi. But even though he no longer went to Xunhua he continued to have followers

there, especially among the Turkic Salars, and tensions between his followers and those of Ma Laichi remained high, a state no doubt fostered on
account of the Qing's continued support of the Khafiyya. And things came
to a head in 1781 when one of Ma Mingxin's followers, Su Forty-Three, led
a group of Jahriyya in an attack on the Khafiyya that left more than one
hundred people dead, including a Qing official. At this turn of events Ma
Mingxin was arrested as a rebel leader and brought to Lanzhou. Su Forty-
Three and his band followed and demanded his release. The Qing official
at the prison rejected their pleas and instead had Ma Mingxin executed.

This action resulted in a full-scale rebellion among Ma Mingxin's followers across northwest China. In response the Manchu court sent Grand
Secretary Agui from Beijing to lead a battalion of troops to suppress the
uprising. After arriving in the west they set about killing all the Jahriyya
leaders and exiling their followers to the frontiers of the Qing Empire. Yet
even after these heavy-handed tactics the Jahriyya rose up again three years
later under the leadership of Ma Mingxin's disciple Tian Wu. His revolt
was also brutally suppressed by Qing forces and inevitably the tensions
between the court and this particular Muslim group continued to fester.
The third leader of the Jahriyya, Ma Datian, for example, was charged with
sedition in 1818 and then died en route to his place of exile in Manchuria.
And this cycle of imperial suppression and Muslim response continued and
reached its final apogee during the devastating Muslim rebellions of the
mid-nineteenth century that wracked both the north and south of China.[56]

To make sense of this spiral of violence between local Muslim groups
and the Qing state we need to recall Qianlong's shift in religious and legal
policies. Prior to the 1760s, although Chinese officials had repeatedly petitioned the court to outlaw Islam entirely in the empire, the Manchu emperors had maintained that Islam fell within the bounds of civilization and
that Muslims should receive the same treatment as all imperial subjects. As
the Qing became involved on one side of this theological dispute between
the Khafiyya and Jahriyya, however, this imperial rhetoric was no longer
tenable. Moreover, as the Qing court began implementing the laws drafted
by Chen Hongmou that discriminated against Muslims based solely on
their religion the Muslim view of the Manchu state deteriorated. This
resulted in a spiral of communal and state violence, and the subsequent or
tandem growth of the supposedly "anti-Qing" Jahriyya. Moreover, on
account of Qing bureaucratic malfeasance the local economies of these

Muslim areas were devastated, and this further spurred the escalating sense
of distrust and alienation.

Nevertheless, tensions really began when the Qianlong emperor and the
Board of Punishments instituted the first anti-Muslim laws in 1762. These
laws followed the earlier policy recommendations of Chen Hongmou and
mandated that all Muslim leaders had to report any inappropriate behavior
within their community to the authorities, and local officials had to report
Muslim criminal acts to the state authorities. As might have been expected,
court records began to fill with Muslim acts of criminality, and local officials inundated the court with reports of Muslim bandits and their intrinsic
propensity for violence. In response, the Qing authorities became even
more suspicious and drafted further regulations concerning Muslims. Thus
Muslims found in groups of three or more with any weapon were deemed
immediately to be criminals. In the 1770s, the Qing court even created a
new criminal act/category, *dou'ou*, "brawling," that could be used as pre-
tense to arrest specifically Muslims. As an inevitable result, Muslims who
might not initially have sided with the Jahriyya teachings joined them in
protesting Qing policy, thus further reinforcing the court's fear of a growing Islamic anti-Qing movement.

As noted above this mutual animosity culminated in 1781 when Ma
Mingxin was executed. Yet it was further exacerbated by faulty intelligence.
Namely, a Qing official sent to quell the violence between the Khafiyya and
Jahriyya informed one group who he thought were Khafiyya that the Qing
would exterminate all followers of the Jahriyya tradition. To his dismay, his
audience turned out to be Jahriyya followers and they summarily killed
him. With the death of another Qing official at the hands of the Jahriyya
the Qing court responded with the "pacification" campaign led by Grand
Secretary Agui. And although the campaign was successful it also bred animosity among the Jahriyya. This anger was further compounded by local
leaders, who, in trying to impress the court, were overly zealous in killing
perceived Muslim enemies of the state. As a result the Jahriyya continued
to grow and thus Tian Wu was able to launch another revolt in 1784.

At this turn of events, the Qianlong emperor was baffled, and he wrote
in a letter to one of his ministers: "Why would Muslims from far and near
join up and follow them like sheep? . . . did news of Li Shiyao's investiga-
tions of Muslims leak out, so rebels could start rumors flying of [a government campaign to] 'exterminate Muslims' as an excuse to incite riots? I

have thought of all these things, but none seems to be the true reason. In the end, why did they rebel? We must get to the bottom of this!"[57]

Whether they got to the bottom of it is unknown. What is clear is that the 1784 rebellion was suppressed, and as an interim solution the Qing instituted a virtual military occupation of northwest China. While it held the peace for the next half century, when Qing forces had to move south in the 1850s to fight the growing Christian Taiping rebellion, internal and external violence erupted again in the northwest, culminating in the devastating Muslim rebellions of the 1860s and 1870s.[58]

It is within this course of events—the introduction of revivalist Islam, the official categorization of Muslims as violent and anti-Qing, and the militarization of northwest China along the border of Mongol territory—that the reappearance of Mongol questions about halal in the eighteenth century need to be situated. Moreover, it is important to recognize that the issue of halal was at this time not simply a Mongol-Muslim issue, as it had been in the empire period, but in the Qing it was also a Buddhist-Muslim issue. Indeed, as noted above, Islam had never been an issue in Mongol sources in the post-Mongol period, nor had it been an issue after the Mongols converted to Buddhism in the late sixteenth century. But in the wake of the Manchu conquest of Muslim Inner Asia in the eighteenth century and the subsequent Jahriyya uprising, the Mongols started for the first time to comment upon the world of Islam.

In particular, they started to draw a distinction between those whom they saw as being Buddhist—Mongols, Tibetans, Chinese, and Manchu—and the Muslims. Of course, this division was based on the nature of the Qing dynasty and its "cultural blocs," which the Mongols reframed solely in terms of religion. Thus unlike in the post-Mongol period when religion was a secondary feature, in the late Qing period it had become the dominant element of identification. One Mongol author, for example, in describing the people of the Qing dynasty notes simply, "As for the Turkestanis, they are a people without the pure majestic Dharma."[59] Of course, the "Turkestanis" were the Moghals, and they were actually related by blood to the Mongols. Indeed, it was precisely for this reason that Shah Khan and 'Abd al-Karim had had relations with Altan Khan even though he was a Buddhist, since at that time the Mongol legacy trumped religion.

In the Qing dynasty, however, this was no longer the case because the Manchus had put the Mongol legacy to rest. As a result, among the Mongols Buddhism had become paramount, and this had the consequence that even ancient blood ties were reconceptualized. Thus rather than identifying with "real" Mongol ancestors, such as the Moghals/Turkestanis, Mongol ritual texts came to assert that "Tibetans, Chinese, and Mongols . . . those three were born from one mother"![60] Within this reenvisioning and redrawing of the boundaries between the Buddhist and Muslim worlds of Inner Asia it is not surprising that the Mongols eventually started drawing upon the *Kālacakratantra*, which as we saw in Chapter 2, was composed largely in reaction to the Muslim advance in eleventh-century India. In the context of the late Qing, however, the Mongols therefore started to use the *Kālacakratantra*'s myth of Shambhala in order to make sense of the present. The 1835 *Pearl Rosary* (*Subud Erike*), for example, turned history on its head by claiming that a prophecy had been given in which Chinggis Khan had been born in order to kill Muslims.[61]

But as we have seen the *Kālacakratantra* also bemoans at length Islamic foodways in relation to Brahmanical norms. "[The barbarians] kill camels, horses, and cattle, and briefly cook their flesh together with blood. They cook beef and amniotic fluid with butter and spice, rice mixed together with vegetables, and forest fruit, all at once on the fire. Men eat that, O king, and drink bird eggs, in the place of the demon [barbarians]."[62]

Yet more to the point, the *Kālacakratantra* also specifically condemned the preparation of halal meat: "Using the mantra of the barbarian deity Bismillah, they will slit the throats of animals with cleavers."[63] For the author(s) of the *Kālacakratantra* this presentation of Muslim butchering practices was not really about halal per se, but as we have seen, one part of their larger confused attempt to link Islam with Vedic ritual sacrifices. Regardless of its original intentions, however, this passage from the *Kālacakratantra* gave Buddhist sanction to the long-standing Mongol aversion to halal. Thus while Mongol sources from this period are filled with anti-Muslim sentiment, the only element that ever confirms Islamic perfidy is halal: "According to those Muslims, they say that you cannot eat the meat of animals that die naturally. To kill an animal according to their own wrong view, one will be saved if, while cutting the neck with a knife, you recite the Lord's Dharani, Bismillah."[64]

And this desire to differentiate Buddhists from Muslims by means of their respective butchering practices is well captured in the work of Lama Shabkar (1781–1851), who even goes so far as to use the Mongol method of slaughtering as a metaphor for Buddhist enlightenment.

I, the renunciate, "Self-liberation of the Six Senses,"
First do a lot of slaughtering for the meat of the banquet:

The young Shepherd—awareness—
Comes from the mountain
Of the sublime Dharma of the Great Perfection,
Herding the nine yaks of the nine vehicles,
The four sheep of the four tantra sections,
And the three goats of the Tripitaka.

Bringing the goats, sheep, and yaks
Into the center of a large enclosure—the vast absolute expanse—
The butcher—omniscient primordial wakefulness—
Sharpens the knife of insight,
Lays one of them down on the ground—firm faith—
And ties it up with a rope—the accumulation of merit.
Cutting the belly open by means of the accumulation of wisdom,
He swiftly severs the main vein of the two veils,
And removes the hide of discursive thoughts.

Cutting up the carcass with the enlightened meaning of the sutras
    and tantras,
He dismembers it with logic and reason,
And chops it into pieces with the hand-axe of the pith instructions.

Then he throws the pieces of the various phenomena
Into the vast cauldron of the absolute nature;
And, placing it on the tripod of the natural presence of the three
    kayas,
Lights the fire of the four boundless thoughts.
He cooks meditation experiences and realization to their ultimate
    end,
And serves this all on a ground cloth—the merging of meditation
    and post-meditation.[65]

Within the context of the late Qing the Mongols and Tibetans had thereby successfully fused the anti-Muslim strands of both the Dharma and the Mongol legacy through the nexus of halal.

The situation among the Mongols, however, was not entirely one of Buddhist anti-Muslim hysteria. Some Mongol authors even included in their works lengthy descriptions of the Muslim world:

Outside their territories there is a stone surrounded with three hundred gates. Between each two gates there is, according to their reckoning, 360 miles, according to Chinese reckoning, 720 miles. The King's palace has 24 gates. The tower of the central palace is constructed of gold, and the palaces in the four directions are made of porcelain of four colours. . . . Every one or two years there is a disastrous wind in that country, and buildings and cities are destroyed. The people are of 12 tribes, with different languages. Gold and silver coins are scattered by the King over men who attain felicity. The people make the lips of their wells, and their water vessels, from gold and silver, and inlay them with all sorts of jewels. . . . To the south of the people of Küngker is a blue stone known as Mecca, the shrine of the heretics. It is about eighty centimeters in size. It is fixed in the air, and, for four or five spans all around, nothing touches the ground. Its height is about that of the hand of a man on horseback.

Near it is the temple of the heretics. It is a huge temple, its inner extent being about five or six bow shots. It has not a single pillar or beam, and it is called the great Rangjung temple. Quite some way from that temple is a shrine of the heretics, known as Mahasuri-yin Bilaya. It has a white stone with a hole in it like the human genitals, and it touches nothing either. The fact is that this, too, is fixed in the air by the force of magnetism.[66]

Although this passage does have its fantastical elements it also reflects the growing awareness of world geography and international politics ushered in by the eighteenth-century works of Tibetan scholars such as Sumba Khenpo and Jikmé Linkpa, who provided firsthand descriptions of Mughal-Ottoman relations and cities like Mecca and Istanbul.[67]

Yet even though such works may have offered the Mongols a different perspective on the Muslim world they did not change their anti-Muslim stance. The author of the above passage in fact went on to summarize his view of the Muslim world by drawing upon the *Kālacakratantra*: "As for what is called the land of Mecca, which is on the bank of the Sita river:

Mecca is a word that means Muslim. Those La Loo are all Muslims. Now, after the present period, the false beliefs of those Muslims will be disseminated more and more, and the majority of the people in this earthly continent will be Muslim. As for the beliefs of the Muslims: they do not eat the meat of the beasts, which have died of themselves. They kill their beasts to the best of their ability according to their false belief, saying that if they cut the throats of the creatures with a razor after having pronounced the dharani of Bismillah their god, they will be delivered."[68] Thus even with all the other events unfolding in eighteenth- and nineteenth-century Qing-dynasty China, the Mongol Buddhists continued to draw a sharp line between themselves and the Muslim world on the basis of halal.

Injannashi and the Question of Islam

There was one Mongol writer, however, who would challenge this status quo by arguing that Muslims and their rituals, including halal, were just like those of the Buddhists. His name was Injannashi (1837–1892), and he was a Mongol nobleman from a distinguished family that had fallen on hard times.[69] Their businesses, including a coal mine, had collapsed; and in seeking solace and meaning in life Injannashi had turned to writing. In so doing he wrote a massive fictionalized account of the life of Chinggis Khan as well as two novels, which following the tradition of rewriting the Ming dynasty novel *Dream of the Red Chamber* (*Hong lou meng*) tell the tale of the Chinese gentry family of Bei Hou. Moreover, each of these works also includes fascinating prefaces laying out Injannashi's own ideas on a range of issues, including that of Islam.[70]

Injannashi's initial comments about Muslims are negative; however, his animosity does not arise from the standard repertoire of Buddhist anti-Muslim polemics that we have seen above. Rather, Injannashi is upset by the fact that Muslims are allowed to take the civil service examination while Mongols are not: "But then, in this Great Qing Empire, regarding those Muslims who submitted to the empire later than the Mongols did, and who did not contribute to the founding of the dynasty as the Mongols did, care is being taken so as not to let the learned among them be neglected by selecting from among them, according to their schooling, persons to employ in ministerial positions. Why are Mongols alone singled out and excluded from this examination system? Therefore, I tried to reason to myself as follows: Is it because the Mongols are so uncouth and stupid that they will never be able to pass the examination, so that no examination system is necessary for them?"[71]

To put this critique into context, we need to recall that the civil service exam was the engine of social status creation and maintenance in late imperial China.[72] Being excluded thus had grave consequences, and for Injannashi this was especially poignant since the central thrust of his work was precisely to advocate for educational reform. Or at least he wanted education for the nobility so that they could retain their status in the changing socioeconomic realities of late nineteenth-century China.[73] Yet, while he does use Muslims as a whipping post in regard to this particular issue, he also looks at Islam in another light, one that is completely at odds with the anti-Muslim tenor of the times.

Injannashi does this by means of a cross-cultural study of ritual. To this end Injannashi begins by comparing various mourning rites starting with a description from the *Wanbaozhuan*, a popular Chinese encyclopedia, which records the following: "there is a small nation by the name Jinwoguo in the environs of the ancient Man nation on an island of the Southern Sea. They make their living by hunting beasts and birds of their mountains and plains, and sometimes this nation is also referred to as the Manluowu. At times, when the ships and boats of China by dint of wind arrive at their shores, the natives come in hordes and seize those on the ship, kill them and eat their flesh. They make utensils out of human skulls and marrow bones. They curse their parents day and night, hoping they will die sooner. When their parents die, they beat great drums and summon their neighbors to come to feast on the flesh of the dead."[74] This description was no doubt disturbing for a Chinese reader, since what could be worse than actually consuming one's parents?[75] For those steeped in the Confucian world of filial piety this was certainly beyond the pale, and the *Wanbaozhuan* readily confirms, "they are a nation who knows not of humanity."

Of course, as we have seen, representing "the other" as monstrous, or as cannibals, is nothing new. Not only did Muslims present Buddhists in this way; so too did the Franciscan friar William of Rubruck. He namely claimed the Tibetans ate their parents "from the pious motive of providing them with no other grave than their own bellies."[76] Indeed, the portrayal of the Jinwoguo in the *Wanbaozhuan*, the view of the Khotanese in the *Ḥudūd al-ʿĀlam*, and Rubruck's Tibet, especially their fascination with cannibalism, are all part of a whole. All of these representations were part of larger discursives that were distancing and even dehumanizing "the other." Thus by challenging such representations Injannashi was very much like modern scholars who investigate the "discourses" shaping representations of "the other" in relation to empire, race, gender, and so on.[77] For Injannashi the main question, however, was why Chinese scholars presented the Jinwoguo in the way they did.

His rather simple and direct answer was that their prejudices arose out of ignorance and selfishness. He thus takes Chinese scholars to task for being unfamiliar with the underlying logic and rationale of this particular mourning rite and approaching it solely from a stance of moral superiority.[78] "Some learned ones believe that only the Middle Kingdom is the kingdom of heaven, and that it alone possesses humanity. They believe this land alone receives the major benefits of sun and moon, and this land alone gives birth to intellects and wise ones, great minds and scholars. They not only explain all the rest to be strange, alien, perverse and evil, peculiar and queer, they even believe this to be true in their hearts."[79] He then goes on to puncture this image by humorously pointing out the absurdity of Chinese scholars who for three thousand years claimed to be at the center of civilization, and yet for all that time continued to miscalculate solar and lunar eclipses—a mistake that Injannashi points out with relish was rectified only with the arrival of the Belgian Jesuit Ferdinand Verbiest at the Kangxi emperor's court in the seventeenth century.

To drive his point home Injannashi continues his critique of misrepresenting "the other" by discussing Mongol and Tibetan burial rites. He thus imagines how a Chinese person may misunderstand a Mongolian cremation as an act of vengeance against one's parents since lamas wave swords and spears over a burning corpse. "Suppose those Chinese from the interior who inter their parents in gold and jade should witness a Mongol cremation, since they do not know the reason, they will likewise say the same thing as about the people of Jinwoguo. They will say that the Mongols, having cursed their parents to death, not only burn their dead, but call upon those red and yellow robed, queue-less,[80] bald and shaven people and make them wield sword and spear over the dead and pour oils over the dead to inflame the fire, whereby they take vengeance upon their dead parents. They certainly will not believe that actually it is a rite to offer the flesh of the dead for the Buddha to partake of it, thereby making them Buddhas."[81] Injannashi thereby returns to his central theme of needing to understand the rationale behind the ritual. One cannot simply look at the external practice; one must elucidate the internal logic.[82]

To do so Injannashi turns to the Tibetan sky burial, which much like cannibalism has been fetishized in both the East and West. Yet rather than exoticizing or condemning this practice he explains the reason behind this rite. He claims that in the Tibetan view, vultures are sacred Dharma protectors and by consuming the flesh of a corpse the sins of the deceased are cleansed and thus the soul will find a good incarnation. Moreover, he makes the same assertion about the Jinwoguo and their necrophagia. "Even those people of Jinwoguo, because of their great population and lack of land and having no domesticated animals, have long since known the taste of human flesh. Therefore when a parent dies, they will call upon their tribes and members of their family to have a great feast, thereby obtaining the merit of making satiated the great hunger of many, and the soul of the dead will go to heaven. To sum it up, all of them possess a kind of mourning rite."[83] In this way Injannashi not only explains the rationale behind the seemingly bizarre ritual of consuming one's deceased parents, but also validates the humanity of the Jinwoguo. As he declares, "even those who devour the flesh of their parents possess justice and goodness. Such being the case, can any teaching be without just principle?"[84]

The idea that any teaching, or religion, must by definition be premised on goodness is Injannashi's central argument. While his view is clearly based on Confucian precedent, especially Mencius, Injannashi takes the traditional Confucian view of inherent human goodness, and the value of ritual for instilling and nurturing positive values, in a new direction by putting it in a comparative context.[85] It is therefore not only Confucian mourning rites that are proper and instill humanity with values, but all mourning rites are valid since they too are inherently premised on both human goodness and the wish to perpetuate it through ritual performances. For Injannashi, the reason this is the case is that in his view a religion would not have followers if that were not the case. "I think the founder of a religion cannot profit . . . [if he] devises a new evil doctrine. What would he gain by it? I think each of these teachings has its good points and never intended to be evil. Only that we know not the fine details of these teachings and theories and true characters, and we believe them to be unacceptable and wrong. Naturally, the founder of a religion cannot say 'My religion is no good; my religion is wrong; the other teachings are right; you all follow them; leave my religion; don't follow my religion; do not study my religion.' Since it is being called a teaching, it is founded for the purpose of teaching people. It simply cannot be evil."[86] Thus in many ways Injannashi's interpretation parallels contemporary introductory textbooks on world religions, which also maintain that all religions have value; none are inherently evil, we simply need to understand them.[87] Or as Injannashi writes: "Is it not simply that customs appear to differ in each place and their concepts seem to be strange to each other, but the aims are all the same?"[88]

Thus all religions and their rites, no matter how difficult to understand from an outsider's perspective, actually derive from human goodness and should therefore be tolerated. "Even the peculiarities of the Muslims, and the customs of the Jinwoguo have their righteousness and goodness. . . . Since all of them are for the good of men, how could there be wrong and malice? I have even talked to some of those learned among the European and Muslim devils, and found they too speak of the cultivation of virtues and self-control. Certainly they do not teach the harming of others with selfishness."[89]

Yet it is not only on the phenomenological level that Injannashi's work parallels the modern study of religion; he also premises his analysis on the ground of skepticism. As he explains whether he was to include "matters of gods and demons and strange magic and sorcery" in his work he proclaims that "since I was born, [I have] never believed in such matters of which there is no proof nor matters which are not in congruence with logic and laws [of nature]."[90] Yet even so, he decided to include them since people believed in them in the past; however, he hopes that "future readers of this work will not think of me as they do of mendacious lamas."[91]

Having established his theoretical paradigm Injannashi finally turns to the volatile issue of Muslim foodways. He writes: "Even those Muslim butchers of sheep and cows, not able to bear simply killing sheep and cows for meat, perform some kind of ritual to direct the souls of the slaughtered animals to heaven, and offer prayers and bless their knives before they proceed to kill. They may not be able to dispatch the slaughtered souls to heaven, but if you compare the present day Chinese and Mongols who simply butcher their animals without any kind of ritual, for meat and profit, those Muslims certainly have good hearts. Those not informed often simply follow the crowd by custom and defame the Muslims as having an animal origin, and say that they adhere to evil teaching and false doctrine. Alas, how unjust this is!"[92] By means of his skeptical and decidedly modern approach Injannashi is thus able to challenge nearly a millennium of Buddhist polemics against Islam and argue that halal practices actually derive out of human goodness.

   To confirm this point he concludes by comparing halal butchering practices with the Tibetan Buddhist practice of praying for rebirth in Buddha
Amitabha's paradise.[93] Even though both religious specialists "are not sure
whether they are able to commit the soul as they hope, they certainly do
not believe that they are committing the soul to hell instead. The intentions
are the same in both cases, except the difference that one [= animal] is
killed and the other [= human] died naturally."[94] Injannashi thus reaffirms
his main thesis based on the theory that all religions and rituals actually
derive from human goodness. "They all seek the best according to their
own custom. The outer aspects may differ but the thought behind them are
the same."[95] In this way Injannashi is finally able to argue that the intentions of both Muslims and Buddhists are inherently the same. By proving
that Buddhists and Muslims are fundamentally the same Injannashi
believed he had overcome not only the problem of prejudice, but also the
problem of difference.

CONCLUSION

A bit of weakness in metaphor is enough for tomorrow.
For the berries to ripen on the fence, and for the sword to break under
the dew.

—Mahmoud Derwish, *Sonnets [VI]*

You are me, and I am you.
Isn't it obvious that we "inter-are"?

—Thich Nhat Han, *Interrelationship*

ALTHOUGH INJANNASHI BELIEVED he had solved the problem of prejudice and difference it is clear that both of these issues are still with us, as is the idea that Buddhism and Islam are inherently different. Indeed, even though Injannashi's metaphor of a common humanity has now been updated within new theoretical frameworks—such as ecumenicalism, multiculturalism, pluralism, and cosmopolitanism—the fundamental issue of how one should deal with "the other" still remains. How such difference is to be articulated and dealt with is, of course, not only an ongoing process, but also a fundamental aspect of the human experience. And in this regard the case of Buddhists and Muslims in Inner Asia is no different.

In the case of the nineteenth century, for example, when Western travelers rediscovered Inner Asia they came across a world sharply divided between Buddhists and Muslims. Indeed, their alienation from one another was so deep and profound that even on such a basic everyday level as tying knots these two groups were different. According to Western travelers one could therefore identify someone's religious affiliation simply by looking at how they tied goods together, or loaded them onto camels.[1] That such a difference existed between the Buddhists and Muslims did not strike the

Western explorers as surprising. They had grown up in the age when modern views of Islam and Buddhism were forged and thus they took it for granted that Buddhism and Islam were radically different. In fact it was precisely this framework that handily explained their greatest discovery: the famous Buddhist monuments of the fabled Silk Road.

In their view the very reason these artistic treasures stood empty and forlorn waiting to be rediscovered was on account of the fanatical Muslims who had violently pushed the Buddhists out of Inner Asia. In fact, was it not precisely such a dynamic that had shaped Buddhist-Muslim interaction ever since the destruction of Nalanda monastery in the early thirteenth century? Thus the fact that Buddhists and Muslims were so alienated from one another that they even tied knots differently simply seemed to make sense. No one even bothered to ask if they had always tied knots differently, or whether this distinction arose at a particular time, or for a particular reason—one perhaps that had nothing to do with religion?

Even if they had asked such questions it is very likely they would have received the answer they expected. Contemporary Buddhists and Muslims in Inner Asia would probably have confirmed that it had always been like this. They would probably have said something along the lines of: we have always been different; we have always been at odds. Indeed, it was along this very same line of reasoning that Tibetan lamas were to make the argument that Muslims should be excluded from the Republic of China. In their view, Muslims were backward and violent and therefore should not be allowed to join the Buddhists in the modern nation-state of China.[2] Thus both the Tibetan lamas and Western explorers were claiming an eternal difference between Buddhism and Islam. Yet, of course, as we have seen in the case of the Tibetan lamas, the origins of this particular Buddhist view of Islam was largely the legacy of the Qing dynasty, during which the Chinese, Mongol, and Tibetan Buddhists were imagined as one group, and the Muslims another. And the same can be said of the Western explorers, who also presented their views in terms of a common narrative, one that invariably pitted the peaceful Buddhists against the militant Muslims.

The aim of this book has been to challenge this story. And as promised in the introduction it was also the aim to use the Buddhist-Muslim encounter in order to explore some interlocking themes, such as how Buddhism and Islam were shaped by their meeting on the Silk Road and what this thousand-year-history may tell us about the possibilities of cross-cultural understanding. While the first of these endeavors has hopefully been

Figure 30. Buddho-Arabic tattoo. Photo: Liljana Elverskog.

achieved in full, it may be an open question whether any grand conclusion can be drawn from this history about the elusive quest for cross-cultural understanding. Hopefully this study, however, has at least revealed the importance of history in this endeavor. Indeed, central to this entire project has been the power of history to overturn common narratives that inform suspicions and prejudices of all sorts. At the same time, however, history does not only overturn received wisdom. It is also the central pillar that upholds the status quo since it explains and justifies the present. Indeed, it is precisely on account of these contradictory possibilities that history beckons to us as a mirror and guide for both the present and future. Thus let us end by leaving the past and thinking instead about the present and future.

Beyond reevaluating our common views about the Dharma and Islam and the history of Eurasian interaction, what does the history of the Buddhist-Muslim encounter tell us about the contemporary world? Can we use any of the issues explored herein—such as the revival of jihad, the artistic representation of Muhammad, Muslim integration, and competing legal systems—in relation to current debates about these very same issues? Or what about the economic rise of Asia and the Middle East? What will this world-altering economic transformation entail not only for the Christian West, but also for the Buddhists and Muslims who will once again meet in oil- and natural-gas-rich Inner Asia? Will Christianity become the religion of the disenfranchised as Buddhism and Islam reclaim their mantle as the religions of the cosmopolitan elite?[3] And more to the point, how in this future age will Buddhists and Muslims understand each other? Will they create a new hybrid culture with lasting resonance as recently evidenced in the Zen-like simplicity of the I. M. Pei–designed Museum of Islamic Art in Doha?[4] Indeed, does the appearance of such enduring monuments, as well as those more ephemeral (figure 30), augur a new age of Buddhist-Muslim cross-cultural exchange? Or will their differences lead to conflict? While the answers to all these questions are unfortunately unknown, it is certainly the case that the history of Buddhist-Muslim interaction is just beginning.

Introduction

Note to epigraphs: Quoted in Efraim Karsh, *Islamic Imperialism: A History* (New Haven: Yale University Press, 2007), 1. Maurice Walshe, *The Long Discourses of the Buddha: A Translation of the Dīgha Nikāya* (Boston: Wisdom Publications, 1995), 156.

1. The importance of this institution in Asian history is well borne out by the current project to rebuild Nalanda with the explicit aim of making it one of the top universities in the world (Jeffery E. Garten, "Real Old School," *New York Times*, December 9, 2006).

2. André Wink, *Al-Hind: The Making of the Indo-Islamic World, Vol. 1: Early Medieval India and the Expansion of Islam 7th–11th Centuries* (Leiden: Brill, 1990), 268.

3. Ronald M. Davidson, *Indian Esoteric Buddhism: A Social History of the Tantric Movement* (New York: Columbia University Press, 2002), 109.

4. On the destruction of Nalanda see H. D. Sankalia, *The Nālandā University* (Delhi: Oriental Publishers, 1976), 244–247.

5. This is the common view in both popular and academic literature. See, for example, Lawrence Sutin, *All Is Change: The Two Thousand-Year Journey of Buddhism to the West* (New York: Little, Brown, 2006), 45–46; and Jerry H. Bentley, *Old World Encounters: Cross-Cultural Encounters and Exchanges in Pre-Modern Times* (New York: Oxford University Press, 1993), 131–133.

6. Steven Darian, "Buddhism in Bihār from the Eighth to the Twelfth Century with Special Reference to Nālandā," *Asiatische Studien/Études asiatiques* 25 (1971): 346.

7. George Roerich, *Biography of Dharmasvāmin (Chag lo tsa-ba Chos-rje-dpal): A Tibetan Monk Pilgrim* (Patna: K. P. Jayaswal Research Institute, 1959), 90.

8. Arthur Waley, "New Light on Buddhism in Medieval India," *Mélanges Chinois et Boudhiques* 1 (1931–1932): 355–376.

9. Kazuo Enoki, "Tsung-le's Mission to the Western Regions in 1378–1382," *Oriens Extremus* 19, 1–2 (1972): 52.

10. R. A. L. H. Gunawardana, *Robe and Plough: Monasticism and Economic Interest in Early Medieval Sri Lanka* (Tucson: University of Arizona Press, 1979), 264.

11. The area studies model plays a role in distorting our understanding of the historical interactions across Eurasia. On the historiographical problems inherent in this model see, for example, Alexander Woodside, *Lost Modernities: China, Vietnam, Korea and the Hazards of World History* (Cambridge: Harvard University Press, 2006), 15, 24–25; and Thomas T. Allsen, *The Royal Hunt in Eurasian History* (Philadelphia: University of Pennsylvania Press, 2006).

12. The demise of Buddhism in India was an issue not only for Indian Buddhists, but also for Buddhists across Asia. In China, for example, the end of Buddhism in India, or its imagined demise, fit Chinese historiography very well, especially since it enabled China and the sacred mountain of Wutai Shan to be reimagined as the center of the Buddhist world (Tansen Sen, *Buddhism, Diplomacy, and Trade: The Realignment of Sino-Indian Relations, 600–1400* [Honolulu: University of Hawai'i Press, 2003], 87).

13. On the issue of Indian historiography and religious identities see Peter van der Veer, *Religious Nationalism: Hindus and Muslims in India* (Berkeley: University of California Press, 1994).

14. This sentiment is well captured in the 1834 work of T. Postens, who writes "that during the Arab conquest 'the most unrelenting cruelty and intolerance appears to have been excercised' (p. 152) and that 'the fanaticism of the Moslems always induces them to make converts instead of ameliorating the condition of the people' (p. 160)" (quoted in Derryl N. MacLean, *Religion and Society in Arab Sind* [Leiden: Brill, 1989], 23).

15. While the Mughals and Islam were, and are, often used to explain India's woes, many Indian nationalists, such as Gandhi, also recognized the need to incorporate Muslims into the vision of modern India. In fact, what the British feared most was the union of Hindus and Muslims, which Gandhi supported (see David Page, *Prelude to Partition: The Indian Muslims and the Imperial System of Control 1920–1932* [New York: Oxford University Press, 1982]). One interesting footnote to this intellectual project of uniting Muslims and Hindus is found in U. Ali's attempt to find the teachings of Islam and Muhammad foreshadowed in the Vedas (*Mohammed in Ancient Scriptures* [Agra: S. R. Brothers, 1936]).

16. Of course, few Indians today are violent Hindu nationalists; most, in fact, recognize India's strength as residing precisely in its multicultural past. See, for example, Amartya Sen's *The Argumentative Indian: Writings on Indian History, Culture and Identity* (New York: Picador, 2006).

17. The literature on orientalism is enormous; however, an overview of this discourse and its continuing relevance can be found in Emran Qureshi and Michael A Sells, eds., *The New Crusades: Constructing the Muslim Enemy* (New York: Columbia University Press, 2003).

18. I borrow the phrase "orientalist fear" from Tim Jon Semmerling's study of how the "evil Arab" stereotype is driven by cultural fears stemming from the perceived challenges Muslims pose to Western national ideologies and myths (*"Evil" Arabs in*

American Popular Film: Orientalist Fear [Austin: University of Texas Press, 2006]). While there is a vast scholarship reevaluating Muslim history and the Muslim–European Christian relationship, some recent noteworthy examples are William Dalrymple's work on the Mughals (*White Mughals: Love and Betrayal in Eighteenth-Century India* [New York: Viking, 2003]; *The Last Mughal: The Fall of a Dynasty: Delhi, 1857* [New York: Knopf, 2007]), Maya Jasanoff's elegy to Lucknow (*Edge of Empire: Lives, Culture, and Conquest in the East, 1750–1850* [New York: Vintage, 2006]), Mark Mazower's similar portrayal of Ottoman Salonica (*Salonica, City of Ghosts: Christians, Muslims and Jews 1430–1950* [New York: Vintage, 2006]), and the catalogue to the Metropolitan Museum of Art's exhibit *Venice and the Islamic World, 828–1797* (ed. Stefano Carboni [New Haven: Yale University Press, 2007]).

19. On the origin of these stereotypes in the scholarship of the nineteenth century see Tomoko Masuzawa, *The Invention of World Religions* (Chicago: University of Chicago Press, 2005), 121–146, 179–180.

20. While the linkage between Buddhism and science began already in the early twentieth century, one of the better-known and popular examples of this approach is Fritjof Capra's *The Tao of Physics: An Exploration of the Parallels Between Modern Physics and Eastern Mysticism* (Berkeley: Shambhala, 1975). For a nuanced interpretation of this phenomenon see Donald S. Lopez, Jr., *Buddhism and Science: A Guide for the Perplexed* (Chicago: University of Chicago Press, 2008).

21. The view of Islam as inherently medieval has become especially prevalent in the international media's presentation of the Taliban. Dexter Filkins, for example, recently described them in this way: "The Talibs were cutting their well-known medieval path" ("Right at the Edge," *New York Times Magazine*, September 7 [2008]: 55).

22. For a convenient overview and collection of material on the Western construction of Buddhism see Donald S. Lopez, Jr., ed., *A Modern Buddhist Bible: Essential Readings from East and West* (Boston: Beacon Press, 2002).

23. David L. McMahan, *The Making of Buddhist Modernism* (New York: Oxford University Press, 2008).

24. On the implications of this particular historiographical model see Jonathan S. Walters, *Finding Buddhists in Global History* (Washington, D.C.: American Philosophical Society, 1998), 8–12; as well as Philip C. Almond, *The British Discovery of Buddhism* (Cambridge: Cambridge University Press, 1988).

25. On the Aryan-Semitic discourses of nineteenth-century scholarship, see Maurice Olender (trans. Arthur Goldhammer), *The Languages of Paradise: Race, Religion, and Philology in the Nineteenth Century* (Cambridge: Harvard University Press, 2008); and Dorothy M. Figueira, *Aryans, Jews, Brahmins: Theorizing Authority Through Myths of Identity* (Albany: State University of New York Press, 2002).

26. An excellent study on the context and meaning of the Taliban's destruction of the Bamiyan Buddhas is Finbarr Barry Flood's "Between Cult and Culture: Bamiyan, Iconoclasm, and the Museum," *Art Bulletin* 84, 4 (2002): 641–659.

Chapter 1. Contact

1. In recent years there has been a steady growth in scholarship on Buddhism in the West; for an introduction to this scholarship see Charles S. Prebish and Martin Baumann, *Westward Dharma: Buddhism Beyond Asia* (Berkeley: University of California Press, 2002).

2. Wealthy western Buddhists are often portrayed not only as objects of ridicule, but also of scorn. See, for example, the dismay and anger at "California Buddhists" in Pankaj Mishra, *An End of Suffering: The Buddha in the World* (New York: Farrar, Straus and Giroux, 2004), 353–371.

3. Although there have been numerous attempts to represent the Buddha as a proto-feminist, the bulk of the material discounts this modern interpretation. See, for example, Liz Watson, *Charming Cadavers: Horrific Figurations of the Feminine in Indian Buddhist Hagiography* (Chicago: University of Chicago Press, 1996); Bernard Faure, *The Power of Denial: Buddhism, Purity and Gender* (Princeton: Princeton University Press, 2003); and Kim Gutschow, *Being a Buddhist Nun: The Struggle for Enlightenment in the Himalayas* (Cambridge: Harvard University Press, 2004).

4. On Buddhism's violent role in Japanese imperialism, for example, see Brian Victoria, *Zen at War* (Burlington: Weatherhill, 1997), as well as James Heissig and John C. Maraldo, eds., *Rude Awakenings: Zen, the Kyoto School and the Question of Nationalism* (Honolulu: University of Hawai'i Press, 1995) and Robert Buswell, "The Zen of Japanese Nationalism," in *Curators of the Buddha: The Study of Buddhism Under Colonialism*, ed. Donald S. Lopez, Jr. (Chicago: University of Chicago Press, 1995), 107–160.

5. Elliot Sperling, "'Orientalism' and Aspects of Violence in the Tibetan Tradition," in *Imagining Tibet: Perceptions, Projections, and Fantasies*, ed. Thierry Dodin and Heinz Räther (Boston: Wisdom Publications, 2003), 318. For more on Tibetan warfare, see Donald LaRocca, *Warriors of the Himalayas: Rediscovering the Arms and Armor of Tibet* (New York: Metropolitan Museum of Art, 2006).

6. In recent years there has been an outpouring of studies on the history of the Shangri-La myth and its impact in both the East and West. See, for example, Peter Bishop, *The Myth of Shangri-La: Tibet, Travel Writing and the Creation of Sacred Landscape* (London: The Athlone Press, 1989); Thierry Dodin and Heinz Räther, *Imagining Tibet: Perceptions, Projections, and Fantasies* (Boston: Wisdom Publications, 2003); Donald S. Lopez, *Prisoners of Shangri-la: Tibetan Buddhism and the West* (Chicago: University of Chicago Press, 1998); Martin Brauen, Renate Koller, and Markus Vock, *Traumwelt Tibet: Westliche Trugbilder* (Berne: Paul Haupt, 2000); and Monica Esposito, *Images of Tibet in the Nineteenth and Twentieth Centuries* (Paris: École française d'Extrême-Orient, 2008).

7. On the violent component of Sinhalese Buddhist nationalism see Stanley J. Tambiah, *Buddhism Betrayed?: Religion, Politics, and Violence in Sri Lanka* (Chicago: University of Chicago Press, 1992); Tessa J. Bartholomeusz and Chandra Richard De

Silva, eds., *Fundamentalism and Minority Identities in Sri Lanka* (Albany: State University of New York Press, 1998); Tessa J. Bartholomeusz, *In Defense of Dharma: Just-War Ideology in Buddhist Sri Lanka* (New York: Routledge Curzon, 2002); Ananda Abeyesekara, "The Saffron Army, Violence, Terror(ism): Buddhism, Identity, and Difference in Sri Lanka," *Numen* 48, 1 (2001): 1–46.

8. One of the few studies exploring Buddhist economic history is Jacques Gernet, *Buddhism in Chinese Society: An Economic History from the Fifth to the Tenth Centuries*, trans. Franciscus Verellen (New York: Columbia University Press, 1998).

9. Scholars have identified two chronologies for the life of the Buddha, the long and the short. For the scholarly debates on the dating of the Buddha see the three-volume collection *The Dating of the Historical Buddha*, ed. Heinz Bechert (Göttingen: Vandenhoeck und Ruprecht, 1991–97).

10. John S. Strong, *The Experience of Buddhism: Sources and Interpretations* (Belmont: Wadsworth, 1995), 9–10.

11. Sheldon Pollock, *The Language of the Gods in the World of Men: Sanskrit, Culture, and Power in Premodern India* (Berkeley: University of California Press, 2006), 51. For a preliminary attempt to address this oversight see Sheldon Pollock, "Axialism and Empire," in *Axial Civilizations and World History*, ed. Johann P. Arnason, S. N. Eisenstadt, and Björn Wittrock (Leiden: Brill, 2005), 400–411.

12. For an overview of these developments and a reevaluation of their impact on the development of early Buddhism, see Greg Bailey and Ian Mabbett, *The Sociology of Early Buddhism* (New York: Cambridge University Press, 2003), 13–107.

13. On the so-called "sixteen great countries" (*soḍaśa mahājanapada*) see Étienne Lamotte, *History of Indian Buddhism: From the Origins to the Śaka Era*, trans. Sara Webb-Boin (Louvain-Paris: Peeters Press, 1988), 7–9. And on how these entities were less historical realities than a "technical term" in Buddhist literature, see Richard F. Gombrich, *Theravada Buddhism: A Social History from Ancient Benares to Modern Colombo* (London: Routledge & Kegan Paul, 1988), 54.

14. For more detailed studies on the shift from these "republics" (*gana-sanghas*) to the more complex political systems of kingdoms and empires, see Romila Thapar, *From Lineage to State: Social Formations in the Mid-first Millennium B.C. in the Ganga Valley* (Bombay: Oxford University Press, 1984); and Uma Chakravarti, *The Social Dimensions of Early Buddhism* (Delhi: Oxford University Press, 1987).

15. On the relationship between iron, changing methods of warfare, and the rise of centralizing states, see Victor H. Mair's study of the rise of the Qin dynasty that first unified China (*The Art of War: Sun Zi's Military Methods* [New York: Columbia University Press, 2007], 37–39).

16. Rudolf W. Müller, *Geld und Geist: Zur Enstehungsgeschichte von Identitätsbewusstein und Rationalität seit der Antike* (Frankfurt: Campus, 1977).

17. Jonathan P. Berkey, *The Formation of Islam: Religion and Society in the Near East* (New York: Cambridge University Press, 2003), 5.

18. Chakravarti, *Social Dimensions*, 19.

19. The *Śārdūlakarṇāvadāna*, which was translated into Chinese in 230 C.E., notes that the Magadhan *mashaka* is equal to twelve grains of gold; and 16 *mashaka* equal one Chinese *jin*. I thank Brian Baumann for this information.

20. Walshe, *Long Discourses of the Buddha*, 236.

21. This passage is from the *Aṅguttara Nikāya* and is quoted in Chakravarti, *Social Dimensions*, 83. For a similar passage see also the *Mahāsīhanāda Sutta* in the *Majjhima Nikāya*, 12.41.

22. Himanshu P. Ray, *The Winds of Change: Buddhism and the Maritime Links of Early South Asia* (Delhi: Oxford University Press, 1994), 132.

23. Jes P. Asmussen, *Xᵘāstvānīft. Studies in Manichaeism* (Copenhagen: Prostant apud Munksgaard, 1965), 150. See also Davidson, *Indian Esoteric Buddhism*, 78.

24. Ray, *The Winds of Change*, 153–154.

25. Gustavo Benavides, "Buddhism, Manichaeism, Markets and Empires," in *Hellenisation, Empire, and Globalisation: Lessons from Antiquity*, ed. Luther H. Martin and Panayotis Pachis (Thessaloniki: Vanias Publications, 2004), 23.

26. For an excellent study on the interaction between the Confucian ideal of the four classes (literati, farmers, artisans, and merchants) in relation to the realities of an expanding economy, see Timothy Brook, *The Confusions of Pleasure: Commerce and Culture in Ming China* (Berkeley: University of California Press, 1999).

27. Patrick Olivelle, *Dharmasutras: The Law Codes of Apastamba, Gautama, Baudhayana, and Vasistha* (New York: Oxford University Press, 1999), 105.

28. Michael J. Walsh, "The Economics of Salvation: Toward a Theory of Exchange in Chinese Buddhism," *Journal of the American Academy of Religion* 75, 2 (2007): 363.

29. I. B. Horner, *Milinda's Questions, Vol. 1* (London: Luzac & Company, Ltd., 1963), 171. On the courtesan tradition of treating men of different backgrounds equally, see Ludwick Sternbach, *Gaṇikā-vṛtta-saṃgrahaḥ or Texts on Courtezans in Classical Sanskrit* (Hoshiapur: Vishveshvarand Institute Publications, 1953), 72–73.

30. Chakravarti, *Social Dimensions*, 99.

31. Over time Buddhist texts came to identify more and more jobs; for example, in the *Dīgha Nikāya* there is a standard list of 25 occupations (Walshe, *Long Discourses of the Buddha*, 93), but in the later *Milandapañhā* there are 75 (Liu Xinru, *Ancient China and Ancient India: Trade and Religious Exchanges AD 1–600* [Delhi: Oxford University Press, 1988], 37).

32. Gustavo Benavides, "Economy," in *Critical Terms for the Study of Buddhism*, ed. Donald S. Lopez, Jr. (Chicago: University of Chicago Press, 2005), 82–83.

33. Fred M. Donner, *Narratives of Islamic Origins: The Beginning of Islamic Historical Writing* (Princeton: Darwin Press, 1998), 147–148, 175–177.

34. G. R. Hawting, *The Idea of Idolatry and the Emergence of Islam: From Polemic to History* (New York: Cambridge University Press, 1999), 13. Patricia Crone and Michael Cook have made the most extreme form of this argument. They have argued that since all the Islamic sources on the early period are late, they should not be used to reconstruct early Muslim history. Instead only contemporary sources in Armenian,

Greek, Syriac, and Hebrew should be used. In doing so they famously made the argument that Islam actually originated as a Jewish messianic movement (*Hagarism: The Making of the Islamic World* [Cambridge: Cambridge University Press, 1977]). For a fuller discussion of this historiographical interpretation see the introduction in Patricia Crone, *Slaves on Horses: The Evolution of the Islamic Polity* (Cambridge: Cambridge University Press, 1980), 1–17.

35. Chase F. Robinson, *Islamic Historiography* (Cambridge: Cambridge University Press, 2003), 11–12.

36. Hawting, *The Idea of Idolatry*, 12–13.

37. For an overview of the "revisionist" readings of the Qur'an see Gabriel Said Reynolds, "Introduction: Qur'ānic studies and its controversies," in *The Qur'ān in Its Historical Context*, ed. Gabriel Said Reynolds (New York: Routledge, 2008), 1–25.

38. Oleg Grabar, *The Shape of the Holy: Early Islamic Jerusalem* (Princeton: Princeton University Press, 1996), 56–71.

39. For a critique of the idea that Islam arose in a world of trade see Patricia Crone, *Meccan Trade and the Rise of Islam* (Oxford: Basil Blackwell, 1987).

40. André Wink, *Al-Hind: The Making of the Indo-Islamic World, Vol. 1: Early Medieval India and the Expansion of Islam 7th–11th Centuries* (Leiden: Brill, 1990), 34.

41. One inevitable consequence of this development was not only that the tribal past came to be idealized, but there also arose the inevitable question of authenticity— which group and set of ideas represented "true Islam." On this issue, see Engseng Ho, *The Graves of Tarim: Genealogy and Mobility Across the Indian Ocean* (Berkeley: University of California Press, 2006), 55–60.

42. This statement is recorded in the work of Mutribi al-Asamm al-Samarqandi, who visited the Mughal court in the late 1620s; see Muzaffar Alam and Sanjay Subrahmanyam, *Indo-Persian Travels in the Age of Discoveries, 1400–1800* (Cambridge: Cambridge University Press, 2006), 127.

43. D. Lombard, "Y a-t-il Une Continuité des Réseaux Marchands Asiatiques?" in *Marchands et Hommes d'Affaires Asiatiques dans l'Océan Indien et la Mer da Chine*, ed. D. Lombard and J. Aubin (Paris: EHESS, 1988), 11–18.

44. Berkey, *The Formation of Islam*, 121.

45. On the role of interstitial groups, especially traders in the rise of Buddhism, Christianity, and Islam, see Benavides, "Economy," 84.

46. See James Heitzman, "Early Buddhism, Trade, and Empire," in *Studies in the Archaeology and Paleoanthropology of South Asia*, ed. Kenneth A. R. Kennedy and Gregory L. Possehl (New Delhi: Oxford and IBH Publishing/American Institute of Indian Studies, 1984), 121–137; and G. M. Bongard-Levin, *Mauryan India* (New Delhi: Sterling, 1985), 133–136; Charles Holcombe, "Trade-Buddhism: Maritime Trade, Immigration, and the Buddhist Landfall in Early Japan," *Journal of the American Oriental Society* 119, 2 (1999): 280–292.

47. On the interconnection between merchants and Buddhist institutions functioning as banks see Himanshu P. Ray, *Monastery and Guild: Commerce Under the*

Satavahanas (Delhi: Oxford University Press, 1986); and Gregory Schopen, "Doing Business for the Lord: Lending on Interest and Written Loan Contracts in the *Mūlasarvāstivada-vinaya*," *Journal of the American Oriental Society* 114 (1994): 527–554.

48. S. A. M. Adshead, *China in World History* (London: Macmillan, 1988), 52, 102.

49. Thomas T. Allsen, *Commodity and Exchange in the Mongol Empire: A Cultural History of Islamic Textiles* (Cambridge: Cambridge University Press, 1997), 105.

50. There has been a great deal of debate about the origin of this artwork and its possible Greek antecedents; see, for example, Stanley K. Abe, "Inside the Wonder House: Buddhist Art and the West," in *Curators of the Buddha: The Study of Buddhism Under Colonialism*, ed. Donald S. Lopez, Jr. (Chicago: University of Chicago Press, 1995), 63–106.

51. On the economic downturn of this period and its broader implications see Philippe Beaujard, "The Indian Ocean in Eurasian and African World-Systems Before the Sixteenth Century," *Journal of World History* 16, 4 (2005): 421–436.

52. For an early positive evaluation of the Hepthalites in a sixth-century Chinese history, see Yang Hsüan-chih, *A Record of Buddhist Monasteries in Lo-yang* (Princeton: Princeton University Press, 1984), 225–228. In terms of Buddhism's fate under the Hepthalites it is also important to note that it was during their reign that the giant Bamiyan Buddhas were erected; see Xavier Tremblay, "The Spread of Buddhism in Serindia: Buddhism Among Iranians, Tocharians, and Turks Before the 13th Century," in *The Spread of Buddhism*, ed. Ann Heirman and Stephen P. Bumbacher (Leiden: Brill, 2007), 88.

53. Étienne de La Vaissière, *Sogdian Traders: A History*, trans. James Ward (Leiden: Brill, 2005), 111.

54. On the rise of the Turks and their involvement in Central Asia see Peter B. Golden, *An Introduction to the History of the Turkic Peoples* (Wiesbaden: Otto Harrassowitz, 1992), 115–154.

55. On the development of the Sanskrit cosmopolis see Pollock, *The Language of the Gods in the World of Men*.

56. Liu, *Ancient India and Ancient China*, 27. This development is confirmed not only by Chinese pilgrim accounts, but also epigraphical evidence; see de la Vaissière, *Sogdian Traders*, 81.

57. Siglinde Dietz, "Buddhism in Gandhara," in *The Spread of Buddhism*, ed. Ann Heirman and Stephen P. Bumbacher (Leiden: Brill, 2007), 60–62.

58. Quoted in Khaliq Ahmad Nizami, "Early Arab Contact with South Asia," *Journal of Islamic Studies* 5, 1 (1994): 56.

59. Wink, *Al-Hind Vol. 1*, 173.

60. On the shift of the trade routes north and the subsequent rise of the Sogdians, who in many ways were simply at the right place at the right time, see La Vaissière's comprehensive study *Sogdian Traders*.

61. Davidson, *Indian Esoteric Buddhism*, 81. On the history of Buddhism in Cen-

tral Asia see Boris A. Litvinsky, *Die Geschichte des Buddhismus in Ostturkestan* (Wiesbaden: Harrassowitz Verlag, 1999).

62. Antonio Forte, "Chinese State Monasteries in the Seventh and Eighth Centuries," in *Echoo Go Tenjiku Koku den kenkyu,* ed. Kuwayama Shoshin (Kyoto: Institute for Research in the Humanities, 1992), 228–231.

63. Ray, *Winds of Change,* 27.

64. Kirin Narayan, *My Family and Other Saints* (Chicago: University of Chicago Press, 2007), 181. On account of the abundance of this trade some have even suggested that the monumental sculptures of the Ethiopian Aksumite kingdom were inspired by Buddhist precedents (Wink, *Al-Hind Vol. 1,* 28); however, most scholars now discount this idea (David W. Phillipson, *Ancient Ethiopia: Its Antecedents and Successors* [London: British Museum, 1998], 64).

65. On the history of Buddhism along the Persian Gulf see the two articles of W. Ball, "Two Aspects of Iranian Buddhism," *Bulletin of the Asia Institute of Pahlavi University* 1 (1976): 103–163; "Some Rock-cut Monuments in Southern Iran," *Iran* 24 (1986): 95–115; and Gianroberto Scarcia, "The 'Vihar' of Qongqor-olong: Preliminary Report," *East and West* 25, 1–2 (1979): 99–104. On the early Buddhist engagement with Iranian culture see A. S. Melikian-Chirvani, "Recherches sur l'architecture de l'Iran bouddhique. I. Essai sur les origines et le symbolisme du stupa iranien," *Le monde iranien et l'Islam* 3, 1 (1975): 1–61; Victor H. Mair, "Three Brief Essays Concerning Chinese Tocharistan, no. B: Early Iranian Influences on Buddhism in Central Asia," *Sino-Platonic Papers* 16 (1990): 131–134; and David A. Scott, "The Iranian Face of Buddhism," *East West* 40 (1990): 43–78; Richard C. Foltz, *Spirituality in the Land of the Noble: How Iran Shaped the World's Religions* (Oxford: Oneworld, 2004): 63–75.

66. On the linkage between the Buddhists in Afghanistan and the new northern route of the Silk Road see Jens-Uwe Hartmann, "Buddhism Along the Silk Road: On the Relationship Between the Buddhist Sanskrit Texts from Northern Turkestan and Those from Afghanistan," in *Turfan Revisited: The First Century of Research into the Arts and Cultures of the Silk Road,* ed. Desmond Durkin-Meisterernst et al. (Berlin: Dietrich Reimer Verlag, 2004), 125–128.

67. This westward migration is confirmed by the Sassanian inscription of Kirder at Naqsh-i Rustam, which specifically mentions Buddhists in eastern Iran (Christopher J. Brunner, "The Middle Persian Inscription of the Priest Kirder at Naqsh-i Rustam," in *Near Eastern Numismatics, Iconography, Epigraphy, and History: Studies in Honour of George C. Miles,* ed. Dickran K. Kouymjian [Beirut: American University of Beirut, 1974], 105–106). For a survey of Buddhist monuments in Afghanistan, see C. S. Upasak, *History of Buddhism in Afghanistan* (Sarnath: Central Institute of Higher Tibetan Studies, 1990); and on the history of Bamiyan see Deborah Klimburg-Salter, *The Kingdom of Bamiyan: Buddhist Art and Culture of the Hindu Kush* (Naples-Rome: Istituto Universitario Orientale, 1989).

68. B. G. Gokhale, "Buddhism in the Gupta Age," in *Essays on Gupta Culture,* ed. Bardwell L. Smith (Delhi: Motilal Banarsidass, 1983), 129–153.

69. Wink, *Al-Hind Vol. 1*, 73.

70. While there is an enormous literature on the *Kamasutra*, an excellent introduction to the text and its meaning is Wendy Doniger, "Reading the '*Kamasutra*': The
Strange and the Familiar," *Daedalus* Spring 2007: 66–78.

71. André Bareau, *Les sectes bouddhiques du Petit véhicule* (Saigon: École française
d'extrême-orient, 1955). Scholars have recently started to use the term Nikaya, meaning "schools," or else "Mainstream," to identify these Buddhist traditions rather than
the more common Hinayana, "little vehicle," which is a derogatory term derived from
Mahayana literature.

72. Jonathan Silk, "What, if Anything, Is Mahāyāna Buddhism? Problems of
Definitions and Classifications," *Numen* 49 (2002): 355–405.

73. Paul Harrison, "Searching for the Origins of the Mahāyāna: What Are We
Looking For?" *Eastern Buddhist* 28 (1995): 65; Jan Nattier, *A Few Good Men: The
Bodhisattva Path According to the Inquiry of Ugra (Ugraparipṛcchā-sūtra)* (Honolulu:
University of Hawai'i Press, 2003); and Daniel Boucher, *Bodhisattvas of the Forest and
the Formation of the Mahāyāna: A Study and Translation of the* Rāṣṭrapālaparipṛcchā-
sūtra (Honolulu: University of Hawai'i Press, 2008).

74. Douglas Osto, *Power, Wealth and Women in Indian Mahāyāna Buddhism: The
Gaṇḍavyūha-sūtra* (New York: Routledge, 2008).

75. For a comprehensive of survey of Mahayana Buddhist thought see Paul Wil-
liams, *Mahāyāna Buddhism: The Doctrinal Foundations* (London: Routledge, 1989).

76. These terms are borrowed from Strong, *Experience of Buddhism*, 181–187.

77. On the importance of this debate in Buddhism, see Peter Gregory, *Sudden
and Gradual: Approaches to Enlightenment in Chinese Thought* (Honolulu: University
of Hawai'i Press, 1987).

78. On the problems related to the appearance of Mahayana Buddhism see Gregory Schopen, *Figments And Fragments Of Mahāyāna Buddhism In India: More Collected
Papers* (Honolulu: University of Hawai'i Press, 2005).

79. Liu, *Ancient India and Ancient China*, 39. On the Buddhist response to these
developments see, for example, Osto, *Power, Wealth and Women in Indian Mahāyāna
Buddhism*.

80. Liu Xinru, *Silk and Religion: An Exploration of Material Life and the Thought
of People, AD 600–1200* (Delhi: Oxford University Press, 1996), 28.

81. "In short, the Buddhist values of the seven treasures and the emphasis on
donating these items developed out of an economic environment where both ruler
and urban dweller sought luxury goods. . . . On the one hand they bestowed prestige
on their owners—the monasteries, the donors, the purchasers influenced by fashion.
On the other hand their production and transaction encouraged substantial economic
activities. Thus Buddhist values reinforced and extended trade while sustaining certain
economic activities even through a period of urban decline" (Liu, *Ancient India and
Ancient China*, 177, 180).

82. See John Kieschnick, *The Impact of Buddhism on Chinese Material Culture*

(Princeton: Princeton University Press, 2003). The introduction of Buddhism did not only affect Chinese material culture, however. It also impacted more intangible things such as how to organize space. See Anne Cheng, "La notion d'espace dans la pensée traditionelle chinoise," in *Aménager l'espace*, ed. Flora Blanchon (Paris: Presses de l'Université de Paris-Sorbonne, 1993), 33–44.

83. Ray, *Winds of Change*, 41–44, 116. On this issue see also Sen, *Buddhism, Diplomacy, and Trade*, chap. 4.

84. Benavides, "Economy," 82.

85. David Gordon White, *The Alchemical Body: Siddha Traditions in Medieval India* (Chicago: University of Chicago Press, 1996), 35.

86. As Davidson has shown in his *Indian Esoteric Buddhism* (chap. 3) the social breakdown of post-Gupta period had six consequences: 1) When the financial support of the business community failed, Buddhists sought support from the new political powers. 2) This resulted in the contraction of Buddhist sites, especially in south India. 3) Women were no longer involved with the Dharma. 4) Buddhist scholars created a radical skepticism, *prasangika madhyamika*, which claimed the high-ground "by virtue of its extremism." 5) Buddhist intellectuals moved away from abhidharma toward Brahmanical epistemology. 6) Because of patronage shifts monasteries became landed fiefs, or "super monasteries" (*mahāvihāra*).

87. David B. Gray, *The Cakrasamvara Tantra* (New York: American Institute of Buddhist Studies, 2007), 9.

88. On the popular views of tantra, see Hugh B. Urban, *Tantra: Sex, Secrecy, Politics, and Power in the Study of Religion* (Berkeley: University of California Press, 2003).

89. White, *The Alchemical Body*, 306.

90. Davidson, *Indian Esoteric Buddhism*, chap. 4.

91. David Gordon White, *Kiss of the Yogini* (Chicago: University of Chicago Press, 2003), 124–125.

92. Gray, *Cakrasamvara Tantra*, 81.

93. Taranatha, *History of Buddhism in India*, trans. Lama Chimpa and Alaka Chattopa-dhyaya (Delhi: Motilal Banarsidas, 1990), 279.

94. Wink, *Al-Hind Vol. 1*, 283.

95. Davidson, *Indian Esoteric Buddhism*, 85.

96. Tremblay, "The Spread of Buddhism in Serindia," 89–97. See also Mariko Namba Walter, "Sogdians and Buddhism," *Sino-Platonic Papers* 174 (2006): 1–66.

97. B. A. Litvinsky, "Outline History of Buddhism in Central Asia," in *Kushan Studies in the USSR: Papers Presented by the Soviet Scholars at the UNESCO Conference on History, Archaeology and Culture of Central Asia in the Kushan Period, Dushanbe 1968*, ed. B. Gafurov et al. (Calcutta: Indian Studies Past and Present, 1970), 57.

98. Benavides, "Buddhism, Manichaeism, Markets and Empires," 34. For an overview on the history and practices of Manichaism see Jason BeDuhn, *The Manichaean Body: In Discipline and Ritual* (Baltimore: Johns Hopkins University Press, 2000).

99. This is, of course, the interpretation found in Manichean sources and is also

echoed in later Muslim sources (see, for example, Juvaini, 'Ala-ad-Din 'Ata-Malik, *The History of the World Conqueror*, trans. John A. Boyle [Manchester: Manchester University Press, 1958], vol. 1, 58). On Bügü Khan's conversion, including an important reevaluation of its history, see Larry V. Clark, "The Conversion of Bügü Khan to Manichaism," in *Studia Manichaica. IV*, ed. R. E. Emmerick, W. Sunderman, P. Zieme (Berlin: Berlin-Brandenburgische Akademie der Wissenschaften, 2000), 82–123.

100. On the history of Buddhism in Kashmir see Jean Nadou, *Les bouddhistes Kasmiriens au moyen age* (Paris: Presses Universitaires de France, 1968); and on its eventual Islamization see Muhammad Ishaq Khan, *Kashmir's Transition to Islam: The Role of Muslim Rishis (Fifteenth to Eighteenth Century)* (New Delhi: Manohar, 2002).

101. On the Bhaumakara see Bimal Chandra Mahapatra, *Buddhism and Socio-Economic Life of Eastern India with Special Reference to Bengal and Orissa (8th–12th Centuries)* (New Delhi: D. K. Printworld, Ltd., 1995).

102. Tilman Frasch, "A Buddhist Network in the Bay of Bengal: Relations Between Bodhgaya, Burma and Sri Lanka, c. 300–1300," in *From the Mediterranean to the China Sea: Miscellaneous Notes*, ed. C. Guillot, D. Lombard, and R. Ptak (Wiesbaden: Harrassowitz Verlag, 1998), 69–92. The linkages across the Buddhist Mediterranean are also reflected in the similarities in the Buddhist art found across these areas; see Denise Patry Leidy, *The Art of Buddhism: An Introduction to Its History and Meaning* (Boston: Shambhala, 2008), 29.

103. Wink, *Al-Hind Vol. 1*, 111.

104. MacLean, *Religion and Society*, 7.

105. Wink, *Al-Hind Vol. 1*, 135. For more on the early history of the Buddhist traders in this area see Ball, "Two Aspects of Iranian Buddhism," 116–122.

106. On the problems of the *Chachnama* and its value as a historical source see Wink, *Al-Hind Vol. 1*, 194–196.

107. R. A. Stein, *Tibetan Civilization* (Stanford: Stanford University Press, 1972), 58–59.

108. J. Harmath and B. A. Litvinsky, "Tokharistan and Gandhara Under Western Turk Rule (650–750)," in *History of Civilizations of Central Asia, Vol. III.*, ed. B. A. Livintsky (Paris: UNESCO Publishing, 1996), 391–401; Frantz Grenet, "Regional Interaction in Central Asia and Northwest India in the Kidarite and Hephthalite Periods," in *Indo-Iranian Languages and People*, ed. Nicholas Sims-Williams (London: Oxford University Press, 2002), 203–224.

109. On this episode in Muslim historiography see S. Maqbul, *India and the Neighbouring Territories in the "Kitab Nuzhat al-Mushtaq fi'Khtiraq al-'Afaq" of al' Sharif al'Idrisi* (Leiden: Brill, 1960), 96–97. The amount of 40,000 pounds is derived from ibn Nadim's *Fihrist*; see Bayard Dodge, *The Fihrist of al-Nadim: A Tenth Century Survey of Muslim Culture* (New York: Columbia University Press, 1970), 829 n. 16.

110. There is a striking parallel with this story and the holding of prisoners in Calcutta, the notorious Black Hole of Calcutta, which was used to justify the British

invasion of India. See Nicholas B. Dirks, *The Scandal of Empire: India and the Creation of Imperial Britain* (Cambridge: Belknap Press, 2006), 1–4, 34.

111. On this episode see MacLean, *Religion and Society*, 65–66.

112. MacLean, *Religion and Society*, 66 (citing the *Chachnama*, 93; and Baladhuri 1866: 437–38).

113. Patricia Crone, *God's Rule—Government and Islam: Six Centuries of Medieval Islamic Political Thought* (New York: Columbia University Press, 2004), 372.

114. Richard Bulliet, *Conversion to Islam in the Medieval Period* (Cambridge: Harvard University Press, 1979). For a critique of Bulliet's methodology see Michael Morony, "The Age of Conversions: A Reassessment," in *Conversion and Continuity: Indigenous Christian Communities in Islamic Lands, Eighth to Eighteenth Centuries*, ed. Michael Gervers and Ramzi Jibran Bikhazi (Toronto: Pontifical Institute of Medieval Studies, 1990), 135–150.

115. Gianroberto Scarcia, "A Preliminary Report on a Persian Legal Document of 470–1078 Found at Bamiyan," *East and West* 14 (1963): 73–85; Klimburg-Salter, *The Kingdom of Bamiyan*, 41; Zemaryalai Tarzai, "Bamiyan 2006: The Fifth Excavation Campaign of Prof. Tarzai's Mission," *Silk Road Studies* 4, 2 (2006): 21.

116. Wink, *Al-Hind Vol. 1*, 149.

117. Yohanan Friedmann, *Tolerance and Coercion in Islam: Interfaith Relations in the Muslim Tradition* (New York: Cambridge University Press, 2003), 84–85.

118. For an overview of the Muslim conquest of Central Asia see Hugh Kennedy, *The Great Arab Conquests: How the Spread of Islam Changed the World We Live In* (Cambridge: Da Capo Press, 2007), 255–323.

119. Wink, *Al-Hind Vol. 1*, 195.

120. Patricia Crone, *Roman, Provincial and Islamic Law: The Origins of the Islamic Patronate* (Cambridge: Cambridge University Press, 1987).

121. Quoted in MacLean, *Religion and Society*, 41.

122. On a similar policy in the British empire see David Cannadine, *Ornamentalism: How the British Saw Their Empire* (New York: Oxford University Press, 2001).

123. MacLean, *Religion and Society*, 42.

124. MacLean, *Religion and Society*, 44.

125. Berkey, *Formation of Islam*, 161.

126. See Jürgen Paul, *Herrscher, Gemeinwesen, Vermitter: Ostiran und Transoxanien in vormongolischer Zeit* (Stuttgart: Steiner, 1996).

127. Wink, *Al Hind Vol. 1*, 112–125.

128. Wink, *Al Hind Vol. 1*, 213–216.

129. S. Razia Jafri, "Description of India (Hind and Sind) in the Works of Al-Iṣṭakhrī, Ibn Ḥauqal and Al-Maqdisī," *Bulletin of the Institute of Islamic Studies* 5 (1961): 8, 14, 18, 33, 36.

130. C. E. Sachau, *The Chronology of Ancient Nations: An English Version of the Arabic Text of the Athar-ul-bakiya of Albiruni, or "Vestiges of the Past," Collected and*

Reduced to Writing by the Author in A.H. 390–1, A.D. 1000 (London: William H. Allen, 1879), 188–189.

131. Quoted in A. S. Melikian-Chirvani, "The Buddhist Ritual in the Literature of Early Islamic Iran," in *South Asian Archaeology 1981*, ed. Bridget Allchin (Cambridge: Cambridge University Press, 1984), 273.

132. Melikian-Chirvani, "The Buddhist Ritual," 273.

133. Mahapatra, *Buddhism and Socio-Economic Life*, 55.

134. See Aziz Ahmad, "Epic and Counter-Epic in Medieval India," *Journal of the American Oriental Society* 83 (1962): 470–476.

135. Some of the more common explanations for the decline of Buddhism in India are: 1) Laxity in monastic discipline. 2) Schism in the samgha. 3) Rise of Tantra and the merging with Hinduism. 4) Lack of a lay Buddhist identity. 5) Hindu intellectual attacks. 6) Doctrine of Suffering. 7) Muslim persecution. 8) Decline of patronage. 9) Royal persecution. 10) Too cerebral and divorced from daily concerns. See, for example, Kanai Lal Hazra, *The Rise and Decline of Buddhism in India* (New Delhi: Munshiram Manoharlal Publishers, 1995).

136. Robert G. Hoyland, *Seeing Islam as Others Saw It: A Survey and Evaluation of Christian, Jewish and Zoroastrian Writings on Early Islam* (Princeton: Darwin Press, 1995), 248; Han-Sung Yang et al., *The Hye Ch'o Diary: Memoir of the Pilgrimage to the Five Regions of India* (Berkeley: Asian Humanities Press, 1989), 52.

137. MacLean, *Religion and Society*, 68.

138. Wink, *Al Hind Vol. 1*, 173.

139. MacLean, *Religion and Society*, 75.

140. Ray, *Winds of Change*, 122.

141. "Spiritual capital" is a term coined by the sociologists Peter L. Berger and Robert W. Heffner, "Spiritual Capital in Comparative Perspective," http://www.spiritualcapitalresearch program.com/pdf/Berger.pdf [n.d., accessed November 24, 2008).

142. On the importance of medical knowledge and healing the sick in the spread of Buddhism, see Kenneth G. Zysk, *Asceticism and Healing in Ancient India: Medicine in the Buddhist Monastery* (New York: Oxford University Press, 1991), and Gregory Schopen, "The Good Monk and His Money in a Buddhist Monasticism of 'The Mahāyāna Period'," *Eastern Buddhist* 12, 1 (2000): 95. Moreover, as is invariably the case with conversion stories a key element is the ability to heal; in the case of Islam in northwest India see, for example, S. Nadvi, "Religious Relations Between Arabia and India," *Islamic Culture* 8 (1934): 204.

143. In thinking about these issues it is also interesting to note that in an Indian law compilation, the *Devalasmṛti* (ca. 800–1000 C.E.), "converting to Islam is only a minor contamination and might be made null and void by a minor ritual" (Andreas Kaplony, "The Conversion of the Turks of Central Asia to Islam as Seen by Arabic and Persian Geography," in *Islamisation de l'Asie centrale: Processus locaux d'acculturation du VIIe au XIe siècle*, ed. Étienne de la Vaissière [Paris: Association pour l'avancement des études iraniennes, 2008], 328).

144. Peter Brown, *Authority and the Sacred: Aspects of Christianization of the Roman World* (New York: Cambridge University Press, 1995), x.

145. Brown, *Authority and the Sacred*, 6.

146. For a nuanced account of Islamization in Central Asia see Devin DeWeese, *Islamization and Native Religion in the Golden Horde: Baba Tükles and Conversion to Islam in Historical and Epic Tradition* (University Park: Pennsylvania State University Press, 1994).

Chapter 2. Understanding

Note to epigraphs: Quoted in Vladimir Minorsky, *Sharaf al-Zamān Tāhir Marvazī on China, the Turks and India* (London: Royal Asiatic Society, 1942), 141. Quoted in John Newman, "Islam in the Kālacakra Tantra," *Journal of the International Association of Buddhist Studies* 21, 2 (1998): 320.

1. The text is *Kitāb al-manbah wa-l-'amal fī sharḥ kitāb al-malal wa-n-naḥl* by Ahmad bin Yahya Murtada (d. 1437 C.E.), which is described in S. Nadvi, "Religious Relations between Arabia and India," *Islamic Culture* 8, 2 (1934): 205–206.

2. Ibn Hauqal, for example, notes that in Sind the majority of the inhabitants are non-Muslim and that the Arabs are only a ruling elite (*Configuration de la terre [Kitāb Ṣūrat al-Arḍ]*, trans. J. H. Kramers and G. Wiet [Paris: Éditions G.-P. Maisonneuve & Larose, 1964], 313). See also S. Razia Jafri, "Description of India (Hind and Sind) in the Works of Al-Iṣṭakhrī, Ibn Ḥauqal and Al-Maqdisī," *Bulletin of the Institute of Islamic Studies* 5 (1961): 8, 14, 18, 32–33, 35–36.

3. For example, Al-Iṣṭakhrī writes, "Here the Muslims and the infidels wear the same type of dress and allow their hair to grow long," quoted in Jafri, "Description of India," 13.

4. M. A. Shaban, *The 'Abbasid Revolution* (Cambridge: Cambridge University Press, 1970), 48.

5. On the history of the Umayyads see G. R. Hawting, *The First Dynasty of Islam: The Umayyad Caliphate A.D. 661–750* (London: Croom Helm, 1986).

6. Christopher I. Beckwith, "The Plan of the City of Peace: Central Asian Iranian Factors in Early 'Abbasid Design," *Acta Orientalia Academiae Scientiarum Hungaricae* 38 (1984): 128–147. For a different view on the origins of Baghdad see Jacob Lassner, *The Shaping of 'Abbasid Rule* (Princeton: Princeton University Press, 1980), 169–183.

7. See Christopher I. Beckwith, "Aspects of the Early History of the Central Asian Guard Corps in Islam," *Archivum Eurasiae Medii Aevi* 4 (1984): 29–43; and Étienne de la Vaissière, "Chakars d'Asie centrale: à propos d'ouvrages recents," *Studia Iranica* 34 (2005): 139–149.

8. Tayeb El-Hibri, *Reinterpreting Islamic Historiography: Harun al-Rashid and the Narrative of the 'Abbasid Caliphate* (New York: Cambridge University Press, 1999), 8.

9. Étienne de la Vaissière, *Samarcande et Samarra: Elites d'Asie centrale dans l'empire abbasside* (Paris: Association pour l'avancement des études iraniennes, 2007).

10. On the history of the Barmakids see Dominique Sourdel, *Le vizirat 'abbaside*

de 739 à 936 (132 à 324 à l'Hégire) (Damascus: Institut français de Damas, 1959), 129–144; and Hugh Kennedy, *When Baghdad Ruled the Muslim World: The Rise and Fall of Islam's Greatest Dynasty* (Cambridge: Da Capo Press, 2004), 37–44, 62–65.

11. This fact led the Arab geographer Ibn al-Faqih to actually compare the Barmakids with the Quraysh who were the guardians of the Ka'ba in pre-Islamic times (Hugh Kennedy, *The Early Abbasid Caliphate: A Political History* [London: Croom Helm, 1981], 101).

12. On the possible reasons for the Barmakid conversion to Islam see C. E. Bosworth, "Abū Ḥafṣ 'Umar Al-Kirmānī and the Rise of the Barmakids," *Bulletin of the School of Oriental and African Studies* 57, 2 (1994): 270.

13. On policies implemented by the Barmakids, see Hugh Kennedy, "The Barmakid Revolution in Islamic Government," *Pembroke Papers* 1 (1990): 89–98.

14. Richard W. Bulliet, "Naw Bahar and the Survival of Iranian Buddhism," *Iran* 14 (1976): 140–145.

15. Dimitri Gutas, *Greek Thought, Arabic Culture: The Graeco-Arabic Translation Movement in Baghdad and Early Abbasid Society* (New York: Routledge, 1998).

16. As David Pingree has pointed out the three traditions are based on Brahmagupta's *Brahmasphutasiddhanta*, Āryabhaṭa's *Khaṇḍakhādyaka*, and Āryabhaṭa's *Āryabhatiya*; see "Al-Biruni's Knowledge of Sanskrit Astronomical Texts," in *The Scholar and the Saint*, ed. Peter J. Chelkowski (New York: New York University Press, 1975), 67–68.

17. Max Meyerhof, "'Ali at-Tabri's 'Paradise of Wisdom,' One of the Oldest Arabic Compendiums of Medicine," *Isis* 16, 1 (1931): 12–13, 42–46. For a list of other Indian medical texts translated into Arabic at this time see Nizami, "Early Arab Contact," 64.

18. Charles Seife, *Zero: The Biography of a Dangerous Idea* (New York: Viking Penguin, 2000), 66–73.

19. Jacques Vernet, "Al-Khwarazmi," in *Encyclopedia of Islam*, 2nd edition, ed. P. J. Bearman et al. (Leiden: Brill, 1960–2005).

20. Majid Fakhry, *A History of Islamic Philosophy* (New York: Cambridge University Press, 1983), 33–34.

21. The Muslim interest in things Indian also famously included the tradition of making swords of wootz steel, which greatly enhanced the military power of the Caliphate (Robert Raymond, *Out of the Fiery Furnace: The Impact of Metals on the History of Mankind* [University Park: Pennsylvania State University Press, 1984], 80).

22. Dodge, *Fihrist*, 828–829.

23. For an important re-interpretation of Buddhist pilgrimage see Toni Huber, "Putting the Gnas Back into Gnas-skor: Rethinking Tibetan Pilgrimage Practice," in *Sacred Spaces and Powerful Places in Tibetan Culture: A Collection of Essays*, ed. Toni Huber (Dharamsala: Library of Tibetan Works and Archives, 1999), 77–104.

24. Dodge, *Fihrist*, 829.

25. On "medieval consubstantiality, for which things seen and words heard are

equally reliable sources of knowledge," see Syed Manzurul Islam, *The Ethics of Travel: From Marco Polo to Kafka* (Manchester: Manchester University Press, 1996).

26. On the discourse of idolatry in the shaping of early Islam see Hawting's *The Idea of Idolatry and the Emergence of Islam: From Polemic to History.*

27. When Muhammad smashed the idols, only the images of Abraham, Mary, and Jesus were preserved inside the Ka'ba (Elaine Wright, *Islam: Faith, Art, Culture, Manuscripts of the Chester Beatty Library* [London: Scala Publishers, 2009], 27).

28. Dodge, *Fihrist,* 829.

29. A. S. Melikan-Chirvani, "The Buddhist Heritage in the Art of Iran," in *Mahāyānist Art After A.D. 900,* ed. William Watson (London: Percival David Foundation of Chinese Art, 1977), 59.

30. Christopher I. Beckwith, *The Tibetan Empire in Central Asia: A History of the Struggle for Great Power Among Tibetans, Turks, Arabs, and Chinese During the Early Middle Ages* (Princeton: Princeton University Press, 1987), 161.

31. Wink, *Al Hind Vol. 1,* 124.

32. Dodge, *Fihrist,* 829–830.

33. Vladimir Minorsky, "Abu Dulaf," in *Encyclopedia of Islam,* 2nd ed., ed. P. J. Bearman et al. (Leiden: Brill, 1960–2005).

34. Dodge, *Fihrist,* 830–831n.20.

35. Grant Parker, *The Making of Roman India* (New York: Cambridge University Press, 2008), 122–125, 251–294.

36. Dodge, *Fihrist,* 831.

37. Jacques Waardenburg, "The Medieval Period, 650–1500," in *Muslim Perceptions of Other Religions: A Historical Survey,* ed. Jacques Waardenburg (New York: Oxford University Press, 1999), 33.

38. This model continues to shape the contemporary "Buddhist-Christian dialogue" that often compares the Bodhisattva and Christ figure. See, for example, Donald S. Lopez, Jr. and Steven C. Rockefeller, eds., *The Christ and the Bodhisattva* (Albany: State University of New York Press, 1987).

39. Roger Jackson, "Terms of Sanskrit and Pali Origin Acceptable as English Words," *The Journal of the International Association of Buddhist Studies* 5 (1982): 141–142. See also Henry Yule and A. C. Burnell, *Hobson-Jobson: A Glossary of Colloquial Anglo-Indian Words and Phrases* (Delhi: Munshiram Manoharlal, 1968 rpt.).

40. Berkey, *Formation of Islam,* 99–100.

41. "Ibrahim b. Adham," in *Encyclopedia of Islam,* 2nd ed., ed. P. J. Bearman et al. (Leiden: Brill, 1960–2005).

42. Robert C. Zaehner, *Hindu and Muslim Mysticism* (London: Athlone, 1960), 86–109.

43. It was presumably translated before 815; see Daniel Gimaret, *Le Livre de Bilawahr et Budasf selon la version arabe ismaélienne* (Geneva: Librarie Droz, 1971), 61. For an edition of the Arabic see Daniel Gimaret, *Kitāb Bilawhar wa Budasf* (Beirut: Dar El-Machreq Éditeurs, 1986).

44. Zeina Matar, "The Buddha Legend: A Footnote from an Arabic Source," *Oriens* (1990): 440–442.

45. Gimaret, *Le Livre de Bilawahr et Budasf*, 3–11.

46. S. M. Stern and S. Walzer, *Three Unknown Buddhist Stories in an Arabic Version* (Oxford: Oxford University Press, 1971), 4–6, 15–24.

47. Carl-A. Keller, "Perceptions of Other Religions in Sufism," in *Muslim Perceptions of Other Religions: A Historical Survey*, ed. Jacques Waardenburg (New York: Oxford University Press, 1999), 184.

48. Stern and Walzer, *Three Unknown Buddhist Stories*, 5.

49. Quoted in E. Esin, "The Turkish Baksi and the Painter Muhammad Kalam," *Acta Orientalia* 32 (1970): 84 n9. The mention of a purple robe is interesting since this color was reserved for monks who received the imperial favor of the Chinese emperor (Antonino Forte, "On the Origin of the Purple *kasaya* in China," *Buddhist Asia* 1 [2003]: 145–166). It may therefore be the case that this description actually refers to one of the Chinese monasteries that existed in Central Asia (see Antonino Forte, "An Ancient Monastery Excavated in Kirgiziya," *Central Asiatic Journal* 38 [1994]: 41–57).

50. Minorsky, *Marvazī*, 42.

51. Dodge, *Fihrist*, 831–832.

52. On the development of the Maitreya myth see the articles in Alan Sponberg and Helen Hardacre, eds., *Maitreya, the Future Buddha* (New York: Cambridge University Press, 1988).

53. On the history of these debates see Jan Nattier, *Once Upon a Future Time: Studies in a Buddhist Prophecy of Decline* (Berkeley: Asian Humanities Press, 1991), 27–144.

54. For a convenient overview of millenarian religious movements in China see Maria Hsia Chang, *Falun Gong: The End of Days* (New Haven: Yale University Press, 2004), 32–59..

55. Robert E. Fisher, *Buddhist Art and Architecture* (London: Thames & Hudson, 1993), 118–119.

56. Simone Gaulier, Robert Jera-Bezard and Monique Maillard, *Buddhism in Afghanistan and Central Asia* (Leiden: Brill, 1976), 12.

57. For an overview and bibliography on the development of the Buddha image and its cult, especially the mistaken assumption of its relation to the Mahayana, see Gregory Schopen, "On Sending the Monks Back to Their Books: Cult and Conservatism in Early Mahāyāna Buddhism," in *Figments and Fragments of Mahāyāna Buddhism in India: More Collected Papers* (Honolulu: University of Hawai'i Press, 2005), 108–153.

58. On the development of Buddhist art during this period see Susan L. Huntington, *The "Pala-Sena" Schools of Sculpture* (Leiden: Brill, 1984).

59. White, *Alchemical Body*, 80.

60. Dodge, *Fihrist*, 832–833.

61. On the development and definition of tantra see David Gordon White, intro-

duction to *Tantra in Practice*, ed. David Gordon White (Princeton: Princeton University Press, 2000), 3–38.

62. Roxanne L. Euben, *Journeys to the Other Shore: Muslim and Western Travelers in Search of Knowledge* (Princeton: Princeton University Press, 2006), 77.

63. On the fall of the Barmakids see J. S. Meisami, "Mas'ūdī on Love and the Fall of the Barmakids," *Journal of the Royal Asiatic Society* (1989): 252–277.

64. This split is seen, for example, in the two major schools of Muslim theology (*kalam*), Asarism and Maturidism; in particular, the total lack awareness of the latter by the former in the earlier period. Much of this, of course, had to do with the fact that Maturidism developed in Central Asia, which at the time was not part of the Islamic heartland and its western orientation. As a result, Asarites were able to ignore the theological arguments of the Maturites. Once the Turks adopted the local tradition of Maturidism, however, the situation became completely reversed. In particular, with the move of the Turks into the Islamic heartland, and their promotion of a Maturi-based Hanafi tradition, Central Asia, rather than Baghdad and other cities in the Caliphate, became the center of Islamic intellectual life. On these developments see Wilferd Madelung, "The Spread of Maturidism and the Turks," in *Religious Schools and Sects in Medieval Islam* (London: Variorum Reprints, 1985), II, 109–168. And on the subsequent importance of Central Asian scholars in the science of *furu'*, the study and elaboration of *shari'a*, in the twelfth and thirteenth centuries, see Robert D. McChesney, "Central Asia's Place in the Middle East: Some Historical Considerations," in *Central Asia Meets the Middle East*, ed. David Menashri (London: Frank Cass, 1998), 37–48.

65. S. M. Yusuf, "The Early Contacts between Islam and Buddhism," in *Studies in Islamic History and Culture* (Lahore: Institute of Islamic Culture, 1970), 42–78. For a similar break in Muslim knowledge about China in the ninth and tenth centuries, see André Miquel, "L'Inde et la Chine vues du coté de l'Islam," in *As Others See Us: Mutual Perceptions, East and West*, ed. Bernard Lewis, Edmund Leites, and Margaret Case (New York: International Society for the Comparative Study of Civilizations, 1985), 285.

66. Richard C. Foltz, "Muslim 'Orientalism' in Medieval Travelogues of India," *Studies in Religion/Sciences Religiouses* 37, 1 (2008): 82.

67. G. Ferrand, *Voyage du marchande arabe Sulayman en Inde et en Chine redigé en 851 suivi de remarques par Abu Zayd Hasan* (Paris: Bossard, 1922), 124.

68. Sen, *Buddhism, Diplomacy and Trade*, 243.

69. On the development of this myth see Carl Ernst, "India as a Sacred Land," in *Religions of India in Practice*, ed. Donald S. Lopez, Jr. (Princeton: Princeton University Press, 1995), 556–564.

70. According to Biruni the Buddhists had been displaced by Manichaeans before Islam arrived in central Asia (E. Sachau, *Alberuni's India* [London: Trübner, 1888], 21)

71. On the development of Tibetan trade toward the East see Elliot Sperling, "The Szechwan-Tibet Frontier in the Fifteenth Century," *Ming Studies* 26 (1988): 38–39.

72. On Tangut and Khitan Buddhism see Ruth W. Dunnell, *The Great State of White and High: Buddhism and State Formation in Eleventh-Century Xia* (Honolulu: University of Hawai'i Press, 1996); and Nancy S. Steinhardt, *Liao Architecture* (Honolulu: University of Hawai'i Press, 1997). On Song Buddhism see Peter Gregory and Daniel Getz, eds., *Buddhism in the Sung* (Honolulu: University of Hawai'i Press, 1999); and Mark Halperin, *Out of the Cloister: Literati Perspectives on Buddhism in Sung China* (Cambridge: Harvard University Asia Center, 2006).

73. On the impact of the Song on the world economy see William H. MacNeill, *The Pursuit of Power: Technology, Armed Force, and Society since A.D. 1000* (Chicago: University of Chicago Press, 1982), 24–62; Janet L. Abu-Lughod, *Before European Hegemony: The World System* A.D. *1250–1350* (New York: Oxford University Press, 1989), 316–348; and A. G. Frank, *ReOrient: Global Economy in the Asian Age* (Berkeley: University of California Press, 1998).

74. See, for example, Friedrich Hirth and W. W. Rockhill, *Chao Ju-kua and His Work on the Chinese and Arab Trade in the Twelfth and Thirteenth Centuries* (St. Petersburg: Imperial Academy of Sciences, 1911; rpt. Taipei: Literature House, 1965).

75. Art historians have been most notable in drawing these connections, especially in regards to the so-called "Inner Asian International Style," which stretched from Afghanistan to Burma. See, for example, Deborah E. Klimburg-Salter and Eva Allinger, *The Inner Asian International Style 12th-14th Centuries: Papers presented at a Panel of the 7th Seminar of the International Association for Tibetan Studies, Graz 1995* (Vienna: Verlag der Österreichischen Akademie der Wissenschaften, 1998).

76. Mimi Hall Yiengpruksawan, "Finding China and Tibet in Classical Japan: The Case of the Amida Hall at Byodoin," unpublished lecture presented at Southern Methodist University, April 12, 2007.

77. Sen, *Buddhism, Diplomacy and Trade*, chaps. 4 and 5.

78. Even though Biruni could not find actual Buddhists he was able to gather information about their cosmology from either Buddhist or Hindu texts as seen in his brief description found in the *Athar al-baqiya*. Unfortunately the text breaks off and thus what Biruni actually knew about Buddhism remains a mystery: "They believe in the eternity of time and the migration of souls; they think that the globe of the universe is flying in an infinite vacuum, that therefore it has a rotary motion, since anything that is round, when thrown off its place, goes downward in a circular motion, as they say. But others of them believe that the world has been created (within time), and maintain that its duration is one million of years, which they divide into four periods, the first of four hundred thousand years, the *Aurea Aetas*" (Sachau, *The Chronology of Ancient Nations*, 189).

79. Sen, *Buddhism, Diplomacy and Trade*, 176.

80. Dodge, *Fihrist*, 837.

81. Minorsky, *Marvazī*, 42.

82. Bruce B. Lawrence, *Shahrastani on the Indian Religions* (The Hague: Mouton, 1971), 103.

83. M. S. Khan, "An Eleventh century Hispano-Arabic Source for Ancient Indian Science and Culture," in *Prof. H. K. Sharwani Felicitation Volume* (Hyderabad: 1975), 357–389.

84. V. Minorsky, "Gardīzī on India," in *Iranica: Twenty Articles* (Tehran: University of Tehran, 1964), 208.

85. For a full translation of Shahrastani's work see *Livre des religions et des sectes*, trans. Daniel Gimaret and Guy Monnot (Leuven: Peeters, 1986). The description of Buddhism is in volume 2, pages 530–533.

86. Lawrence, *Shahrastani*, 42–43.

87. Lawrence, *Shahrastani*, 108.

88. Lawrence, *Shahrastani*, 113–114.

89. Minorsky, *Marvazī*, 42.

90. Paul E. Walker, "The Doctrine of Metempsychosis in Islam," in *Islamic Studies Presented to Charles J. Adams*, ed. Wael B. Hallaq and Donald P. Little (Leiden: Brill, 1991), 219–238.

91. On Plato and his *Phaedrus* see Gannanath Obeyesekere, *Imagining Karma: Ethical Transformation in Amerindian, Buddhist and Greek Rebirth* (Berkeley: University of California Press, 2002), 253–318.

92. On the Muslims in Tang dynasty China see Edward H. Schafer, "Iranian Merchants in T'ang Dynasty Tales," in *Semitic and Oriental Studies*, ed. Walter J. Fischel (Berkeley: University of California Press, 1951), 403–422; Chen Dasheng, "Persian Settlements in Southeastern China during the T'ang, Sung and Yüan Dynasties," in *Encyclopedia of Islam*, 2nd ed., ed. P. J. Bearman et al. (Leiden: Brill, 1960–2005).

93. On this rebellion and its impact on the Muslim community of Canton see Howard S. Levy, *Biography of Huang Ch'ao* (Berkeley: University of California Press, 1961), 113–121; and George F. Hourani, *Arab Seafaring in the Indian Ocean in Ancient and Early Medieval Times* (Princeton: Princeton University Press, 1951), 64–75.

94. The extent of this trade is well borne out by the fact that in Tibetan geographical conceptualizations "the West," meaning the Caliphate, was understood simply as "a land of merchants" (Arianne MacDonald, "Note sur la diffusion de la 'théorie des Quatre Fils du Ciel' au Tibet," *Journal asiatique* 250 [1962]: 539).

95. Ibn Ḥauqal, *Configuration de la terre*, 447. On the Muslim-Tibetan musk trade see also Ferrand, *Voyage du marchande arabe Sulayman*, 109–111; and Corneille Jest, "Valeurs d'echange en Himalaya et au Tibet: lambre et le musc," in *De la voute celeste au terroir, du jardin au foyer*, ed. Lucien Bernot et al. (Paris: Éditions de l'École des Hautes Études en Sciences Sociales, 1987), 227–238; and, more recently, Anna Akasoy and Ronit Yoeli-Tlalim, "Along the Musk Routes: Exchanges between Tibet and the Islamic World," *Asian Medicine: Tradition and Modernity* 3, 2 (2007): 217–240; and Anya King, "The Musk Trade and the Near East in the Early Medieval Period" (unpublished Ph.D. dissertation, Indiana University, 2007).

96. Edwin O. Reischauer, *Ennin's Diary: The Record of a Pilgrimage to China in Search of the Law* (New York: Ronald Press, 1955), 70.

97. On Tibet in the early Muslim world see Douglas M. Dunlop, "Arab Relations with Tibet in the Eighth and Early Ninth Centuries A.D.," *Islam Tetkikleri Enstitüsü Dergisi* 5 (1973): 301–318; and Christopher I. Beckwith, "The Location and Population of Tibet According to Early Islamic Sources," *Acta Orientalia Academiae* 43 (1989): 163–170.

98. A. P. Martinez, "Gardīzī's Two Chapters on the Turks," *Archivum Eurasiae Medii Aevi* 2 (1982): 128–131.

99. Vladimir Minorsky, *Ḥudūd al-'Ālam 'The Regions of the World': A Persian Geography 372 A.H.–982 A.D.* (London: Luzac and Co., 1970), 92.

100. Minorsky, *Ḥudūd al-'Ālam*, 93–94.

101. V. Minorsky, "A False Jayhāni," in *Iranica: Twenty Articles* (Tehran: University of Tehran, 1964), 216–223.

102. Minorsky, *Marvazī*, 28.

103. Nadvi, "Religious Relations," 202.

104. Ferrand, *Voyage du marchande arabe Sulayman*, 68, 113. See also Ingeborg Palke, "Die Chinareise des Sulaiman at-Tagir," *Zeitschrift für Geschichte der arabisch-islamischen Wissenschaften* 5 (1989), 190–224.

105. Ferrand, *Voyage du marchande arabe Sulayman*, 68, 71.

106. See, for example, the well known episode recounted by ibn Nadim about the Central Asian Muslim ruler who did not kill a group of Manichaeans because the "Manichaean" emperor of China threatened that in retaliation he would kill the Muslims in China (Dodge, *Fihrist*, 802–803; on this episode see V. Minorsky, "Tamīm ibn Baḥr's Journey to the Uyghurs," *Bulletin of the School of Oriental and African Studies* 12, 2 [1948]: 303). The idea of a Manichaean China is also found in Marvazī (Minorsky, *Marvazī*, 15), while the Persian *Ḥudūd al-'Ālam* notes that "Most of them are Manichaeans (*din-i Mani*), but their king is a Buddhist" (Minorsky, 84). In trying to explain why Muslims continued to mistakenly claim that China was Manichean, one scholar has offered several possible explanations such as the legend that Mani supposedly escaped to China, or else it may have been a confusion with the Uygur khan's conversion. It is also possible that Mani's fame as a painter became connected with the legendary skill of Chinese artisans, or else it derived from Muslim familiarity with the south-coast Manicheans who survived until the fifteenth century. Lastly, it may simply have been a confusion between the two religions since both seemed similar to outsiders; see Michal Biran, *The Empire of the Qara Khitai in Eurasian History: Between China and the Islamic World* (New York: Cambridge University Press, 2005), 175–76.

107. On the Western engagement with Confucianism see Lionel M. Jensen, *Manufacturing Confucianism: Chinese Traditions and Universal Civilizations* (Durham: Duke University Press, 1997).

108. See Stanley Weinstein, *Buddhism Under the T'ang* (Cambridge: Cambridge

University Press, 1987); and T. H. Barrett, *Taoism under the T'ang: Religion and Empire During the Golden Age of the Chinese* (London: Wellsweep, 1996).

109. On the multivalency of Chinese religious life see, for example, Michel Strickmann, "India in the Chinese Looking Glass," in *The Silk Route and the Diamond Path*, ed. Deborah E. Klimburg-Salter (Los Angeles: UCLA Art Council, 1979), 52–63; and Stephen F. Teiser, introduction to *Religions of China in Practice*, ed. Donald S. Lopez, Jr. (Princeton: Princeton University Press, 1996), 3–40.

110. Minorsky, *Marvazī*, 25.

111. Arthur F. Wright, "Fo-t'u-teng: A Biography," *Harvard Journal of Asiatic Studies* 11 (1948): 321–371.

112. John Kieschnick, *The Eminent Monk: Buddhist Ideals in Medieval Chinese Hagiography* (Honolulu: University of Hawai'i Press, 1997), 67–111. In the late imperial period, however, the state limited the role of Buddhists in rainmaking rituals, see Jeffrey Snyder-Reinke, *Dry Spells: State Rainmaking and Local Governance in Late Imperial China* (Cambridge: Harvard University Asia Center, 2009), 58–59.

113. Minorsky, *Ḥudūd al-ʿĀlam*, 85.

114. Sarah E. Fraser. *Performing the Visual: The Practice of Buddhist Wall Painting in China and Central Asia, 618–960* (Stanford: Stanford University Press, 2004), 20–21, 172.

115. For an overview of Khotan and Khotanese Buddhism see Prods Oktor Skjaervø, "Khotan, An Early Center of Buddhism in Chinese Turkestan," in *Buddhism Across Boundaries: Chinese Buddhism and the Western Regions*, ed. Jan Nattier and John McRae (Taipei: Foguangshan Foundation for Buddhist & Culture Education, 1999), 265–344.

116. Minorsky, *Ḥudūd al-ʿĀlam*, 85.

117. On the Buddhist worship of relics see Kevin Trainor, *Relics, Ritual, and Representation in Buddhism: Rematerializing the Sri Lankan Theravada Tradition* (New York: Cambridge University Press, 1997); David Germano and Kevin Trainor, eds., *Embodying the Dharma: Buddhist Relic Veneration in Asia* (Albany: State University of New York Press, 2004); and John S. Strong, *Relics of the Buddha* (Princeton: Princeton University Press, 2004).

118. Minorsky, *Ḥudūd al-ʿĀlam*, 85.

119. "Khotan is situated between two rivers. In its limits (*Ḥudūd*) live wild people who are man-eaters" (Minorsky, *Ḥudūd al-ʿĀlam*, 85).

120. On the Qarakhanid dynasty see Peter B. Golden, "The Karakhanids and Early Islam," in *The Cambridge History of Early Inner Asia*, ed. Denis Sinor (New York: Cambridge University Press, 1990), 343–370.

121. Maḥmūd al-Kāšgarī, *Compendium of the Turkic Languages (Diwan Lugat at-Turk) Volume 1*, ed. and trans. Robert Dankoff and James Kelly (Cambridge: Harvard University Press, 1982), 270. Although this poem describes an attack on the Uygurs it most likely actually refers to the Qarakhanid conquest of Khotan, see Robert Dankoff,

"Three Turkic Verse Cycles Relating to Inner Asian Warfare," *Harvard Ukranian Studies* 3–4, 1 (1979–1980): 161.

122. White, *Alchemical Body*, 7.

123. White, *Alchemical Body*, 73 ff.

124. Taranatha, *History*, 319–320.

125. Taranatha, *History*, 326–327.

126. Taranatha, *History*, 328.

127. F.W. Thomas, "Buddhism in Khotan: Its Decline According to Two Tibetan Accounts," in *Sir Asutosh Mookherjee Silver Jubilee Volumes* (Calcutta: Calcutta University Press, 1927), 30–52. For more on the so-called "Kauśāmbī Legend" in Khotan see Nattier, *Once Upon a Future Time*, 188–204.

128. Quoted in Newman, "Islam in the Kālacakra Tantra," 312.

129. On the sparsity of references to Islam in Indian literature and epigraphy as a whole from the seventh to eleventh century see Brajadulal Chattopadhyaya, *Representing the Other? Sanskrit Sources and the Muslims* (New Delhi: Manohar, 1998), 92–97.

130. David Scott, "Buddhism and Islam: Past to Present Encounters and Interfaith Lessons," *Numen* 42, 2 (1995): 143.

131. Even though scholars disagree on the time and place of the *Kālacakratantra*'s intial appearance (between the ninth and eleventh centuries; and northwest and east India), a central element of the work is the tension between Buddhism and Islam. See Giacomella Orofino, "Apropos of Some Foreign Elements in the Kālacakratantra," in *Tibetan Studies: Proceedings of the 7th Seminar of the IATS, Graz, 1995*, ed. H. Krasser et al. (Vienna: Österreichische Akademie der Wissenschaften, 1997), 717–724; and Newman, "Islam in the Kālacakra Tantra," 332.

132. Newman, "Islam in the Kālacakra Tantra," 334.

133. On the myth of Shambhala see Edwin Bernbaum, *The Way to Shambhala: A Search for the Mythical Kingdom Beyond the Himalayas* (Los Angeles: Jeremy P. Tarcher, 1980); and Lubos Belka, "The Myth of Shambhala: Visions, Visualizations, and the Myth's Resurrection in the Twentieth Century in Buryatia," *Archiv Orientální* 71, 3 (2003): 247–262.

134. John Newman, "Eschatology in the Wheel of Time Tantra," in *Buddhism in Practice*, ed. Donald S. Lopez, Jr. (Princeton: Princeton University Press, 1995), 284–289.

135. Newman, "Islam in the Kālacakra Tantra," 325.

136. Leonard W. J. van der Kuijp, "The Earliest Indian Reference to Muslims in a Buddhist Philosophical Text of *circa* 700," *Journal of Indian Philosophy* 34 (2006): 196–200.

137. Newman, "Islam in the Kālacakra Tantra," 334–335.

138. Newman, "Islam in the Kālacakra Tantra," 343–344.

139. Newman, "Islam in the Kālacakra Tantra," 342.

140. "The influence of Islamic Ptolemaic theory upon Indian astronomy can be

traced back to Munjala in the tenth century." David Pingree, *Jyotiḥśāstra: Astral and Mathematical Literature* (Wiesbaden: Otto Harrassowitz, 1981), 34.

141. Newman, "Islam in the Kālacakra Tantra," 336 n. 46.

142. I thank Brian Baumann for this information.

143. Robert Hillenbrand, "Madrasa III. Architecture," in *Encyclopedia of Islam*, 2nd ed., ed. P. J. Bearman et al. (Leiden: Brill, 1960–2005).

144. Géza Fehévári, "Islamic Incense-burners and the Influence of Buddhist Art," in *The Iconography of Islamic Art: Studies in Honour of Robert Hillenbrand*, ed. Bernard O'Kane (Edinburgh: Edinburgh University Press, 2005), 127. See also A. S. Melikian-Chirvani, "The Buddhist Heritage in the Art of Iran," in *Mahāyānist Art After AD 900*, ed. William Watson (London: Percival David Foundation, 1971), 56–73.

145. Christopher I. Beckwith, "The Introduction of Greek Medicine into Tibet in the Seventh and Eighth Centuries," *Journal of the American Oriental Society* 99, 2 (1979): 297–313; and Christopher I. Beckwith, "The Medieval Scholastic Method in Tibet and the West," in *Reflections on Tibetan Culture: Essays in Memory of Turrell V. Wylie*, ed. L. Epstein and R. Sherbourne (New York: E. Mellen Press, 1990), 307–313.

146. Ronit Yoeli-Tlalim, "On Urine Analysis and Tibetan Medicine's Connections with the West," in *Studies in the History of Tibetan Medicine*, ed. Frances Garrett, Mona Schrempf, and Sienna Craig (Sankt Augustin: International Institute for Tibetan and Buddhist Studies, forthcoming); Dan Martin, "Greek and Islamic Medicines' Historical Contact with Tibet: A Reassessment in View of Recently Available but Relatively Early Sources on Tibetan Medical Eclecticism," unpublished paper presented at the Islam and Tibet Conference, November 18, 2006, Warburg Institute, London.

147. White, *Alchemical Body*, 106.

148. On the history of magic squares see the three articles by Schuyler Cammann, "Evolution of Magic Squares in China," *Journal of the American Oriental Society* 80 (1960): 116–124; "Old Chinese Magic Squares," *Sinologica* 7 (1962): 14–53; "Islamic and Indian Magic Squares," *History of Religion* 8 (1968/1969): 181–209, and 271–299.

149. Karl R. Schaeffer, *Enigmatic Charms: Medieval Arabic Book Printed Amulets in American and European Libraries and Museums* (Leiden: Brill, 2006), 5.

150. On the development of printing in Buddhist China see T. H. Barrett, *The Woman Who Discovered Printing* (New Haven: Yale University Press, 2008).

151. Jonathan M. Bloom, *Paper Before Print: The History and Impact of Paper in the Islamic World* (New Haven: Yale University Press, 2001), 32–45. On the impact of paper in Muslim Inner Asia see David J. Roxburgh, *The Persian Album 1400–1600: From Dispersal to Collection* (New Haven: Yale University Press, 2005), 159–165.

152. See, for example, both the Chinese blockprinted amulets (figs. 140–143, 147, 148, 150, 153), and the mid-tenth century amulets with both Chinese and Sanskrit mantras (figs. 149, 151, 152) in Roderick Whitfield, *The Art of Central Asia: The Stein Collection in the British Museum Vol. 2, Paintings from Dunhuang II* (London: Kodansha International and The Trustees of the British Museum, 1983). On the development of Buddhist amulets in relation to Daoism in early China see Michel Strickmann,

Chinese Magical Medicine (Stanford: Stanford University Press, 2002), 1–193; and Christine Mollier, *Buddhism and Taoism Face to Face: Scripture, Ritual, and Iconographic Exchange in Medieval China* (Honolulu: University of Hawai'i Press, 2008). On the use of amulets in the Buddhist tradition see Stanley J. Tambiah, *The Buddhist Saints of the Forest and the Cult of Amulets: A Study in Charisma, Hagiography, Sectarianism, and Millennial Buddhism* (Cambridge: Cambridge University Press, 1984).

153. The revival of exchange between the East and West in the twelfth century, especially on account of the Qara Khitai, is explored more in the next chapter; however, in the context of printing technology it is important to note that it was at this same time that the blockprinting of cloth appeared in India (Phyllis Granoff, "Luxury Goods and Intellectual History: The Case of Printed and Woven Multicolored Textiles in Medieval India," *Ars Orientalis* 34 [2004]: 151–171), and that this material was then sold to the Muslim world (Ruth Barnes, *Indian Block-Printed Textiles in Egypt: The Newberry Collection in the Ashmolean Musuem, Oxford* [Oxford: Clarendon Press, 1997]).

154. Nik Douglas, *Tibetan Tantric Charms and Amulets: 230 Examples Reproduced from Original Woodblocks* (New York: Dover Publications, 1978).

155. Francis Richard, *Splendeurs persanes: Manuscrits de XIIe au XVIIe siècle* (Paris: Bibliothèque nationale de France, 1997), 37.

156. Another aspect of this transmission that needs further study is the development of blockprinted Hajj certificates, which also seems to derive from Buddhist practices. See Dominique Sourdel and Janine Sourdel-Thomine, "Une collection médiévale de certificates de pèlerinage à la Mekke conservés à Istanbul," in *Études médiévales et patrimonie Turc: Volume publié à l'occasion du centième anniversaire de la naissance de Kemal Atatürk*, ed. Janine Sourdel-Thomine (Paris: Éditions du Centre National de la Recherche Scientifique, 1983), 167–273; and Şule Aksoy and Rachel Milstein, "A Collection of Thirteenth-Century Illustrated Hajj Certificates," in *M. Ugur Derman Festschrift: Papers Presented on the Occasion of his Sixty-fifth Birthday*, ed. Irvin Cemil Schick (Istanbul: Sabanci Universitesi, 2000), 101–134.

157. Charles Melville, "*Padshah-i Islam*: The Conversion of Sultan Mahmud Ghazan Khan," *Pembroke Papers* 1 (1990): 163.

158. J. de Somogyi, "A *Qasida* on the Destruction of Baghdad by the Mongols," *Bulletin of the School of Oriental and African Studies* 7 (1933–5): 41–48; J. A. Boyle, "The Death of the Last 'Abbasid Caliph of Baghdad: A Contemporary Muslim Account," *Journal of Semitic Studies* 6 (1961): 145–161; and G. M. Wickens, "Nasir ad-Din Tusi on the Fall of Baghdad: A Further Study," *Journal of Semitic Studies* 7 (1962): 23–35.

Chapter 3. Idolatry

Note to epigraph: *Buddha Abhiseka*, quoted in Donald K. Swearer, *Becoming the Buddha: The Ritual of Image Consecration in Thailand* (Princeton: Princeton University Press, 2004), 162–164.

1. C. E. Bosworth, "An Alleged Embassy from the Emperor of China to the Amir Nasr b. Ahmad: A Contribution to Samanid Military History," in *Yad-name-ye Irani-ye Minorsky*, ed. Mojtaba Minovi and Iraj Afshar (Tehran: Tehran University, 1969), 19.

2. Bosworth, "An Alleged Embassy," 20.

3. Bosworth, "An Alleged Embassy," 21.

4. Bosworth, "An Alleged Embassy," 21–22.

5. See, however, the curious case of the Ming dynasty emperor Zhengde (r. 1506–1521), who reportedly converted to Islam (Toh Hoong Teik, "Shaykh 'Alam: The Emperor of Early Sixteenth-Century China," *Sino-Platonic Papers* 110 [2000]: 1–20). Chinese Muslim historiography also claims that the founder of the Ming dynasty was Muslim (Zvi ben-dor Benite, "'The Marrano Emperor': The Mysterious Bond Between Zhu Yuanzhang and His Muslims," in *Long Live the Emperor! Uses of the Ming Founder Across Six Centuries of East Asian History*, ed. Sarah Schneewind [Minneapolis: Society for Ming Studies, 2008], 275–308).

6. C. E. Bosworth, *The Ghaznavids: Their Empire in Afghanistan and Eastern Iran 994–1040* (Edinburgh: Edinburgh University Press, 1963), 4–23.

7. As noted by David Sneath these migrations did not entail the movement of entire peoples and the displacement of local peoples; rather, it was largely the political elites of various groups who moved and then consolidated their power in new regions. See *The Headless State: Aristocratic Orders, Kinship Society, and Misrepresentations of Nomadic Inner Asia* (New York: Columbia University Press, 2007), 159–167.

8. Peter B. Golden, "The Migrations of the *Oguz*," *Archivum Ottomanicum* 4 (1972): 78–80.

9. On the Islamic response to this Turkic invasion see David Cook, *Studies in Muslim Apocalyptic* (Princeton: The Darwin Press, 2002), 84–91.

10. S. Vryonis, Jr., *The Decline of Medieval Hellenism in Asia Minor and the Process of Islamization from the Eleventh through the Fifteenth Century* (Berkeley: University of California Press, 1971), 70–120.

11. C. E. Bosworth, "The Political and Dynastic History of the Iranian World (A.D. 1000–1217)," in *The Cambridge History of Iran*, ed. J. A. Boyle (Cambridge: Cambridge University Press, 1968), 1–202.

12. Tha'alibi, *The Book of Curious and Entertaining Information*, trans. C. E. Bosworth (Edinburgh: Edinburgh University Press, 1968), 141.

13. Tha'alibi, *The Book*, 141.

14. Sunil Sharma, *Persian Poetry at the Indian Frontier: Mas'ūd Sa'd Salmān of Lahore* (New Delhi: Permanent Black, 2000), 12.

15. Melikian-Chirvani, "The Buddhist Ritual," 274.

16. Richard N. Frye, *The History of Bukhara* (Cambridge: Mediaeval Academy of America, 1954), 20.

17. Bo Gyllensvärd, "The Buddha Found at Helgö," in *Excavations at Helgö XVI:*

Exotic and Sacral Finds, ed. Helen Clarke and Kristina Lamm (Stockholm: Almqvist & Wiksell, 2004), 5–14.

18. S. Yoshinobu, "Sung Foreign Trade: Its Scope and Organization," in *China Among Equals: The Middle Kingdom and Its Neighbors, 10th–14th Centuries*, ed. Morris Rossabi (Berkeley: University of California Press, 1983), 104–106.

19. The classic treatment of this phenomenon is Joseph Fletcher, "Turco-Mongolian Monarchic Tradition in the Ottoman Empire," in *Eucharisterion: Essays Presented to Omeljan Pritsak*, ed. I. Sevcenko and F. E. Sysyn (Cambridge: Ukranian Research Institute, 1979–1980): 237–242.

20. On the legend of Prester John see the articles in C. F. Beckingham and B. Hamilton, *Prester John, the Mongols and the Ten Lost Tribes* (Aldershot: Variorum, 1996); as well as Peter Jackson, "Prester John Redivivus: A Review Article," *Journal of the Royal Asiatic Society* 3, 7 (1997): 424–432. For another Christian response to the coming of the Mongols see Robert E. Lerner, *The Powers of Prophecy: The Cedar of Lebanon Vision from the Mongol Onslaught to the Dawn of the Enlightenment* (Berkeley: University of California Press, 1983).

21. Christopher Tyerman, *God's War: A New History of the Crusades* (London: Allen Lane, 2006), 62–78.

22. Michal Biran, "True to Their Ways: Why the Qara Khitai Did Not Convert to Islam," in *Mongols, Turks and Others: Eurasian Nomads and the Sedentary World*, ed. Reuven Amitai and Michal Biran (Leiden: Brill, 2005), 175–200.

23. Biran, *Qara Khitai*, 211.

24. The same view of both India and China was also to develop later in Europe. See, for example, David Porter, *Ideographica: The Chinese Cipher in Early Modern Europe* (Stanford: Stanford University Press, 2001).

25. Biran, *Qara Khitai*, 100.

26. A. K. S. Lambton, "Justice in the Medieval Persian Theory of Kingship," *Studia Islamica* 17 (1962): 91–119.

27. Biran, *Qara Khitai*, 171.

28. Thomas T. Allsen, "Mongolian Princes and Their Merchant Partners 1200–1260," *Asia Major* 3, 2 (1989): 86–94.

29. Biran, *Qara Khitai*, 174.

30. On the early Guge kingdom see Roberto Vitali's *The Kingdoms of Gu.Ge Pu.Hrang: According to Mnga'.Ris Rgyal.Rabs by Gu.Ge Mkhan.Chen Ngag.Dbang Grags.Pa* (London: Serindia Publications, 1997); and *Records of Tho.Ling: A Literary and Visual Reconstruction of the "Mother" Monastery in Gu.ge* (Dharamsala: Amnye Machen Institute, 1999), 7–36.

31. André Wink, *Al-Hind: The Making of the Indo-Islamic World, Vol. 2: The Slave Kings and the Islamic Conquest: 11th–13th Centuries* (Leiden: Brill, 1997), 149.

32. Richard M. Eaton, "Temple Desecration and Indo-Muslim States," in *Beyond Turk and Hindu: Rethinking Religious Identities in Islamicate South Asia*, ed. David

Gilmartin and Bruce B. Lawrence (Gainesville: University of Florida Press, 2000), 246–281.

33. Wink, *Al Hind Vol. 2*, 147.

34. Dan Martin, "Tibet at the Center: A Historical Study of Some Tibetan Geographical Conceptions Based on Two Types of Country-Lists Found in Bon Histories," in *Tibetan Studies: Proceedings of the 6th Seminar of the International Association for Tibetan Studies, Fagernes 1992, Vol. 1*, ed. Per Kvaerne (Oslo: The Institute for Comparative Research in Human Culture, 1994), 532, fig. 9.

35. Toni Huber, *The Holy Land Reborn: Pilgrimage and the Tibetan Reinvention of Buddhist India* (Chicago: University of Chicago Press, 2008), chaps. 3 and 4. More recently, however, as Huber also shows in his study, this phenomenon has recently reversed itself. Namely, on account of numerous factors, including Buddhist modernism and their own exile, Tibetans now see India as the Holy Land.

36. Leonard van der Kuijp, *The Kālacakra and the Patronage of Buddhism by the Mongol Imperial Family* (Bloomington: Indiana University, Department of Central Eurasian Studies, 2004).

37. Although sources are lacking from the Yuan period, there are important works from the latter period. In the case of Southeast Asia, for example, we have the work of Muhammad Rabi, who in the 1680s was sent by Shah Sulaiman of Iran to the court of King Narai in Thailand. John O'Kane has published a partial translation of this work (*The Ship of Sulaiman* [New York: Columbia University Press, 1972]), and Alam and Subrahmanyam have recently published an excellent study on Rabi (*Indo-Persian Travels in the Age of Discoveries, 1400–1800*, 159–174). Similarly, during the Qing period, Chinese Muslim thinkers also grappled with the Dharma. The most famous example was Liu Zhi, who compared the Daoist concept of *wuwei* (non-action), the Buddhist concept of emptiness, and the Chinese Islamic concept of *Zhenyi*, the True and One (see James D. Frankel, "Liu Zhi's Journey Through Ritual Law to Allah's Chinese Name: Conceptual Antecedents and Theological Obstacles to the Confucian-Islamic Harmonization of the *Tianfang Dianli*," Ph.D. diss., Columbia University, 2005).

38. Juvaini, *History of the World Conqueror*, 64–65.

39. Another strategy used to legitimate the Mongols was to parallel them with the great pre-Muslim Iranian kings as found in Firdausi's *Shah name*. Abolala Soudavar, for example, has argued that the incidents selected for illustration in the Great Mongol *Shahnama* were chosen for the parallels between them and events in Mongol history ("The Saga of Abu-Sa'id Bahador Khan. The Abu-Sa'idnamé," in *The Court of the Il-khans 1290–1340*, ed. Julian Raby and Teresa Fitzherbert [Oxford: Oxford University Press, 1996], 95–211). On this topic see also the four articles of A. S. Melikian-Chirvani, "Le *Shah-name*, la gnose soufie et le pouvoir mongol," *Journal asiatique* 222 (1984): 249–338; "Le Livre des rois, miroir du destin, I," *Studia Iranica* 17, 1 (1988): 7–46; "Le Livre des rois, miroir du destin, II: Takht-e Soleyman et la symbolique du *Shah-mame*," *Studia Iranica* 20, 1 (1991): 33–148; "Conscience du passé et résistance

culturelle dans l'Iran mongol," in *L'Iran face à la domination mongole*, ed. Denise Aigle (Tehran: Institut Français de Recherche en Iran, 1997), 135–177; as well as Sheila S. Blair, "A Mongol Envoy," in *The Iconography of Islamic Art: Studies in Honour of Robert Hillenbrand*, ed. Bernard O'Kane (Edinburgh: Edinburgh University Press, 2005), 45–46.

40. Biran, *Qara Khitai*, 198.

41. H. G. Raverty, *Tabakat-i-Nasiri: A General History of the Muhammadan Dynasties of Asia, including Hindustan, from A.H. 194 [810 A.D.], to A.H. 658 [1260 A.D.], and the Irruption of the Infidel Mughals into Islam* (London: Gilbert & Rivington, 1881), 1157–1159.

42. Igor de Rachewiltz, "Turks in China Under the Mongols: A Preliminary Investigation of Turco-Mongol Relations in the 13th and 14th Centuries," in *China Among Equals: The Middle Kingdom and Its Neighbors, 10th–14th Centuries*, ed. Morris Rossabi (Berkeley: University of California Press, 1983), 287. On the historiography of Güyüg see Kim Hodong, "A Reappraisal of Güyüg Khan," in *Mongols, Turks and Others: Eurasian Nomads and the Sedentary World*, ed. Reuven Amitai and Michal Biran (Leiden: Brill, 2005), 309–338.

43. Peter Zieme, *Religion und Gesellschaft im Uigurischen Königreich von Qoco* (Opladen: Westdeutscher Verlag, 1992).

44. For an overview of this literature see Johan Elverskog, *Uygur Buddhist Literature* (Turnhout: Brepols, 1997).

45. E. I. Kychanov, "Tibetans and Tibetan Culture in the Tangut State Hsi Hsia (982–1227)," in *Proceedings of the Csoma de Körös Memorial Symposium*, ed. Louis Ligeti (Budapest: Akadémiai Kiadó, 1978), 205–211; Elliot Sperling, "Lama to the King of Hsia," *The Journal of the Tibet Society* 7 (1987): 31–50; Ruth Dunnell, "The Hsia Origins of the Yüan Institution of Imperial Preceptor," *Asia Major* 5 (1992): 85–111; Elliot Sperling, "Rtsa-mi Lo-tsa-ba Sangs-rgyas grags-pa and the Tangut Background to Early Mongol-Tibetan Relations," in *Tibetan Studies. Proceedings of the 6th Seminar of the International Association of Tibetan Studies, Fagernes 1992*, ed. Per Kvaerne (Oslo: Institute for Comparative Research in Human Culture 1994), 801–824; Xie Jisheng, "A Unique Tangut Thangka in the Wuwei City Museum: Study of a *thangka* Discovered in the Tara Cave Temple," in *Studies in Sino-Tibetan Buddhist Art: Proceedings of the Second International Conference on Tibetan Archaeology and Art, Beijing, September 3–6, 2004*, ed. Xie Jisheng, Shen Weirong, and Liao Yang (Beijing: China Tibetology Publishing House, 2006), 427–458.

46. On the building of Buddhist monuments during the reign of Ögedei see, F. W. Cleaves, "The Sino-Mongolian Inscription of 1346," *Harvard Journal of Asiatic Studies* 15 (1952): 1–123.

47. On Mongol religious policy during the empire period see Christopher P. Atwood, "Validation by Holiness or Sovereignty: Religious Toleration as Political Theology in the Mongol World Empire of the Thirteenth Century," *The International History Review* 23, 2 (2004): 237–256; and Peter Jackson, "The Mongols and the Faith

of the Conquered," in *Mongols, Turks and Others: Eurasian Nomads and the Sedentary World*, ed. Reuven Amitai and Michal Biran (Leiden: Brill, 2005), 245–290.

48. Joseph Thiel, "Der Streit der Buddhisten und Taoisten zur Mongolenzeit," *Monumenta Serica* (1961): 1–81.

49. Juvaini, *History of the World Conqueror*, 52.

50. Biran, *Qara Khitai*, 177 n. 53.

51. Juvaini, *History of the World Conqueror*, 60, 70–74.

52. Guillaume de Rubrouck, *The Mission of Friar William: His Journey to the Court of the Great Khan Möngke 1253–1255*, trans. Peter Jackson (London: Hakluyt Society, 1990), 151.

53. *Nom* derives from the Greek νομυσ and was transmitted by the Sogdians into Inner Asia where it became the standard translation for both "Dharma" and "book."

54. Juvaini, *History of the World Conqueror*, 60.

55. Thomas T. Allsen, "Mahmud Yalavac (?–1254), Mas'ud Beg (?–1289), 'Ali Beg (?–1280); Bujir (fl. 1206–1260)," in *In the Service of the Khan: Eminent Personalities of the Early Mongol-Yüan Period*, ed. Igor de Rachewiltz et al. (Wiesbaden: Harrassowitz Verlag, 1993), 122–135.

56. Morris Rossabi, "The Muslims in the Early Yüan Dynasty," in *China Under Mongol Rule*, ed. John D. Langlois, Jr. (Princeton: Princeton University Press, 1981), 265.

57. Juvaini, *History of the World Conqueror*, 207.

58. Juvaini, *History of the World Conqueror*, 223. See also Herbert Franke, "Eine Mittelalterliche chinesische Satire auf die Mohammedaner," in *Der Orient in der Forschung: Festschrift für Otto Spies zum 5 April 1966*, ed. Wilhelm Hoenerbach (Wiesbaden: Otto Harrassowitz, 1967), 202–208.

59. Juvaini, *History of the World Conqueror*, 225. The same story is also in Juzjani; see 1110–1111.

60. Maurizio Peleggi, "Shifting Alterity: The Mongol in the Visual and Literary Culture of the Late Middle Ages," *The Medieval History Journal* 4, 1 (2001): 21–22; Richard C. Foltz, "Ecumenical Mischief Under the Mongols," *Central Asiatic Journal* 43 (1999): 42–69.

61. Peter Jackson, "The Dissolution of the Mongol Empire," *Central Asiatic Journal* 32 (1978): 235. On the Buddhist impact on the later Yuan see Herbert Franke, "Tibetans in Yüan China," in *China Under Mongol Rule*, ed. John D. Langlois, Jr. (Princeton: Princeton University Press, 1981), 326–328; and Shoju Inaba, "An Introductory Study on the Degeneration of Lamas: A Geneaological and Chronological Note on the Imperial Preceptors in the Yüan Dynasty," in *A Study of Kleśa: A Study of Impurity and the Purification in the Oriental Religions*, ed. G. H. Sasaki (Tokyo: Shimizukobundo, 1975), 19–57.

62. Allsen, *Commodity and Exchange*, 50. Although it was Möngke who greatly advanced Mongol power in Islamic lands Muslim sources surprisingly do not hold him in contempt. The introduction of the *qubchir* tax, however, was roundly despised

by the Muslims because it seemed to function very much like the Islamic *jizya* poll tax (Thomas T. Allsen, *Mongol Imperialism: The Policies of the Grand Qan Möngke in China, Russia and the Islamic Lands, 1251–1259* [Berkeley: University of California Press, 1987]: 167–168).

63. On the relationship between Khubilai Khan and Pakpa Lama see Dieter Schuh, *Erlasse und Sendschreiben mongolischer Herrscher für tibetische Geistliche* (Skt. Augustin: VGH Wissenschaftsverlag, 1977); Janos Szerb, "Glosses on the Oeuvre of Bla-ma 'Phags pa: II. Some Notes on the Events of the Years 1251–1254," *Acta Orientalia Hungarica* 34 (1980): 263–285; Constance Hoog, *Prince Jin-gim's Textbook of Tibetan Buddhism* (Leiden: Brill, 1983); and Herbert Franke, *Chinesischer und Tibetischer Buddhismus im China der Yüanzeit* (Munich: Kommission für Zentralasiatische Studien/Bayerische Akademie der Wissenschaften, 1996).

64. On the transmission of Muslim science and culture into Yuan China see, for example, Kodo Tasaka, "An Aspect of Islam Culture Introduced into China," *Memoirs of the Research Department of the Toyo Bunko* 16 (1957): 35–74; and Paul D. Buell and Eugene N. Anderson, *A Soup for the "Qan": Chinese Dietary Medicine of the Mongol Era as Seen in Hu Szu-Hui's "Yin-Shan Cheng-Yao"* (London: Kegan Paul International, 2000).

65. For an overview of the role Muslim scholars played in Yuan astronomy see Brian Baumann, *Divine Knowledge: Buddhist Mathematics According to the Anonymous Manual of Mongolian Astrology and Divination* (Leiden: Brill, 2008), 299–307.

66. On Nasir al-Din's career in the Il-khanid court see George Lane, *Early Mongol Rule in Thirteenth-Century Iran: A Persian Renaissance* (London: Routledge, 2003), chap. 7; and F. J. Ragep, *Nasr al-Din Tusi's Memoir of Astronomy (al-Tadhkira fi 'ilm al-hay'a)* (New York: Springer-Verlag, 1993), 13–15.

67. Quoted in S. M. Grupper, "The Buddhist Sanctuary-Vihara of Labnasagut and the Il-Qan Hülegü: An Overview of Il-Qanid Buddhism and Related Matters," *Archivum Eurasiae Medii Aevi* 13 (2004): 31–32. Hülegü's devotion to Buddhism is also found in another Christian Armenian source from 1267: "For he was deceived by the astrologers and priests of some images called Sakmonia, who has been, they say, God for 3,040 years. He will still have another 37 tomans, a toman being 10,000. Then, they say, another Mondri [Maitreya] will carry him away. They called Toyin these priests in whom he believed and at whose command he went out to war, or did not go out. They said, 'You will long remain in your body, and when you attain a great old age, you will be put on another new body.' They had him build a temple for those images. He used to go there to pray, and they worked whatever witchcraft they decried on him." (Robert W. Thomson, "The Historical Compilation of Vardan Arewelc'i," *Dumbarton Oaks Papers* 43 [1989]: 221).

68. Tegüder converted as a youth to Islam and when he took the throne he ruled as Sultan Ahmad (r. 1282–84); however, his reign was a disaster and his conversion had no impact on the Mongol elite, who drove him out of power. See Reuven Amitai, "The Conversion of Tegüder Ilkhan to Islam," *Jerusalem Studies in Arabic and Islam*

25 (2001): 15–43; and Judith Pfeiffer, "Conversion to Islam Among the Ilkhans in Muslim Narrative Traditions: The Case of Ahmad Tegüder," Ph.D. diss., University of Chicago, 2003.

69. Jamal J. Elias, *The Throne Carrier of God: The Life and Thought of 'Ala' ad-dawla as-Simnani* (Albany: State University of New York Press, 1995), 18, 26.

70. Rashiduddin Fazlullah, *Jami'u't-tawarikh: Compendium of Chronicles, A History of the Mongols, Part Three*, trans. W. M. Thackston (Cambridge: Harvard University, Department of Near Eastern Languages and Civilizations, 1999), 664.

71. Melville, "Padishah," 171–172. On the conversion of Il-khans and the misguided link often made between Sufism and Mongol shamanism see Reuven Amitai, "Sufis and Shamans: Some Remarks on the Islamization of the Mongols in the Ilkhanate," *Journal of the Economic and Social History of the Orient* 42, 1 (1999): 27–46.

72. On the anti-Buddhist and anti-Christian activities of Ghazan's influential advisor Nauraz see Jean Aubin, *Emirs mongols et vizirs persans dans les remous de l'acculturation* (Leuven: Peeters, 1995), 61–68.

73. DeWeese, *Islamization*, 95–100.

74. A. P. Martinez, "The Third Portion of the Story of Gazan Xan in Rasidu'd-Din's *Ta'rix-e Mobarak-e Gazani*," *Archivum Eurasiae Medii Aevi* 6 (1986[1988]): 56–72.

75. The classic example of this phenomenon occurred in mid-ninth-century Tang dynasty China; see Kenneth Ch'en, "The Economic Background of the Hui-ch'ang Suppression of Buddhism," *Harvard Journal of Asiatic Studies* 19, 1–2 (1956): 67–105. See also Bosworth's comments about the Ghaznavids as not only the "hammers of the pagan Hindus," but also the "bringers into circulation within the eastern Islamic economy of the temple treasures of India" (*The Later Ghaznavids: Splendour and Decay, The Dynasty in Afghanistan and Northern India 1040–1186* [New York: Columbia University Press, 1977], 32).

76. Karl Jahn, *Rashid al-Din's History of India* (The Hague: Mouton, 1965), xxxiii.

77. The impact of Hülegü's 1258 destruction of Baghdad on the Muslim *imaginaire* cannot be underestimated. As one scholar has noted the entire crusader movement is but a footnote in comparison to Hülegü's conquest. Moreover, this episode has been most powerfully resuscitated within the contemporary jihadi movement since "the Mongol metaphor . . . is central to the revolutionary theory as developed by the Sayyid Qutb school" (E. Sivin, *Radical Islam: Medieval Theology and Modern Politics* [New Haven: Yale University Press, 1985], 57). See also Johannes Jansen, "Ibn Taymiyyah and the Thirteenth Century: A Formative Period of Modern Muslim Radicalism," *Quadreni di Studi Arabi* 5–6 (1987–1988): 391–396.

78. Juvaini was not simply a collaborator. He had divided loyalties between the Mongols and his conquered compatriots. See Teresa Fitzherbert, "Portrait of a Lost Leader: Jalal al-Din Khawarazmshah and Juvaini," in *The Court of the Il-khans 1290–1340*, ed. Julian Raby and Teresa Fitzherbert (Oxford: Oxford University Press, 1996),

69–75. On the role of the Juvaini family in Il-khanid Iran see Lane, *Early Mongol Rule in Thirteenth-Century Iran*, chap. 6.

79. Juvaini, *History of the World Conqueror*, 15–16.

80. Farhad Dafarty, *The Assassin Legends: Myths of the Isma'ilis* (London: I. B. Tauris, 1994), 36–44. On Hülegü's destruction of the Nizari State see Farhad Daftary, *The Isma'ilis: Their History and Doctrines* (Cambridge: Cambridge University Press, 1990), 421–430.

81. A. K. Lambton, "Changing Concepts of Justice and Injustice from the 5th/11th Century to the 8th/14th Century in Persia: The Saljuq Empire and the Ilkhanate," *Studia Islamica* 68 (1988): 50.

82. Lambton, "Changing Concepts of Justice and Injustice," 60.

83. Judith Pfeiffer, "Conversion Versions: Sultan Öljeytü's Conversion to Shi'ism (709/1309) in Muslim Narrative Sources," *Mongolian Studies* 22 (1999): 35–67.

84. For the historical context of Ibn Taymiyya's fatwas and his critique of the Mongols see Thomas Raff, *Remarks on an Anti-Mongol Fatwa by Ibn Taimiya* (Leiden: Self-published, 1973), 38–59; and Denise Aigle, "The Mongol Invasions of Bilād al-Shām by Ghāzān Khān and Ibn Taymīyah's Three 'Anti-Mongol' Fatwas," *Mamluk Studies Review* 11, 2 (2007): 89–120.

85. Reuven Amitai, "Ghazan, Islam and Mongol Tradition: A View from the Mamluk Sultanate," *Bulletin of the School of Oriental and African Studies* 59 (1996): 9.

86. D. Aigle, "Le grand *jasaq* de Genghis-khan, l'empire, la culture mongole et la shari'a," *Journal of the Economic and Social History of the Orient* 47, 1 (2004): 31–79; D. Aigle, "Loi mongole *vs* loi islamique: Entre mythe et réalité," *Annales: Histoire, Sciences sociales* 59, 5–6 (2004): 971–996.

87. David Cook, *Understanding Jihad* (Berkeley: University of California Press, 2005), 64–65.

88. For an overview of the unflattering contemporary views on Ibn Taymiyya see Donald P. Little, "Did Ibn Taymiyya Have a Screw Loose?" *Studia Islamica* 41 (1975): 93–111.

89. Muhammad U. Menon, *Ibn Taimīya's Struggle Against Popular Religion* (The Hague: Mouton, 1976); Jean R. Michot, *Musique et danse selon Ibn Taymiyya: Le Livre du Sama^c et de la Danse* (Kitab al'Sama ^c wa'l-Raqs) *compilé par le shaykh Muḥammad al-Manbijī* (Paris: J. Vrin, 1991); Niels Henrik Olesen, *Culte des saints et pélerinage chez Ibn Taymiyya* (Paris: P. Geuthner, 1991).

90. Perween Hassan, "The Footprint of the Prophet," *Muqarnas* 10 (1993): 341.

91. For an overview on the relationship between the local Persian rulers and the Mongols see Lane, *Early Mongol Rule in Thirteenth-Century Iran*, chap. 5.

92. A. P. Martinez, "Change in Chancellery Languages and Language Changes in General in the Middle East, with Particular Reference to Iran in the Arab and Mongol Periods," *Archivum Eurasiae Medii Aevi* 7 (1987–1991): 107–108.

93. Aubin, *Emirs mongols et vizirs persans*, 31–38.

94. Karl Jahn, "Paper Currency in Iran," *Journal of Asian History* 4 (1970): 120–

135; Judith Kolbas, *The Mongols in Iran: Chingiz Khan to Uljaytu 1220–1309* (New York: Routledge, 2006), 290.

95. Birgitt Hoffman, "The Gates of Piety and Charity: Rasid al-Din Fadl Allah as Founder of Pious Endowments," in *L'Iran face à la domination mongole*, ed. Denise Aigle (Tehran: Institut Français de Recherche en Iran, 1997), 189–202.

96. For the most detailed account of Rashid al-Din's life see Birgitt Hoffman, *Waqf im mongolischen Iran: Rashiduddins Sorge um Nachrum und Seelenheil* (Stuttgart: Franz Steiner Verlag, 2000), 53–91.

97. On some of the historiographical issues related to the *Jami' al-tawarikh* see David O. Morgan, "Rašid al-Din and Gazan Khan," in *L'Iran face à la domination mongole*, ed. Denise Aigle (Tehran: Institut Français de Recherche en Iran, 1997), 179–188.

98. Abolala Soudavar, "The Han-Lin Academy and the Persian Royal Library-Atelier," in *History and Historiography of Post-Mongol Central Asia and the Middle East: Studies in Honor of John E. Woods*, ed. Judith Pfeiffer and Sholeh A. Quinn (Wiesbaden: Harrassowitz Verlag, 2006), 467–483.

99. Robert Hillenbrand, "The Arts of the Book in Ilkhanid Iran," in *The Legacy of Genghis Khan: Courtly Art and Culture in Western Asia, 1256–1353*, ed. Linda Komaroff and Stefano Carboni (New Haven: Yale University Press, 2002), 150.

100. On the *History of India* see the collected articles on the text by Karl Jahn as well as his complete German translation: *Rashid al-Din's History of India* and *Die Indiengeschichte des Rašid ad-Din* (Vienna: Verlag der Österreichischen Akademie der Wissenschaften, 1980).

101. Allsen, *Culture and Conquest*, 92.

102. Luciano Petech, *Central Tibet and the Mongols: The Yüan-Sa-skya Period of Tibetan History* (Rome: Istituto italiano per il Medio ed Estremo Oriente, 1990).

103. Vitali, *The Kingdoms of Gu.Ge Pu.Hrang*, 418–419.

104. Elliot Sperling, "Hülegü and Tibet," *Acta Orientalia Academicae Scientiarum Hungaricae* 44 (1990): 153.

105. Jahn, *History of India*, xxxvii.

106. Jahn, *Indiengeschichte*, 93.

107. Jahn, *Indiengeschichte*, 100. As noted above the Buddhists from the Tangut could well have been Tibetans, but they could also have been Kashmiri like Kamalaśrī himself. See Leonard van der Kuijp, "Jayānanda: A Twelfth Century *Guoshi* from Kashmir Among the Tangut," *Central Asiatic Journal* 37, 3–4 (1993): 188–197.

108. Geng Shimin and Zhang Baoxi, "Yuan huihuwen 'Zhong xiu wen shu si bei,' chu shi," *Kaogu xuebao* 2 (1986): 253–264. On the importance of Maitreya in Uygur Buddhism see Klaus Röhrborn and András Róna-Tas, *Spätformen des zentralasiatischen Buddhismus. Die altuigurische Sitātapatrā-dhāraṇī* (Göttingen: Nachrichten der Akademie der Wissenschaften zu Göttingen, 2005), 240–241.

109. Masahiro Shogaito, "On Uighur Elements in Buddhist Mongolian Texts," *Memoirs of the Research Department of the Toyo Bunko* 49 (1991): 27–49; and Michael

C. Brose, "Uyghur Technologists of Writing and Literacy in Mongol China," *T'oung Pao* 91 (2005): 396–435.

110. Herbert Franke, "A Note on the Multilinguality in China Under the Mongols: The Compilers of the Revised Buddhist Canon, 1285–87," in *Opuscala Altaica: Essays Presented in Honor of Henry Schwarz*, ed. Edward H. Kaplan and Donald W. Whisenhunt (Bellingham: Western Washington University, 1994), 286–298.

111. Gregory Schopen, "Hīnayāna Texts in a 14th Century Persian Chronicle," *Central Asiatic Journal* 26 (1982): 228–235.

112. See, for example, his presentation of the thirty-two marks of a great man and the list of ten sins (Jahn, *Indiengeschichte*, 73, 77).

113. Jahn, *History of India*, xlviii.

114. Sheila R. Canby, "Depictions of Buddha Śakyamuni in the *Jami' al-Tavarikh* and the *Majma' al-Tavarikh*," *Muqarnas* 10 (1993): 299–310.

115. See, for example, the story of Nanda from the *Saṁgāmāvacara Jātaka* in chapter 9 (Jahn, *Indiengeschichte*, 82–83).

116. Stephen F. Teiser, *Reinventing the Wheel: Paintings of Rebirth in Medieval Buddhist Temples* (Seattle: University of Washington Press, 2007), 50–75.

117. On the importance of healthy and beautiful bodies in opposition to those with deformities in Buddhist discourse and karma theory see John Powers, *A Bull of a Man: Images of Masculinity, Sex and the Body in Indian Buddhism* (Cambridge: Harvard University Press, 2009).

118. Max Scherberger, *Das Mi'ragname: Die Himmel-und Höllenfahrt des Propheten Muhammad in der osttürkischen Überlieferung* (Würzburg: Ergon Verlag, 2003), 123–128, 131–132.

119. For a detailed study of this manuscript and its possible Buddhist influences see Christiane J. Gruber, *The Timurid "Book of Ascension" (Miʿrajnama): A Study of Text and Image in a Pan-Asian Context* (Rome: Ediciones Patrimonio, 2008): 313–326.

120. On the importance of heaven and hell in the Buddhist tradition see Bryan J. Cuevas and Jacqueline I. Stone, *The Buddhist Dead: Practices, Discourses, Representations* (Honolulu: University of Hawai'i Press, 2007); and Bryan J. Cuevas, *Travels in the Netherworld: Buddhist Popular Narratives of Death and the Afterlife in Tibet* (Oxford: Oxford University Press, 2008).

121. In addition to describing this translation style, Schopen has also identified two other Sanskrit Nikaya texts used by Rashid al-Din: the description of heaven in chapter 8 is from the *Vasishta Sūtra*, and the question and answers of chapter 16 are from the *Devata Sūtra* ("Hīnayana Texts," 226–227).

122. The interpretation of Buddhist concepts with Islamic terminology (e.g. *wuṣūl, ittiḥād, tanasukh, khalwatīyān*) is also found in the work of Simnani. I thank Devin DeWeese for sharing with me his unpublished work on Simnani, wherein he makes this point.

123. Jahn, *Indiengeschichte*, 78.

124. Jahn, *Indiengeschichte*, 94.

125. Rashid al-Din's argument that the Buddha was a prophet with a book was probably not widely accepted among other Muslims. Simnani, for example, who is the other Muslim scholar of the Il-khanid age who engaged extensively with Buddhists argued precisely that the reason Buddhist mystics fail is because "they pursue a path according to their own personal opinions and not the guidance of a prophet" (Elias, *The Throne Carrier of God*, 110).

126. Jahn, *History of India*, xcviii.

127. Jahn, *History of India*, lxxiv.

128. Rashid al-Din's presentation also differs in this regard from that of Simnani, who either condemns Buddhists for not truly understanding their own teachings, or else praises the one Buddhist, Bakshi Parinda, whose view of "icons" was actually in accord with Islamic understandings (Elias, *The Throne Carrier of God*, 18, 26).

129. On the development of the Pure Land tradition in China see Julian F. Pas, *Visions of Sukhavati: Shan-Tao's Commentary on the Kuan Wu-Liang-Shou-Fo Ching* (Albany: State University of New York University, 1995).

130. T 365, *Skt. *Amitayur-dhyana Sutra*. On this work see Pas, *Visions of Sukhavati*.

131. Jahn, *History of India*, lxxi. See also the story of Uddalaka's ascent to the Buddha Amitabha's paradise (*History of India*, xcv).

132. The worship of Guanyin is also espoused in Chapter 10: "It is said that there is a being, an angel, Lokeshara, in Chinese named: Kuanshi[yin], whose task is to liberate souls from the imperfect animal form and to raise them to the human stage. Lokesvara redeems the perfect souls unceasingly from the imperfect bodies" (Jahn, *History of India*, lxiv).

133. Chün-fang Yü, *Kuan-yin: The Chinese Transformation of Avalokitesvara* (New York: Columbia University Press, 2001), 324. Compare also the similarities in the following description of the *Kāraṇḍavyūha Sūtra* and the quotation from the *Compendium*: "The eleven-headed and thousand-armed Kuanyin enters Avici Hell and transforms it into a realm of coolness and clarity. The sutra does not dwell on the gruesome details of hells except to describe the Avici hell as being encircled by rings of iron walls that are constantly heated by a blazing fire. There is also a hell, which consists of an enormous cauldron in which sinners constantly bob up and down in the scalding water in the manner of boiled beans. But when Kuan-yin enters, the fire is immediately extinguished and the cauldron is smashed to pieces. Moreover, the fire pit is changed into a precious pond filled with large lotus flowers as big as cartwheels. All hell becomes paradise, dazzlingly bright light shines forth. Kuan-yin enters the great citadel of the Hungry ghosts and saves them as well . . . they achieve rebirth in the Pure Land of Bliss" (Yü, *Kuan-yin*, 324–325).

134. Jahn, *History of India*, lxxii.

135. Jahn, *History of India*, lxxiii.

136. Johan Elverskog, "The Mongolian *Big Dipper Sūtra*," *Journal of the International Association of Buddhist Studies* (2007): 87–124.

137. One measure of this interaction was that in the thirteenth century the New Year in Iran was not celebrated at the vernal equinox according to the Islamic calendar, but was celebrated six weeks before the spring equinox in keeping with the Chinese calendar. See Charles Melville, "The Chinese Uighur Animal Calendar in Persian Historiography of the Mongol Period," *Iran* 32 (1994): 83–98.

138. These informants helped Rashid al-Din write his history of China; see Herbert Franke, "Some Sinological Remarks on Rašid al-Din's History of China," *Oriens* 4 (1951), 21–26.

139. Karl Jahn, "Rashid al-Din and Chinese Culture," *Central Asiatic Journal* 14 (1970): 134–147.

140. Elverskog, *Uygur Buddhist Literature*, # 25, 26, 34, 54. See also Peter Zieme, *Magische Texte des uigurischen Buddhismus* (Turnhout: Brepols, 2005), 115–150, 179–185. On the complicated nature of Buddhist transmission in Inner Asia see also the Old Tibetan translation of the Chinese Guanyin text, *Qianshou qianyan Guanshiyin pusa guangda yuannan wuai Dabeixin tuoluoni jing* (T 1060), in György Kara, "An Old Tibetan Fragment on Healing from the Sūtra of the Thousand-Eyed and Thousand-Handed Great Compasionate Bodhisattva Avalokiteśvara in the Berlin Turfan Collection," in *Turfan Revisited: The First Century of Research into the Arts and Cultures of the Silk Road*, ed. Desmond Durkin-Meistererernst et al. (Berlin: Dietrich Reimer Verlag, 2004), 141–146.

141. Jampa L. Panglung, "Die tibetische Version des Siebengestirn-Sūtra," in *Tibetan History and Language: Studies Dedicated to Uray Géza on His 70th Birthday*, ed. E. Steinkellner (Vienna: Arbeitskreis für Tibetische und Buddhistische Studien, 1991), 399–416.

142. This story is found in a range of Buddhist literature, including the *Apādana*, *Mahāvastu*, *Divyāvadanā*, *Ekottarikāgama* (T 125), *Da Zhidu lun* (T 1508), *Fenbie gongde lun* (T 1507), and the *Mahākaruṇapuṇḍarīka* (T 380). See Jonathan A. Silk, *Riven by Lust: Incest and Schism in Indian Buddhist Legend and Historiography* (Honolulu: University of Hawai'i Press, 2009), 115–122.

143. Jan Nattier, "Namowa buddhay-a: A Note on the Sources of the Mongolian Kanjur," unpublished paper presented at the Annual Meeting of the American Oriental Society, New Haven, Conn., 1986.

144. Another small linguistic piece of evidence in this regard is the use of the Uygur-Mongolian *saril* (Skt. *carira*) for relics in the description of Adam's Peak (Jahn, *Indiengeschichte*, 75). A similar linguistic analysis confirming the presence of Uygurs in Iran can be found in Grupper's study of the term Labnasgut ("The Buddhist Sanctuary," 35–36); and Simnani's use of the Uygur terms *nom* for Dharma and *burkhan* for Buddha (I thank Devin DeWeese for this information).

145. On this problem see Johan Elverskog, *Buddhism, History and Power: The Jewel Translucent Sutra and the Formation of Mongol Identity* (Ph.D. diss., Indiana

University, 2000), 1–10; Teiser, *Reinventing the Wheel*, 42–49; and Natalie Köhle, "Why did the Kangxi Emperor Go to Wutai Shan? Patronage, Pilgrimage, and the Place of Tibetan Buddhism at the Early Qing Court," *Late Imperial China* 29, 1 (2008): 102–105.

146. Jahn, *History of India*, lx–lxi. See also the Buddha's explanation on the monks' relation to donated food, which not only elevates tantric practitioners above the other two Buddhist traditions, but also promotes vegetarianism. "To the sect of the Sravakas and Pratyekabuddhas, he said that they must earn their food by begging; and if then food of animal nature was thrown into their beggar's bowl, they should not enquire as to its origin but should eat all, whatever it might be, to pacify the stomach. And to the sect of the Samyaksambuddhas he said, 'Since ye have attained the power of discrimination between good and evil, ye must yourselves know what to do, what may be eaten, and that animals may not be tortured. But if ye are hungry and are given a dead animal or one that has been put to death, eat it then, but in no case may ye grant permission for animals to be killed'" (Jahn, *History of India*, lxi).

147. On the mistaken linkage between Buddhism and vegetarianism in the West see Tristram Stuart, *The Bloodless Revolution: A Cultural History of Vegetarianism from 1600 to Modern Times* (London: W. W. Norton, 2006), 46, 124, 127, 523 n. 3.

148. John Kieschnick, "Buddhist Vegetarianism in China," in *Of Tripod and Palate: Food, Politics, and Religion in Traditional China*, ed. Roel Sterckx (New York: Palgrave Macmillan, 2005), 186–194. On the importance of vegetarianism as a marker of Chinese Buddhist identity see Francesca Tarocco, *The Cultural Practices of Modern Chinese Buddhism: Attuning the Dharma* (New York: Routledge, 2007), 31–39.

149. Jahn, *Indiengeschichte*, 101.

150. Kurtis R. Schaeffer and Leonard W. J. van der Kuijp, *An Early Tibetan Survey of Buddhist Literature: The* Bstan pa rgyas pa rgyan gyi nyi 'od *of Bcom ldan ral gri* (Cambridge: The Harvard Oriental Series, 2009): 9–41.

151. See, for example, Sheila S. Blair and Jonathan M. Bloom, *The Art and Architecture of Islam, 1250–1800* (New Haven: Yale University Press, 1994), 24–36.

152. This classification is based upon Oleg Grabar, *Mostly Miniatures: An Introduction to Persian Painting* (Princeton: Princeton University Press, 2000), 43–45.

153. On these works see Priscilla Soucek, "An Illustrated Manuscript of al-Biruni's *Chronology of Ancient Nations*," in *The Scholar and the Saint: Studies in Commemoration of Abu'l-Rayhan al-Biruni and Jalal al-Din al-Rumi*, ed. Peter J. Chelkowski (New York: New York University Press, 1975), 103–168.

154. Güner Inal, "Some Miniatures of the *Jami'al-Tavarikh* in Istanbul, Topkapi Museum, Hazine Library No. 1654," *Ars Islamica* 5 (1963): 163–176; David Talbott, *The Illustrations to the "World History" of Rashid al-Din* (Edinburgh: Edinburgh University Press, 1976); Basil Gray, *The World History of Rashid al-Din: A Study of the Royal Asiatic Society Manuscript* (London: Faber & Faber, 1978); Sheila S. Blair, *A Compendium of Chronicles: Rashid ad-Din's Illustrated History of the World* (London: The Nour Foundation, 1995).

155. Marianna Shreve Simpson, *The Illustrations of an Epic: The Earliest Shahname Manuscripts* (New York, 1979).

156. Richard Ettinghausen, "Persian Ascension Miniatures," *Academia Nazionale dei Lincei, Rendiconti* 12 (1957): 360–383; Oleg Grabar and Sheila S. Blair, *Epic Images and Contemporary History: The Illustrations of the Great Mongol Shahname* (Chicago: University of Chicago Press, 1980).

157. Linda Komaroff and Stefano Carboni, *The Legacy of Genghis Khan: Courtly Art and Culture in Western Asia, 1256–1353* (New Haven: Yale University Press, 2002).

158. Johann Christoph Bürgel, *The Feather of the Simurgh: The "Licit Magic" of the Arts in Medieval Islam* (New York: New York University Press, 1988), 14.

159. Daan van Reenen, "The *Bilderverbot*, a New Survey," *Der Islam* 67, 1 (1990): 27–77.

160. Oleg Grabar, *The Illustrations of the Maqamat* (Chicago: University of Chicago Press, 1984), 150.

161. Marshall Hodgson, *The Venture of Islam: Conscience and History in a World Civilization*, 3 vols. (Chicago: University of Chicago Press, 1974), 255.

162. Grabar, *Maqamat*, 147.

163. On the architectural changes ushered in during this period see, for example, Yasser Tabbaa, *The Transformation of Islamic Art During the Sunni Revival* (London: I. B. Tauris, 2002).

164. Oleg Grabar, "The Illustrated *Maqamat* of the Thirteenth Century: the Bourgeoisie and the Arts," in *Islamic Visual Culture, 1100–1800* (Burlington: Ashgate Variorum, 2006), 167–186.

165. Basil Gray, "Fourteenth-century Illustrations of the Kalilah and Dimnah," *Ars Islamica* 8 (1940): 136–138; David S. Rice, "The Oldest Illustrated Arabic Manuscript," *Bulletin of the School of Oriental and African Studies* 22 (1954): 207–223; Esin Atil, *Kalila wa Dimna: Fables from a Fourteenth Century Arabic Manuscript* (Washington, D.C.: Smithsonian, 1981); Jill S. Cowan, *Kalila wa Dimna: An Animal Allegory of the Mongol Court* (New York: Oxford University Press, 1989).

166. A. S. Melikian-Chirvani, *Le roman de Varqe et Golsah: Essai sur les rapports de l'esthétique plastique dans l'Iran pré-mongol, suivi de la tradition du poème* (Paris: Artes Asiatique numéro spécial XXII, 1970).

167. M. S. Ipsiroglu, *Painting and Culture of the Mongols* (New York: Harry N. Abrams, 1964), 38. On the illustrated scientific manuscripts see the five essays on the topic in Anna Contadini's *Arab Painting: Text and Image in Illustrated Arabic Manuscripts* (Leiden: Brill, 2007), 25–91.

168. Grabar, *Maqamat*, 140.

169. On the multifarious Chinese influences on Persian painting see Basil Gray, "Chinese Influence in Persian Painting: 14th and 15th Centuries," in *The Westward Influence of Chinese Arts from the 14th to the 18th Century*, ed. William Watson (London: Percival David Foundation of Chinese Art, 1988), 11–19; Nancy S. Steinhardt, "Chinese Ladies in the Istanbul Albums," in *Between China and Iran: Paintings from*

Four Istanbul Albums, ed. Ernst J. Grube and Eleanor Sims (London: Percival David Foundation of Chinese Art, 1988), 77–84; Basil Gray, "The Chinoiserie Elements in the Paintings in the Istanbul Albums," in *Between China and Iran: Paintings from Four Istanbul Albums*, ed. Ernst J. Grube and Eleanor Sims (London: Percival David Foundation of Chinese Art, 1988), 85–89; Yukai Kadoi, "Cloud Patterns: The Exchange of Ideas Between China and Iran Under the Mongols," *Oriental Art* 48 (2002): 25–36.

170. Linda Komaroff, "The Transmission and Dissemination of a New Visual Language," in *The Legacy of Genghis Khan: Courtly Art and Culture in Western Asia, 1256–1353*, ed. Linda Komaroff and Stefano Carboni (New Haven: Yale University Press, 2002), 183.

171. Grabar, *Mostly Miniatures*, 43.

172. James C. Y. Watt, "A Note on Artistic Exchanges in the Mongol Empire," in *The Legacy of Genghis Khan: Courtly Art and Culture in Western Asia, 1256–1353*, ed. Linda Komaroff and Stefano Carboni (New Haven: Yale University Press, 2002), 72–73.

173. Emil Esin, "Two Miniatures from the Collection of Topkapi," *Ars Orientalia* 5 (1963): plate 1. The "Buddhist influence," although a negative one, can also be seen in the Muslim paintings that represent the destruction of idols, which look like Buddha statues. See, for example, the painting of Abraham destroying the Sabian idols in al-Biruni's *Athar al-Baqiya* (Soucek, "An Illustrated Manuscript," figure 5); and Muhammad casting down the idols from the roof of the Ka'ba in Mirkhwand's univeral history, the *Rawdat as-Safa* of 1595, which is reproduced as figure four in chapter 1.

174. It has also been suggested that the "strip composition" of Il-khanid art derives from the Central Asian paintings of the Buddha's life story (Ipsiroglu, *Painting and Culture*, 42). On the possibility of other Uygur influences see Esin, "Two Miniatures," 156–157 n. 2; ; Emel Esin, "A Pair of Miniatures from the Miscellany Collections of Topkapi," *Central Asiatic Journal* 21, 1 (1977): 13–35; and Emel Esen, "On the Relationship Between the Iconography in Muslim Uygur Manuscripts and Buddhist Uygur Eschatology," in *Altaistic Studies*, ed. Gunnar Jarring and Staffan Rosén (Stockholm: Almqvist, 1985), 37–52.

175. While it would be enticing to include here the famous and enigmatic paintings of Siyah Qalam, "Black Pen," as evidence of possible Buddhist or Central Asian influences, this does not seem appropriate because these works are both from a later period and based on different influences. See Michael Rogers, "Siyah Qalam," *Marg* 41 (1987–1988): 21–38; and Nancy S. Steinhardt, "Siyah Qalem and Gong Kai: An Istanbul Album Painter and a Chinese Painter of the Mongolian Period," *Muqarnas* 4 (1987): 59–71.

176. On the centrality of visuality in Mahayana Buddhism see David L. McMahan, *Empty Vision: Metaphor and Visionary Imagery in Mahāyāna Buddhism* (London: Routledge Curzon, 2002).

177. "The Prophet is depicted enthroned at the beginning of a copy of the *Marzu-bannama* (Book of Margrave) transcribed in Baghdad in 1299, and cycles of illustrations of Muhammad's life appear in manuscripts from the Il-khanid period—including an undated copy of Abu al-Fadl Muhammad Bal'ami's history, the 1307 copy of al-Biruni's treatise, and several copies of Rashid al-Din's *Compendium of Chronicles*" (Sheila S. Blair, "The Religious Art of the Ilkhanids," in *The Legacy of Genghis Khan: Courtly Art and Culture in Western Asia, 1256–1353*, ed. Linda Komaroff and Stefano Carboni [New Haven: Yale University Press, 2002], 117).

178. Such destruction, however, was never universal. Nevertheless, a most fascinating example in this regard is found in the account of an auction held in Anatolia in 1655 as recorded by the Ottoman writer Evliya Çelebi. Namely, when potential bidders were able to peruse the sale items beforehand one individual defaced an illustrated manuscript; however, rather than being praised for his piety the man was accused of being a philistine and then lashed and stoned as a punishment. See Robert Dankoff, *Evliya Çelebi in Bitlis: The Relevant Section of the Seyahatname* (Leiden: Brill, 1990), 294–297.

179. Hillenbrand, "The Arts of the Book," 150.

180. Priscilla P. Soucek, "The Life of the Prophet: Illustrated Versions," in *Content and Context of Visual Arts in the Islamic World*, ed. Priscilla P. Soucek, (University Park: Pennsylvania State University Press, 1988), 193–217; Robert Hillenbrand, "Images of Muhammad in al-Biruni's *Chronology of Ancient Nations*," in *Persian Painting from the Mongols to the Qajars: Studies in Honour of Basil W. Robinson*, ed. Robert Hillenbrand (New York: I. B. Tauris, 2000), 133–135.

181. The use of images to teach the Dharma was especially prevalent in China; see Victor H. Mair, "Records of Transformation Tableaux (*Pien-hsiang*)," *T'oung Pao* 72 (1986): 3–43; Victor H. Mair, *Painting and Performance: Chinese Picture Recitation and Its Indian Genesis* (Honolulu: University of Hawai'i Press, 1989); Wu Hung, "What is *Bianxiang?*—On the Relationship Between Dunhuang Art and Dunhuang Literature," *Harvard Journal of Asiatic Studies* 52, 1 (1992): 111–192.

182. This passage is from the *Mūlasarvāstivāda Vinaya*, quoted in Teiser, *Reinventing the Wheel*, 55–56.

183. David Jackson, *A History of Tibetan Painting: The Great Tibetan Painters and Their Traditions* (Wien: Verlag der Österreichischen Akademie der Wissenschaften, 1996), 70.

184. On the linkages between Tibet and Inner Asia as reflected in the portraits of the donors at Alchi monastery see Eleanor Sims, with Boris Marshak and Ernst J. Grube, *Peerless Images: Persian Painting and Its Sources* (New Haven: Yale University Press, 2002), 22–24; and on the Perso-Muslim influence at Alchi see F. B. Flood, "Mobility and Mutation: Iranian Hunting Themes in the Murals of Alchi, Western Himalayas," *South Asian Studies* 7 (1991): 21–35. For surveys of early Buddhist art in western Tibet see Romi Khosla, *Buddhist Monasteries in the Western Himalaya* (Kathmandu: Ratna Pustak Bhandar, 1979); Roger Goepper and Jaroslav Poncar, *Alchi:*

Ladakh's Hidden Buddhist Sanctuary, the Sumtsek (Boston: Shambhala Publications, 1996); Deborah E. Klimburg-Salter, *Tabo: A Lamp for the Kingdom, Early Indo-Tibetan Buddhist Art in the Western Himalaya* (New York: Thames & Hudson, 1998).

185. Grabar, *Mostly Miniatures*, 95.

186. Jane Casey Singer, "Painting in Central Tibet, ca. 950–1400," *Artibus Asiae* 54, 1/2 (1994): 135.

187. In this context, however, it should be noted that the development of Tibetan paintings with feet and hands upon them developed in particular with the writings of Pakmo Drukpa (1110–1170) and his student Jigten Sumgo (1143–1217), who founded the Drigungpa, the lineage with whom the Mongols in Iran were allied. See Kathryn H. Selig Brown, "Early Footprint Thangkas, 12th–14th Century," *The Tibet Journal* 27, 1–2 (2003): 71–112; and Kathryn H. Selig Brown, *Eternal Presence: Handprints and Footprints in Buddhist Art* (Katonah: Katonah Museum of Art, 2004), 19.

188. Blair, "Patterns of Patronage and Production," 53. See also Terry Allen, "Byzantine Sources for the *Jami' al-tawarikh* of Rashid al-Din," *Ars Orientalia* 15 (1985): 121–136.

189. Raff, *Remarks on an Anti-Mongol Fatwa*, 63.

190. Blair, "Religious Art of the Ilkhanids," 112–114.

191. M. Molé, "Les Kubrawiya entre le Sunnisme et Shiisme aux Huitième et Neuvième Siècles de l'Hégire," *Revue des Études Islamiques* 29 (1961): 76–90.

192. Pfeiffer, "Conversion Versions," 45–46.

193. See, for example, B. W. Robinson, *Fifteenth-Century Persian Painting: Problems and Issues* (New York: New York University Press, 1991); and Thomas W. Lentz and Glenn D. Lowry, *Timur and the Princely Vision: Persian Art and Culture in the Fifteenth Century* (Washington, D.C.: Smithsonian Institution Press, 1989). On the adoption of the Timurid's artistic culture by the Uzbeks, see Maria Eva Subtelny, "Art and Politics in Early Sixteenth Century Central Asia," *Central Asiatic Journal* 27, 1 (1983): 121–148.

194. See, for example, Mirza Haydar's comments about the origin of Islamic painting during the Il-khans in his *Tarikh-i-Rashidi: A History of the Khans of Moghulistan*, trans. W. M. Thackston (Cambridge: Harvard University, Department of Near Eastern Studies, 1996), 130.

Chapter 4. Jihad

Note to epigraph: *Mahāprajñāpāramitopadeśa*, quoted in Paul Demiéville, "Le boudhisme et la guerre," in *Choix d'études bouddhiques* (Leiden: Brill, 1973), 266–267.

1. The problem of alcoholism was so severe among the Moghuls that on one jihad against the Yellow Uighurs the troops were too drunk to carry out the mission (Mirza Haydar Dughlat, *Tarikh-i-Rashidi: A History of the Khans of Moghulistan*, trans. W. M. Thackston [Cambridge: Harvard University, Department of Near Eastern Studies, 1996], 219). On the problem of alcoholism among the Mongols and its origin in the

empire period, see Thomas T. Allsen, "Ögedei and Alcohol," *Mongolian Studies* 29 (2007): 3–12.

2. Haydar Dughlat, *Tarikh-i-Rashidi*, 256.

3. A Moghul invasion in 1447–1448 was, according to Tibetan sources, repelled by the famous iron-bridge-building lama Tangton Gyalpo (1385–1464?); see Luciano Petech, "Ta-ts'e, Gu-ge, Pu-ra?: A New Study," in *Selected Papers on Asian History* (Rome: Istituto Italiano per il medio ed estresmo oriente, 1988), 385.

4. Haydar Dughlat, *Tarikh-i-Rashidi*, 76, 253. On the idea of Tibet being the center of the Buddhist world in Ming-dynasty China, see Hoong Teik Toh, *Tibetan Buddhism in Ming China* (Ph.D. diss., Harvard University, 1994), 44–58.

5. Haydar Dughlat, *Tarikh-i-Rashidi*, 256.

6. Haydar Dughlat, *Tarikh-i-Rashidi*, 267–268.

7. Haydar Dughlat, *Tarikh-i-Rashidi*, 268.

8. Haydar Dughlat, *Tarikh-i-Rashidi*, 276.

9. Mirza Haydar would invade Ladakh again in 1545 and 1548, when he would appoint Mullah Hasan to rule there as governor; however, when Mirza Haydar died in 1551 Muslim rule in Ladakh also came to an end (Luciano Petech, *The Kingdom of Ladakh c. 950–1842 A.D.* [Rome: Istituto Italiano per il medio ed estresmo oriente, 1977], 27–28).

10. Michal Biran, "The Mongol Transformation: From the Steppe to Eurasian Empire," *Medieval Encounters* 10 (2004): 339–361.

11. On the historiographical implications of choosing a starting point see Bernard Lewis, *From Babel to Dragomans: Interpreting the Middle East* (New York: Oxford University Press, 2004), 389.

12. On the migration of the Uygurs and their development in Turfan and Shazhou see James Russell Hamilton, *Les Ouighours à l'époque des Cinq Dynasties d'après les documents chinois* (Paris: Presses Universitaires de France, 1955); Elisabeth Pinks, *Die Uiguren von Kan-chou in der frühen Sung-Zeit (960–1028)* (Wiesbaden: Harrassowitz, 1968); and Lilla Russell-Smith, *Uygur Patronage in Dunhuang: Regional Art Centres on the Northern Silk Road in the Tenth and Eleventh Centuries* (Leiden: Brill, 2005), 31–76.

13. H. J. Klimkeit, "Christians, Buddhists and Manicheans in Medieval Central Asia," *Buddhist-Christian Studies* 1 (1981): 46–50.

14. Takao Moriyasu, "On the Uighur Buddhist Society at Ciqtim in the Turfan During the Mongol Period," in *Splitter aus der Gegend von Turfan: Festschrift für Peter Zieme anläßlich seines 60. Geburtstags*, ed. Mehmet Ölmez and Simone-Christiane Raschmann (Istanbul: Türk Dilleri Arastirmalari Dizisi, 2002), 156. For an overview of the theories about the development of Uygur Buddhism see Takao Moriyasu, "Chronology of West Uighur Buddhism: Re-examination of the Dating of the Wall-paintings in Grünwedel's Cave No. 8 (New: No. 18), Bezelik," in *Aspects of Research into Central Asian Buddhism: In Memoriam Kogi Kudara*, ed. Peter Zieme (Turnhout: Brepols, 2008), 191–194.

15. I borrow the term "steppe intelligentsia" from Paul D. Buell, "Cinqai (*ca.* 1169–1252)," in *In the Service of the Khan: Eminent Personalities of the Early Mongol-Yüan Period (1200–1300)*, ed. Igor de Rachewiltz et al. (Wiesbaden: Harrassowitz, 1993), 95.

16. Thomas T. Allsen, "The Yüan Dynasty and the Uighurs of Turfan in the 13th Century," in *China Among Equals: The Middle Kingdom and Its Neighbors, 10th–14th Centuries*, ed. Morris Rossabi (Berkeley: University of California Press, 1983), 243–280.

17. Abdurishid Yakup, "Two Alliterative Uighur Poems from Dunhuang," *Linguistic Research* 17–18 (1999): 11–12.

18. Abdurishid Yakup, "On the Interlinear Uyghur Poetry in the Newly Unearthed Nestorian Text," in *Splitter aus der Gegend von Turfan: Festschrift für Peter Zieme anläßlich seines 60. Geburtstags*, ed Mehmet Ölmez and Simone-Christiane Raschmann (Istanbul: Türk Dilleri Arastirmalari Dizisi, 2002), 415.

19. For examples of Uygur Buddhist resistance to Islam see Semih Tezcan, *Das uigurische Insadi-Sutra* (Berlin: Akademie Verlag, 1974), 71–72; and Semih Tezcan and Peter Zieme, "Antiislamische Polemik in einem alttürkischen buddhistischen Gedicht aus Turfan," *Altorientalische Forschungen* 17, 1 (1990): 146–151.

20. Peter Zieme and György Kara, *Ein uigurisches Totenbuch: Naropas Lehre in uigurischer Übersetzung von vier tibetischen Traktaten nach Sammelhandschrift aus Dunhuang British Museum Or. 8212 (109)* (Wiesbaden: Harrassowitz, 1979), 27–29, 161–162.

21. Herbert Franke, "Mittelmongolische Glossen in einer arabischen Astronomischen Handschrift von 1366," *Oriens* 31 (1988): 95–118. On the scientific contents of al-Sanjufini's *zij* see E. S. Kennedy and Jan Hogendijk, "Two Tables from an Arabic Astronomical Handbook for the Mongol Viceroy of Tibet," in *A Scientific Humanist: Studies in Memory of Abraham Sachs*, ed. Erie Leichty et al. (Philadelphia: The University Museum, 1988), 233–242; E. S. Kennedy, "Eclipse Predictions in Arabic Astronomical Tables Prepared for the Mongol Viceroy of Tibet," *Zeitschrift für Geschichte der Arabisch-Islamischen Wissenschaften* 4 (1990): 60–80.

22. Peter B. Golden, "The World of the Rasūlid Hexaglot," in *The King's Dictionary: The Rasūlid Hexaglot: Fourteenth Century Vocabularies in Arabic, Persian, Turkic, Greek, Armenian, and Mongol*, ed. Peter B. Golden (Leiden: Brill, 2000), 14–18. On the growth of interest in other languages during the Mongol empire see also Thomas T. Allsen, "The Rasūlid Hexaglot in Its Eurasian Cultural Context," in *The King's Dictionary: The Rasūlid Hexaglot: Fourteenth Century Vocabularies in Arabic, Persian, Turkic, Greek, Armenian, and Mongol*, ed. Peter B. Golden (Leiden: Brill, 2000), 25–48.

23. On the negative role the "Mongol yoke" plays in Russia's imagination see Orlando Figes, *Natasha's Dance: A Cultural History of Russia* (New York: Metropolitan Books, 2002), 358–429.

24. See, for example, John Darwin, *After Tamerlane: The Global History of Empire Since 1405* (London: Bloomsbury Press, 2008).

25. Thomas T. Allsen, "Sharing Out the Empire: Apportioned Lands Under the

Mongols," in *Nomads in the Sedentary World*, ed. Anatoly M. Khazanov and André Wink (Richmond: Curzon Press, 2001), 172–190.

26. Jean Richard, "La conversion de Berke et les debuts de l'islamisation de la horde d'or," *Revue des Études Islamiques* 35 (1967): 173–184; István Vásáry, "'History and Legend' in Berke Khan's Conversion to Islam," in *Aspects of Altaic Civilization III*, ed. Denis Sinor (Bloomington: Indiana University, Research Institute for Inner Asian Studies, 1990): 230–252; Devin DeWeese, "Problems of Islamization in the Volga-Ural Region: Traditions About Berke Khan," in *Proceedings of the International Symposium on Islamic Civilisation in the Volga-Ural Region, Kazan, 8–11 June 2001*, ed. Ali Çaksu and Radik Mukhammetshin (Istanbul: Research Centre for Islamic History, Art and Culture, 2004), 3–13.

27. Charles J. Halperin, "The Kipchak Connection: The Ilkhans, the Mamluks and Ayn Jalut," *Bulletin of the School of Oriental and African Studies* 63, 2 (2000): 229–245.

28. On the conflict between these two see Reuven Amitai Preiss, *Mongols and Mamluks: The Mamluk-Ilkhanid War, 1260–1281* (Cambridge: Cambridge University Press, 1995).

29. Amitai Preiss, *Mongols and Mamluks*, 81.

30. For a comprehensive study on the relations between the Mongols and Christian Europe see Peter Jackson, *The Mongols and the West, 1221–1410* (Harlow: Pearson Longman, 2005).

31. Amitai Preiss, *Mongols and Mamluks*, 80.

32. Michal Biran, *Qaidu and the Rise of the Independent Mongol State in Central Asia* (Richmond: Curzon, 1997).

33. Peter Jackson, "From Ulus to Khanate: The Making of the Mongol States c. 1220–c. 1290," in *The Mongol Empire and Its Legacy*, ed. Reuven Amitai-Preiss and David O. Morgan (Leiden: Brill, 1999), 12–38.

34. See, for example, Herbert Franke, "Sino-Western Contacts Under the Mongol Empire," *Journal of the Royal Asiatic Society* (Hong Kong Branch) 6 (1966): 49–72.

35. See, for example, Thomas T. Allsen, "Biography of a Cultural Broker: Bolad Ch'eng-Hsiang in China and Iran," in *The Court of the Ilkhans, 1290–1340*, ed. Julian Raby and Teresa Fitzherbert (Oxford: Oxford University Press, 1996), 7–22.

36. See, for example, Eric Vogelin, "Mongol Orders of Submission to European Powers, 1245–1255," *Byzantion* 15 (1940–1941): 378–411.

37. György Kara, "Mediaeval Mongol Documents from Khara Khoto and East Turkestan in the St. Petersburg Branch of the Institute of Oriental Studies," *Manuscripta Orientalia* 9, 2 (2003): 28–30.

38. On this issue see Beatrice Forbes Manz, "The Development and Meaning of Chaghatay Identity," in *Muslims in Central Asia: Expressions of Identity and Change*, ed. Jo-Ann Gross (Durham: Duke University Press, 1992), 27–45.

39. Igor de Rachewiltz, *The Secret History of the Mongols: A Mongolian Epic Chronicle of the Thirteenth Century* (Leiden: Brill, 2006), § 202, 758–761.

40. Chaghatai's anti-Muslim policies are brought most vociferously to the fore in the work of Juzjani; see, for example, H. G. Raverty, *The Tabakat-i-Nasiri of Minhaj-i-Saraj, Abu-Umar-i-Usman: A General History of the Muhammadan Dynasties of Asia, including Hindustan from A. H. 194 (810 A. D.) to A. H. 658 (1260 A. D.), and the irruption of the infidel Mughals into Islam* (London: Gilbert & Rivington, 1881), 1144–1148.

41. On the earlier development of this view of Chaghatai in the context of Möngke's 1250s purge of the Chaghatai lineage see Christopher P. Atwood, "Informants and Sources for the *Secret History of the Mongols*," *Mongolian Studies* 29 (2007): 34–36.

42. The following material is based on Michal Biran, "The Chaghadaids and Islam: The Conversion of Tarmashirin Khan (1331–34)," *Journal of the American Oriental Society* 122, 4 (2002): 742–752.

43. See, for example, R. D. McChesney, "Zamzam Water on a White Felt Carpet: Adapting Mongol Ways in Muslim Central Asia, 1550–1650," in *Religion, Customary Law, and Nomadic Technology*, ed. Michael Gervers and Wayne Schlepp (Toronto: Toronto Studies in Central and Inner Asia, 2000), 63–80.

44. Dai Matsui, "A Mongolian Decree from the Chaghataid Khanate Discovered at Dunhuang," in *Aspects of Research into Central Asian Buddhism: In Memoriam Kogi Kudara*, ed. Peter Zieme (Turnhout: Brepols, 2008), 159–178; Dai Matsui, "Revising the Uigur Inscriptions of the Yulin Caves," *Nairiku Ajia gengo no kenkyu* 23 (2008): 30–41.

45. Biran, "Chaghataids and Islam," 750.

46. The term "Moghul" reflects the Persian and Arabic adaptation of the Turkic rendering of "Mongol," and is the term used to identify the dynastic lineage of Chaghatai that ruled Central Asia from the fourteenth to seventeenth century. Unfortunately, it is also the term commonly used to refer to the descendants of Babur who ruled in India, though more often than not it is misspelled as "Mughal," which is apparently an English adaptation of Indian pronunciation. Regardless, however, it is a misnomer, since the descendants of Babur never used this term themselves. They saw themselves as Timurids (see Lisa Balabanlilar, "The Lords of the Auspicious Conjunction: Turco-Mongol Imperial Identity on the Subcontinent," *Journal of World History* 18, 1 [2007]: 1–39). And to make matters even more complicated, we should note that as the descendants of Chaghatai came to be known as the Moghuls, the term Chaghatai came to be applied to the Timurids and their written language.

47. On the transition of the Timurids from a nomadic empire to an urban state focused on both agriculture and Islamic shrines, see Maria E. Subtelny, *Timurids in Transition: Turko-Persian Politics and Acculturation in Medieval Iran* (Leiden: Brill, 2007).

48. On the conversion of Tughlugh Temür see Kim Hodong, "The Early History of the Moghul Nomads: The Legacy of the Chaghatai Khanate," in *The Mongol Empire and Its Legacy*, ed. Reuven Amitai-Preiss and David O. Morgan (Leiden: Brill, 1999), 301–307.

49. On the history of the Kataki and the connection between Sufism and urban renewal see Kim Hodong, "Muslim Saints in the 14th to the 16th Centuries of Eastern Turkestan," *International Journal of Central Asian Studies* 1 (1996): 287–296, 314–319.

50. K. M. Maitra, *A Persian Embassy to China: Being an Extract from Zubdatu't Tawarikh of Hafiz Abru* (New York: Paragon Book Reprint Corp., 1970), 14–15.

51. Luo Yuejiong, *Xian bin lü* (Beijing: Zhonghua shuju, 1983). I thank Abdurishid Yakup for this reference.

52. On the rise of Tamerlane see Beatrice F. Manz, *The Rise and Rule of Tamerlane* (New York: Cambridge University Press, 1989), 41–89.

53. On these political struggles see John Dardess, *Conquerors and Confucians: Aspects of Political Change in Late Yüan China* (New York: Columbia University Press, 1973).

54. Johan Elverskog, *The Pearl Rosary: Mongol Historiography in Early Nineteenth Century Ordos* (Bloomington: Mongolia Society, 2007), 60 n. 189.

55. The following material is based upon essays in Herbert Franke and Denis Twitchett, *The Cambridge History of China, Vol. 6: Alien Regimes and Border States, 907–1368* (New York: Cambridge University Press, 1994) and L. Carrington Goodrich and Chaoyang Fang, *Dictionary of Ming Biography, 1368–1644* (New York: Columbia University Press, 1976).

56. On the development of Chinese law under the Mongols see Bettine Birge, *Women, Property, and Confucian Reaction in Sung and Yuan China: 960–1368* (Cambridge: Cambridge University Press, 2002).

57. On the Mongol response to this predicament, in particular their attempt at reclaiming this new territory by means of the cult of Chinggis Khan, see Johan Elverskog, "The Legend of Muna Mountain," *Inner Asia* 8, 1 (2006): 99–122.

58. For the court debates and different Ming views on the Mongols see Henry Serruys, *Sino-Mongol Relations During the Ming, I: The Mongols in China During the Hung-wu Period (1368–1398)* (Brussels: Institut Belge des Hautes Études Chinoises, 1959); Sechin Jagchid and Van Jay Symons, *Peace, War, and Trade Along the Great Wall: Nomadic-Chinese Interaction Through Two Millennia* (Bloomington: Indiana University Press, 1989); and Alastair Johnston, *Cultural Realism: Strategic Culture and Grand Strategy in Chinese History* (Princeton: Princeton University Press, 1995).

59. The Ming hatred of the Mongols would reach its most pathological extreme during the later reign of the Jiajing emperor (r. 1522–1566), who mandated that the Chinese characters for "barbarians" (i.e., Mongols) should be written in the smallest possible characters in all official records (James Geiss, "The Chia-ching Reign, 1522–1566," in *The Cambridge History of China, Vol. 8: 1*, ed. F. W. Mote and D. Twitchett [Cambridge: Cambridge University Press, 1988], 441).

60. Hidehiro Okada, "Origins of the Dörben Oyirad," *Ural-Altaische Jahrbücher* 7 (1987): 181–211; Junko Miyawaki, "The Birth of Oyirad Khanship," *Central Asiatic Journal* 41 (1997): 39–41.

61. Jasper Becker, *City of Heavenly Tranquility: Beijing in the History of China* (New York: Oxford University Press, 2008), 18.

62. On the Ming-Mongol horse trade, see Henry Serruys, *Sino-Mongol Relations During the Ming, III: Trade Relations: The Horse Fairs* (Brussels: Institut Belge des Hautes Études Chinoises, 1975).

63. Elliot Sperling, "The Szechwan-Tibet Frontier in the Fifteenth Century," *Ming Studies* 26 (1988): 37–55. On earlier Sino-Tibetan trade see Paul J. Smith, *Taxing Heaven's Storehouse: Horses, Bureaucrats, and the Destruction of the Sichuan Tea Trade, 1074–1224* (Cambridge: Council on East Asian Studies, 1991).

64. Johan Elverskog, *The Jewel Translucent Sutra: Altan Khan and the Mongols in the Sixteenth Century* (Leiden: Brill, 2003), 148–149 n. 257.

65. Morris Rossabi, "Ming Foreign Policy: The Case of Hami," in *China and Her Neighbours: Borders, Visions of the Other, Foreign Policy 10th to 19th Century*, ed. Sabine Dabringhaus and Roderich Ptak (Wiesbaden: Harrassowitz, 1997), 79–97.

66. In fact, this westward orientation extended all the way to Egypt, where Oirad men served in the army and Oirad women were joyfully accepted as wives by the Mamluk elite; see Linda S. Northrup, *From Slave to Sultan: The Career of Al-Manṣūr Qalāwūn and the Consolidation of Mamluk Rule in Egypt and Syria (678–689 A.H./ 1279–1290 A.D.)* (Stuttgart: Franz Steiner Verlag, 1998), 117–118, 191.

67. André Wink, *Al-Hind: The Making of the Indo-Islamic World, Vol. 1, Early Medieval India and the Expansion of Islam 7th–11th Centuries* (Leiden: Brill, 1990), 331.

68. Joseph F. Fletcher, "China and Central Asia, 1368–1884," in *The Chinese World Order*, ed. John K. Fairbank (Cambridge: Harvard University Press, 1968), 205–219. On the interaction between the Timurids and the Ming see also Morris Rossabi, "A Translation of Ch'en Ch'eng's *Hsi-Yu Fan-kuo Chih*," *Ming Studies* 17 (1983): 49–59.

69. Maitra, *A Persian Embassy*, 39.

70. Maitra, *A Persian Embassy*, 46–49. A similar paean to "infidel" artistry is found in another account of one of Shahrukh's embassies, namely, Abdul-Razzaq Samarqandi's account of his mission to south India between 1442 and 1445: "We reached the village of Pednur, the buildings of which were like unto the houris and palaces of paradise. There is an idol temple. . . . Without exaggeration it can be said that no description of that building could do it justice. . . . It is as pleasant as the Garden of Iram. . . . In the midst of this space was a platform as tall as a man, made of beautiful dressed stone, the blocks so expertly and delicately set one on another that one might think it was of a single block. . . . There were so many designs and so much depiction made with sharp stylus in that granite that it was beyond description. From top to bottom of that structure there was not the space of a hand free of *firangi* and *khatai* designs. . . . In that place morning and evening, after their unacceptable worship, they play instruments and dance. All the men of the village have duties to perform there, and votive offerings are brought there, and votive offerings are brought

from distant cities. In the belief of these infidels it is the Ka'ba of the guebres" (W. M. Thackston, *A Century of Princes: Sources on Timurid History and Art* [Cambridge: Aga Khan Program for Islamic Architecture, 1989], 306–307). For positive Muslim views of "infidel" art in the later Mughal period see also Carl Ernst, "Admiring the Works of the Ancients: The Ellora Temples as Viewed by Indo-Muslim Authors," in *Beyond Turk and Hindu: Rethinking Religious Identities in Islamicate South Asia* (Gainesville: University of Florida Press, 2000), 98–120.

71. Masami Hamada, "Jihād, Hijra, et 'devoir du sel' dans l'histoire du Turkestan Oriental," *Turcica* 33 (2001), 38.

72. "By the end of Jumada II (July 11th) they arrived at Turfan. Majority of the inhabitants of this town were unbelievers and worshipped idols. They had large idol-temples of superb beauty inside which there were many idols, some of them having been made newly and others old. In foreground of the platform there was a big image which was asserted by them to be the statue of Sakyamuni" (Maitra, *A Persian Embassy*, 12–13).

73. Joseph F. Fletcher, "The Naqshbandiyya in Northwest China," in *Studies on China and Islamic Central Asia,* ed. Beatrice Manz (Aldershot: Variorum, 1995), XI, 5.

74. The origin of the Naqshbandiyya's focus on *shari'a* can be traced back to the fourteenth-century Khojagānī Sufis; see Devin DeWeese, "Khojagānī Origins and the Critique of Sufism: The Rhetoric of Communal Uniqueness in the *Manāqib* of Khoja ᶜAli ᶜAzīzān Rāmītanī," in *Islamic Mysticism Contested: Thirteen Centuries of Controversies and Polemics,* ed. Frederick De Jong and Bernd Radtke (Leiden: Brill, 1999), 496, 507, 518.

75. For a concise overview of the Mongol impact on the Muslim world see Michal Biran, *Chinggis Khan* (Oxford: Oneworld Publications, 2007), 74–136.

76. Devin DeWeese, "The Influence of the Mongols on the Religious Consciousness of Thirteenth Century Europe," *Mongolian Studies* 5 (1978): 41–78.

77. On the eternal struggle between external or internal solutions to human problems and their metaphors see Edward Slingerland, *Effortless Action: Wu-wei as Conceptual Metaphor and Spiritual Ideal in Early China* (Oxford: Oxford University Press, 2003).

78. Devin DeWeese, "'Stuck in the Throat of Chingiz Khan': Envisioning the Mongol Conquests in Some Sufi Accounts from the 14th to 17th Centuries," in *History and Historiography of Post-Mongol Central Asia and the Middle East: Studies in Honor of John E. Woods,* ed. J. Pfeiffer and S. A. Quinn (Wiesbaden: Harrassowitz, 2006), 23–60.

79. On the spiritual and historical struggles between the Yasaviyya and Naqshbandiyya see Devin DeWeese, "The *Masha'-ikh-i* Turk and the *Khojagan*: Rethinking the Links Between the Yasavi and Naqshbandi Sufi Traditions," *Journal of Islamic Studies* 7, 2 (1996): 180–207.

80. On this shrine and its connection with Yasavi historiography see Devin DeWeese, "Sacred Places and 'Public' Narratives: The Shrine of Ahamd Yasavi in

Hagiographical Traditions of the Yasavi Sufi Order, 16th–17th Centuries," *Muslim World* 90 (2000): 353–376.

81. Beatrice F. Manz, "Tamerlane and the Symbolism of Sovereignty," *Iranian Studies* 21, 1–2 (1988): 105–122.

82. David Roxburgh, *Turks: A Journey of a Thousand Years, 600–1600* (London: Royal Academy of Arts, 2005), 196–197.

83. This particular phrase ("sharr-i rusūm-i bīgānegān") is found in several Naqshbandiyya letters (Jo-Ann Gross and Asom Urunbaev, *The Letters of Khwāja 'Ubayd Allāh Aḥrār and His Associates* [Leiden: Brill, 2002]: 114, 128, 166).

84. Kim Hodong, "The Rise and Fall of the Hami Kingdom (ca. 1389–1513)," in *Land Routes of the Silk Roads and the Cultural Exchanges Between the East and West Before the 10th Century* (Beijing: New World Press, 1996). One should also note that at Toyuq the Uygur Buddhist cave temples became the seat of Sufi dervishes "who considered the caves to be the abode of the 'Seven Sleepers' of Islamic hagiography" (Scott, "Buddhism and Islam," 146).

85. Another facet of this process of religious conversion was the incorporation of Buddhist stories into the Muslim tradition. For example, the story of a sandstorm from Xuanzang's pilgrimage through Central Asia became part of Kataki Sufi lore (Masami Hamada, "Islamic Saints and Their Mausoleums," *Acta Asiatica* 34 [1978]: 81–83). Moreover, the so-called "Uwaysi" Sufis had a legend about a sufi named Muhibb-i Kuhmar ("Lover of the Mountain Snake") and a holy snake that was apparently modeled on a Buddhist snake story connected with the philosopher Nagurjuna (Julian Baldick, *Imaginary Muslims: The Uwaysi Sufis of Central Asia* [New York: I. B. Tauris, 1993], 163–165). The same kind of appropriation of Buddhist elements into Islam also happened in Java; see A. H. Johns, "From Buddhism to Islam: An Interpretation of the Javanese Literature of the Transition," *Comparative Studies in Society and History* 9, 1 (1966): 40–50.

86. Haydar, *Tarikh-i-Rashidi*, 35–36, 48.

87. Joseph F. Fletcher, "China and Central Asia, 1368–1884," in *The Chinese World Order*, ed. John K. Fairbank (Cambridge: Harvard University Press, 1968), 216–218. On the continued trade through the fifteenth century see Hiroshi Watanabe, "An Index of Embassies and Tribute Missions from Islamic Countries to Ming China (1368–1644) as Recorded in the *Ming Shih-lu* Classified According to Geographic Area," *Memoirs of the Research Department of the Toyo Bunko* 33 (1975): 285–348; and F. W. Cleaves, "The Sino-Mongolian Edict of 1453 in The Topkapi Sarayi Müsezi," *Harvard Journal of Asiatic Studies* 13, 3–4 (1950): 431–446.

88. Juten Oda, "Uighuristan," *Acta Asiatica* 34 (1978): 43.

89. Henry Serruys, "Early Lamaism in Mongolia," *Oriens Extremus* 10 (1962): 189–191.

90. Sh. Bira, "Qubilai Qa'an and 'Phags-pa bLa-ma," in *The Mongol Empire and Its Legacy*, ed. Reuven Amitai-Preiss and David O. Morgan (Leiden: Brill, 1999), 240–249.

91. Herbert Franke, "Tibetans in Yüan China," in *China Under Mongol Rule*, ed. John D. Langlois, Jr. (Princeton: Princeton University Press, 1981), 308. For studies of this Buddhist model of rule among the Mongols and Tibetans see Janos Szerb, "Glosses on the Oeuvre of Bla-ma 'Phags-pa: III. The 'Patron-Patronized' Relationship," in *Soundings in Tibetan Civilization*, ed. Barbara Nimri Aziz and Matthew T. Kapstein (Delhi: Manohar, 1985), 165–173; David S. Ruegg, "*Mchod yon, yon mchod and mchod gnas/yon gnas*: On the Historiography and Semantics of a Tibetan Religio-social and Religio-political Concept," in *Tibetan History and Language*, ed. Ernst Steinkeller (Vienna: Arbeitskreis für Tibetische und Buddhistische Studien Universität Wien, 1991), 441–453; David S. Ruegg, "The Precept-Donor (*yon mchod*) Relation in Thirteenth Century Tibetan Society and Polity, Its Inner Asian Precursors and Indian Models," in *Tibetan Studies*, ed. H. Krasser et al. (Vienna: Österreichische Akademia der Wissenschaft, 1997), 857–872.

92. Serruys, "Early Lamaism in Mongolia," 181–216; Henry Serruys, "Additional Note on the Origin of Lamaism in Mongolia," *Oriens Extremus* 13 (1966): 165–173; Elliot Sperling, "Notes on References to 'Bri-Gung-pa-Mongol Contact in the Late Sixteenth and Early Seventeenth Centuries," in *Tibetan Studies: Proceedings of the 5th Seminar of the International Association of Tibetan Studies*, ed. Ihara Shoren and Yamaguchi Ziuho (Narita: Naritasan Shinsoji, 1992), 741–750.

93. On the Ming court's involvement with Tibetan lamas see Toh, *Tibetan Buddhism in Ming China*; Natalie Köhle, "Why Did the Kangxi Emperor Go to Wutai Shan? Patronage, Pilgrimage, and the Place of Tibetan Buddhism at the Early Qing Court," *Late Imperial China* 29, 1 (2008): 77–84; Peter Schwieger, "A Document of Chinese Diplomatic Relations with East Tibet During the Ming Dynasty," in *Tibetstudien: Festschrift für Dieter Schuh zum 65. Geburtstag*, ed. Petra Maurer and Peter Schwieger (Bonn: Bier'sche Verlaganstallt, 2007), 209–226; Shen Weirong, "On the History of Gling tshang Principality of mDo khams During the Yuan and Ming Dynasties: Studies on Sources Concerning Tibet in *Ming Shilu* (I)," in *Tibetstudien: Festschrift für Dieter Schuh zum 65. Geburtstag*, ed. Petra Maurer and Peter Schwieger (Bonn: Bier'sche Verlaganstallt, 2007), 227–266; Dora C. Y. Ching, "Tibetan Buddhism and the Creation of the Imperial Image," in *Culture, Courtiers, and Competition: The Ming Court (1368–1644)*, ed. David M. Robinson (Cambridge: Harvard University Asia Center, 2008), 321–364; and David M. Robinson, "The Ming Court and the Legacy of the Yuan Mongols," in *Culture, Courtiers, and Competition: The Ming Court (1368–1644)*, ed. David M. Robinson (Cambridge: Harvard University Asia Center, 2008), 365–421.

94. The Oirad seizure of the emperor had profound consequences for the Ming (F. W. Mote, "The T'u-mu Incident of 1449," in *Chinese Ways in Warfare*, ed. Frank Kierman, Jr., and John K. Fairbank [Cambridge: Harvard University Press, 1974], 243–272). One scholar has even claimed that it changed forever the Ming intellectual world (Chu Hung-lam, "Intellectual Trends in the Fifteenth Century," *Ming Studies* 27 [1989]: 9).

95. On these developments see Elverskog, *The Jewel Translucent Sutra*, 129–179.

96. David Robinson, "Politics, Force and Ethnicity in Ming China: Mongols and the Abortive Coup of 1461," *Harvard Journal of Asiatic Studies* 59 (1999), 95.

97. Jürgen Paul, *Die politische und soziale Bedeutung der Naqsbandiyya in Mittelasien im 15. Jahrhundert* (Berlin: Walter de Gruyter, 1991).

98. On the political and financial power of Khoja Ahrar in both Central Asia and India see Muzaffar Alam, "The Mughals, the Sufi Shaikhs and the Formation of Akbari Dispensation," *Modern Asian Studies* 43, 1 (2009): 143–154.

99. Jürgen Paul, "Forming a Faction: The *Ḥimāyat* System of Khwaja Ahrar," *International Journal of Middle East Studies* 23, 4 (1991): 533–548.

100. Morris Rossabi, "The Decline of the Central Asian Caravan Trade," in *The Rise of Merchant Empires: Long Distance Trade in the Early Modern World, 1350–1750*, ed. James D. Tracy (New York: Cambridge University Press, 1990), 351–370.

101. Fletcher, "The Naqshbandiyya," 6–7.

102. Elverskog, *The Jewel Translucent Sutra*, 48–53.

103. Johan Elverskog, "The Story of Zhu and the Mongols of the 17th Century," *Ming Studies* 50 (2004): 39–76.

104. Hidehiro Okada, "Dayan Khan in the Battle of Dalan Terigün," in *Gedanke und Wirkung: Festschrift zum 90. Geburtstag von Nikolaus Poppe*, ed. W. Heissig and K. Sagaster (Wiesbaden: Harrassowitz, 1989), 262–270.

105. Louis Hambis, "Note sur l'installation des Mongols dans la Boucle du Fleuve Jaune," in *Mongolian Studies*, ed. Louis Ligeti (Amsterdam: B. R. Grüner, 1970), 167–179.

106. During Altan Khan's two-year campaign to the west in 1558–1560, for example, even though he invaded Tibet he showed no interest in pursuing tantric Buddhism; see Elverskog, *The Jewel Translucent Sutra*, 108.

107. On the confrontation between the Qing and European powers see, for example, James L. Hevia, *Cherishing Men from Afar: Qing Guest Ritual and the Macartney Embassy of 1993* (Durham: Duke University Press, 1995); James L. Hevia, *English Lessons: The Pedagogy of Imperialism in Nineteenth-Century China* (Durham: Duke University, 2003); Lydia H. Liu, *The Clash of Empires: The Invention of China in Modern World Making* (Cambridge: Harvard University Press, 2006).

108. On the history and meaning of the Great Wall see Nicola DiCosmo, *Ancient China and Its Enemies: The Rise of Nomadic Power in East Asian History* (Cambridge: Cambridge University Press, 2002); and Arthur Waldron, *The Great Wall of China: From Myth to History* (Cambridge: Cambridge University Press, 1990).

109. B. J. ter Haar, *The White Lotus Teachings in Chinese Religious History* (Leiden: Brill, 1992), 152–153.

110. Elverskog, *The Jewel Translucent Sutra*, 98 n. 104.

111. Carney T. Fisher, "Smallpox, Salesmen, and Sectarians: Ming-Mongol Relations in the Jiajing Reign (1522–67)," *Ming Studies* 25 (1988): 1–23.

112. Johan Elverskog, "Tibetocentrism, Religious Conversion and the Study of

Mongolian Buddhism," in *The Mongolia-Tibet Interface: Opening New Research Terrains in Inner Asia*, ed. Hildegaard Diemberger and Uradyn Bulag (Leiden: Brill, 2007), 59–81.

113. The Mongolian term "White Turbans" used to refer to the Muslims of Inner Asia was borrowed from the Chinese (see Paul Pelliot, "Le Hōja et le Sayyid Husain de l'Histoire des Ming," *T'oung pao* 38 [1948]: 130–132).

114. Elverskog, *The Jewel Translucent Sutra*, 168–169.

115. F. W. Cleaves, "Aqa Minu," *Harvard Journal of Asiatic Studies* 24 (1962–1963): 64–81.

116. Elverskog, *The Jewel Translucent Sutra*, 109–110.

117. Fletcher, "The Naqshbandiyya," 9.

118. Serruys, "Early Lamaism in Mongolia," 202–213.

119. On these developments see Zahiruddin Ahmad, *Sino-Tibetan Relations in the Seventeenth Century* (Rome: Istituto Italiano per il Medio ed Estremo Oriente, 1970).

120. For an overview of the Ming dynasty's last century see Brook, *The Confusions of Pleasure: Commerce and Culture in Ming China* (Berkeley: University of California Press, 1999), 153–237.

121. Nurhaci (1559–1626), the founder of the Manchu state, had already received tantric initiation and appointed his "guru," Olug Darkhan Nangso, as Dharma-master of the Manchu realm in 1621. Nurhaci also had seven large monasteries built near his residence of Hetu Ala (i.e., Yenden, the old capital) in the 1620s (Sabine Dabringhaus, "Chinese Emperors and Tibetan Monks: Religion as an Instrument of Rule," in *China and Her Neighbours: Borders, Visions of the Other, Foreign Policy 10th to 19th Century China*, ed. Sabine Dabringhaus and Roderich Pitak [Wiesbaden: Harrassowitz, 1997], 122). These building projects were then followed by those of his successor, Hong Taiji (1592–1643), who had the famous Mahakala Temple constructed in 1635, which was a paragon of Manchu imbrication with Buddhism and the Mongol legacy. Not only was the temple to house a copy of the Buddhist canon in Mongolian, but also the remains of Ligdan Khan, the last Chinggisid ruler's guru, Sharba Khutugtu, and most importantly, the famous Mahakala statue. Khubilai Khan had given this statue to Pakpa Lama during the Yuan dynasty, and when Ligdan Khan's family submitted to the Manchus they presented it as tribute. The importance of this statue, with its historical linkages and ritual significations, was profoundly important for the Manchu claim to be seen as the rightful heirs of Mongol Buddhist rule; and thus in 1643 Hong Taiji initiated an extension of this important temple complex. In 1645 this project was complete with four temples and adjoining stupas having been built to encircle the Mahakala Temple, the imperial palace, and the Manchu capital of Mukden within a mandala. As Samuel Grupper notes, "this architectonic representation of the Buddhist cosmological order (an arrangement reminiscent of the ensemble of Bsam yas at the old Tibetan imperial precinct of Brag mar) celebrated [Hong Taiji's] succession as cakravartin, defined Manchu dynastic right, and set the Manchu capital and realm

under the protection of Mahakala" ("Manchu Patronage and Tibetan Buddhism During the First Half of the Ch'ing Dynasty," *Journal of the Tibet Society* 4 [1984]: 53).

122. A third group led by the Torghud left the area in 1630 and established themselves on the Volga River in southern Russia. They became the Kalmyks.

123. Christopher P. Atwood, "Titles, Appanages, Marriages, and Officials: A Comparison of Political Forms in the Zünghar and Thirteenth-Century Mongol Empires," in *Imperial Statecraft: Political Forms and Techniques of Governance in Inner Asia, Sixth-Twentieth Centuries*, ed. David Sneath (Bellingham: Western Washington University, 2006), 211–214.

124. For a convenient overview of the Great Fifth's career see Samten G. Karmay, "The Fifth Dalai Lama and His Reunification of Tibet," in *Lhasa in the Seventeenth Century: The Capital of the Dalai Lamas*, ed. Françoise Pommaret (Leiden: Brill, 2003), 65–80; and Elliot Sperling, "Tibet's Foreign Relations During the Epoch of the Fifth Dalai Lama," in *Lhasa in the Seventeenth Century: The Capital of the Dalai Lamas*, ed. Françoise Pommaret (Leiden: Brill, 2003), 119–132.

125. Elliot Sperling, "Awe and Submission: A Tibetan Aristocrat at the Court of Qianlong," *International History Review* 20, 2 (1998): 325–335. On Qing policy toward Tibet in the eighteenth century see Luciano Petech, *China and Tibet in the Early 18th Century* (Leiden: Brill, 1950).

126. Yumiko Ishihama, "A Study of the Seals and Titles Conferred by the Dalai Lamas," in *Tibetan Studies: Proceedings of the Fifth Seminar of the International Association of Tibetan Studies*, ed. Shoren Ihara and Zuiho Yamaguchi (Narita: Naritasan Shinsoji, 1992), 501–514.

127. On the consequences of this assault for the Kagyü lineage, especially its retreat to the Sino-Tibetan borderlands see Karl Debreczeny, "Dabaojigong and the Regional Tradition of Ming Sino-Tibetan Painting in the Kingdom of Lijiang," in *Buddhism Between Tibet and China*, ed. Matthew T. Kapstein (Boston: Wisdom Publications, 2009), 97–152.

128. Even though the Great Fifth did eventually wield control over Tibet, to a large extent the institutionalization of the Dalai Lama and his ritual and political authority was the legacy of the regent Sangye Gyatso, who wrote more than seven thousand pages on this topic (Kurtis R. Schaeffer, "Ritual, Festival and Authority Under the Fifth Dalai Lama," in *Power, Politics, and the Reinvention of Tradition: Tibet in the Seventeenth and Eighteenth Centuries*, ed. Bryan J. Cuevas and Kurtis R. Schaeffer [Leiden: Brill, 2006], 188).

129. Elliot Sperling, " 'Orientalism' and Aspects of Violence in the Tibetan Tradition," in *Imagining Tibet: Perceptions, Projections, and Fantasies*, ed. Thierry Dodin and Heinz Räther (Boston: Wisdom Publications, 2003), 318.

130. Zuiho Yamaguchi, "The Sovereign Power of the Fifth Dalai Lama: *sPrul sku* gZims-khang-gong-ma and the Removal of Governor Nor-bu," *Memoirs of the Research Department of the Toyo Bunko* 53 (1995): 1–28.

131. Although "Western scholars [have] long since prepared an obituary" for the

Jonangpa, the tradition still continues to thrive at monasteries like Chöjé in Dzamtang (Elliot Sperling, "Tibetan Buddhism, Perceived and Imagined, along the Ming-Era Sino-Tibetan Frontier," in *Buddhism Between Tibet and China*, ed. Matthew T. Kapstein [Boston: Wisdom Publications, 2009], 156)

132. Gerhard Emmer, "Dga' Ldan Tshe Dbang Dpal Bzang Po and the Tibet-Ladakh-Mughal War of 1679–84," in *The Mongolia-Tibet Interface: Opening New Research Terrains in Inner Asia*, ed. Uradyn E. Bulag and Hildegaard G. M. Diemberger (Leiden: Brill, 2007), 81–107.

133. From the 1733 biography of Sonam Tobgyé, *dPal-mi'i dbang po'i rtogs-pa brjod-pa 'jig-rten kun-tu dga'-ba'i gtam*, quoted in Luciano Petech, "The Tibetan-Ladakhi-Moghul War (1679–1683)," in his *Selected Papers on Asian History* (Rome: Istituto Italiano per il Medio ed Estremo Oriente, 1988), 33.

134. On the history of these two competing lineages see Alexandre Papas, *Soufisme et politique entre Chine, Tibet, et Turkestan: Étude sur les Khwajas Naqshbandis du Turkestan Oriental* (Paris: Librarie d'Amérique et d'Orient, 2005).

135. Thierry Zarcone, "Sufism from Central Asia Among the Tibetans in the 16th–17th Centuries," *Tibet Journal* 20, 3 (1995): 102–105.

136. Hidehiro Okada and Junko Miyawaki, "The *Biography of Zaya Pandita*, the Greatest Oirad Monk," in *Biographies of Eminent Mongol Buddhists*, ed. Johan Elverskog (Sankt Augustin, Germany: International Institute for Tibetan and Buddhist Studies, 2008), 27–45.

137. James A. Millward, *Eurasian Crossroads: A History of Xinjiang* (New York: Columbia University Press, 2007), 77.

138. On the Manchu conquest of the Zünghars see Peter C. Perdue, *China Marches West: The Qing Conquest of Central Eurasia* (Cambridge: Belknap Press, 2005).

Chapter 5. Halal

Note to epigraph: *Yuan Shi*, based on the translation in F. W. Cleaves, "The Rescript of Qubilai Prohibiting the Slaughtering of Animals by Slitting the Throat," *Journal of Turkish Studies* 16 (1992): 69.

1. On the Mongol capital see Hok-lam Chan, *Legends of the Building of Old Peking* (Hong Kong: Chinese University Press, 2007).

2. A. C. Moule and Paul Pelliot, *Marco Polo, The Description of the World, Vol. 1* (London: George Routledge & Sons, 1938), 216.

3. Based on the translation in Cleaves, "The Rescript of Qubilai," 72–73.

4. Paul Ratchnevsky, "Rašid ad-Din über de Mohammendaner-Verfolgungen in China unter Qubilai," *Central Asiatic Journal* 14 (1970): 163–180.

5. J. A. Boyle, *The Successors of Genghis: Translated from the Persian of Rashid al-Din* (New York: Columbia University Press, 1971), 294.

6. Boyle, *The Successors of Genghis*, 294.

7. Apparently based on the passages "kill those who join other gods with God" (Qur'an 4:5) and "attack those who join other gods with God in all" (Qur'an 4:36).

8. Boyle, *The Successors of Genghis*, 295.

9. The Great God was Möngke Tengri, "Eternal Tengri," the supreme god in the Mongol pantheon, who had given the blessing upon Chinggis Khan to rule the world. And in recognition of this fact, as Hamid al-Din rightly points out, every letter and decree issued by the Mongols begins with the phrase "By the blessing/power of Eternal God," for in their view the Mongol conquests and world domination were the will of Möngke Tengri (see Nicholas Poppe, *Mongolian Monuments in the hP'ags-pa Script*, trans. J. R. Krueger [Wiesbaden: Harrassowitz, 1957]; and Sgrol-dkar et al., *Xizang lishi dangan huicui* [A collection from the Historical Archives of Tibet] [Beijing: Cultural Relics Publishing House, 1995], no. 1, 2, 5, 6. A slightly different form is found in the Pakpa script letter published by Paul Pelliot ["Monkha denri-yin khuchun-dur kha'an u su-dur"] in Giuseppe Tucci, *Tibetan Painted Scrolls* [Rome: Librera dello Stato, 1949], 623). Of course, confusion invariably arose when this Mongol religious vision was translated into a Western religious framework, such as in William of Rubruck's translation of Möngke Khan's letter to Louis IX that begins: "This is the order of the everlasting God [Möngke Tengri]. 'In Heaven there is only one eternal God [Möngke Tengri]'" (Rubruck, *The Mission of Friar William*, 248; see also Eric Vogelin, "Mongol Orders of Submission to European Powers, 1245–1255," *Byzantion* 15 [1940–1941]: 391). Christians, of course, understood this to mean the Christian God, not Möngke Tengri. But that was not the case. Güyüg Khan in fact made this clear in a letter he sent to the Pope explaining why the Mongols will not convert to Christianity: "Because they [the Christians] did not obey the word of God [Möngke Tengri]." And it was precisely such religious confusion that Hamid al-Din used to his advantage when discussing the theory of jihad with Khubilai Khan. Indeed, his argument eloquently captures the point made in the previous chapter about jihad always being reinterpreted in new historical contexts.

10. Elizabeth Endicott-West, "Merchant Associations in Yuan China: The *Ortaq*," *Asia Major* 2 (1989): 127–145.

11. Christopher P. Atwood, *Encyclopedia of Mongolia and the Mongols* (New York: Facts on File, 2004), 253.

12. From the recently discovered 1346 *Zhizheng Tiaoge* published by Han'gukhak Chungang Yon'guwon p'yon (Seoul: Hymonisut'u, 2007). I thank Kim Hodong for this translation.

13. Paul Buell, "A Cautionary Tale: Činqqis Qan as the Third Man," *Mongolian Studies* 29 (2007): 55–66.

14. The best history of Chinggis Khan's life and career is still Paul Ratchnevsky, *Genghis Khan: His Life and Legacy* (Oxford: Basil Blackwell, 1991). On the question of the representation of Chinggis Khan see Jack Weatherford, *Genghis Khan and the Making of the Modern World* (New York: Crown, 2004).

15. Christopher P. Atwood, "The Date of the *Secret History* Reconsidered," *Journal of Song-Yuan Studies* 37 (2007): 1–48.

16. Christopher P. Atwood, "Informants and Sources for the *Secret History of the Mongols*," *Mongolian Studies* 29 (2007): 34–36.

17. "When they first rose to power they made a yasa that no one should slaughter animals by cutting their throats but should slit open their breasts after the Mongols' own fashion" ('Ala-ad-Din 'Ata-Malik Juvaini, *The History of the World Conqueror*, trans. John A. Boyle [Manchester: Manchester University Press, 1958], 260).

18. Juvaini, *History of the World Conqueror*, 206.

19. Juvaini, *History of the World Conqueror*, 272.

20. For an overview of the ongoing debate on the nature and history of the "Great Yasa" see David Morgan, "The 'Great *Yasa* of Chinggis Khan' Revisited," in *Mongols, Turks, and Others: Eurasian Nomads and the Sedentary World*, ed. Reuven Amitai and Michal Biran (Leiden: Brill, 2005), 291–308.

21. A. Bausani, "Religion Under the Mongols," in *The Cambridge History of Iran, Vol. 5: The Saljuq and Mongol Periods*, ed. J. A. Boyle (Cambridge: Cambridge University Press, 1968), 548.

22. J. A. Boyle, "Dynastic and Political History of the Il-Khans," in *The Cambridge History of Iran, Vol. 5: The Saljuq and Mongol Periods*, ed. J. A. Boyle (Cambridge: Cambridge University Press, 1968), 346.

23. Coincidentally, when Ahmad was finally investigated after his murder "Khubilai was convinced of the Muslim minister's guilt and so had his corpse exhumed and hung in a bazaar; then he allowed his dogs to attack it" (Morris Rossabi, "The Reign of Khubilai Khan," in *The Cambridge History of China, Vol. 6: Alien Regimes and Border States, 907–1368*, ed. Herbert Franke and Denis Twitchett [New York: Cambridge University Press, 1994], 474).

24. On the Song Chinese response to the Mongol conquest see, for example, John Chaffee, *Branches of Heaven: A History of the Imperial Clan of Sung China* (Cambridge: Harvard University Asia Center, 1999), 242–259.

25. On the importance of maintaining imperial authority in regard to this incident see Kim Hodong, "A Portrait of a Christian Official Under Mongol Rule: Life and Career of 'Isa Kelemechi (1227–1308)," unpublished paper presented at the workshop, "The Mongols and Christianity," Ulaanbaatar, Mongolia, August 10–12, 2007.

26. Craig Clunas, *Empire of Great Brightness: Visual and Material Cultures of Ming China, 1368–1644* (Honolulu: University of Hawai'i, 2007), 82. For a historical overview of blue-and-white porcelain see John Carswell, *Blue and White: Chinese Porcelain Around the World* (London: Art Media Resources, 2000).

27. A convenient overview of Hui history and its "four tides" of development—the early period, the Qing revival, modernist reforms, and ethnic nationalism—can be found in Dru C. Gladney, *Muslim Chinese: Ethnic Nationalism in the People's Republic* (Cambridge: Council on East Asian Studies, 1996), 21–63.

28. Thomas T. Allsen, *Commodity and Exchange in the Mongol Empire: A Cultural History of Islamic Textiles* (Cambridge: Cambridge University Press, 1997), 30–45.

29. James A. Millward and Laura J. Newby, "The Qing and Islam on the Western

Frontier," in *Empires at the Margins: Culture, Ethnicity, and Frontier in Early Modern China*, ed. Pamela Kyle Crossley, Helen F. Siu, and Donald S. Sutton (Berkeley: University of California Press, 2006), 124–125.

30. Vincent Goossaert, "The Beef Taboo and the Sacrificial Structure of Late Imperial Chinese Society," in *Of Tripod and Palate: Food, Politics, and Religion in Traditional China*, ed. Roel Sterckx (New York: Palgrave Macmillan, 2005), 244.

31. Although vegetarianism is much lauded in Tibetan Buddhist literature (e.g., Shabkar Tsogdruk Rangdrol, *The Life of Shabkar: The Autobiography of a Tibetan Yogin*, trans. Matthieu Ricard et al. [Albany: State University of New York Press, 1994]: 195, 327, 411, 541–542, 582, 585), most Tibetans still eat meat. For an example of how Tibetans circumvent the karmic consequences of killing animals for food see Geoff Childs, *Tibetan Diary: From Birth to Death and Beyond in a Himalayan Valley of Nepal* (Berkeley: University of California Press, 2004), 125–128.

32. Valentin A. Riasanovsky, *Fundamental Principles of Mongol Law* (Bloomington: Indiana University Press, 1965), 83.

33. While there is extensive scholarship on the importance of foodways in defining religious, cultural, and ethnic boundaries, some works relevant to this study are Claudine Fabre-Vassas, *The Singular Beast: Jews, Christians, and the Pig*, trans. Carol Volk (New York: Columbia University Press, 1997); Uradyn E. Bulag, *Nationalism and Hybridity in Mongolia* (Oxford: Oxford University Press, 1998), 194–211; Maris Boyd Gillette, *Between Mecca and Beijing: Modernization and Consumption Among Urban Chinese Muslims* (Stanford: Stanford University Press, 2000), 114–166; and Robert F. Campany, "The Meanings of Cuisines of Transcendence in Late Classical and Medieval China," *T'oung Pao* 91 (2005): 1–6.

34. The promotion of pork by the Spanish authorities continued for some time, especially among the Moriscos, those Muslims who had converted to Christianity. In particular, the Spanish state and their ecclesiastical supporters continually feared that their conversion was never truly authentic. Thus in order to ensure that this was not the case church leaders such as Fray Luis de Aliagra, the confessor of Phillip III (1578–1621), argued that being a good Christian entailed not only attending mass and confessing, but also eating pork and drinking wine (James B. Tueller, *Good and Faithful Christians: Moriscos and Catholicism in Early Modern Spain* [New Orleans: University Press of the South, 2002], 171, 223).

35. Jason Goodwin, *Lords of the Horizons: A History of the Ottoman Empire* (New York: Henry Holt, 1998), 230; and Maria Balinska, *The Bagel: The Surprising History of a Modest Bread* (New Haven: Yale University Press, 2008), 41–43.

36. Richard A. Lobban, Jr., "Pigs and Their Prohibition," *International Journal of Middle East Studies* 26, 1 (1994): 57–75.

37. K. M. Maitra, *A Persian Embassy to China: Being an Extract from Zubdatu't Tawarikh of Hafiz Abru* (New York: Paragon Book Reprint Corp., 1970), 106.

38. On the Muslim use of pork to distinguish themselves from Buddhists in Thai-

land see Angela Burr, "Pigs in Noah's Ark: A Muslim Origin Myth from Southern Thailand," *Folklore* 90, 2 (1979): 178–185.

39. Ruy Gonzalez de Clavijo, *Clavijo: Embassy to Tamerlane, 1403–1406*, trans. Guy Le Strange (London: George Routledge & Sons, 1928), 223.

40. Fletcher has argued that this name may also have been a play-on-words between the family name of the Ming dynasty's founder, *Zhu* 朱, and the Chinese word for pig, *zhu* 豬 ("China and Central Asia," 349 n. 20).

41. Ma Huan, *Ying-yai Sheng-lan: The Overall Survey of the Ocean's Shores [1433]*, trans. J. V. G. Mills (Cambridge: Cambridge University Press, 1970), 138.

42. On the origins of the Manchus see Mark C. Elliott, *The Manchu Way: The Eight Banners and Ethnic Identity in Late Imperial China* (Stanford: Stanford University Press, 2001), 1–33.

43. Frederic Wakeman, Jr., *The Great Enterprise: The Manchu Reconstruction of Imperial Order in Seventeenth-Century China* (Berkeley: University of California Press, 1985), 202–203.

44. On the Qing conquest of the Chinese Muslims see Morris Rossabi, "Muslim and Central Asian Revolts," in *From Ming to Ch'ing: Conquest, Region and Continuity in Seventeenth-Century China*, ed. Jonathan D. Spence and John E. Wills, Jr. (New Haven: Yale University Press, 1979), 185–194.

45. Kate Teltscher, *The High Road to China: George Bogle, the Panchen Lama, and the First British Expedition to Tibet* (New York: Farrar, Straus and Giroux, 2006).

46. Johan Elverskog, *Our Great Qing: The Mongols, Buddhism and the State in Late Imperial China* (Honolulu: University of Hawai'i Press, 2006), chap. 4.

47. Jonathan N. Lipman, "'A Fierce and Brutal People': On Islam and Muslims in Qing Law," in *Empire at the Margins: Culture, Ethnicity, and Frontier in Early Modern China*, ed. P. K. Crossley, H. F. Siu, and D. S. Sutton (Berkeley: University of California Press, 2006), 88.

48. Lipman, "'A Fierce and Brutal People,'" 89.

49. Lipman, "'A Fierce and Brutal People,'" 89.

50. For an exhaustive study of Chen Hongmou's career and his vision of the "civilizing mission" see William T. Rowe, *Saving the World: Chen Hongmou and Elite Consciousness in Eighteenth Century China* (Stanford: Stanford University Press, 2001), esp. chap. 12.

51. The following historical summary is based on Jonathan N. Lipman, *Familiar Strangers: A History of Muslims in Northwest China* (Seattle: University of Washington Press, 1997), 114–115; the articles collected in Joseph F. Fletcher, *Studies on Chinese and Islamic Inner Asia*, ed. Beatrice Manz (Aldershot: Variorum, 1995); A. D. W. Forbes, "Ma Ming-hsin," in *Encyclopedia of Islam*, 2nd ed., ed. P. J. Bearman et al. (Leiden: Brill, 1960–2005), V, 850–852; and Anthony Garnaut, "Pen of the Jahriyya: A Commentary of *The History of the Soul* by Zheng Chengzhi," *Inner Asia* 8 (2006): 29–50.

52. On the development of Sino-Islamic culture in the Qing period, see Zvi Ben-

Dor Benite, *The Dao of Muhammad: A Cultural History of Muslims in Late Imperial China* (Cambridge: Harvard East Asia Center, 2005), 5–19.

53. Joseph F. Fletcher, "The Naqshabandiyya in Northwest China," in *Studies on China and Islamic Central Asia*, ed. Beatrice Manz (Aldershot: Variorum, 1995), XI:13–14.

54. On the history of silent versus vocal *dhikr* in the Naqshbandi tradition see Jürgen Paul, "Organization and Doctrine: The Khwājagān/Naqshbandīya in the First Generation After Baha'uddin," *Anor* 1 (Halle/Berlin: Das Arabische Buch, 1998): 18–30.

55. A similar conflict between a Buddhist state and Wahhabi-inspired Muslims also occurred on the Malay peninsula in the eighteenth and nineteenth centuries (Victor Lieberman, *Strange Parallels: Southeast Asia in Global Context, c. 800–1830, Vol. 1, Integration on the Mainland* [New York: Cambridge University Press, 2003], 334).

56. On the Hui rebellions in the south, see David G. Atwill, *The Chinese Sultanate: Islam, Ethnicity, and the Panthay Rebellion in Southwest China, 1856–1873* (Stanford: Stanford University Press, 2005).

57. Lipman, *Familiar Strangers*, 114–115.

58. On these rebellions, especially that of Yaqub Beg, see Kim Hodong, *Holy War in China: The Muslim Rebellion and State in Chinese Central Asia, 1864–1877* (Stanford: Stanford University Press, 2004).

59. Jimbadorji, *Bolor Toli*, ed. Liu Jinsuo (Beijing: Ündüsüten-ü keblel-ün qoriya, 1984), 366.

60. *Ünegen-ü sang orosiba*, mss., 2r (Zhongguo Menggu wen guji zongmu bianhui, *Catalogue of Ancient Mongolian Books and Documents of China* [Beijing: Beijing Tushuguan Chubanshe, 1999], no. 3529). The same passage is found in both Ulaanbaatar *Ünegen-ü sang* manuscripts published by Charles Bawden, "The 'Offering the Fox' Again," *Zentralasiatische Studien* 10 (1976): 453. The Oirat manuscript, on the other hand, claims they had the same father; see Charles Bawden, "An Oirat Manuscript of the 'Offering the Fox,'" *Zentralasiatische Studien* 12 (1978): 7–34.

61. Johan Elverskog, *The Pearl Rosary: Mongol Historiography in Early Nineteenth Century Ordos* (Bloomington: Mongolia Society, 2007), 36–37.

62. John Newman, "Islam in the Kalacakra Tantra," *Journal of the International Association of Buddhist Studies* 21, 2 (1998): 319.

63. Newman, "Islam in the Kalacakra Tantra," 334.

64. *Sambala-yin oron-u teüke orosiba* [History of the Land of Shambhala], MS p. 19 (Zhongguo Menggu wen guji zongmu bianhui, *Catalogue of Ancient Mongolian Books*, no. 4633).

65. Shabkar, *The Life of Shabkar*, 196.

66. Jimbadorji, *Bolor Toli*, 367.

67. See Micheal Aris, "India and the British According to a Tibetan Text of the Later Eighteenth Century," in *Tibetan Studies: Proceedings of the 6th Seminar of the IATS, Fagernes 1992*, ed. Per Kvaerne (Oslo: The Institute for Comparative Research

in Human Culture, 1994), 7–25; Michael Aris, '*Jig-med-gling-pa's 'Discourse on India'*
of 1787: A Critical Edition and Annotated Translation of the Cho-phyogs rgya-gar-gyi
gtam brtag-pa brgyad-kyi me-long (Tokyo: International Institute for Buddhist Studies
of ICABS, 1996); and Matthew Kapstein, "Just Where on Jambudvipa Are We? New
Geographical Knowledge and Old Cosmological Schemes in 18th Century Tibet," in
Forms of Knowledge in Early Modern South Asia, ed. Sheldon Pollock (Durham: Duke
University Press, forthcoming).

68. Jimbadorji, *Bolor Toli*, 368.

69. For the biographical details of Injannashi's life see John Gombojab Hangin,
*Köke Sudur (The Blue Chronicle): A Study of the First Mongolian Historical Novel by
Injannasi* (Wiesbaden: Harrassowitz, 1973), 1–14.

70. On the literary context of these prefaces see A. Craig Clunas, "The Prefaces to
Nigen Dabqur Asar and their Chinese Antecedents," *Zentralasiatische Studien* 14, 1
(1980): 139–194.

71. Hangin, *Köke Sudur*, 63.

72. Benjamin A. Elman, *A Cultural History of Civil Examinations in Late Imperial
China* (Berkeley: University of California Press, 2000), xi.

73. Johan Elverskog, "Injannashi, the Anti-Cervantes," in *Biographies of Eminent
Mongol Buddhists*, ed. Johan Elverskog (Sankt Augustin, Germany: International Institute for Tibetan and Buddhist Studies, 2008), 75–98.

74. Hangin, *Köke Sudur*, 95.

75. On the discourses of eating and cannibalism in China see Gang Yue, *The
Mouth That Begs: Hunger, Cannibalism, and the Politics of Eating in Modern China*
(Durham: Duke University Press, 1999).

76. Rubruck, *The Mission of Friar William*, 158.

77. On the anthropological fascination with cannibalism see Peggy R. Sandave,
Divine Hunger: Cannibalism as a Cultural System (Cambridge: Cambridge University
Press, 1988); Laurence R. Goldman, *The Anthropology of Cannibalism* (Westport: Ber-
gin & Garvey, 1999); Francis Parker et al., *Cannibalism and the Colonial World* (Cambridge: Cambridge University Press, 2004); Gananath Obeyesekere, *Cannibal Talk: The
Man-Eating Myth and Human Sacrifice in the South Seas* (Berkeley: University of California Press, 2005).

78. On the problem of moral superiority and the study of religion see Robert
Orsi's study on the common approaches to the Christian snakehandlers of the Ameri-
can south ("Snakes Alive: Religious Studies Between Heaven and Earth," in his
*Between Heaven and Earth: The Religious Worlds People Make and the Scholars Who
Study Them* [Princeton: Princeton University Press, 2005]: 177–203).

79. Hangin, *Köke Sudur*, 96.

80. On the importance of the queue in Qing society, see Philip Kuhn, *Soulstealers:
The Chinese Sorcery Scare of 1768* (Cambridge: Harvard University Press, 1990); Wei-
kun Cheng, "Politics of the Queue: Agitation and Resistance in the Beginning and End

of Qing China," in *Hair: Its Power and Meaning in Asian Cultures*, ed. Alf Hiltebeitel and Barbara Miller (Albany: State University of New York Press, 1998), 123–142.

81. Hangin, *Köke Sudur*, 98.

82. For a contemporary study that adopts the same approach in its investigation of the Chinese legal practice of *lingchi* see Timothy Brook, Jérôme Bourgon, and Gregory Blue, *Death by a Thousand Cuts* (Cambridge: Harvard University Press, 2008), chaps. 3–5.

83. Hangin, *Köke Sudur*, 99.

84. Hangin, *Köke Sudur*, 99.

85. For an excellent interpretation of Mencius see Slingerland, *Effortless Action*, 131–173; and on comparing religious practices see Robert F. Campany, "Xunzi and Durkheim as Theorists of Ritual Practice," in *Discourse and Practice*, ed. Frank Reynolds and David Tracy (Albany: State University of New York Press, 1992), 86–103.

86. Hangin, *Köke Sudur*, 97.

87. On the historical development of the comparative study of religion see, for example, Eric J. Sharpe, *Comparative Religion: A History* (La Salle: Open Court, 1986).

88. Hangin, *Köke Sudur*, 99.

89. Hangin, *Köke Sudur*, 99, 100.

90. Hangin, *Köke Sudur*, 75–76.

91. Hangin, *Köke Sudur*, 76. Injannashi's critique of contemporary lamas is part of the anti-clericalism of the late nineteenth-century Qing dynasty. On this phenomenon see Vincent Goossaert, ed., *Anticléricalisme en Chine*, special issue of *Extrême-Orient, Extrême-Occident* 24 (2002).

92. Hangin, *Köke Sudur*, 96–97.

93. On the worship of Amitabha in Tibet, see Matthew T. Kapstein, "Pure Land Buddhism in Tibet?" in *Approaching the Land of Bliss: Religious Praxis in the Cult of Amitabha*, ed. Richard Payne and Kenneth Tanaka (Honolulu: University of Hawai'i Press, 2004), 16–41; and Georgios Halkias, "Pure-Lands and Other Visions in Seventeenth-Century Tibet: A *Gnam chos sadhana* for the Pure-land Sukhavati Revealed in 1658 by Gnam chos Mi 'gyur rdo rje (1645–1667)," in *Power, Politics, and the Reinvention of Tradition: Tibet in the Seventeenth and Eighteenth Centuries*, ed. Bryan J. Cuevas and Kurtis R. Schaeffer (Leiden: Brill, 2006), 103–128.

94. Hangin, *Köke Sudur*, 97.

95. Hangin, *Köke Sudur*, 97–98.

Conclusion

1. Peter Fleming, *News from Tartary: A Journey from Peking to Kashmir* (London: Jonathan Cape, 1936), 201. I thank Philippe Forêt for bringing to my attention the case of different Muslim and Buddhist knots.

2. Gray Tuttle, *Tibetan Buddhists in the Making of Modern China* (New York: Columbia University Press, 2005), 143–144.

3. On the shift of Christianity to the Southern Hemisphere, see, for example, Phillip Jenkins, *The Next Christendom: The Coming of Global Christianity* (New York: Oxford University Press, 2002).

4. Nicolai Ouroussoff, "For I. M. Pei, History Is Still Happening," *New York Times*, December 14, 2008.

Index

ACKNOWLEDGMENTS

D URING THE WRITING of this book I attended the seminar of a
noted Polish sociologist who, during his lecture, chided American
scholars for thanking their families in their acknowledgments. For
him this was slightly ridiculous. Instead he advocated that one should thank
those scholars found in the bibliography.

While I sympathize with this sentiment, I nevertheless begin by thanking my wife, Liljana, who on short notice allowed to me to turn our family
life upside-down, so that I, with our son in tow, could head off to Sweden
and set about writing this book. Without her unflagging support and
understanding, writing these pages would never have been possible.

Heading off to Sweden, of course, was not simply done on a whim.
Rather, I was fortuitously invited to join a group of scholars working on
Inner Asia at the Swedish Collegium for Advanced Study, and for this I
deeply thank Barbro Klein, Staffan Rosén, and Björn Wittrock. Indeed,
without the respite from teaching and everyday academic work that this
opportunity afforded it is unlikely that this project could ever have been
attempted. For creating and maintaining such a scholar's utopia, I therefore
wish to thank the directors and staff at SCAS for making my stay in Uppsala
so enjoyable and productive.

At the same time it should also be noted that the manuscript I wrote in
the hallowed halls of the Linneanum had its origins back in my teenage
years when I was enthralled by the writers of the Beat Generation and came
across Brion Gysin's early mixing of Arabic and Chinese calligraphy. Of
course, how this youthful curiosity blossomed into this book is a long story.
Yet it is one that could not have happened without the guidance and support of all the teachers I have had the good fortune to work with at the
University of California, Berkeley, the Naropa Institute, the Karmapa Institute, Tribhuvan University, Middlebury College, and Indiana University,

Bloomington. Without having had the good fortune to meet all of these teachers I would never have had the intellectual wherewithal to try to bring my childhood fantasies to academic reality.

Forging this reality, however, was not a solo affair. Numerous colleagues have helped me think about and shape my argument through discussions and the endless emailing of various queries, and I thank them all, but I especially want to thank those who offered valuable comments on earlier drafts of this work: Thomas Allsen, Chris Atwood, Brian Baumann, Devin DeWeese, Ayman El-Desouky, Philippe Forêt, Kim Hodong, Victor Mair, Aleksandr Naymark, Morris Rossabi, Bruce Tindall, Gray Tuttle, Dan Waugh, and Abdurishid Yakup.

Portions of this work were also presented at various conferences, and colloquia, and I wish to thank everyone who invited me, and to those who provided helpful comments and criticisms during my presentations at the Warburg Institute, Uppsala University, Rice University, the University of Toronto, McMaster University, the University of Southern California, and Harvard University.

I also want to thank all those who helped with the images and maps found throughout the book: Helen Abbott, Ian Aberle, Rudolph Abraham, Rodney Ast, Norman Belza, Jonathan Bloom, Geoff Childs, Michael Crow, Karl Debreczeny, Melvyn Goldstein, Amy Hofland, Linda Komaroff, Donald LaRocca, Angelo Lui, Auste Mickunaite, Maggie Murphy, Jennifer Lee, Ruth Long, Sandra Powlette, Jane Siegel, Eric Sommer, Volker Thewalt, Johannes Thomann, Jade Tran, Jenna Turner, Lynda Unchern, Sinéad Ward, Doris Weiner, and Shiyuan Yuan. Moreover, I wish to thank James Quick of the Office of Research and Graduate Studies at Southern Methodist University, as well as Dean Peter Moore, for providing funds to help defray the cost of reproducing these images.

Last, I want to thank everyone involved in the actual creation of this book beginning with Victor Mair, who quite literally took my manuscript under his wing as he was heading out the door. Since then he has been a constant source of encouragement and sage advice. I also thank Peter Agree and the staff at Penn Press, especially Ashley Nelson, Noreen O'Connor-Abel, Jennifer Malloy, and Sandra Haviland, for making the final stretch of this project such a joy.

And finally, I want to thank all of the scholars whose work is cited in the notes. Without their pioneering work this project could not have been brought to fruition.